The
Essayist

Also by Sheridan Baker

The Complete Stylist, SECOND EDITION
The Practical Stylist, SECOND EDITION
Problems in Exposition: Supplementary Exercises for
The Complete Stylist *and* The Practical Stylist
(WITH DWIGHT STEVENSON)

The
Essayist

Second Edition

SHERIDAN BAKER
The University of Michigan

 Thomas Y. Crowell Company • New York • Established 1834

Designed by Angela Foote

FRONT COVER ILLUSTRATION:
"Herodotus Crowned by Apollo." Detail of woodcut
on title page of *Historiarum libri IX* (Venice, 1494),
edited by Giovanni and Gregorio de Gregoriis.
(Bibliothèque Nationale)

Acknowledgments

2 3 4 5

Jeremy R. Azrael, "Murder Trial in Moscow," *The Atlantic Monthly*, May 1962.
Jeremy Azrael is Professor of Political Science and Chairman of the Committee on
Slavic Area Studies at the University of Chicago.

James Baldwin, "Fifth Avenue Uptown: A Letter from Harlem," in *Nobody Knows
My Name* by James Baldwin. Copyright © 1960 James Baldwin. Reprinted by
permission of the publisher, The Dial Press. Originally published in *Esquire.*

Gordon E. Bigelow, "A Primer of Existentialism," *College English*, December
1961. Copyright © 1961 by the National Council of Teachers of English. Reprinted by permission of the publisher and Gordon E. Bigelow.

Harrison Brown, "After the Population Explosion," *Saturday Review*, June 26,
1971. Copyright © 1971 Saturday Review, Inc. Harrison Brown teaches at the
California Institute of Technology.

Henry Seidel Canby, "Sentence Maker," in *Thoreau* (Boston: Houghton Mifflin
Company, 1939).

"Get-Out-If-You-Can!," The Center for the Study of Democratic Institutions, The
Fund for the Republic, Inc. Reprinted with permission from The Center for the
Study of Democratic Institutions in Santa Barbara, California.

G. K. Chesterton, "Science and the Savages," in *Heretics*. Reprinted by permission
of The Bodley Head Ltd.

Cyril Connolly, "Blueprint for a Silver Age: Notes on a Visit to America," *Harper's
Magazine*, December 1947.

Loren Eiseley, "The Real Secret of Piltdown," in *The Immense Journey*. Copyright © 1955 by Loren Eiseley. Reprinted from *The Immense Journey*, by Loren
Eiseley by permission of Random House, Inc.

Wolcott Gibbs, from "Triple-Threat Man," *The New Yorker*, January 4, 1958.
Copyright © 1958 The New Yorker Magazine, Inc.

Theodore M. Greene, "Man out of Darkness: Religion Has Not Lost Its Power," *The Atlantic Monthly*, April 1949. Copyright © 1949 by The Atlantic Monthly Company, Boston, Mass. Reprinted with permission.

Louis J. Halle, "The Student Drive to Destruction," *The New Republic*, October 19, 1968. Reprinted by permission of The New Republic, copyright © 1968, Harrison-Blaine of New Jersey, Inc.

Erich Heller, "The Importance of Nietzche," in *The Artist's Journey into the Interior and Other Essays* by Erich Heller. Copyright © 1964, 1965 by Erich Heller. Reprinted by permission of Random House, Inc.

Ernest Hemingway, from *Death in the Afternoon.* Copyright 1932 Charles Scribner's Sons; renewal copyright © 1960 Ernest Hemingway.

Eric Hoffer from *The True Believer* (Harper & Row, 1951). Reprinted by permission of Harper & Row, Publishers, Inc.

Richard Hofstadter, "Democracy and Anti-Intellectualism in America," *The Michigan Alumnus Quarterly Review* (now *The Michigan Quarterly Review*), August 8, 1953. Reprinted with permission from The Michigan Quarterly Review.

Sidney Hook, "The War Against the Democratic Process," *The Atlantic Monthly*, February 1969. Copyright © 1969 by The Atlantic Monthly Company, Boston, Mass. Reprinted with permission.

Aldous Huxley, from *Point Counter Point*. Copyright 1928 by Aldous Huxley. Reprinted by permission of Harper & Row, Publishers, Inc.

Rufus M. Jones, "The Mystic's Experience of God," in *Jubilee: One Hundred Years of the Atlantic*. Copyright © 1942 by The Atlantic Monthly,

James Joyce, from *A Portrait of the Artist as a Young Man*. Copyright 1916 by B. W. Heubsch, renewed 1944 by Nora Joyce. Reprinted by permission of The Viking Press, Inc.

Norman Mailer, "What Is Wrong with the City?" *The New York Times Magazine*, May 18, 1969. Copyright © 1969 by The New York Times Company. Reprinted by permission of The New York Times Company, the author, and the author's agent, Scott Meredith Literary Agency, Inc.

Dwight Macdonald, "8½: Fellini's Obvious Masterpiece," in *Dwight Macdonald on Movies* (Englewood Cliffs, New Jersey: Prentice-Hall, Inc., 1969). Copyright © 1969 by Dwight Macdonald. Reprinted by permission of the author.

Joseph Mitchell, from "The Beautiful Flower," *The New Yorker*, June 4, 1955. Copyright © 1955 The New Yorker Magazine, Inc.

Daniel P. Moynihan, "Nirvana Now," *The American Scholar*, Vol. 36, No. 4, Autumn, 1967. Copyright © 1967 by the United Chapters of Phi Beta Kappa. Reprinted by permission of the publishers.

George Orwell, "Shooting an Elephant," in *Shooting an Elephant and Other Essays* by George Orwell. Copyright 1945, 1946, 1949, 1950, by Sonia Brownell Orwell. Reprinted by permission of Harcourt Brace Jovanovich, Inc., and Secker & Warburg.

Alan Patton, "The Challenge of Fear," *Saturday Review*, September 9, 1967. Copyright © 1967 Saturday Review, Inc.

Richard Poirier, "The War Against the Young: Its Beginnings," in *The Performing Self: Compositions and Decompositions in the Languages of Contemporary Life* by Richard Poirier. Copyright © 1971 by Oxford University Press, Inc. Reprinted by permission.

Harold Rosenberg, "The Cubist Epoch," *The New Yorker*, May 8, 1971. Reprinted by permission; copyright © 1971 The New Yorker Magazine, Inc.

George Santayana, "Cervantes," in *Essays in Literary Criticism of George Santayana* edited by Irving Singer. Reprinted by permission of Charles Scribner's Sons. Copyright © 1956 Charles Scribner's Sons.

Edward Sapir, "Language and Literature," in *Language* by Edward Sapir, copyright, 1921, by Harcourt Brace Jovanovich, Inc.; copyright, 1949, by Jean V. Sapir. Reprinted by permission of the publisher.

Albert Schweitzer, "The Evolution of Ethics," *The Atlantic Monthly*, November 1958. The National Arts Foundation arranged for the publication of "The Evolution of Ethics" in the United States. Translation from the German by Mrs. Carleton Smith.

George Bernard Shaw, from "Epilogue" to *Pygmalion*. Reprinted by permission of The Society of Authors, on behalf of the Bernard Shaw Estate.

Henry Silver, "Better Writing," *PMLA*, March 1951. Reprinted by permission of the Modern Language Association of America.

Lois Z. Smith, "An Experimental Investigation of Young Children's Interest and Expressive Behavior Responses to Single Statement, Verbal Repetition, and Ideational Repetition of Content in Animal Stories," *Child Development*, I (1930), 232–38, 245–47. Reprinted by permission of The Society for Research in Child Development, Inc.

Walter T. Stace, "Man Against Darkness," *The Atlantic Monthly*, September 1948. Copyright © 1948 by The Atlantic Monthly Company, Boston, Mass. Reprinted with permission.

Diana Trilling, "Celebrating with Dr. Leary," *Encounter*, June 1967. Reprinted by permission of the author.

Austin Warren, from "Henry James: Symbolic Imagery in the Later Novels," in *Rage for Order* (Chicago: University of Chicago Press, 1948). Reprinted by permission of the author.

Eudora Welty, "Review of *The Underground Man*," *The New York Times Book Review*, February 14, 1971. Copyright © 1971 by The New York Times Company. Reprinted by permission.

E. B. White, "A Slight Sound at Evening," (Allen Cove, Summer 1954) in *The Points of My Compass* by E. B. White. Copyright, 1954 by E. B. White. Originally appeared in *The Yale Review* under the title "Walden—1954." Reprinted by permission of Harper & Row, Publishers, Inc.

Virginia Woolf, "How Should One Read a Book?," in *The Second Common Reader* by Virginia Woolf, copyright, 1932, by Harcourt Brace Jovanovich, Inc.; copyright © 1960, by Leonard Woolf. Reprinted by permission of Harcourt Brace Jovanovich, Inc. and The Hogarth Press Ltd.

Charles E. Wyzanski, "A Federal Judge Digs the Young," *Saturday Review*, July 20, 1968. Copyright © 1968 Saturday Review, Inc.

To Buffy, Libby, and Bill

Preface

These essays—now newly selected, arranged, and augmented to face the new questions stirring in modern society—take the student progressively through the questions of expository writing. They illustrate how a thesis may organize his points at a stroke, how a structure is built, how the paragraph, the sentence, and the word may work their various wiles. They include the autobiographical essay and, since nothing so tunes our linguistic precision, the ironic essay—and specimens of how *not* to write. I conclude with some examples of variety in evidence and the author's voice, and a return to the fundamental questions of our times. Readers of *The Practical Stylist* and *The Complete Stylist*, and the many users of the first edition of *The Essayist*, will recognize the rhetorical approach.

As before, the book aims for the one practical point: how to write an essay. I do not ignore the lively and important ideas these essays develop; indeed, I make frequent suggestions for thinking about them. Nevertheless, the book's rhetorical aim—the *how* of writing—puts these ideas under practical management. Each of the twelve sections takes up a rhetorical problem and holds to it until the end, forgoing for the moment other targets of opportunity. To keep the aim sharp, I show the student in a general way what to look for as he begins each section; and at the end, instead of the usual "questions for study," I suggest ways for applying in his own writing the principles he has just seen demonstrated. To talk thus primarily about writing—how this essay was put together, how the student might put one together himself—relieves the teacher most blessedly from being sociologist, psychologist, anthropologist, and seer; and it actually seems to teach the student how to write. Not that I see reading only as grist for the writer's mill. Talk about the writing, and the ideas emerge—and the big questions of meaning and truth as well.

Each section renews the consideration, in one way or another, of what the modern world believes and disbelieves, its faiths and failures. Virginia Woolf and Cyril Connolly illustrate how marvelously the literate mind can respond to the world it imagines and the world it sees; Norman Mailer and Alan Paton, how the creative writer can face modern political issues; and Dwight Macdonald, Eudora Welty, and Harold Rosenberg, how the critic achieves fresh insights through the analysis of creative work occurring in various forms. I include a number of classics of the classroom, partly because they have taught well, but mostly because they are valuable. The thoughts of a Thoreau, for example, or a Schweitzer, go deep enough for a lifetime. Like White, I believe that every student in the universe should know Thoreau; he once gave me a permanent turn, too, and I think I have learned more about writing from him than from anyone.

Which brings me to my final point. In an age that preaches a keeping up with the linguistic Joneses, the student needs help from outside. He will learn nothing from the herd but to go along; he needs to see the virtues in other voices and other times. By worrying over the gristle in a Thoreau, Swift, or Carlyle, he may perhaps discover how to give today's very different idiom an occasional blessing of fiber and fire. Consequently, I have sought a wide variety of excellence in the readings, including, among the modern voices, samples from other ages, and urging exercises in imitating complex styles. And though I have tried to stick to the rhetorical point, I have nevertheless also sought a certain clash of idea and subject, from essay to essay, to stir up the sediment of language and idea both, and to leave the student something to sift for his own essay of the week.

There are thirty-six complete essays—more than enough for close study in any one semester—and illustrations from eleven other authors as well. Yet I believe the book compact enough for the student to use and study without having to carry it back to market at the semester's end four-fifths unread.

The essays are reproduced exactly as they appeared in the texts cited, except that obvious typographical spelling errors have been corrected, all book titles italicized, and some minor styling inconsistencies changed.

SHERIDAN BAKER

Contents

1 Thesis: The Argumentative Edge   1

     How Should One Read a Book?   VIRGINIA WOOLF   2

Clum —— *A Primer of Existentialism*   GORDON E. BIGELOW   11

2 Structure: Middle Tactics   23

     The War Against the Young: Its Beginnings
       RICHARD POIRIER   24

     The Student Drive to Destruction   LOUIS J. HALLE   41

     A Federal Judge Digs the Young
       CHARLES E. WYZANSKI JR.   47

     The War Against the Democratic Process
Clum —— SIDNEY HOOK   53

3 Middle Tactics: The Vector of Interest   63

Man Against Darkness   W. T. STACE   *65*

Man Out of Darkness: Religion Has Not Lost Its Power
THEODORE M. GREENE   *76*

Celebrating with Dr. Leary   DIANA TRILLING   *85*

The Mystic's Experience of God   RUFUS M. JONES   *103*

Plato and Bacon   THOMAS BABINGTON MACAULAY   *106*

4 Paragraphs: Beginning, Middle, End   114

Language and Literature   EDWARD SAPIR   *115*

Cum —*Cervantes*   GEORGE SANTAYANA   *122*

Nirvana Now   DANIEL P. MOYNIHAN   *128*

5 Sentences: A Notebook of Styles   145

I. THE SIMPLE SENTENCE

from *The True Believer*   ERIC HOFFER   *146*

from *Triple-Threat Man*   WOLCOTT GIBBS   *147*

II. COORDINATION

from *The Beautiful Flower*   JOSEPH MITCHELL   *148*

Better Writing   HENRY M. SILVER   *149*

III. SUBORDINATION

from *Death in the Afternoon*
ERNEST HEMINGWAY   *150*

from *Henry James: Symbolic Imagery in the
Later Novels*   AUSTIN WARREN   *151*

IV. PARALLELS AND PERIODIC PROSE

Of Studies   FRANCIS BACON   *152*

from *Liberal Knowledge*
JOHN HENRY NEWMAN   *153*

from *A Portrait of the Artist as a Young Man*
JAMES JOYCE   *154*

V. THE LONG AND SHORT

from *Point Counter Point*   ALDOUS HUXLEY   *155*

from *Epilogue to Pygmalion*
GEORGE BERNARD SHAW   *156*

6 Sentences in Exposition 159

The Evolution of Ethics ALBERT SCHWEITZER 160
The Real Secret of Piltdown LOREN EISLEY 169
Science and Savages G. K. CHESTERTON 177
Sentence Maker HENRY SEIDEL CANBY 181

7 Words: The Figurative Dimension 188

Where I Lived, and What I Lived For
HENRY DAVID THOREAU 190
A Slight Sound at Evening E. B. WHITE 201
The Importance of Nietzsche ERICH HELLER 209

8 The Autobiographical Essay 226

Shooting an Elephant GEORGE ORWELL 227
Fifth Avenue Uptown: A Letter from Harlem
JAMES BALDWIN 233

9 The Horrors of Exposition: Too
Much or Too Little 242

An Experimental Investigation LOIS Z. SMITH 243
Get-Out-If-You-Can!
AMERICAN TRADITIONS PROJECT 252

10 The Ironic Essay 256

A Modest Proposal JONATHAN SWIFT 257
Coleridge THOMAS CARLYLE 264
After the Population Explosion HARRISON BROWN 271

11 The Critical Review 281

8½: Fellini's Obvious Masterpiece
DWIGHT MACDONALD 282
The Underground Man EUDORA WELTY 295
The Cubist Epoch HAROLD ROSENBERG 301

12 Evidence and the Author's Voice   308

   Murder Trial in Moscow   JEREMY R. AZRAEL *309*

   What Is Wrong with the City?   NORMAN MAILER *321*

   Democracy and Anti-Intellectualism in America
     RICHARD HOFSTADTER *330*

   Blueprint for a Silver Age   CYRIL CONNOLLY *350*

   The Challenge of Fear   ALAN PATON *361*

How Should One Read a Book? VIRGINIA WOOLF · *2*
A Primer of Existentialism GORDON E. BIGELOW · *11*

Thesis
The Argumentative Edge

These two essays might be called direct "exposition"—a simple laying out of the subject for all to view. Actually, neither is so direct nor so simple. Each writer has gone beyond mere description to say something specific *about* his subject. Believing something about his subject that he wants you also to believe—a proposition to be proved, a thesis—each writer has in fact written something like a proposal instead of a mere ex-

1

planation. Each has given his subject a slight edge of argument, and with it a sense of direction, of interesting purpose.

Mrs. Woolf's essay is slightly more edged than Mr. Bigelow's. Her belief about how one should read is closer to argument than is Mr. Bigelow's belief about the significance of existentialism. And yet Mrs. Woolf's belief, her thesis, is not so clearly stated nor so easily grasped: her polite intelligence keeps her from forcing the edge of her argument at us and makes her essay seem more purely expository than it is. Ask yourself, as you read, what her central thesis is, and find her own clearest statement of it.

Mr. Bigelow's essay is about as direct an exposition as one will find. He is simply defining and clarifying a concept. But notice how he too presents an argumentative edge, saying in effect: "This subject is important, yet imperfectly understood; you need to understand it to read the books of your times."

How Should One Read a Book?
Virginia Woolf

In the first place, I want to emphasise the note of interrogation at the end of my title. Even if I could answer the question for myself, the answer would apply only to me and not to you. The only advice, indeed, that one person can give another about reading is to take no advice, to follow your own instincts, to use your own reason, to come to your own conclusions. If this is agreed between us, then I feel at liberty to put forward a few ideas and suggestions because you will not allow them to fetter that independence which is the most important quality that a reader can possess. After all, what laws can be laid down about books? The battle of Waterloo was certainly fought on a certain day; but is *Hamlet* a better play than *Lear*? Nobody can say. Each must decide that question for himself. To admit authorities, however heavily furred and gowned, into our libraries and let them tell us how to read, what to read, what value to place upon what we read, is to destroy the spirit of freedom which is the breath of those sanctuaries. Everywhere else we may be bound by laws and conventions—there we have none.

But to enjoy freedom, if the platitude is pardonable, we have of course to control ourselves. We must not squander our powers, helplessly and ignorantly, squirting half the house in order to water a single rose-bush; we must train them, exactly and powerfully, here on the very spot. This, it may be, is one of the first difficulties that faces us in a library. What is "the very spot"? There may well seem to be nothing but a conglomeration and huddle of confusion. Poems and novels, histories and memoirs, dictionaries and bluebooks; books written in all languages by men and women of all tempers, races, and ages jostle each other on the shelf. And outside the donkey brays, the women gossip at the pump, the colts gallop across the fields. Where are we to begin? How are we to bring order into this multitudinous chaos and so get the deepest and widest pleasure from what we read?

It is simple enough to say that since books have classes—fiction, biography, poetry—we should separate them and take from each what it is right that each should give us. Yet few people ask from books what books can give us. Most commonly we come to books with blurred and divided minds, asking of fiction that it shall be true, of poetry that it shall be false, of biography that it shall be flattering, of history that it shall enforce our own prejudices. If we could banish all such preconceptions when we read, that would be an admirable beginning. Do not dictate to your author; try to become him. Be his fellow-worker and accomplice. If you hang back, and reserve and criticise at first, you are preventing yourself from getting the fullest possible value from what you read. But if you open your mind as widely as possible, then signs and hints of almost imperceptible fineness, from the twist and turn of the first sentences, will bring you into the presence of a human being unlike any other. Steep yourself in this, acquaint yourself with this, and soon you will find that your author is giving you, or attempting to give you, something far more definite. The thirty-two chapters of a novel— if we consider how to read a novel first—are an attempt to make something as formed and controlled as a building: but words are more impalpable than bricks; reading is a longer and more complicated process than seeing. Perhaps the quickest way to understand the elements of what a novelist is doing is not to read, but to write; to make your own experiment with the dangers and difficulties of words. Recall, then, some event that has left a distinct impression on you—how at the corner of the street, perhaps, you passed two people talking. A tree shook; an electric light danced; the tone of the talk was comic, but also tragic; a whole vision, an entire conception, seemed contained in that moment.

But when you attempt to reconstruct it in words, you will find that it breaks into a thousand conflicting impressions. Some must be subdued; others emphasized; in the process you will lose, probably, all grasp upon the emotion itself. Then turn from your blurred and littered pages to the opening pages of some great novelist—Defoe, Jane Austen, Hardy. Now you will be better able to appreciate their mastery. It is not merely that we are in the presence of a different person—Defoe, Jane Austen, or Thomas Hardy—but that we are living in a different world. Here, in *Robinson Crusoe*, we are trudging a plain high road; one thing happens after another; the fact and the order of the fact is enough. But if the open air and adventure mean everything to Defoe they mean nothing to Jane Austen. Hers is the drawing-room, and people talking, and by the many mirrors of their talk revealing their characters. And if, when we have accustomed ourselves to the drawing-room and its reflections, we turn to Hardy, we are once more spun round. The moors are round us and the stars are above our heads. The other side of the mind is now exposed—the dark side that comes uppermost in solitude, not the light side that shows in company. Our relations are not towards people, but toward Nature and destiny. Yet different as these worlds are, each is consistent with itself. The maker of each is careful to observe the laws of his own perspective, and however great a strain they may put upon us they will never confuse us, as lesser writers so frequently do, by introducing two different kinds of reality into the same book. Thus to go from one great novelist to another—from Jane Austen to Hardy, from Peacock to Trollope, from Scott to Meredith—is to be wrenched and uprooted; to be thrown this way and then that. To read a novel is a difficult and complex art. You must be capable not only of great fineness of perception, but of great boldness of imagination if you are going to make use of all that the novelist—the great artist—gives you.

But a glance at the heterogeneous company on the shelf will show you that writers are very seldom "great artists"; far more often a book makes no claim to be a work of art at all. These biographies and autobiographies, for example, lives of great men, of men long dead and forgotten, that stand cheek by jowl with the novels and poems, are we to refuse to read them because they are not "art"? Or shall we read them, but read them in a different way, with a different aim? Shall we read them in the first place to satisfy that curiosity which possesses us sometimes when in the evening we linger in front of a house where the lights are lit and the blinds are not yet drawn, and each floor of the house shows us a different section of human life in being? Then we are consumed with curiosity about the lives of these people—the servants gossiping, the gentlemen dining, the girl dressing for a party, the old woman at the window with her knitting. Who are they, what are they, what are their names, their occupations, their thoughts, and adventures?

Biographies and memoirs answer such questions, light up innumerable such houses; they show us people going about their daily affairs, toiling, failing, succeeding, eating, hating, loving, until they die. And sometimes as we watch, the house fades and the iron railings vanish and we are out at sea; we are hunting, sailing, fighting; we are among savages and soldiers; we are taking part in great campaigns. Or if we like to stay here in England, in London, still the scene changes; the street narrows; the house becomes small, cramped, diamond-paned, and malodorous. We see a poet, Donne, driven from such a house because the walls were so thin that when the children cried their voices cut through them. We can follow him, through the paths that lie in the pages of books, to Twickenham; to Lady Bedford's Park, a famous meeting-ground for nobles and poets; and then turn our steps to Wilton, the great house under the downs, and hear Sidney read the *Arcadia* to his sister; and ramble among the very marshes and see the very herons that figure in that famous romance; and then again travel north with that other Lady Pembroke, Anne Clifford, to her wild moors, or plunge into the city and control our merriment at the sight of Gabriel Harvey in his black velvet suit arguing about poetry with Spenser. Nothing is more fascinating than to grope and stumble in the alternate darkness and splendour of Elizabethan London. But there is no staying there. The Temples and the Swifts, the Harleys and the St. Johns beckon us on; hour upon hour can be spent disentangling their quarrels and deciphering their characters; and when we tire of them we can stroll on, past a lady in black wearing diamonds, to Samuel Johnson and Goldsmith and Garrick; or cross the channel, if we like, and meet Voltaire and Diderot, Madame du Deffand; and so back to England and Twickenham—how certain places repeat themselves and certain names!—where Lady Bedford had her Park once and Pope lived later, to Walpole's home at Stawberry Hill. But Walpole introduces us to such a swarm of new acquaintances, there are so many houses to visit and bells to ring that we may well hesitate for a moment, on the Miss Berrys' doorstep, for example, when behold, up comes Thackeray; he is the friend of the woman whom Walpole loved; so that merely by going from friend to friend, from garden to garden, from house to house, we have passed from one end of English literature to another and wake to find ourselves here again in the present, if we can so differentiate this moment from all that have gone before. This, then, is one of the ways in which we can read these lives and letters; we can make them light up the many windows of the past; we can watch the famous dead in their familiar habits and fancy sometimes that we are very close and can surprise their secrets, and sometimes we may pull out a play or a poem that they have written and see whether it reads differently in the presence of the author. But this again rouses other questions. How far, we must ask ourselves, is a book influenced by its writer's life—how far is it safe to let the man interpret the writer? How far shall we resist or give way to the sympathies and antipathies that the man himself rouses in us—so sensitive are words, so receptive of the character of the author? These are questions that press upon us when we read lives and letters, and we must answer them for ourselves, for nothing can be more fatal than to be guided by the preferences of others in a matter so personal.

But also we can read such books with another aim, not to throw light on literature, not to become familiar with famous people, but to refresh and exercise our own creative powers. Is there not an open window on the right hand of the bookcase? How delightful to stop reading and look out! How stimulating the scene is, in its unconsciousness, its irrelevance, its perpetual movement—the colts galloping round the field, the woman filling her pail at the well, the donkey throwing back his head and emitting his long, acrid moan. The greater part of any library is nothing but the record of such fleeting moments in the lives of men, women, and donkeys. Every literature, as it grows old, has its rubbish-heap, its record of vanished moments and forgotten lives told in faltering and feeble accents that have perished. But if you give yourself up to the delight of rubbish-reading you will be surprised, indeed you will be overcome, by the relics of human life that have been cast out to moulder. It may be one letter—but what a vision it gives! It may be a few sentences—but what vistas they suggest! Sometimes a whole story will come together with such beautiful humour and pathos and completeness that it seems as if a great novelist had been at work, yet it is only an old actor, Tate Wilkinson, remembering the strange story of Captain Jones; it is only a young subaltern serving under Arthur Wellesley and falling in love with a pretty girl at Lisbon; it is only Maria Allen letting fall her sewing in the empty drawing-room and sighing how she wishes she had taken Dr. Burney's good advice and had never eloped with her Rishy. None of this has any value; it is negligible in the extreme; yet how absorbing it is now and again to go through the rubbish-heaps and find rings and scissors and broken noses buried in the huge past and try to piece them together while the colt gallops round the field, the woman fills her pail at the well, and the donkey brays.

But we tire of rubbish-reading in the long run. We tire of searching for what is needed to complete the half-truth which is all that the Wilkinsons, the Bunburys, and the Maria Allens are able to offer us. They had not the artist's power of mastering and eliminating; they could not tell the whole truth even about their own lives; they have disfigured the story that might have been so shapely. Facts are all that they can offer us, and facts are a very inferior form of fiction. Thus the desire grows upon us to have done with half-statements and approximations; to cease from searching out the minute shades of human character, to enjoy the greater abstractness, the purer truth of fiction. Thus we create the mood, intense and generalised, unaware of detail, but stressed by some regular, recurrent beat, whose natural expression

is poetry; and that is the time to read poetry when we are almost able
to write it.

> Western wind, when wilt thou blow?
> The small rain down can rain.
> Christ, if my love were in my arms,
> And I in my bed again!

The impact of poetry is so hard and direct that for the moment there
is no other sensation except that of the poem itself. What profound
depths we visit then—how sudden and complete is our immersion!
There is nothing here to catch hold of; nothing to stay us in our flight.
The illusion of fiction is gradual; its effects are prepared; but who
when they read these four lines stops to ask who wrote them, or con-
jures up the thought of Donne's house or Sidney's secretary; or en-
meshes them in the intricacy of the past and the succession of generations? The poet is always our contemporary. Our being for the moment
is centered and constricted, as in any violent shock of personal
emotion. Afterwards, it is true, the sensation begins to spread in wider
rings through our minds; remoter senses are reached; these begin to
sound and to comment and we are aware of echoes and reflections. The
intensity of poetry covers an immense range of emotion. We have only
to compare the force and directness of

> I shall fall like a tree, and find my grave,
> Only remembering that I grieve,

with the wavering modulation of

> Minutes are numbered by the fall of sands,
> As by an hour glass; the span of time
> Doth waste us to our graves, and we look on it;
> An age of pleasure, revelled out, comes home
> At last, and ends in sorrow; but the life,
> Weary of riot, numbers every sand,
> Wailing in sighs, until the last drop down,
> So to conclude calamity in rest,

or place the meditative calm of

> whether we be young or old,
> Our destiny, our being's heart and home,
> Is with infinitude, and only there;
> With hope it is, hope that can never die,
> Effort, and expectation, and desire,
> And something evermore about to be,

beside the complete and inexhaustible loveliness of

> The moving Moon went up the sky,
> And nowhere did abide:
> Softly she was going up,
> And a star or two beside—

or the splendid fantasy of

> And the woodland haunter
> Shall not cease to saunter
>   When, far down some glade,
> Of the great world's burning,
> One soft flame upturning,
> Seems, to his discerning,
>   Crocus in the shade,

to bethink us of the varied art of the poet; his power to make us at once actors and spectators; his power to run his hand into character as if it were a glove, and be Falstaff or Lear; his power to condense, to widen, to state, once and for ever.

"We have only to compare"—with those words the cat is out of the bag, and the true complexity of reading is admitted. The first process, to receive impressions with the utmost understanding, is only half the process of reading; it must be completed, if we are to get the whole pleasure from a book, by another. We must pass judgment upon these multitudinous impressions; we must make of these fleeting shapes one that is hard and lasting. But not directly. Wait for the dust of reading to settle; for the conflict and the questioning to die down; walk, talk, pull the dead petals from a rose, or fall asleep. Then suddenly without our willing it, for it is thus that Nature undertakes these transitions, the book will return, but differently. It will float to the top of the mind as a whole. And the book as a whole is different from the book received currently in separate phrases. Details now fit themselves into their places. We see the shape from start to finish; it is a barn, a pig-sty, or a cathedral. Now then we can compare book with book as we compare building with building. But this act of comparison means that our attitude has changed; we are no longer the friends of the writer, but his judges; and just as we cannot be too sympathetic as friends, so as judges we cannot be too severe. Are they not criminals, books that have wasted our time and sympathy; are they not the most insidious enemies of society, corrupters, defilers, the writers of false books, faked books, books that fill the air with decay and disease? Let us then be severe in our judgments; let us compare each book with the greatest of its kind.

There they hang in the mind, the shapes of the books we have read solidified by the judgments we have passed on them—*Robinson Crusoe, Emma, The Return of the Native.* Compare the novels with these— even the latest and least of novels has a right to be judged with the best. And so with poetry—when the intoxication or rhythm has died down and the splendour of words has faded, a visionary shape will return to us and this must be compared with *Lear,* with *Phèdre,* with *The Prelude;* or if not with these, with whatever is the best or seems to us to be the best in its own kind. And we may be sure that the newness of new poetry and fiction is its most superficial quality and that we have only to alter slightly, not to recast, the standards by which we have judged the old.

It would be foolish, then, to pretend that the second part of reading, to judge, to compare, is as simple as the first—to open the mind wide to the fast flocking of innumerable impressions. To continue reading without the book before you, to hold one shadow-shape against another, to have read widely enough and with enough understanding to make such comparisons alive and illuminating—that is difficult; it is still more difficult to press further and to say, "Not only is the book of this sort, but it is of this value; here it fails; here it succeeds; this is bad; that is good." To carry out this part of a reader's duty needs such imagination, insight, and learning that it is hard to conceive any one mind sufficiently endowed; impossible for the most self-confident to find more than the seeds of such powers in himself. Would it not be wiser, then, to remit this part of reading and to allow the critics, the gowned and furred authorities of the library, to decide the question of the book's absolute value for us? Yet how impossible! We may stress the value of sympathy; we may try to sink our own identity as we read. But we know that we cannot sympathise wholly or immerse ourselves wholly; there is always a demon in us who whispers, "I hate, I love," and we cannot silence him. Indeed, it is precisely because we hate and we love that our relation with the poets and novelists is so intimate that we find the presence of another person intolerable. And even if the results are abhorrent and our judgments are wrong, still our taste, the nerve of sensation that sends shocks through us, is our chief illuminant; we learn through feeling; we cannot suppress our own idiosyncrasy without impoverishing it. But as time goes on perhaps we can train our taste; perhaps we can make it submit to some control. When it has fed greedily and lavishly upon books of all sorts—poetry, fiction, history, biography—and has stopped reading and looked for long spaces upon the variety, the incongruity of the living word, we shall find that it is changing a little; it is not so greedy, it is more reflective. It will begin to bring us not merely judgments on particular books, but it will tell us that there is a quality common to certain books. Listen, it will say, what shall we call *this?* And it will read us perhaps *Lear* and then perhaps the *Agamemnon* in order to bring out that common quality. Thus, with our taste to guide us, we shall venture beyond the particular book in search of qualities that group books together; we shall give them names and thus frame a rule that brings order into our perceptions. We shall gain a further and a rarer pleasure from that discrimination. But as a rule only lives when it is perpetually broken by contact with the books themselves—nothing is easier and more stultifying than to make rules which exist out of touch with facts, in a vacuum—now at last, in order to steady ourselves in this difficult attempt, it may be well to turn to the very rare writers who are able to enlighten us upon literature as an art. Coleridge and Dryden and Johnson, in their considered criticism, the poets and novelists themselves in their unconsidered sayings, are often surprisingly relevant; they light up and solidify the vague ideas that have been tumbling in the misty depths of our minds. But they are only able to help us if we come to them laden with questions and suggestions won honestly in the course of our own reading. They can do nothing for us if we herd ourselves under their authority and lie down like sheep in the shade of a hedge. We can only understand their ruling when it comes in conflict with our own and vanquishes it.

If this is so, if to read a book as it should be read calls for the rarest qualities of imagination, insight, and judgment, you may perhaps conclude that literature is a very complex art and that it is unlikely that we shall be able, even after a lifetime of reading, to make any valuable contribution to its criticism. We must remain readers; we shall not put on the further glory that belongs to those rare beings who are also critics. But still we have our responsibilities as readers and even our importance. The standards we raise and the judgment we pass steal into the air and become part of the atmosphere which writers breathe as they work. An influence is created which tells upon them even if it never finds its way into print. And that influence, if it were well instructed, vigorous and individual and sincere, might be of great value now when criticism is necessarily in abeyance; when books pass in review like the procession of animals in a shooting gallery, and the critic has only one second in which to load and aim and shoot and may well be pardoned if he mistakes rabbits for tigers, eagles for barndoor fowls, or misses altogether and wastes his shot upon some peaceful cow grazing in a further field. If behind the erratic gunfire of the press the author felt that there was another kind of criticism, the opinion of people reading for the love of reading, slowly and unprofessionally, and judging with great sympathy and yet with great severity, might this not improve the quality of his work? And if by our means books were to become stronger, richer, and more varied, that would be an end worth reaching.

Yet who reads to bring about an end, however desirable? Are there not some pursuits that we practise because they are good in themselves, and some pleasures that are final? And is not this among them? I have sometimes dreamt, at least, that when the Day of Judgment dawns and the great conquerors and lawyers and statesmen come to receive their rewards—their crowns, their laurels, their names carved indelibly upon imperishable marble—the Almighty will turn to Peter and will say, not without a certain envy when He sees us coming with our books under our arms, "Look, these need no reward. We have nothing to give them here. They have loved reading."

A *Primer of Existentialism*
Gordon E. Bigelow

For some years I fought the word by irritably looking the other way whenever I stumbled across it, hoping that like dadaism and some of the other "isms" of the French *avant garde* it would go away if I ignored it. But existentialism was apparently more than the picture it evoked of uncombed beards, smoky basement cafes, and French beatniks regaling one another between sips of absinthe with brilliant variations on the theme of despair. It turned out to be of major importance to literature and the arts, to philosophy and theology, and of increasing importance to the social sciences. To learn more about it, I read several of the self-styled introductions to the subject, with the baffled sensation of a man who reads a critical introduction to a novel only to find that he must read the novel before he can understand the introduction. Therefore, I should like to provide here something most discussions of existentialism take for granted, a simple statement of its basic characteristics. This is a reckless thing to do because there are several kinds of existentialism and what one says of one kind may not be true of another, but there is an area of agreement, and it is this common ground that I should like to set forth here. We should not run into trouble so long as we understand from the outset that the six major themes outlined below will apply in varying degrees to particular existentialists. A reader should be able to go from here to the existentialists themselves, to the more specialized critiques of them, or be able to recognize an existentialist theme or coloration in literature when he sees it.

A word first about the kinds of existentialism. Like transcendentalism of the last century, there are almost as many varieties of this *ism* as there are individual writers to whom the word is applied (not all of them claim it). But without being facetious we might group them into two main kinds, the *ungodly* and the *godly*. To take the ungodly or atheistic first, we would list as the chief spokesmen among many others Jean-Paul Sartre, Albert Camus, and Simone de Beauvoir. Several of this important group of French writers had rigorous and significant experience in the Resistance during the Nazi occupation of France in World War II. Out of the despair which came with the collapse of their nation during those terrible years they found unexpected strength in the single indomitable human spirit, which even under severe torture could maintain the spirit of resistance, the unextinguishable ability to say "No." From this irreducible core in the human spirit, they erected after the war a philosophy which was a twentieth-century variation of the philosophy of Descartes. But instead of saying "I think, therefore I am," they said "I can say No, therefore I exist." As we shall presently see, the use of the word "exist" is of prime significance. This group is chiefly responsible for giving existentialism its status in the popular mind as a literary-philosophical cult.

Of the godly or theistic existentialists we should mention first a mid-nineteenth-century Danish writer, Søren Kierkegaard; two contemporary French Roman Catholics, Gabriel Marcel and Jacques Maritain; two Protestant theologians, Paul Tillich and Nicholas Berdyaev; and Martin Buber, an important contemporary Jewish theologian. Taken together, their writings constitute one of the most significant developments in modern theology. Behind both groups of existentialists stand other important figures, chiefly philosophers, who exert powerful influence upon the movement—Blaise Pascal, Friedrich Nietzsche, Henri Bergson, Martin Heidegger, Karl Jaspers, among others. Several literary figures, notably Tolstoy and Dostoievsky, are frequently cited because existentialist attitudes and themes are prominent in their writings. The eclectic nature of this movement should already be sufficiently clear and the danger of applying too rigidly to any particular figure the general characteristics of the movement which I now make bold to describe:

1. Existence before essence. Existentialism gets its name from an insistence that human life is understandable only in terms of an individual man's existence, his particular experience of life. It says that a man *lives* (has existence) rather than *is* (has being or essence), and that every man's experience of life is unique, radically different from everyone else's and can be understood truly only in terms of his involvement in life or commitment to it. It strenuously shuns that view which assumes an ideal of Man or Mankind, a universal of human nature of which each man is only one example. It eschews the question of Greek philosophy, *"What is mankind?"* which suggests that man can be defined if he is ranged in his proper place in the order of nature; it asks instead the question of Job and St. Augustine, *"Who am I?"* with its suggestion of the uniqueness and mystery of each human life and its emphasis upon the subjective or personal rather than the objective or impersonal. From the outside a man appears to be just another natural creature; from the inside he is an entire universe, the center of infinity. The existentialist insists upon this latter radically subjective view, and from this grows much of the rest of existentialism.

2. *Reason is impotent to deal with the depths of human life.* There are two parts to this proposition—first, that human reason is relatively weak and imperfect, and second, that there are dark places in human life which are "nonreason" and to which reason scarcely penetrates. Since Plato, Western civilization has usually assumed a separation of reason from the rest of the human psyche, and has glorified reason as suited to command the nonrational part. The classic statement of this separation appears in the *Phaedrus,* where Plato describes the psyche in the myth of the chariot which is drawn by the white steeds of the emotions and the black unruly steeds of the appetites. The driver of the chariot is Reason who holds the reins which control the horses and the whip to subdue the surging black steeds of passion. Only the driver, the rational nature, is given human form; the rest of the psyche, the nonrational part, is given a lower, animal form. This separation and exaltation of reason is carried further in the allegory of the cave in the *Republic.* You recall the sombre picture of human life with which the story begins: men are chained in the dark in a cave, with their backs to a flickering firelight, able to see only uncertain shadows moving on the wall before them, able to hear only confused echoes of sounds. One of the men, breaking free from his chains, is able to turn and look upon the objects themselves and the light which casts the shadows; even, at last, he is able to work his way entirely out of the cave into the sunlight beyond. All this he is able to do through his reason; he escapes from the bondage of error, from time and change, from death itself, into the realm of changeless eternal ideas or Truth, and the lower nature which had chained him in darkness is left behind.

Existentialism in our time, and this is one of its most important characteristics, insists upon reuniting the "lower" or irrational parts of the psyche with the "higher." It insists that man must be taken in his wholeness and not in some divided state, that whole man contains not only intellect but also anxiety, guilt, and the will to power—which modify and sometimes overwhelm the reason. A man seen in this light is fundamentally ambiguous, if not mysterious, full of contradictions and tensions which cannot be dissolved simply by taking thought. "Human life," said Berdyaev, "is permeated by underground streams." One is reminded of D. H. Lawrence's outburst against Franklin and his rational attempt to achieve moral perfection: "The Perfectability of Man! . . . The perfectability of which man? I am many men. Which of them are you going to perfect? I am not a mechanical contrivance. . . . It's a queer thing is a man's soul. It is the whole of him. Which means it is the unknown as well as the known. . . . The soul of man is a dark vast forest, with wild life in it." The emphasis in existentialism is not on idea but upon the thinker who has the idea. It accepts not only his power of thought, but his contingency and fallibility, his frailty, his body, blood, and bones, and above all his death. Kierkegaard emphasized the distinction between *subjective* truth (what a person *is*) and *objective* truth (what the person *knows*), and said that we encounter the true self not in the detachment of thought but in the involvement and agony of choice and in the pathos of commitment to our choice. This distrust of rational systems helps to explain why many existential writers in their own expression are paradoxical or prophetic or gnomic, why their works often belong more to literature than to philosophy.

3. *Alienation or estrangement.* One major result of the dissociation of reason from the rest of the psyche has been the growth of science, which has become one of the hallmarks of Western civilization, and an ever-increasing rational ordering of men in society. As the existentialists view them, the main forces of history since the Renaissance have progressively separated man from concrete earthy existence, have forced him to live at ever higher levels of abstraction, have collectivized individual man out of existence, have driven God from the heavens, or what is the same thing, from the hearts of men. They are convinced that modern man lives in a fourfold condition of alienation: from God, from nature, from other men, from his own true self.

The estrangement from God is most shockingly expressed by Nietzsche's anguished cry, "God is dead," a cry which has continuously echoed through the writings of the existentialists, particularly the French. This theme of spiritual barrenness is a commonplace in literature of this century, from Eliot's "Hollow Man" to the novels of Dos Passos, Hemingway, and Faulkner. It often appears in writers not commonly associated with the existentialists as in this remarkable passage from A *Story-Teller's Story,* where Sherwood Anderson describes his own awakening to his spiritual emptiness. He tells of walking alone late at night along a moonlit road when,

I had suddenly an odd, and to my own seeming, a ridiculous desire to abase myself before something not human and so stepping into the moonlit road, I knelt in the dust. Having no God, the gods having been taken from me by the life about me, as a personal God has been taken from all modern men by a force within that man himself does not understand but that is called the intellect, I kept smiling at the figure I cut in my own eyes as I knelt in the road. . . .

There was no God in the sky, no God in myself, no conviction in myself that I had the power to believe in a God, and so I merely knelt in the dust in silence and no words came to my lips.

In another passage Anderson wondered if the giving of itself by an entire generation to mechanical things was not really making all men impotent, if the desire for a greater navy, a greater army, taller public buildings, was not a sign of growing impotence. He felt that Puritanism and the industrialism which was its offspring had sterilized modern life, and proposed that men return to a healthful animal vigor by renewed contact with simple things of the earth, among them untrammeled sexual expression. One is reminded of the unkempt and delectable raffishness of Steinbeck's *Cannery Row* or of D. H. Lawrence's quasi-religious doctrine of sex, "blood-consciousness" and the "divine otherness" of animal existence.

Man's estrangement from nature has been a major theme in literature at least since Rousseau and the Romantic movement, and can hardly be said to be the property of existentialists. But this group nevertheless adds its own insistence that one of modern man's most urgent dangers is that he builds ever higher the brick and steel walls of technology which shut him away from a health-giving life according to "nature." Their treatment of this theme is most commonly expressed as part of a broader insistence that modern man needs to shun abstraction and return to "concreteness" or "wholeness."

A third estrangement has occurred at the social level and its sign is growing dismay at man's helplessness before the great machine-like colossus of industrialized society. This is another major theme of Western literature, and here again, though they hardly discovered the danger or began the protest, the existentialists in our time renew the protest against any pattern or force which would stifle the unique and spontaneous in individual life. The crowding of men into cities, the subdivision of labor which submerges the man in his economic function, the burgeoning of centralized government, the growth of advertising, propaganda, and mass media of entertainment and communication— all the things which force men into Riesman's "Lonely Crowd"—these same things drive men asunder by destroying their individuality and making them live on the surface of life, content to deal with things rather than people. "Exteriorization," says Berdyaev, "is the source of slavery, whereas freedom is interiorization. Slavery always indicates alienation, the ejection of human nature into the external." This kind of alienation is exemplified by Zero, in Elmer Rice's play "The Adding Machine." Zero's twenty-five years as a bookkeeper in a department store have dried up his humanity, making him incapable of love, of friendship, of any deeply felt, freely expressed emotion. Such estrangement is often given as the reason for man's inhumanity to man, the explanation of injustice in modern society. In Camus' short novel, aptly called *The Stranger*, a young man is convicted by a court of murder. This is a homicide which he has actually committed under extenuating circumstances. But the court never listens to any of the relevant evidence, seems never to hear anything that pertains to the crime itself; it convicts the young man on wholly irrelevant grounds—because he had behaved in an unconventional way at his mother's funeral the day before the homicide. In this book one feels the same dream-like distortion of reality as in the trial scene in *Alice in Wonderland*, a suffocating sense of being enclosed by events which are irrational or absurd but also inexorable. Most disturbing of all is the young man's aloneness, the impermeable membrane of estrangement which surrounds him and prevents anyone else from penetrating to his experience of life or sympathizing with it.

The fourth kind of alienation, man's estrangement from his own true self, especially as his nature is distorted by an exaltation of reason, is another theme having an extensive history as a major part of the Romantic revolt. Of the many writers who treat the theme, Hawthorne comes particularly close to the emphasis of contemporary existentialists. His Ethan Brand, Dr. Rappaccini, and Roger Chillingworth are a recurrent figure who represents the dislocation in human nature which results when an overdeveloped or misapplied intellect severs "the magnetic chain of human sympathy." Hawthorne is thoroughly existential in his concern for the sanctity of the individual human soul, as well as in his preoccupation with sin and the dark side of human nature, which must be seen in part as his attempt to build back some fullness to the flattened image of man bequeathed to him by the Enlightenment. Whitman was trying to do this when he added flesh and bone and a sexual nature to the spiritualized image of man he inherited from Emerson, though his image remains diffused and attenuated by the same cosmic optimism. Many of the nineteenth-century depictions of man represent him as a figure of power or of potential power, sometimes as daimonic, like Melville's Ahab, but after World War I the power is gone; man is not merely distorted or truncated, he is hollow, powerless, faceless. At the time when his command over natural forces seems to be unlimited, man is pictured as weak, ridden with nameless dread. And this brings us to another of the major themes of existentialism.

4. *"Fear and trembling," anxiety.* At Stockholm when he accepted the Nobel Prize, William Faulkner said that "Our tragedy today is a general and universal physical fear so long sustained by now that we can even bear it. There are no longer problems of the spirit. There is only one question: When will I be blown up?" The optimistic vision of the Enlightenment which saw man, through reason and its extensions in science, conquering all nature and solving all social and political problems in a continuous upward spiral of Progress, cracked open like a melon on the rock of World War I. The theories which held such high hopes died in that sickening and unimaginable butchery. Here was a concrete fact of human nature and society which the theories could not contain. The Great Depression and World War II deepened the sense of dismay which the loss of these ideals brought, but only with the atomic bomb did this become an unbearable terror, a threat of instant annihilation which confronted all men, even those most insulated by the thick crust of material goods and services. Now the most unthinking person could sense that each advance in mechanical technique carried not only a chromium and plush promise of comfort but a threat as well.

Sartre, following Kierkegaard, speaks of another kind of anxiety which oppresses modern man—"the anguish of Abraham"—the necessity which is laid upon him to make moral choices on his own responsibility. A military officer in wartime knows the agony of choice which forces him to sacrifice part of his army to preserve the rest, as does a man in high political office, who must make decisions affecting the lives of millions. The existentialists claim that each of us must make moral decisions in our own lives which involve the same anguish. Kierkegaard finds that this necessity is one thing which makes each life unique, which makes it impossible to speculate or generalize about human life, because each man's case is irretrievably his own, something in which he is personally and passionately involved. His book *Fear and Trembling* is an elaborate and fascinating commentary on the Old Testament story of Abraham, who was commanded by God to sacrifice his beloved son Isaac. Abraham thus becomes the emblem of man who must make a harrowing choice, in this case between love for his son and love for God, between the universal moral law which says categorically, "thou shalt not kill," and the unique inner demand of his religious faith. Abraham's decision, which is to violate the abstract and collective moral law, has to be made not in arrogance but in fear and trembling, one of the inferences being that sometimes one must make an exception to the general law because he is (existentially) an exception, a concrete being whose existence can never be completely subsumed under any universal.

5. *The encounter with nothingness.* For the man alienated from God, from nature, from his fellow man and from himself, what is left at last but Nothingness? The testimony of the existentialists is that this is where modern man now finds himself, not on the highway of upward Progress toward a radiant Utopia but on the brink of a catastrophic precipice, below which yawns the absolute void, an uncompromised black Nothingness. In one sense this is Eliot's Wasteland inhabited by his Hollow Man, who is

> Shape without form, shade without color
> Paralyzed force, gesture without motion.

That is what moves E. A. Robinson's Richard Cory, the man who is everything that might make us wish that we were in his place, to go home one calm summer night and put a bullet through his head.

One of the most convincing statements of the encounter with Nothingness is made by Leo Tolstoy in "My Confession." He tells how in good health, in the prime of life, when he had everything that a man could desire—wealth, fame, aristocratic social position, a beautiful wife and children, a brilliant mind and great artistic talent in the height of their powers, he nevertheless was seized with a growing uneasiness, a nameless discontent which he could not shake or alleviate. His experience was like that of a man who falls sick, with symptoms which he disregards as insignificant; but the symptoms return again and again until they merge into a continuous suffering. And the patient suddenly is confronted with the overwhelming fact that what he took for mere indisposition is more important to him than anything else on earth, that it is death! "I felt the ground on which I stood was crumbling, that there was nothing for me to stand on, that what I had been living for was nothing, that I had no reason for living. . . . To stop was impossible, to go back was impossible; and it was impossible to shut my eyes so as to see that there was nothing before me but suffering and actual death, absolute annihilation." This is the "Sickness Unto Death" of Kierkegaard, the despair in which one wishes to die but cannot. Hemingway's short story, "A Clean, Well-Lighted Place," gives an unforgettable expression of this theme. At the end of the story, the old waiter climbs into bed late at night saying to himself, "What did he fear? It was not fear or dread. It was a nothing which he knew too well. It was all a nothing and a man was nothing too. . . . Nada y pues nada, y nada y pues nada." And then because he has experienced the death of God he goes on to recite the Lord's Prayer in blasphemous despair: "Our Nothing who are in Nothing, nothing be thy nothing. . . ." And then the Ave Maria, "Hail nothing, full of nothing. . . ." This is stark, even for Hemingway, but the old waiter does no more than name the void felt by most people in the early Hemingway novels, a hunger they seek to assuage with alcohol, sex, and violence in an aimless progress from bar to bed to bull-ring. It goes without saying that much of the despair and pessimism in other contemporary authors springs from a similar sense of the void in modern life.

6. *Freedom.* Sooner or later, as a theme that includes all the others, the existentialist writings bear upon freedom. The themes we have outlined above describe either some loss of man's freedom or some threat to it, and all existentialists of whatever sort are concerned to enlarge the range of human freedom.

For the avowed atheists like Sartre freedom means human autonomy. In a purposeless universe man is *condemned* to freedom because he is the only creature who is "self-surpassing," who can become something other than he is. Precisely because there is no God to give purpose to the universe, each man must accept individual responsibility for his own becoming, a burden made heavier by the fact that in choosing for himself he chooses for all men "the image of man as he ought to be." A man *is* the sum total of the acts that make up his life—no more, no less—and though the coward has made himself cowardly, it is always possible for him to change and make himself heroic. In Sartre's novel, *The Age of Reason,* one of the least likable of the characters, almost overwhelmed by despair and self-disgust at his homosexual tendencies, is on the point of solving his problem by mutilating himself with a razor, when in an effort of will he throws the instrument down, and we are given to understand that from this moment he will have mastery over his aberrant drive. Thus in the daily course of ordinary life must men shape their becoming in Sartre's world.

The religious existentialists interpret man's freedom differently. They use much the same language as Sartre, develop the same themes concerning the predicament of man, but always include God as a radical factor. They stress the man of faith rather than the man of will. They interpret man's existential condition as a state of alienation from his essential nature which is God-like, the problem of his life being to heal the chasm between the two, that is, to find salvation. The mystery and ambiguity of man's existence they attribute to his being the intersection of two realms. "Man bears within himself," writes Berdyaev, "the image which is both the image of man and the image of God, and is the image of man as far as the image of God is actualized." Tillich describes salvation as "the act in which the cleavage between the

essential being and the existential situation is overcome." Freedom
here, as for Sartre, involves an acceptance of responsibility for choice
and a *commitment* to one's choice. This is the meaning of faith, a faith
like Abraham's, the commitment which is an agonizing sacrifice of one's
own desire and will and dearest treasure to God's will.

A final word. Just as one should not expect to find in a particular writer
all of the characteristics of existentialism as we have described them, he
should also be aware that some of the most striking expressions of
existentialism in literature and the arts come to us by indirection, often
through symbols or through innovations in conventional form. Take
the preoccupation of contemporary writers with time. In *The Sound
and the Fury,* Faulkner both collapses and expands normal clock time,
or by juxtapositions of past and present blurs time into a single
amorphous pool. He does this by using various forms of "stream of
consciousness" or other techniques which see life in terms of unique,
subjective experience—that is, existentially. The conventional view of
externalized life, a rational orderly progression cut into uniform segments by the hands of a clock, he rejects in favor of a view which sees
life as opaque, ambiguous, and irrational—that is, as the existentialist
sees it. Graham Greene does something like this in *The Power and the
Glory.* He creates a scene isolated in time and cut off from the rest of
the world, steamy and suffocating as if a bell jar had been placed over
it. Through this atmosphere fetid with impending death and human
suffering, stumbles the whiskey priest, lonely and confused, pursued by
a police lieutenant who has experienced the void and the death of God.

Such expressions in literature do not mean necessarily that the authors are conscious existentialist theorizers, or even that they know the
writings of such theorizers. Faulkner may never have read Heidegger
—or St. Augustine—both of whom attempt to demonstrate that time is
more within a man and subject to his unique experience of it than it is
outside him. But it is legitimate to call Faulkner's views of time and life
"existential" in this novel because in recent years existentialist theorizers have given such views a local habitation and a name. One of the
attractions, and one of the dangers, of existential themes is that they
become like Sir Thomas Browne's quincunx: once one begins to look
for them, he sees them everywhere. But if one applies restraint and
discrimination, he will find that they illuminate much of contemporary
literature and sometimes the literature of the past as well.

Suggestions for Writing

1. Write a sentence that states Mrs. Woolf's point more sharply and inclusively than she herself has done in any one sentence, perhaps something like "In reading a book one should _____ because _____."

2. Write an essay on the subject "On Becoming Mrs. Woolf." You will start, of course, by pointing out to your readers that this is an exercise recommended by Mrs. Woolf herself ("Do not dictate to your author; try to become him"). But first you must find a central thesis, perhaps trying out, in your mind or in class, one of the following:

   a. Becoming Mrs. Woolf is an uneasy experience.

   b. Becoming Mrs. Woolf is an exciting experience.

In developing either of these, you would consider the intensity of her imagination and the question of how she perceives reality—the braying of the donkey and the women at the pump; the moment at the corner when the tree shook; the times when, through books, experience can seem a mansion, a ship, or a diamond-paned house; the question about "the very spot"; the urgency where "there is no staying"; the fleeting moments, hers and those the library contains. You might go on to explain to your readers what Mrs. Woolf does with windows, with mirrors, with the donkey, with the humorous rose bush turned to dead petals as we wait "for the dust of reading to settle." You will certainly want to explain what she is picturing when she mentions "the dark side of the mind," and why the phrase is both familiar and exciting.

3. Write a direct expository essay explaining to your readers Mrs. Woolf's theory of values. Begin by remarking that Mrs. Woolf's values—that is, what she values in literature—at first seem confusing, even contradictory. She seems to say that no one should judge, that all things have their different and individual values; yet she clearly believes that *Lear* is better than *Hamlet,* and that the good judge would agree. Then end your introductory paragraph with a good expository thesis, well edged—something like "Mrs. Woolf believes in absolute standards, but knowing that standards are hard to apply, she admits into heaven the mere joy of reading."

   Try to use, in your essay, three of her words you have not used before—*multitudinous, impalpable, trudging, heterogeneous, fancy, malodorous,* and so forth.

4. Write an essay defining some ordinary concept—like education, loyalty, success, love. Develop your explanation from the arguable thesis "Though commonly used, commonly misunderstood." Show what the thing you are defining is not, and what it truly is.

5. Write an essay on the thesis "Mrs. Woolf shows existentialist tendencies" using evidence only from "How Should One Read a Book?"

6. Write an essay on the thesis "Life on this campus would be better if, in choosing for himself, everyone followed Sartre's rule of choosing for all men 'the image of man as he ought to be.'" Try to use three or four striking words from Bigelow—*gnomic, raffishness, dislocation, amorphous, steamy.* Try one sentence like Bigelow's "The crowding of men into cities . . ." (p. 15). Work in somewhere one Shakespearian allusion, as Bigelow does in his final paragraph when he quotes indirectly and subtly from the following familiar lines in *A Midsummer Night's Dream:*

> And, as imagination bodies forth
> The forms of things unknown, the poet's pen
> Turns them into shapes, and gives to airy nothing
> A local habitation and a name.

The War Against the Young: Its Beginnings RICHARD POIRIER · *24*
The Student Drive to Destruction LOUIS J. HALLE · *41*
A Federal Judge Digs the Young CHARLES E. WYZANSKI, JR. · *47*
The War Against the Democratic Process SYDNEY HOOK · *53*

Structure

Middle Tactics

These essays illustrate not only how an argument provides a sharp thesis, pointing a clear line through the whole essay, but also how a writer deploys the *pro*'s and *con*'s of his argument in the body, or "middle," of his essay. Again, as you read, look for a specific statement of thesis in each. Read the essays through once, to get your bearings. Then, to acquire a feeling for middle tactics, go through again, marking all words and phrases—*but, now to be sure*, and the like—that signal the turns from one side of the question to the other. You might bracket as *pro* all portions of the essay affirming the author's thesis and *con* all admissions in favor of the opposition. The two diagrams under Suggestions for Writing included at the end of this section may help you to see the tactical principles.

The War Against the Young:
Its Beginnings
Richard Poirier

The social systems which organize and rationalize contemporary life have always been ingeniously armed for the day when youth would rebel against the essentially pastoral status assigned to it. Despite pamperings until recently unimaginable, despite economic briberies and various psychological coercions, the rebellion has broken out. Predictably, the response to it is a gradual escalation involving a more naked use of the tactics that were supposed to prevent, but which also helped to provoke, the crisis in the first place: patronizations, put-downs, and tongue-lashings, along with offers of a place in the governing system (if only the system is left intact) and promises that in any case the future itself holds the solution to whatever now seems to be the trouble. If this technique sounds familiar in its mixture of brutality and pacification, in its combination of aggression and absorption, noted by Edgar Freidenberg in his brilliant analysis of the adult treatment of the adolescent minority, if it sounds vaguely like methods used in other and related domestic and foreign conflicts, then the point is obvious: our society is unfortunately structured, in the prevalent forms of its language and thinking, in ways designed to suppress some of the most vital elements now struggling into consciousness and toward some awareness of their frustrated powers.

This struggle is essentially a cultural one, regardless of the efforts by older people to make political use of it or to place it, unflatteringly, within the terms of traditional politics, particularly cold-war politics. The intellectual weapons used in the war against youth are from the same arsenal—and the young know this—from which war is being waged against other revolutionary movements, against Vietnam, against any effective justice, as distinguished from legislative melodrama, in matters of race and poverty. These weapons, as I've suggested, are by no means crude. They scarcely look at times like weapons at all, and many of the people most adroit in handling them, writers and teachers as well as politicians, aren't even aware that they are directing against youth arguments of a kind used also to rationalize other policies which they consider senseless and immoral. Aside from the political necessities of candidates, why is it that people who can be tough-mindedly idealistic in opposition to our actions in Vietnam or to our treatment of the powerless, talk about youth and think about the rebellion of youth in a manner implicit in the mentality that produces and excuses these other barbarities? The reason, I think, is that most people don't want to face the possibility that each of these troubles grows from the same root and can be traced back to the same habits of mind within each of us and within the social organisms to which we have lent ourselves. They prefer isolated and relatively visible sources for such difficulties, along with the illusion that each of them is susceptible to accredited forms of political or economic cleansing. By contrast, it is the conviction of the most militant young people, and of some older ones, that any solutions will require a radical change in the historical, philosophical, and psychological assumptions that are the foundations of any political or economic system. Some kind of cultural revolution is therefore the necessary prelude even to our capacity to think intelligently about political reformation.

Oddly enough, the young are proved right, in this supposition at least, by the nature of the attacks made against them. I don't mean attacks from the likes of Reagan and Wallace, but those coming from becalmed and sensible men, whose moderation is of a piece with their desire to increase the efficiency of the present system. At work in these attacks are the same tendencies of thought and language that shape the moderate, rationalizing analyses of the other nightmares I've mentioned.

Maybe the most prevalent of these tendencies is the insistence on a language that is intellectually "cool," a language aloof from militant or revolutionary vocabularies which in their exclusion sound excessive, exaggerated, and unserviceable. This cool language is not at all dull or plodding. On the contrary, it's full of social flair; it swings with big words, slang words, naughty words, leaping nimbly from the "way out" to the "way in"—it really holds the world together, hips and squares alike. The best working example is the style of *Time* magazine, and it wasn't surprising to find there a piece full of compliments to what were called in the title "Anti-Revolutionaries." With the suave observation that writers like these "who prefer rationality to revolution are by no means conservative," they honored three distinguished commentators on youth and other scenes. One of the three, Benjamin DeMott, a professor of English at Amherst, diversely active as a novelist, critic, and educational innovator, had earlier written an essay in the Sunday *New York Times Magazine* on the style of what he called the "spirit of overkill" among some of his fellow writers, especially those of the revolutionary fringe like Paul Goodman, Andrew Kopkind, and Susan Sontag.

According to DeMott, writing of the sixties in 1968, the verbal violence of this decade "was" (and I'll get to the significance of this past tense in a moment) "pressed not at new 'enemies' but at old ones already in tatters." Just at a glance one had to wonder why "enemies," new or old, were assigned the unreality of quotation marks. Had the semblance of negotiations made the war in Vietnam disappear as an "enemy"? Does he mean racial injustice? the horrors of urban life? the smothering effects of educational institutions of which he is himself one of the most astute critics? I'm afraid these enemies aren't so easily dispelled. The degree to which they press against DeMott's own "cool" dismissal of them is in fact made evident, with engaging innocence, in the very form of his essay. In order to find a requisite dispassion for his own style, as against what he mistakenly takes for the dominant style of this decade, he must project himself to the end of the century and then look back at us. Like other critics of our violence, he is himself already visiting the famous year 2000, programming for which, as we are cautioned by a number of distinguished economists, sociologists, and technicians, will only be disrupted by people who fail to remain politely soft-spoken amid the accumulating squalor, blood, and suffering of their lives.

This peculiar form of address, by which we are asked to hear our present as if it were our past, suggests yet another and more subtle method of repression—the futuristic—now especially popular in the social sciences. A notably unembarrassed practitioner, and yet another writer commended by the article in *Time* magazine, is Zbigniew Brzezinski, director of the Research Institute on Communist Affairs at Columbia, a sometime member of the Policy Planning Staff of the State Department, and head of Hubert Humphrey's "task force" on foreign affairs for the 1968 election. Also concerned because revolutionary loudmouths and their young adherents are incited by the past rather than the future—keep in mind that there is no present, in case you thought it was hurting someone—Brzezinski published two futuristic position papers in the *New Republic:* "The American Transition," and more recently, "Revolution and Counterrevolution (But Not Necessarily About Columbia!)." These were later incorporated into his book *Between Two Ages.* Happily bounding over invisible rainbows, Brzezinski lets us know that, like it or not, we are already becoming a "technetronic society," and any old-fashioned doctrinal or ideological habits—as if ideology wouldn't be inherent in his imagined social systems—will get us into real, permanent troubles instead of temporary ones. We'll fail to adapt, that is, to "the requirements of the metamorphic age," and thus miss the chance to create a "meritocratic democracy" in which "a community of organization-oriented, application-minded intellectuals [can relate] itself more effectively to the political system than their predecessors." We need only stay calm, and admittedly such language is not designed to excite us, since "improved governmental performance, and its increased sensitivity to social needs is being stimulated by the growing involvement in national affairs of what Kenneth Boulding has called the Educational and Scientific Establishment (EASE)."

Deifications have of course always been announced by capitalization. As in religion, so in politics: an "excessive" concern for the present is a sure way of impairing your future. We are, remember, "between two ages." If, in the one case, you might as well surrender your will to God, in the other you might as well surrender it to EASE, or, getting back to DeMott patiently waiting there at the turn of the century, to "the architects of the Great Disengagement," with "their determination to negotiate the defusing of The Words as well as of The Bombs." But I'm afraid it's merely symptomatic of how bad things are now that many of those who want the young and the rebellious to be more quiet follow the antique example of Hubert Humphrey: they speak to the young not about the past, not even about the present, but about some future, which, as prognosticators, they're already privileged to know. They are There; the revolutionists are living in the Past. And who is here and now, living, suffering, and impassioned in the present? Apparently no one, except maybe a few of what Brzezinski likes to call the "historical irrelevants."

If the young are inarticulate, if, when they do try to expound their views, they sound foolish, are these, and other examples of adult thinking and writing which I'll get to presently, somehow evidences of superior civilization, something to be emulated, the emanations of a system worth saving from revolution? Such arguments and such uses of language—almost wholly abstracted from the stuff of daily life as it is lived in this year, these months, this week—do not define but rather exemplify the cultural and linguistic crisis to which the young are responding with silence even more than with other demonstrations of their nearly helpless discontent. "Power, or the shadow cast by power, always ends in creating an axiological writing," as the French critic Roland Barth puts it, "in which the distance which usually separates fact from value disappears within the space of a word." To prefer "rationality" to "revolution" is good *Time* magazine language. It can't be faulted except by those who feel, as I do, that a revolution is probably necessary if rationality is to be restored to a society that thinks it has been operating rationally. If the young are "revolutionary," and if this is the reverse of "rational," what, then, is the nature of the rationality they're attacking? Quite aside from science fiction passing for history in the writings we've just looked at, are the practices of the United States government with regard to most issues of race, ecology, poverty, the war, the gun laws, or even the postal service rational? Is it rational to vote an increase of money for Vietnam, and on the same hot day in July cut appropriations for the summer employment of young Blacks and Puerto Ricans, thus helping to encourage a bloody summer at home while assuring one abroad?

These are all, as Brzezinski would point out, complex issues, and according to him, they will not be solved by "historical irrelevants," by those who, with revolutionary fervor, are yearning, as he would have it, for the simplicities of the past and who therefore "will have no role to play in the new technetronic society." But what has decided, since I know no people who have, that we want his "technetronic society," that it is desirable or inevitable? Who decides that it is necessary or even good for certain issues to be construed as complex and therefore susceptible only to the diagnosticians who would lead such a society? Why have certain issues become complex and who is served by this complexity? Why is the life we already lead, mysterious and frightening as it is, to be made even more so by the ridiculous shapes conjured up in Brzezinski's jaw-breaking terminologies? Some issues are not simple, which does not mean that some others are not unnecessarily complex. It is clear to everyone that Vietnam is "complex." But it is equally clear that it need not, for us, have become complex; that it might not even have existed as an issue, except for those members of EASE who helped justify our continued presence there. Maybe the secret is that it is really "easy" to be complex.

The funniest and in a way the most innocent example of this kind of no-thinking passing in sound and cadence for responsible, grown-up good sense is offered by George Kennan. The third figure heralded for his rationality in the *Time* article, Kennan is a renowned historian, a former ambassador to the Soviet Union, and the author of yet another containment policy, this one for youth. Kennan's specialty is what might be called "the argument from experience," easily slipping into "the argument from original sin." "The decisive seat of evil in this world," he tells us in *Democracy and the Student Left*, a published debate between him and nearly forty students and teachers, "is not in social and political institutions, and not even, as a rule, in the ill-will or iniquities of statesmen, but simply in the weakness and imperfection of the human soul itself." No one can deny a proposition so general, but surely only someone who likes for other reasons to plead the inescapable complexity of issues could propose such an idea to people wondering how the hell we got into Vietnam or why millions of poor in a country so rich must go hungry every day, and why every summer New York becomes not Fun but Plague City.

Kennan has, of course, had direct experience with other revolutions and with other people who have ignored the imperfections of the human soul simply by denying its existence. No wonder it often sounds, then, as if the militant young are merely his chance at last to give a proper dressingdown to the kind of fellows who brought on the Russian Revolution, his historical analogies being to that extent, at least, more complimentary to the young than Brzezinski's evocation of Luddites and Chartists. "I have heard it freely confessed by members of the revolutionary student generation of Tsarist Russia," Kennan rather huffily reports, "that, proud as they were of the revolutionary exploits of their youth, they never really learned anything in their university years; they were too busy with politics." Earlier, from Woodrow Wilson at his prissiest, he describes an ideal "at the very center of our modern institutions of higher learning": it is a "free place," in Wilson's words, "itself a little world; but not perplexed, living with a singleness of aim not known without; the home of sagacious men."

It was such sagacious men, apparently, since it surely was not the rampaging students, who decided that this ideal place should also house ROTC units, defense projects, recruiters from Dow Chemical, and agents of the CIA. An ideal institution freed of those perplexities —which evidently do not bother Mr. Kennan—is precisely what the students have been agitating for. It is not possible to think about learning now without being, as he pejoratively puts it, "busy with politics." The university officials and the government have seen to that. But again, Kennan probably doesn't regard ROTC as a political presence on campus; students are "busy with politics" not in the precious hours wasted on drill and military science, but only while agitating against these activities, which are mostly useless even from a military point of view. Out of this mess of verbal and moral assumptions, the finest and stiffest blossom is the phrase "freely confessed": imagine having the gall to tell someone outright that as a student you hadn't even done your assignments while trying to overthrow a corrupt and despotic government. Doubtless that government also preferred its universities "not perplexed" by anything related to the conduct of public affairs.

Compared with the futuristic modes of Brzezinski and DeMott, Kennan's mode of argument is at least honest about seeing the present only as if it were the past. In its rather ancient charm it isn't nearly so dangerously effective as still other less explicitly theological, less passionate, more academically systematized methods now in vogue for abridging youthful radicalism or transcendentalism. Consider for example what might be called the tight-contextual method. This is particularly useful in putting campus rioters in their place, their violence always being in excess of any local cause (as if people of draft age or surrounded by a ghetto should care to be exacting about the precise sources of discontent) and in explaining why we cannot withdraw from Vietnam. That country gets reduced, in this form of argument, to some thousands of vaguely identified friends whom we cannot desert, though their worth is even more difficult to locate than is their presence during combat operations.

Of course this kind of analysis works wonders on anything as worldwide and variously motivated as student or youth protest. Unanswerably the students at Columbia are not the students in Paris or Czechoslovakia or even Berkeley. Like the leaders in any generation, the rebellious students are only a small minority of the young, a minority even of the student bodies they belong to. There are local, very special reasons not only for the motivations of each group but for each of the different acts of each group. What is astonishing, however, is that they all do act, that they are all acting now, that the youth of the world almost on signal have found local causes—economic, social, political, academic ones—to fit an apparently general need to rebel. So universal and simultaneous a response to scarcely new causes reveals in the young an imaginative largeness about the interconnection of issues, an awareness of their wider context, of a world in which what in former decades would have been a local war is now symptomatic, as is poverty and the quality of life in our cities, of where the dominant forms of thinking have taken us. Again, it can be said that the young are in effect rebelling against precisely the kinds of analysis that are inadequate to explain what the young are up to. More terrifying than the disorder in the streets is the disorder in our heads; the rebellion of youth, far from being a cause of disorder, is rather a reaction, a rebellion against the disorder we call order, against our failure to make sense of the way we live now and have lived since 1945.

Yet another form of restrictive or deflationary analysis—and appropriately the last I'll consider here, though I'll have more to say about it in the final chapter—is a special favorite of literary critics and historians as well as politicians: the anti-apocalyptic. Implicit in some of the methods we've already looked at, this one dampens revolutionary enthusiasms with the information that history has recorded such efforts before and also recorded their failure—the Abolitionists, the young Bolsheviks, the Luddites. All claims to uniqueness are either tarnished by precedent or doomed to meaninglessness. We've been through it all, and are now doing the best we can, given—and here we're back at the borders of Original Sin—our imperfect state of being. In the treatment of militant groups, this type of argument is especially anxious to expose any elitist or fascist tinge in the young, with their stress on a chimerical "participatory democracy" or their infantile assumption that the worst must be allowed to happen—let us say the election of George Wallace —if ever the inherent horrors of the "System," and thus the necessities of revolution, are to become apparent to everyone. Some people do talk this way; some people always have. But only a minority of the articulate and protesting young lend themselves to anything so politically programmatic. Such arguments are wholly peripheral to the emergence of youth as a truly unique historical force for which there are no precedents.

Youth is an essentially nonpolitical force, a cultural force, that signals, while it can't by itself initiate, the probable beginnings of a new millennium, though hardly the one described in the Book of Revelation. If only because of its continuously fluid, continuously disappearing and emerging membership, it is incapable of organizing itself into shapes suitable to the political alliances that can be made by other, more stable minority groups like the blacks. It has no history; it may never have one, but it is that shared experience of all races which may come finally to dominate our imagination of what we are.

What is happening to the youth of the world deserves the freest imagination, the freest attention that older people are capable of giving. It requires an enormously strenuous, and for most people, probably impossible, intellectual effort. Working within the verbal and conceptual frames—a sadly appropriate word—against which the rebellion of youth is in large part directed, we must try to invent quite different ways of seeing, imagining, and describing. So complicated is the task linguistically that it is possible to fail merely because of the vocabulary with which, from the best intentions, we decide to try. It is perhaps already irrelevant, for example, to discuss the so-called student revolt as if it were an expression of "youth." The revolt might more properly be taken as a repudiation by the young of what adults call "youth." It may be an attempt to cast aside the strangely exploitative and at once cloying, the protective and impotizing concept of "youth" which society foists on people who often want to consider themselves adults. Is it youth or is it the economic and sexual design of adult society that is being served by what Erik Erikson calls the "moratorium," the period when people under twenty-one are "allowed" to discover their identities without at the same time having to assume adult responsibilities?

Quite painfully, the young have suddenly made us aware that the world we have been seeing isn't necessarily the world at all. Not only that France in the spring of 1968 didn't turn out to be the France anyone knew, but that even the young weren't necessarily that thing we call "young." It is no longer a matter of choice therefore: we must learn to know the world differently, including the young, or we may not know it until it explodes, thus showing forth its true nature, to follow the logic of Marx, only in the act and at the moment of breakdown.

Before asking questions about the propriety and programs of young militants who occupy buildings, burn cars, and fight the police, let's first ask what kind of world surrounds these acts. Let's not conceive of the world as a place accidentally controlled by certain people whose wickedness or stupidity has been made evident by disaster, or as the scene of injustices whose existence was hidden from us. Because to do so implies that we are beguiled rather than responsible, responsible, I mean, even for specific things that we do not know are happening. We're in danger of becoming like the Germans before the war who afterward turned to their children with dismay, then surprise, then amnesia. Such analogies to our present situation, and even more to an anticipated one, are not exact, but they are becoming increasingly less remote with each new crime bill contrived by the office of Attorney General Mitchell.

The world we now live in cannot get any better merely by changing its managers or improving some of its circumstances, however. It exists as it does because of the way we think about one another and because of our incapacity, so far at least, to learn to think differently. For those who fought in it and who are now the middle generation and parents of the young, World War II gave absolutely the worst kind of schooling. It trained us to think in extraordinarily simplistic terms about politics and history. One might even say that it made people my age strangely apolitical and ahistorical. We were convinced that evil resided in Nazism and Fascism, and that against these nothing less than total victory was acceptable. The very concept of total victory or unconditional surrender was part of a larger illusion that all wickedness was entrenched in certain groups, circumstances, and persons, and very subtly these were differentiated even from the people or the nations where they found hospitality. The Morgenthau plan had no chance of success, and not simply because it was economically unfeasible in proposing the creation of an agrarian state between the West and the East. It would have had the even more tactically dangerous effect of blaming a *people* for a war. Thereby two embarrassing questions would have been raised: either that the Germans were really a separate kind of people, or, if not, that they were like us, and must therefore have had some understandable provocation for acting as they did. And what could that provocation have been if not something for which we too had a responsibility? No—better just talk about the eradication of Nazism and warlords.

Like all wars, World War II blinded us to the conditions at home that required our attention, and so did the cold war that followed: for nearly twenty-five years we looked at foreign devils rather than domestic ills. The consequences were even worse in our thinking, however, or rather in our not thinking, about the true sources and locations of our trouble. They are within ourselves and within the mechanisms of our own society. One reason why those in the parental generation cannot understand the rebellion of the young is that our own "rebellion" was managed for us, while for the young now it is instinctive and invented and unprogrammed. Our protest movement was the war itself, the crusade against Nazism, Fascism, and Japanese imperialism. In many ways our youth didn't matter to the world. I went into the infantry in 1943 at seventeen, fought in Germany, and came out in 1946 imagining that I'd helped cleanse the globe and could therefore proceed to make up for lost personal time at the university, where a grateful government paid my expenses.

If the war absorbed and homogenized the political feelings of the millions like me who are now the parents of people nearly old enough to be drafted for a quite different kind of war, the G.I. Bill of Rights gave us an experience of college and university life different from any before or since. The G.I. Bill was legislation of enormous political and social importance. It allowed the first huge influx into colleges, university, and later into the academic profession, of people who for financial and social reasons weren't before recognized as belonging to the group which represents youth as our society likes to imagine it—the students. But given their backgrounds, which made them poignantly anxious to take advantage of an opportunity they never thought available, much less a right, given their age, service experience, sexual maturity, and often marriage, this influx of a new kind of student had a stabilizing rather than a disrupting effect. We were maybe the first really serious mass of students who ever entered the academy, designed up till then, and still designed, to prolong immaturity until the ridiculous age of twenty-one or later.

If we were serious, it was in a bad sense, I'm afraid: we wanted so much to make it that we didn't much question the value of what we were doing. I'm not surprised that so few people my age are radical even in temperament. My fellow academicians who came through the process I've described have fitted all too nicely into the Anglophilic gentility of most areas of academic life, into the death-dealing social manners promoted by people who before the war could afford the long haul of graduate as well as undergraduate education. Much more than the reputed and exaggerated effect of television and other media in creating a self-conscious community of the young (effects shared, after all, by people in their thirties and forties), it is the peculiar nature of World War II and of subsequent schooling experience which separates the older from the younger but still contiguous groups.

In thinking about the so-called generation gap, then, I suggest that people my age think not so much about the strangeness of the young but about their own strangeness. Why is it "they" rather than "we" who are unique? By what astonishing arrogance do people my age propose to themselves the program described in the *New York Times* Sunday Book Review by a critic, John Simon, who wrote that during the summer he would support McCarthy and that "beyond that, full-time opposition to radical or reactionary excesses in the arts and criticism strikes me as proper and sufficient activity for a critic. And political enough, too, in its ultimate implications." The ultimate implications are dead center. Dead because what can anyone mean now by an "excess," and from where does one measure it unless, like the person in question, he entertains, as do most of my contemporaries, the illusion that he has emerged a representative of True Nature?

Only when the adult world begins to think of itself as strange, as having a shape not entirely necessary, much less lovely, only when it begins to see that insofar as the world has been made visible to us in forms and institutions, a lot of it isn't *there*, maybe less than half of it—only then can we begin to meet the legitimate anguish of the young with something better than the cliché that they have no program. Revolutionaries seldom do. One can be sick and want health, jailed and want freedom, inwardly dying and want a second birth without a program. For what the radical youth want to do is to expose the mere contingency of facts which have been considered essential. That is a marvelous service, a necessary prelude to our being able, any of us, to think of a program which is more than merely the patching up of social systems that were never adequate to the people they were meant to serve.

Liberal reformers, no matter how tough, won't effect and might even forestall the necessary changes. In our universities, for example, there is no point in removing symptoms and leaving the germs. It is true, as the young have let us know with a zest that isn't always convenient even to sympathizers like myself, that our universities are too often run by fat cats, that renowned professors are bribed by no or little

teaching, that a disproportionate amount of teaching is done by un-
selfish but miserably underpaid and distracted graduate assistants, that,
as a consequence of this imbalance, research of the most exciting kind
has very little immediate bearing on curriculum, which remains much
as it has for the past fifty years, and that, as Martin Duberman elo-
quently shows in *The Uncompleted Past*, authoritarianism in curriculum and in teaching, not to be confused with being an authority in a
subject, is so much a part of our educational system that university
students arrive already crippled even for the freedom one is prepared
to give them. These conditions exist in a pattern of idiotic requirements
and childish, corrupting emoluments not simply because our universities are mismanaged. The mismanagement has itself a prior cause which
is to be found in the way most people think about scholarship and its
relation to teaching—a question which is a kind of metaphor for the
larger one of the relations between the generations: what conditions
permit the most profitable engagements between an older mind that is
trained and knowledgeable and a younger one anxious to discover itself but preconditioned by quite different cultural circumstances?

These circumstances have, of course, always differed between one
generation and another, but never so radically as now. Never before
have so many revered subjects, like literature itself, seemed obsolete
in any strict compartmental form; never before have the divisions between such subjects as anthropology, sociology, and languages seemed
more arbitrary and harmful to intelligent inquiry; and seldom in the
history of modern civilization has there been a greater need felt by
everyone for a new key to our mythologies, a key we nervously feel is
about to be found. For if we are at a moment of terror we are also at a
moment of great expectation and wonder, for which the young have a
special appetite. To meet this challenge, the universities need to dis-
mantle their entire academic structure, their systems of courses and
requirements, their notion of what constitutes the proper fields and
subjects of academic inquiry.

Most people who teach have in their heads some ideal university,
and mine would be governed by a single rule: there is nothing that does
not need to be studied in class, including, of course, the oddity of studying in a class. Everything and everybody, the more randomly selected
the better, has to be subjected to questions, especially dumb questions,
and to the elicitation of answers. The point is that nothing must be
taken for other than "strange," nothing must be left alone. Study the
morning paper, study the teacher, study the listless slouching of students—half-dead already at eighteen. But above all, those working in
advanced research sponsored at any university would also let capable
students study that research and ask questions about it. And if in fact

some things cannot be taught, then that in itself should be the subject of inquiry.

The hierarchies that might evolve would be determined on a wholly pragmatic basis: for subjects, by the amount of effort and time needed to make something yield up the dimensions of its mystery; for any way of thinking, by the degree to which it raises a student to eye level with the potentialities of a subject, the degree to which it can tune his ears into it. Above all, the university would be a place where curricula are discovered anew perhaps every year or so. The argument that the demands of an existing student body cannot be allowed to determine policy for succeeding ones would mean the reverse of what it now means: not that changes are difficult to effect, but that they would be effected year after year, if necessary, to meet the combined changes of interest in students and faculty. Given the sluggishness of most people, the results of such a policy would not be nearly as chaotic or exciting as one might imagine. Indeed, what would be hoped for is more disruption, and therefore more questioning and answering than one would ever get.

In confronting oppositions from youth as in other matters short of Vietnam, Lyndon Johnson was a genius in that his most decent impulses, and he had some, didn't merely serve, weren't merely synchronized with, but were indistinguishable from his often uncanny political instinct for pacifying any opposition, for castrating any force that threatened to move the system off the center track which carried him to power. While demonstrations at Columbia were making Hubert Humphrey sick "deep inside," and Nixon was reportedly saying that if there were a second Columbia uprising he wouldn't have to care whom he had to run against, LBJ was proposing that the vote be given to all people between eighteen and twenty-one. But the terrible price of the political logic he so masterfully handled is at once made evident if we ask what many of the young, and not simply the militant ones, will find to vote for. They are to join the electorate just when it is at last stagnating from our national satisfaction with the mere manipulation and redistribution of the poisons within us. So ingeniously is the center still in control of the manipulative forces, that there will not be a turn to the right within our political system (anyone who thinks Nixon is of the right is merely trying to jazz up our political life), and no one within the system represents the left. The danger sign will be abstention, political indifference, a decision not to care very much who wins, not to participate in a process that affords only negative choices.

When any large number of people demonstrate their indifference to the choices offered them, they tend to invent others that exist outside the going "democratic" process. They tend to gravitate toward some species of the "participatory democracy" for which the elitist young are most severely criticized. It was at least fortunate that Johnson's voting-age proposal couldn't be enacted in time for the young people of eighteen to twenty-one to enter a political imbroglio so contemptibly arranged as the 1968 election. It would only have further convinced them of the necessity for some kind of non-democratic movement to replace the farce of democracy in which they'd have been asked to take part, and it would have allowed their critics to assign to them some blame for the consequences of the indifference among the older electorate. The indifference grows on the momentum supplied not by the young but by the nature of our public life. The now not uncommon proposition that our problems are no longer manageable within existing political systems, and that we need an Authority empowered to decide what is best for us, cannot be ascribed merely to youth, Herbert Marcuse, Vietnam, race, violence, or any combination of these. The emerging failure of confidence in our way of managing ourselves and our interests in the world is the consequence of a political process now overwhelmed by the realities it has tried to hide.

Instinctively, the militant young are involved less in a political rebellion, where demands for their "program" would be relevant, than in an attack on the foundations of all of our current political programming. The issues they raise and the issues they personify are essentially anthropological, which brings us to the cultural rather than the political importance of the proposal to move the voting age back from twenty-one to eighteen. The importance can be dramatized, with no intention of melodrama, by predicting that within twenty years or so it will be necessary to propose, if not to pass, a voting age of sixteen. Like other mere changes of policy, changes in voting age should not be taken as a sign that we are suddenly to be governed by new or radical modes of thinking. Rather, such reforms signal the accumulated power of forces which our operative modes of thinking have before tried to ignore and which they will now try to make invisible by absorption.

But with the mass of youth (nearly half the population is now under twenty-five) our society is faced with an unprecedented difficulty in the application of this essentially social technique. For when it comes to the young, society is not simply absorbing a group which, like the Irish or labor, duplicates in its social organization each part of the dominant group. To give something like adult or historic identity to a mass that has up to now been relegated to the position of "youth" means a disruptive change in the concept of human identity, of when that identity is achieved, of what it properly should contribute to history.

The time scheme that governs our ideas of adolescence, youth, and maturity has changed many times in history since the sixteenth century —Juliet was fourteen, and early in the eighteenth century the age of consent was ten—but it was adjusted to the convenience of an extraordinarily small ruling minority which was in turn submissive to familial regulations. For the first time in history a change of this kind is being made on demand from a powerful mass of young people freed of familial pieties, and never before has a society worked as strenuously as ours, through a mesh of mythologies, to hold these young people back, in an unmercifully prolonged state of adolescence and of what we call "youth." Especially in the United States, the representative and most talented young—the students—have for generations been forced not to take themselves seriously as men and women.

So far, the rebellion has accomplished at least one thing: it has succeeded in demoting "collegiate types" (and the sickly reminiscent values they injected into later life) from glamour to absurdity. The change is not complete, and it never will be. Whole campuses are holdouts, some quite distinguished ones, where the prep-school ethos remains dominant, while at others the overwhelming number of young clods makes it difficult for the few students who really are alive even to find one another, much less establish an *esprit* that can enliven more than a small circle. Still, recent agitations have confirmed some of the advances made by the earlier generation of students under the G.I. Bill and cleared still more room on American campuses for the kind of young person who does want to enter history at eighteen, and who is therefore contemptuous of society's cute and reassuring idea of the collegiate—with Lucille Ball as ideal House Mother. Such historical self-consciousness on the part of university students has been fairly common in Europe and in England, where, as shown by Peter Stansky and William Abrahams in *Journey to the Frontier,* students in the thirties could feel that the "journey" to the Spanish Civil War did not follow but rather began at Oxford and Cambridge. But the differences are obvious, and, again, relate to class and family: children of the English upper classes were educated to feel historical, and what distinguished them from lower-class boys was that from boyhood their "careers" meant something to the political and historical career of England. Only rarely, and almost exclusively at Harvard, does this phenomenon occur in American universities. Education in American universities has generally been a combination of utilitarian course work and play-acting, "getting ready" to be an adult, even if it meant still getting ready at twenty-two.

The shattering of this pattern has been the work of a complex of forces that include students within the larger power bloc of youth, with its enormous influence on dress and mores, and, perhaps above all, its success in the fields of entertainment. By force of numbers and energy alone, the young have created images which older people are now quite anxious to endow with a sexual-social significance which they before refused to find in the activity of "kids." Put another way, youth has ceased to fulfill the "literary" role which American society has been anxious to assign them. They no longer supply us with a pastoral, any more than the "darkies" do, and this is a serious, though to me a most satisfying cultural deprivation for which no replacement has yet been discovered.

Every civilization has to invent a pastoral for itself, and ours has been an idea of youth and of adolescence which has become socially and economically unprofitable, demographically unmanageable, and biologically comic. By a pastoral I mean any form of life which has, by common consent, been secured from the realities of time and history. Some form of pastoral is absolutely essential: it helps stabilize the cycles of individual lives and of civilizations. Its function is an idealizing, simplifying one: it secures certain elemental human attributes from the contaminations of time and of historical involvement. But if the logic of pastoral is to protect certain attributes, its ulterior motive is to keep the human embodiment of these attributes in their proper place, servants rather than participants in daily business where "real" men really face complex reality.

Insofar as America's imagination of itself can be inferred from literature, from popular entertainment, from fashions, conventions, and educational theory, it can be said that we have used youth as a revenge upon history, as the sacrificial expression of our self contempt. Youth has been the hero of our civilization, but only so long as it has remained antagonistic to history, only so long as it has remained a literary or mythological metaphor.

War, the slaughter of youth at the apparent behest of history, is the ultimate expression of this feeling. The American hatred of history, of what it does to us, gets expressed in a preposterous and crippling idealization of youth as a state as yet untouched by history, except as a killer, and in a corresponding incapacity to understand the demand, now, by the best of the young, to be admitted into it. More hung up on youth than any nation on earth, we are also the more determined that youth is not to enter into history without paying the price of that adulteration we call adulthood. To justify what grown-ups have made of our young, virgin, uncontaminated land, it's as if we are compelled to show that what happened was necessary. Exceptions would prove our human culpability for what is otherwise ascribed to history, and so all that is best in our land must either be kept out of history or tarnished by it. Like our natural wonders, youth will be allowed to exist only on condition that it remain, like some natural preserve, outside the processes that transform everything else into waste.

Surely the destination of our assets needn't be so bleak, so inexorable, so neurotically determined. It will now be seen whether or not we are to exhaust our youth, whether or not in its vulnerability, its continually evaporating and exposed condition, it can resist being made grist for the mill. Because youth is not a historically grounded pressure group, aware of its history, jealous of its progress, continuous and evolving. It is rather what we, all of us, sometimes are. I have avoided any precise definition of youth because it refers to the rare human condition of exuberance, expectation, impulsiveness, and, above all, of freedom from believing that all the so-called "necessities" of life and thought are in fact necessities. This condition exists most usefully, for the nation and the world, in people of a certain age, specifically in those who have attained the physical being that makes them wonderfully anxious to create life, to shape life, to enter into life rather than have it fed into them. It is the people of this age, members of what Freidenberg calls the "hot-blooded minority," who are in danger of obliteration as representatives of youth. It is impossible for them to remain youth, in any sense that would profit the rest of society, and also enter into history on the hateful terms now offered them by our political, economic, and technological system. Lyndon Johnson knew instinctively what he was up to when, calling for a vote for people of this age, he remarked that they deserved it because they are "adults in every sense."

Fine, if that means we now change our concept of adulthood to include an eighteen-year-old Bob Dylan rather than an eighteen-year-old Nixon, some creep valedictorian. But that isn't what he had in mind. LBJ hadn't changed his way of thinking about youth, adulthood, or anything else. He was merely responding to this fantastic cultural opportunity the way our leaders respond to any such opportunity for change: they merely make more room in the house with as little inconvenience as possible to the settled inhabitants. All the voting proposal means, and this will have some amusing as well as sad consequences, is that the term youth will be lifted from those who threatened us with it, and then held in reserve for the time, not far off, when it can be quietly left on the narrow shoulders of what we now call adolescents. Some tinkering will be necessary here and there, of course. The Adolescent Clinic at Children's Hospital in Boston chooses the ages thirteen to nineteen for its patients, but those who've seen some of the ten-to-twelve-year-olds who sneak in tell me that if the ranks of adolescence are to be depleted to fill the vacated positions of youth, these in turn will be quickly occupied by Robert Coles's children of crisis. This will seem a facetious prediction to people who like to think they are reasonable.

So, what I'm saying is that if young people are freeing themselves from a repressive myth of youth only to be absorbed into a repressive, even though modified, myth of adulthood, then youth in its best and truest form, of rebellion and hope, will have been lost to us, and we will have at last wasted some of the very best of ourselves.

The Student Drive to Destruction
Louis J. Halle

"We shall destroy because we are a force." observed Arkady. . . .
"Yes, a force is not to be called to account." . . .
"Allow me, though," began Nikolai Petrovitch. "You deny everything; or, speaking more precisely, you destroy everything. But one must construct too, you know."
"That's not our business now. The ground wants clearing first."
—Turgenev, *Fathers and Sons*

To understand the implications of the students' revolt for the future of our civilization one should place it in its historical setting. As a movement of rejection it represents the nihilism that has been developing for over a century now, to the point where it is at last becoming the dominant intellectual drive of our time.

The word "nihilism" was introduced into the common language in 1862, when Turgenev published his *Fathers and Sons*, a compassionate novel dealing with the gap between the generations. Bazarov, the young nihilist who is its hero, represents the revolt of the new generation against the old, against its whole traditional culture.

By the second half of the nineteenth century that traditional culture was losing such innate authority as it had once had. It was the possession of a ruling élite, expressed in the affectation of high ideals that took no account either of the findings of science or of the impoverished lives of the great majority of people, on whose labor the élite lived. Nihilism, in these circumstances, was not entirely without point. According to Bazarov's disciple, the student Arkady, "a nihilist is a man who does not bow down before any authority, who does not take any principle on faith, whatever the reverence in which it may be enshrined." Such nihilism stood for a frank recognition of reality, for a society based on science rather than on an obsolete idealism.

Those who affected the culture that the original nihilists opposed took an optimistic view of human nature—that is, they made a polar distinction between their own noble nature, which was soulful, and the nature of the brute beasts. Man, in their view, was essentially divine, created in the image of his maker, and if he had fallen into evil he was still capable of the redemption that they, themselves, pretended to represent. The nihilists, responding to the initial impact of Darwinism, denied this distinction between men and beasts. (Turgenev began writing his great novel just as *The Origin of Species* was published.) For the piously optimistic view of human nature they substituted a new view in the name of scientific realism. Their denial that man was the divine creature he pretended to be took a particularly persuasive form, at last, in the works of Freud and the Freudians, who concluded that men are governed by the destructive forces that represent their basic animal nature, however either sublimation or hypocrisy may cover them up.

Throughout the Victorian Age ladies and gentlemen had pretended to be exempt from the bestial impulses that are, in fact, common to us all. The way new generations were produced was an unmentionable secret, not to be acknowledged—above all, to be kept from the members of the new generation until, inevitably, they at last learned about it in the shame of the wedding night.

With the revolt against Victorianism that followed World War I, Freudianism became a religion among the advanced intellectuals. The zeal with which it was adopted and preached in the 1920's can be understood only if one appreciates the release from former shame and inhibitions that it provided. Those of the new generation who had secretly entertained "wicked thoughts," believing that decent people did not have them, suddenly learned that everyone had them, including their hypocritical elders. The Freudian psychoanalyst, to whom so many of these people now turned, relieved them of the moral burden they had borne. They confessed to him and he took away the shame. The experience was that of an ineffable liberation.

There were other forms of liberation as well, stemming from the thesis that everyone should rid himself of his inhibitions, inhibitions associated with the hypocritical tradition of the Victorian generation. The extreme exponents of this thesis organized free-love camps and nudist communities. For the most part, however, what it produced was greater verbal frankness, together with a more relaxed and informal relationship between the sexes. Women got off the pedestal that had held them at such a distance from men, and by dressing and behaving so as to reduce the differences between the sexes they made possible a camaraderie with men that, a generation earlier, would have been regarded as improper. (They gave themselves a flat-chested appearance by means of the newly invented brassieres, which were simply tight bands; they cut their hair short, and they smoked cigarettes.) All this was the beginning of what we call permissiveness.

These two trends—the disposition to regard man as essentially beastly, and permissiveness—have both continued through the half century since the First World War, until they have at last reached the predominance they are manifesting today. Today, books advancing the thesis that man is a predatory aggressor by nature are welcomed and acclaimed by the intellectual community. At the same time, all censorship and most of the traditional restrictions on sexual indulgence are denounced.

There is a paradox of disastrous implications here. At the same time that man is represented as being an aggressive beast, incapable of moral responsibility, the inhibitions that society has hitherto imposed on his freedom to indulge his nature are to be removed.

Throughout the history of political philosophy, an optimistic view of human nature has been associated with the advocacy of freedom, a pessimistic view with authoritarianism. The pessimistic view that Plato took, in consequence of the disasters that popular rule had just brought upon Athens, was the basis of the authoritarianism advocated in *The Republic*. In ancient China, the optimistic view of human nature led the Mohists to advocate a society based on love rather than force, while the pessimistic view led the Legalists to advocate a police state. Russian authoritarianism, alike under the czars and their successors, is associated with the accepted view that men are destructive creatures who, if only for their own sakes, have got to be held down.

Our own Western tradition of liberalism, which goes back through Thomas Jefferson to John Locke, was justified by the optimistic view of man's nature that prevailed in the eighteenth century. This is also true of the Jacobin tradition, which goes back through Karl Marx to Rousseau. Marx was explicit in his conception of human nature as basically creative rather than destructive. Consequently, he looked forward to the day when, capitalism having been liquidated, the coercive state would wither away, after which men would enjoy in perpetuity perfect freedom for the indulgence of their natural creativity.

In the face of the logic these cases exemplify, how can one explain the present advocacy of permissiveness by those who regard man as an irremediably greedy, aggressive, and predatory beast? This stands opposed to the logic I have cited, which also takes the form of the principle that men can be free only to the extent that they make a disciplined use of their freedom. It is only where men are prepared to deal tolerantly with the diversity among them, and to abide voluntarily by "the rules of the game," that freedom is possible. Where men will not tolerate the expression of opinions different from their own, and where they refuse to accept decisions reached in accordance with "the rules of the game," the impositions of the police state become unavoidable.

Anyone who has raised children knows, from direct experience, that freedom is a function of the capacity for socially responsible and considerate behavior.

It is the tradition of civility in the United States and Britain, expressed in self-restraint, that has hitherto made possible the relative freedom enjoyed by their peoples, and it is the extreme moderation of the Swiss in resolving their internal differences, which are great, that makes possible the freedom they enjoy today. Here we have demonstrations of the fact that human nature, at an advanced stage of civilization, is capable of such self-discipline as a free society requires.

If one looks at the mixed historical record of mankind, or if one consults one's own experience of the people one has known, it is quite impossible to believe that man is either all bad or all good. He may be properly described, it seems to me, as a beast with a soul. Even if I were willing to concede that the evil was predominant in him—in the sense that he was governed by his animal appetites, by a desire to destroy, by a lust for power—even so, if there is only one spark in the darkness of his nature, there is, in that spark, a basis for unlimited hope. In spite of the fashionable anthropology of our day, which identifies him as a predatory beast, it seems to me clear that man, in his evolution, has already made noticeable progress in rising above the level of his pre-human ancestors.

This is a view for which abundant evidence could be adduced, but it is not a view that can gain a hearing today because it is, for the depressing reasons I have already cited, so unwelcome to those who represent the intellectual fashions of our day. If I should write a book showing that man, like the great carnivores, is predatory by his unchangeable nature, I could be sure that it would be widely read and acclaimed; but if I wrote a book that took an optimistic and teleological view of man's evolution, regarding it as an ascent from the level of the beasts to something ethically and spiritually higher, it would hardly be well received and few would read it. The burden of living up to a high standard is something men can do without. I do not think that this situation will change in what remains of this century, for we seem to be in one of those long periods when civilization, in decline, produces the kind of thinking appropriate to such decline. But if the Phoenix ever rises again, its rise will be accompanied by the general optimism that periods of progress always produce.

Men tend to be what they think they are. If they accept a view of themselves as self-indulgent they will tend to be self-indulgent; if they accept a view of themselves as morally responsible beings they will tend to be morally responsible. I do not think that the widespread denial of social inhibitions on human behavior, which we call permissiveness, is altogether unrelated to the prevalent view of what our human nature really is. Here is a logic that does, in fact, associate the two trends of our time: the hopeless view of our human nature and the assault on social inhibitions. If we are really pigs, rather than fine ladies and gentlemen, then we should not be asked to behave like fine ladies and gentlemen. We should be free to use language regarded as obscene, and there should be no restrictions on theatrical exhibitions of sexual and sadistic practices, no matter how sickening some of them may be. (Whatever may be said in favor of freedom for obscenity, I submit that it is not on the same level of importance as the freedoms guaranteed by the first ten amendments of our Constitution.)

I do not offer this, however, as the primary explanation of how it is that those who regard man as fundamentally bestial are, nevertheless, the advocates of permissiveness. A further explanation is that they are not really interested in the maintenance or enlargement of a régime of freedom that, on the one hand, they tend to take for granted (having never experienced anything else), and that, on the other, does not in itself cure the intractable problems of our societies. The causes they nominally espouse are not necessarily causes they believe in, but mere pretexts for action that has other ends than their success. Any number of activist students admit in private that when they shout for Marx or Mao or Castro that does not mean they care anything about what these figures stand for. They do not carry intellectual responsibility that far. Some of the student leaders have, on occasion, made clear that what they really want is power for themselves (thereby exemplifying the fashionable anthropological view of human nature). At other times they have not bothered to deny that destruction is, for them, an end in itself—relieving them, as such, of any need to think beyond it. If they invoke causes that are genuinely idealistic and progressive, such as human equality or freedom, they do so for tactical purposes only. They invoke them as pretexts on the basis of which they can confuse men of good will and rally the forces of destruction. When German student leaders led their followers, last September, in a violent physical assault on the Leipzig Book Fair, the reason they gave was that the directors of the Fair had chosen President Senghor of Senegal as the recipient of the Fair's peace prize when they might have chosen, instead, Mr. Stokely Carmichael, the apostle of violence. Here the cynicism is patent.

No one, I gather, doubts the intelligence of these student leaders, however gullible their followers may be. In preferring violence to free speech they know, as the Nazi leaders knew, that its success would spell the end of such free speech as I am exercising in this article. When they deliberately and skillfully provoke a bewildered police force into acts of brutality, and then denounce its "fascism," they know the equivocation in which they are indulging. When they denounce the authorities of New York City as being the rulers of a "police state," and oppose them on that basis, they know that a police state is what their movement, if carried to the lengths they intend, would bring about.

It is no answer to say that there are real and important matters for grievance. Of course there are! The point is that the proponents of violence are not really acting, as they pretend, to eliminate these matters. Their leaders, at least, know that, if there are stupid professors (a grievance one student offered me as justification for violent demonstrations), destroying the universities is not the way to get intelligent ones. They know that white discrimination against blacks will not be overcome by a course of action that makes votes for Wallace and pushes the American society in the direction already taken by South Africa. The leaders who know these things are acting cynically, however idealistic what they are doing may seem to older intellectuals who think themselves back in 1848.

Violence and destruction for its own sake prepares the way for the police state, as violence and destruction in Germany prepared the way for Hitler's dictatorship. Specifically, they prepare the way for brutal and ignorant leaders to assume the power of a state that, in our case, possesses a nuclear armament with which it could destroy the world. For those who pursue destruction as an end in itself, the possibilities are now unlimited.

One thing that separates my generation from the generation of my children is the experience it has had of the great depression and of the decade during which the tyranny of the fascist police state seemed likely to engulf the world. My generation has vivid knowledge of how easily the structure of civilization can collapse, and of how terrible the consequences can be in terms of human suffering. Our children, on the other hand, have at best read about these experiences in history books. All that most of them have experienced at first hand is full employment, unlimited opportunity to make a living, and the remarkable freedom of speech and behavior that they have enjoyed in an increasingly permissive society. (On the Berkeley campus, a couple of years ago, I saw earnest-looking boys and girls, righteous indignation written on their faces, sitting behind a table marked "Committee for Sexual Libertinism," and I wondered who was preventing them from simply going ahead and engaging in it.)

I cannot imagine that many of those who say they are willing to face the eventuality of a police state, as the consequence of their actions, would not change their minds if ever they found themselves living under one. I have emphasized the element of cynicism in their conduct —but it is accompanied by an innocence of either experience or knowledge that contributes to their moral irresponsibility. (It was Irwin Cobb who said: the trouble with the younger generation is that it hasn't read the minutes of the last meeting.)

I have no doubt that, if mankind is on a long upward path over the millennia, that path will continue to be marked, in the future as in the past, by great crashes of civilization. I cannot quite believe that one of these crashes will spell a final end to the hopes of mankind; but we are now entering a period of human history when new dangers, produced by scientific progress, require us to exercise a greater self-control than ever before. It is not impossible, as a consequence of the breakdown in the discipline of civilization, that Mr. George Wallace or someone like him will become President of the United States in 1973, with responsibility for its international relations and with control over its nuclear armament.

I have talked to students who believe that the basic procedure of democracy is represented by violence in the streets, and that freedom means doing whatever one pleases. To the extent that each generation is responsible for educating the next, my generation must regard itself as a notable failure.

A Federal Judge Digs the Young
Charles E. Wyzanski, Jr.

It is rather strange that the generation gap is thought of as something to be regretted. In my book, conformity is generally more to be regretted, and a search for unity is already a denial of the diversity of human life. The creativity of God as he created Adam involved a gap. And indeed, it is the kind of challenge that comes from the electricity which crosses the gap that makes life meaningful.

Long ago, in a not very different spirit, the ancient Greek philosopher Heraclitus said, "That which opposes, also fits"; and while what he said may proleptically have had Freudian implications, it is ordinarily thought he was talking of a bow and arrow. I don't know whether the young are the arrow, but I am quite certain that there is no reason for anybody to regret the kind of challenge which comes from difference. Indeed, could there be a clearer indication of a static and decadent civilization than one in which each generation followed the pattern of the previous one?

We are, of course, well aware that this is no ordinary change from one generation to another. Indeed, what we are going through can be compared only with what happened at the end of the eighteenth century, with the American and French Revolutions; what happened in 1848, or nearly happened; what happened in 1917. We are in a great cataclysmic change, one of the most profound in world history, and lucky we are to live in this period.

Harold Howe 2d, U.S. Commissioner of Education, talked recently about the possibility that the colleges were to blame, not the students, for what has been going on at Ohio State, Columbia, Boston University, in Paris and Italy. Wherever you are, you cannot pick up the morning paper without finding that the student revolt is spreading in every corner of the globe. In Paris, in Germany, with the attack on Axel Springer and his newspapers; in Italy, with its closed universities; at Barnard, where *The New York Times* exposed a single child and her parents to an invasion of privacy that it would have condemned editorially if anybody else had done it; at Boston University, where a courageous president told the students they were right about their demand for a larger representation of Negroes in the student body; at Radcliffe College, where students are seeking to be admitted to the board of trustees; at Columbia University, where one can see how justified students were in resenting a proposed gymnasium that would have a separate entrance for Harlem residents and which would be built on land leased at a ridiculously low price. Mr. Howe is right—perhaps the colleges should look at themselves as well as their students.

Certain aspects of the student revolt are much overrated by the commercial press and money-seeking exploiters: sex, drugs, and dress. Most people know what hypocrites the previous generation were. They did not have to wait for the biography of Strachey to know that Keynes and the Bloomsbury set, who determined the intellectual tone of the first quarter of the twentieth century, were hardly in the Sunday school copybook tradition. What Proust and Robert de Montesquiou represented, as we have recently been told in clear language, is that France was not different from Britain. And what person who lived as a young man between World War I and World War II wants to file a certificate as to the errors of Professor Kinsey?

We did not have to wait for the young generation in order to be aware that from the beginning of mankind premarital and post-marital sex have not been lived according to the graven tablets handed down to Moses. What is it that made sex such a dangerous activity in earlier years? Was it not conception and venereal disease? And are they not both, by technological advance, much altered in our society? What reason have we to be so certain, so terribly certain, that sexual chastity is the most desirable state at all stages of a man's and a woman's life? I don't believe it. Neither did the Greeks. Neither did the Asians. A particular Western sect, inspired by a religious leader without sexual experience, foisted that notion on the Western world. Is it not time to reconsider that idea?

And what of drugs? I make no case in behalf of marijuana, but who could tell how many more people have died on the roads in the last year as a result of marijuana than as a result of alcohol. Who could tell me more people have died as a result of marijuana than as a result of cancer caused by cigarette smoking? Is there anybody who doubts that the commercial motives of our society promote the sale of tobacco and the sale of alcohol, and that anybody who came from Mars or Venus or some remote place would find it absolutely impossible to decide on what basis we as a society had outlawed marijuana and not tobacco or alcohol? Have you any doubt in your own mind that it is merely habit and profit that make us of the older generation so content to live in a society where alcohol and tobacco freely circulate, and marijuana is outlawed?

Oh, we go to church, do we? Why? For social and commercial reasons and for consolation in time of trouble. But do we go with faith and conviction and discipline and self-denial? Which of us? From the day that Darwin and Huxley opened the doors and science walked into the church and we walked out, which of us had that kind of faith which represents a deep commitment to that denial and sacrifice and discipline which are the essence of religion?

It is quite right that the young should talk about us as hypocrites. We are. And it is quite right that they should note that our hypocrisy is embedded in our materialism.

So we are critical of the young. Have they not far more reason to be critical of us? And what have we done to get them on the right path from the beginning? Most of us were quite content to have them undergo a permissive kind of education in which not merely the *quadrivium* and the *trivium*, but the whole core of humanistic learning was not part of their deep education. We allowed them pretty much, in their early primary and secondary stages, to have the kind of education from their schools and their peers which they wanted because we were not sufficiently convinced of our own beliefs. And they knew it.

We brought them up in a society in which we no longer believed in either the carrot or the stick. Nor did they. Our society afforded them as children, in their occupations as babysitters and otherwise, a salary rate sufficient to assure them a minor kind of affluence and independence. They walked as they pleased because they had the money, the very root of independence. Then, vastly and suddenly, and quite rightly, we expanded the total educational system so that we flooded the colleges and the universities of the nation at a rate at which nobody could possibly absorb.

Mark Hopkins at one end of the log and the student at the other? Doesn't it sound like a prehistoric fable? Which university student today is in a one-to-one relationship with anybody on the faculty? Which one has any kind of personal relationship in a large university? Was it not certain that men and women of any character would resent these institutions and seek some sort of outlet other than the formal ones in which they were treated like commuters in a subway train?

What is to be said about these young people, plus and minus? And those of us who sit where we hear both sides or many sides of the question know that truth is never or almost never all on one side. Let us give the young, first of all, credit for being right about their concern. They, at least, know that there can never be, in a growing society, a philosophy of consensus. They realize, to return to Heraclitus, that "strife is the source of all things." Growth implies discord as well as advance.

What the young care about is a deeper kind of democracy than some of us have been willing to accept. The French in their immortal division talked of liberty, equality, and fraternity. May one not say that in my generation the accent was heavy on the first? And we do not need to turn to Lord Acton to know that he who emphasizes liberty is he who is already privileged. Liberty means one thing if you are already in the top place and something very different if you are low on the scale.

Many know the classic remark of Mr. Justice Maule, phrased somewhat differently by Anatole France, when Justice Maule was faced by a divorce case in the nineteenth century. At that time in England you were free to get a divorce if you took a very lengthy and expensive proceeding in the Probate, Divorce, and Admiralty Court. And there was before Justice Maule a poor man, poor of purse and poor of spirit, who had not gotten a divorce but had married again. Justice Maule said, "It is the glory of England that the law courts are open alike to the rich and the poor." The glory of the law which treats alike the rich and the poor is no glory. It is a sham. And the society which pretends that it gives liberty to all without being concerned with equality and fraternity is a sham.

The young are quite right that equality and fraternity are necessary for democracy and a kind of understanding of what people are like. We in this country stand too close to know how right the young are. If you look from a distance at what goes on in the United States, there is much sense in the concern that the young have about our total order. It is no accident that the young and the Negro are allied, and this is not pure sentimentalism. It is an awareness that in our civilization the litmus paper is black.

The young marched with the black, and now the young are not wanted. The black do not want us, nor are they wrong. One of the things that we must face up to, just as a parent must face up to it with respect to a child, is that when one is struggling for freedom and identity, sometimes one must do it alone. The rejected, sympathetic, kindly person—the parent or white man—does not understand; but it is his fault. It is part of the process of growing up to grow on your own.

There are those who don't like the phrase "black power." It's a very correct phrase. Anyone who really studies democracy will find out that democracy is pluralistic in character. It is those already in power who scorn the pressure groups. But it is pressure groups—whether they be voter leagues formed by women, labor unions formed by workers, black organizations formed by colored people—that in the end count and enter into the total social fabric. Democracy is a struggle based not only on high ideals; it is power against power. There is an overarch of principle, but the overarch is to hold the ring firm while the contestants battle it out within the limits authorized by the organized society.

The young are not wrong, either, in their wonder about the scope of violence. I tread on very dangerous ground here, and I beg indulgence as a quasi-historian and not as a judge. I ask you to reflect carefully on the Boston Tea Party, on John Brown and the raid on Harpers Ferry, on the sit-down strikes in 1937 in the plants of General Motors. Every one of these was a violent, unlawful act, plainly unlawful. In the light of history, was it plainly futile? There are occasions on which an honest man, when he looks at history, must say that through violence, regrettable as it is, justice of a social kind has worked itself out. Does that mean that I think that violence is right? Most certainly I answer ambiguously. I cannot know; none of us can know until long after this time has gone. But I warn those who think that violence is right because history, in the three instances that I have cited, and many others that one might mention, has shown that violence worked—I warn them that violence will lead to McCarthy I or McCarthy II. To which Senator's philosophy, if either, will this nation respond?

What I invite is caution. The young are right not to take too seriously our statement that they must always behave lawfully, but we who are older are also right to say, "We have lived through reaction, and we know what a price you will pay if you are wrong. And we remind you of the words of Charles Morgan that liberty is a room which can be defined only by the walls which enclose it." The young have a great responsibility. They cannot define liberty except in terms of limitation. Believe me, I do it every day!

The ultimate problem which the young face is whether they have the courage to be radical enough to face the implications of what they are doing. I fear not one bit what they have done so far, provided they go further.

In that wonderful play, even if it was a failure on Broadway, by Peter Ustinov, called *Halfway Up the Tree*, there was a British colonial officer who went abroad and left behind his wife and his two children. One was his son who went to Oxford and dressed like a hippie and was having a homosexual relationship with another fellow while they were carrying around a guitar which neither of them could play. The daughter was pregnant, by which of several men she wasn't sure. The colonial fellow returned—he was of my venerable age—and he wasn't disturbed by what his young had done, but he was a little concerned that the boy didn't know how to play the guitar and the girl didn't know how to keep house. If they had taken the first step, they must be prepared for the second. To show them how he felt about it, he went and lived up in a tree and took care of his own food needs and learned how to play the guitar. Well, it is all quite in point.

The young can be as radical as they like, but they must carry the consequence. It isn't enough to overthrow us. They have to establish themselves. It is one of the elements of life that there will be an establishment. They may not like ours—and I don't think they much care for the Communist one because they have seen how that works—but have they thought through what kind of establishment they want?

I am quite sure that one of the things they will have to do is to rearrange the property structure of this nation. As any good lawyer will tell you, property is only an idea—*meum* and *teum*. *Meum* and *teum* are just a lawyer's idea. The things themselves are things. They don't belong to anybody except as we create the relationship.

There is no doubt that our social structure now works in a most undesirable way. Among the 80 per cent—and it is pretty nearly that—who have the benefits of our system, it works surprisingly well. Effort, at least if followed in paths of conformity, will in the long run yield affluence and security. Or at any rate, one will have an automobile! But if one is in the lowest 20 per cent, he is caught. He may proceed to gain a little, but the gap between him and the 80 per cent is not like the generation gap; it is like the gap between the under-developed and the developed nations—constantly growing and creating tensions and creating an envy which will surely lead to disaster.

I speak not in favor of a negative income tax, about which I understand far too little. Nor do I endorse a particular measure of any sort of redistribution or any particular kind of program of health, education, and welfare. I merely say to those who are young that it isn't enough to love your neighbor. You had better be concerned about how your neighbor will be in a position to love you.

What I have talked about doesn't get very close to specifics. But I do know something about what life presents. It presents a riddle that has no answer and never will. In Erwin Schrödinger's phrase, it is a circle that always will have a gap.

Each generation is faced with a challenge of making some kind of sense out of its existence. In advance it knows from the Book of Job and the Book of Ecclesiastes and the Greek drama that there will be no right answer. But there will be forms of answer. There will be a style. As ancient Greece had the vision of *arete* (the noble warrior), as Dante and the Medievalists had the vision of the great and universal Catholic Church, even as the founding fathers of the American Republic had the vision of the new order which they began, so for the young the question is to devise a style—not one that will be good *semper et ubique*, but one for our place and our time, one that will be a challenge to the very best that is within our power of reach, and one that will make us realize, in Whitehead's immortal terms, that for us the only reality is the process.

The War Against the Democratic Process
Sidney Hook

In the past we used to believe that we could turn for intellectual guidance to our colleges and universities as relatively disinterested centers of inquiry in matters of law and liberty. But alas! Colleges and universities have themselves become embattled storm centers of controversy not only about the presuppositions of the democratic process but about the nature and goals of the university. A few years ago a movement in educational circles advocated that the study of communism, fascism, and other forms of totalitarianism be incorporated into the curriculum of our colleges, that we teach in a scholarly and objective fashion about the fighting faiths and subversive stratagems of the enemies of a free society. Judging by the behavior of student bodies from one end of the country to the other in refusing to give a hearing to points of view which they do not share, and their resort to direct, often violent, action to impose their demands on the academic community, we have failed for the most part to teach students properly even about the meaning of democracy—its logic, ethics, and discipline.

What I wish to consider is some misconceptions both of the democratic process and of the educational process which have contributed to current confusions, darkened counsel, and lamed effective action. Indeed, there is a real danger that unless they are exposed, they may inflame disorders in both school and society. The disconcerting thing is that these misconceptions are being circulated not by demagogues and rabble-rousers, appealing to the vigilante spirit, but by members of the intellectual establishment, individuals in a position of influence and power both in the academy and judiciary. It was said of Florence Nightingale that she began her great reforms of the hospitals of her day with the maxim that whatever hospitals accomplish, they should at least not become centers for the spread of disease. Similarly, it is not too much to expect that one who professes to live by the word of reason should not encourage propaganda by the deed, that educators not apologize for or extenuate violence on the campus, and members of the judiciary not incite to lawlessness.

It is dismaying, for example, to hear Dr. Harvey Wheeler of the Center for the Study of Democratic Institutions characterize rioting as "an American way of life" and speak of its "creative uses."

"Direct action," he says in the *Saturday Review* (May 11, 1968), "the sort that now issues in violence too often [no objection is voiced to its often issuing in violence]—must be given fuller Constitutional protection."

What does this talk about "direct action" mean for which constitutional protection is demanded? Mr. Wheeler is saying that if students, impatient with the refusal of the faculty and/or administration to grant their demands, seize a building and bar access to classes by other students and teachers, they should have *legal* protection for their action. "Violence" would be the attempt to prevent lawless students from preventing other students from carrying on their legitimate educational business. In Wheeler's view, if the faculty or students invite a speaker of whom some other students disapprove, who bar his access to the campus or physically harass him until he leaves, the disrupters should have legal protection against any disciplinary measures.

"Direct action" clearly goes far beyond the expression of orderly dissent and protest. It may be too much to expect that dissent and protest be reasoned or reasonable. But is it too much to ask that it be orderly and peaceful? If so, it is as obvious as anything can be that this call for the constitutional protection of "direct action" is an invitation to chaos. Suppose one group of students resorted to "direct action" against the "direct action" of another group of students. Since the law must be equitably enforced, it could not prevent any group from preventing those who would prevent others from carrying on. What we would have is a kind of academic Hobbesian war of all against all, with the police standing idly by as those in pursuit of the good, the true, and the beautiful pursue and decimate each other.

In a democratic society in which the legal process has not broken down, to advise citizens to resort to "direct action" to get their way is to employ a calculatedly ambiguous expression. It is a covert appeal to the use of violence. When anyone urges "direct action" on students in a university, in which due process cannot be strictly legal but must be interpreted as the use of rational procedures, he is in effect urging the substitution of mob action for the rule of reason.

After all, what is "direct action" as distinct from "indirect action"? It is action which short-cuts deliberation and consultation in order to produce confrontation. Even when passive, its consequences may be harmful to person and property. Union picketing is a right under the First Amendment only when it is *peaceful*. But direct action is not necessarily peaceful any more than resistance is. That is why it is a clear evasion, and further evidence of confusion, when Mr. Wheeler equates his new constitutional right to direct action with the demand that "we must have a new Constitutional right to civil disobedience." A constitutional right, like any legal right, is a claim made by an individual or group which the state must be ready to enforce. Would the state then protect the "direct action" of Southern racists standing in the doorway of integrated school buildings to prevent Negro children from entering? How then could the law enforce the constitutional rights of these children? The law itself would suffer a breakdown from a new disease—legal schizophrenia.

It is a striking phenomenon that more has been written about civil disobedience in the last few years than in the entire period of American history which preceded it. But the nature of civil disobedience in the political democratic process has been radically misunderstood by many, and when these misunderstandings are applied to the academic world, the results border on the grotesque.

There are two fundamental misapprehensions about civil disobedience in general which have seriously misled many. The first is the assumption that each law in a democratic community posits as a legitimate question to every citizen whether to obey that law or to disobey it.

What is overlooked is the fact that, except on rare occasions, the prior allegiance of the *democrat* is to the legitimacy of the process by which the law is adopted. There is always, to be sure, a moral right to reject the whole democratic process on revolutionary or counterrevolutionary grounds, but we are now speaking of civil disobedience in a *democracy*. The democrat cannot make an issue of obeying or not obeying *every* law without repudiating the principle of majority rule and the democratic process to which that rule is integral. It is only on a matter of the gravest moral importance that he will be civilly disobedient, and the limits of his civil disobedience, *if he wishes to remain a democrat and operate within the democratic system*, will be drawn at that point in which the consequences of civil disobedience threaten to destroy the democratic system. That is why there is a presumption that a good citizen will obey the law which passes by majority vote of his fellow citizens or their representatives, even if he happens to be on the losing side. Why else have a vote? The implicit obligation is that the decision, freely made, after discussion, is *prima facie* binding. It is also clear that despite this *prima facie* obligation, any democrat may find *some* decision so unjust that he publicly refuses to obey it, and confident that he is not destroying the democratic system, he accepts the legal consequences of his refusal. But he cannot make *every* law of which he disapproves, *every* vote which has gone against him, a matter of conscientious brooding, of potential commitment to civil disobedience or defiance.

An analogy may make this clear. In the ethical universe of discourse and behavior, we assume that the truth must be told. But only a fanatic will assume that we must tell the truth all the time; and we can all conceive of circumstances in which a moral man will tell a lie. Yet, if anyone therefore inferred that as a moral man he must *always* grapple with the option to speak the truth or not to speak the truth whenever a question is put to him, he would either be the victim of doubting mania or would be disclosing the fact that he was not a moral man, but a confidence man. There is a *prima facie* obligation to speak the truth, even if, in order to save a human life or a woman's honor (to use an old-fashioned phrase), one must sometimes lie.

The trouble with much of the literature on civil disobedience is that in recognizing that it is *sometimes* justifiable, it does not recognize the presumptive validity (not wisdom) to a democrat of laws passed by means of the democratic process. (Whoever, like Thoreau, says that as an individual he will obey society's laws when he can benefit by them but will not accept its laws when they limit his freedom of action or offend his conscience is a freeloader.)

The second misconception of civil disobedience has far more dangerous fruits. The civilly disobedient democrat violates the law and accepts punishment in order to bear witness, to re-educate the majority by provoking them to second thoughts. Having failed to persuade his fellow citizens about the wisdom or justice of some measure by using all the methods open to him through the democratic process, he cannot honestly use civil disobedience as a strategy to prevent the majority of his fellow citizens from achieving their ends. A citizen may refuse to pay a tax which he regards as morally objectionable and go to jail to bring about the repeal of the tax; he has no right to prevent others from paying it. A student may refuse to take a course required of him and may suffer the consequences; he has no right to prevent other students who wish to take it from doing so. He may even strike and urge other students to join him, but he has no right to prevent his fellow students from attending class if they so desire.

What I particularly wish to challenge is the application of the principles of civil disobedience to the university as fundamentally misconceived. The university is not a political community. Its business is not government but primarily the discovery, publication, and teaching of the truth. Its authority is based *not* on numbers or the rule of the majority, but on knowledge. Although it can function in a spirit of democracy, it cannot be organized on the principle of one man, one vote, or, if it takes its educational mission seriously, of equal vote for student and faculty in the affairs of the mind or even with respect to organizational and curricular continuity. The fact that a society is politically organized as a democracy does not entail that all its other institutions be so organized—its families, its orchestras, museums, theaters, churches, and professional guilds.

I think that we may expect that all the institutions in a political democracy function in a *democratic spirit,* and by that I mean that all participants of any institution should be regarded as persons, should be heard, listened to, consulted with. But the responsibility for *decision* cannot be shared equally without equating inexperience with experience, ignorance with expertness, childishness with maturity. The assumption of a political democracy is that there are no experts in wisdom, that each citizen's vote is as good as any other's. If we make the same assumption about universities, and define a citizen of that community as anyone who functions in any capacity on the campus, we may as well shut up educational shop.

All this is denied, directly or indirectly, by the president since 1966 of the State University of New York New College at Old Westbury, Mr. Harris Wofford, Jr., who in a recent address to the American Bar Association maintained that our chief danger in college and country is not civil disobedience, but "undue obedience to law."

Why does Mr. Wofford believe that our students suffer from undue obedience and that they should be encouraged to accept "the theory and practice of civil disobedience"? He admits that "speech, lawful assembly or peaceful petition for the redress of grievances . . . [is] permitted in most of our colleges and universities." He asserts that "the right of students or faculties or visitors to advocate anything on our campuses—Nazism, Communism, sexual freedom, the legalization of marijuana, black supremacy, the war in Viet Nam, the victory of the Viet Cong . . . is generally accepted by academic administrators."

Surely this takes in a lot of ground. Why isn't this enough? Why, if students have the right to speech—which, in effect, means they can talk to faculty and administration about anything—and can make a reasonable case, do they need to be encouraged to resort to direct action? Speech means the possibility of communication. Reasonable speech means the likelihood that procedures can be established in which grievances can be heard and settled. What academic rules exist, and where, comparable with the Nazi laws against Jews and Alabama laws against Negroes, which, as Mr. Wofford claims, an "increasing number of our students feel a basic need to destroy"? Certainly not at Berkeley or Columbia.

Mr. Wofford fails to cite any. But with respect to both the community and the academy, he does say, "We need to develop a different and stronger dialectic than mere words and periodic elections." What can this mean except, when a thorny issue arises, a resort to direct action that corrupts words by making them merely "mere" and by defeating the popular will? What can this mean except a resort to violence in order to get one's way after mere words have proved unavailing? Mr. Wofford wants "to encourage civil disobedience and discourage violence." But having justified civil disobedience as a method of resisting or *preventing* the occurrence of what is regarded as evil, rather than as a self-sacrificial educational act of *teaching* what is evil, he is in effect countenancing student violence, although he claims he is not.

There are some ritualistic liberals, Mr. Wofford among them, who make a sharp distinction between human rights and property rights, and profess relative unconcern about illegal interference with property rights, especially the lawless occupation of public premises. In some contexts this distinction may be illuminating, particularly in legislative decisions where the public interest sometimes conflicts with large vested interests in corporate property. But in the educational context it is misleading and specious. Is the right to learn a human right or a property right? When a handful of students seize buildings at Berkeley or Columbia and prevent the great mass of other students from learning, is a property right or a human right being violated? When a teacher's or administrator's office is being occupied and vandalized, is not this a grave violation of his human right to exercise his profession, an arrogant abridgment of his freedom of movement? When his files are rifled and his letters are destroyed or published, is not this the gravest violation of the personal right of privacy?

The democratic spirit in institutions of higher education has its locus not in any specific mechanisms of voicing ideas, opinions, judgments, or requests on any relevant matter of educational concern, but in the realities of participation. I know of few institutions in which participation of students in the discussion of issues is not welcomed—and where it is not, it seems to me to be elementary educational wisdom as well as discretion on the part of the faculty to see that the situation is remedied as soon as possible. But once it is present, there is no place for the violence and lawlessness which paralyzed Columbia University last spring and which are currently being prepared for other universities.

We have noted an understandable uneasiness about the presence of violence on university campuses on the part of Mr. Wheeler and Mr. Wofford, betrayed by their ambiguous and inconsistent remarks about direct action. We must, however, consider finally a more forthright defense of violence in the academy, recently presented by, of all people, a leading figure in the federal judiciary, Judge Charles Wyzanski, Jr., apropos of his discussion of the Columbia imbroglio in the *Saturday Review* (July 20, 1968). Judge Wyzanski begins his discussion by expressing agreement with Harold Howe II, former U.S. Commissioner of Education, that "the colleges were to blame, not the students, for what has been going on at Ohio State, Columbia, Boston University, in Paris and Italy." This is not an auspicious beginning, for to couple such disparate events and to imply that colleges at home and abroad are equally to blame, or are blame-worthy in the same way, is to overlook the fact that European students revolted against conditions of squalor and material scarcities not found anywhere in the United States except perhaps in small denominational colleges in the South. On no important American college campus that has spawned violence have students suffered the material deprivations and the rigid authoritarian rules of the French and Italian university systems.

Justice Wyzanski in his specific reference to Columbia University asserts that the students were right in resenting the proposed gymnasium in Harlem. Let us grant *arguendo* that students were justified in feeling resentment, although no poll was taken at the time to determine whether they wanted a new gymnasium; nor was a poll of Harlem residents taken to determine whether they preferred the existence of the stone outcropping in its barren uselessness to the presence of the gymnasium with its impressive, even if limited, facilities. The pertinent question is not whether the students were justified in feeling resentment, but whether they were justified in expressing their resentment as they did. To mention just a few things, were they justified in (1) invading and seizing five university buildings, (2) holding an assistant dean captive and threatening him with violence, (3) pillaging the personal files of the president, (4) committing acts of arson, (5) carrying out widespread vandalism costing in the neighborhood of $350,000, (6) destroying records as well as valuable research papers, (7) publicly denouncing the dean of Columbia College before the assembled students with some of the choicest gutter obscenities, and (8) to cite only one action symbolic of the practices of the gutter as well as its languages, spitting in the face of Vice President David Truman, who, as dean of the college the previous year, had received a standing ovation from both students and faculty for opening up new lines of communication between the administration and the student body?

Suppose for a moment that Judge Wyzanski were to make an important legal decision that some citizens of the community resented. This is not an unusual occurrence. What would we normally say if they expressed their resentment at Judge Wyzanski's decision in a manner comparable with the behavior of the resentful students toward the Columbia administrators? Would we content ourselves in saying that these citizens were justified in feeling resentment—as well they may! —and remain silent, as Judge Wyzanski has, about the horrendous method of expressing it? Grant that the dignity of the academic process cannot be compared with the awful majesty of the judicial process. But in either case, is not the basic or paramount issue not the fact of the resentment, however justified, but the violent disruption of the educational or legal process? Whatever the alleged grievances of the small group of students at Columbia, did they warrant the flagrant violence and other forms of lawlessness of which Judge Wyzanski seemingly approved? This is the issue of transcendent educational, political, and moral importance. It is disregarded when he asks about violence not whether it was morally justified or historically necessary but merely whether it was futile or successful. The student violence was obviously successful at Columbia. Is this all we need to know to judge it?

One final word about responsibility. There are those who dismiss the entire concept of responsibility as meaningless on the ground that all causation is ultimately reducible to the influence of objective conditions on human behavior. I know of no one who can consistently exclude reference to responsibility from his talk and thought. At the time of Little Rock, Arkansas, had someone blamed the riotous behavior of the white racists against Negro women and children on the conditions in which they were nurtured, we would have dismissed such an explanation as evasive apologetics. Not all brought up under the same conditions rioted. Sometimes conditions reduce men to a state of being which makes moral judgment on human behavior irrelevant. But whoever would explain away the assaults against academic due process as the result not of deliberate action, but merely of the state of the world or the nation, of the Vietnam War or the draft, has barred his own way to understanding the problems we face in attempting to extend human freedom under law both in schools and in society. Whatever the conditions are, so long as we are recognizably human we are all responsible for our actions; and sometimes for the conditions under which we act, too, but, of course, not in the same way, and not to the same degree.

One sign of responsibility is the making of an intelligent response not only to events that have occurred but to the possibilities of what might occur. The faculties and student bodies of this country can measure up to their responsibilities only by addressing themselves now, separately and cooperatively, not so much to the conquest of power in the academy or general community but primarily to the problems of achieving the best liberal education possible under the imperfect conditions of American society.

Suggestions for Writing

1. Write an essay attacking or defending one point in the controversy about youth: Poirier's concept of "pastoralism," Halle's point about moral irresponsibility, Wyzanski's about hypocrisy, Hook's about democracy. Use a *simple pro-and-con structure*, as follows. Write an introductory paragraph that ends with an assertion of your thesis: "Although often high-handed and ever destructive, today's activitists are rejuvenating democracy." Now write a paragraph of concession to the "con" viewpoint: "Of course, some of their methods have been called fascistic." And so on to the end of the paragraph, including every conceivable objection. Then back to your main line: "But democracy depends basically on moral awareness and justice." The structure might be diagramed something like this:

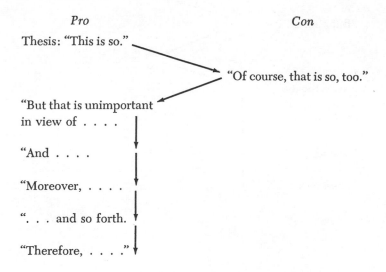

2. Write an essay supporting one of the four essayists against one of the others: "Although Mr. A makes a strong case, Mr. B is nearer the truth of the matter." Now, since the opposition is more considerable, use a *complex*

pro-and-con structure—a series of *con*'s and *pro*'s—to demolish the opposition point by point. Each paragraph may be a small argument that presents the opposition, then knocks it flat. Swing your argument back and forth, using phrases like *To be sure, I admit,* and *On the other hand*—making sure to end each swing on your own side. Then add a good thumping paragraph of conclusion. The structural line might look something like this:

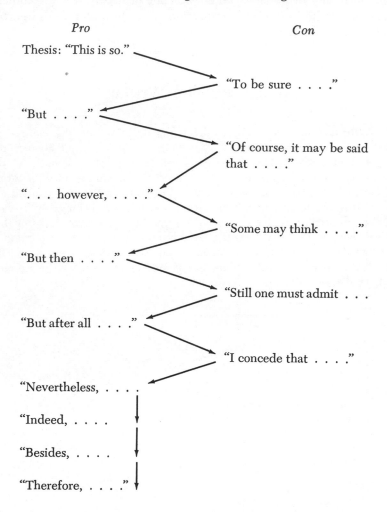

Man Against Darkness w. t. stace · 65
*Man Out of Darkness: Religion Has Not Lost Its
   Power* theodore m. grefne · 76
Celebrating with Dr. Leary diana trilling · 85
The Mystic's Experience of God rufus m. jones · 103
Plato and Bacon thomas babington macaulay · 106

Middle Tactics

The Vector of Interest

An essay's beginning and its end are important,
since they set the thesis and round it to conclusion. We shall look at beginnings and ends closely
in the next chapter, when we consider the different kinds of paragraph. But the middle, the bulk
of the essay, requires tactics that may differ considerably from the *pro*'s and *con*'s we have already seen. The five essays in this section will illustrate some of the differences. Their theses lie
deeper than controversy; the opposition is more

like a shadowy bystander, lending little of the structural force to be seen in controversial argument. But the essays will also show that one tactical principle underlies any effective structural order a writer can think of: to keep the reader interested, save the best for last.

Since the reader sees more clearly at each step into the essay, his interest naturally declines. The writer must therefore push upward to keep the vector of the reader's interest at least on the horizontal, with no sag and preferably with an upward swing:

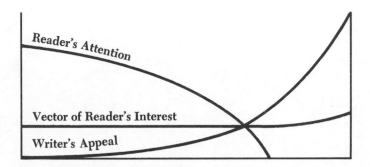

Therefore, in developing the middle of an essay, make each item more interesting than its predecessor, saving best till last.

This is the ideal. Study these five selections to see how well the writers have fulfilled it. Notice also the different kinds of order. After a paragraph on Sartre to clarify his thesis, Stace uses a historical arrangement to illustrate his first point, moving backward in time from Russell to Darwin to Plato, and then forward again to Galileo and modern man. Next he shifts to a reasonable progression, from what he thinks least important (religion) to what he thinks most important (moral courage). Greene progresses from "science" to "spirit"; Diana Trilling augments the natural drama of a programmed evening with some deepening speculation. Jones, too, moves from least to most: from mundane mysticisms to knowledge of God, with its "slow laboratory effects." Notice his thesis (second paragraph), and the way his demonstration so snugly fits it.

Though the selection from Macaulay stands on its own thesis ("To understand Bacon's contribution compare him with Plato"), it is really the middle of a longer essay. Macaulay, too, follows an order of rising interest. But more especially, notice his tactics of contrast. He does not write all about Plato, then all about Bacon. He develops his contrast not author by author, but idea by idea, making each idea bear on *both* authors— a phrase for one, a phrase for the other; a paragraph for one, a paragraph for the other. This is an essential tactical point in any extended contrast.

Man Against Darkness
W. T. Stace

1

The Catholic bishops of America recently issued a statement in which they said that the chaotic and bewildered state of the modern world is due to man's loss of faith, his abandonment of God and religion. For my part I believe in no religion at all. Yet I entirely agree with the bishops. It is no doubt an oversimplification to speak of *the* cause of so complex a state of affairs as the tortured condition of the world today. Its causes are doubtless multitudinous. Yet allowing for some element of oversimplification, I say that the bishops' assertion is substantially true.

M. Jean-Paul Sartre, the French existentialist philosopher, labels himself an atheist. Yet his views seem to me plainly to support the statement of the bishops. So long as there was believed to be a God in the sky, he says, men could regard him as the source of their moral ideals. The universe, created and governed by a fatherly God, was a friendly habitation for man. We could be sure that, however great the evil in the world, good in the end would triumph and the forces of evil would be routed. With the disappearance of God from the sky all this has changed. Since the world is not ruled by a spiritual being, but rather by blind forces, there cannot be any ideals, moral or otherwise, in the universe outside us. Our ideals, therefore, must proceed only from our own minds; they are our own inventions. Thus the world which surrounds us is nothing but an immense spiritual emptiness. It is a dead universe. We do not live in a universe which is on the side of our values. It is completely indifferent to them.

Years ago Mr. Bertrand Russell, in his essay *A Free Man's Worship*, said much the same thing.

> Such in outline, but even more purposeless, more void of meaning, is the world which Science presents for our belief. Amid such a world, if anywhere; our ideals henceforward must find a home. . . . Blind to good and evil, reckless of destruction, omnipotent matter rolls on its relentless way; for man, condemned today to lose his dearest, tomorrow himself to pass through the gate of darkness, it remains only to cherish, ere yet the blow falls, the lofty thoughts that ennoble his little day; . . . to worship at the shrine his own hands have built; . . . to sustain alone, a weary but unyielding Atlas, the world that his own ideals have fashioned despite the trampling march of unconscious power.

It is true that Mr. Russell's personal attitude to the disappearance of religion is quite different from either that of M. Sartre or the bishops or myself. The bishops think it a calamity. So do I. M. Sartre finds it "very distressing." And he berates as shallow the attitude of those who think that without God the world can go on just the same as before, as if nothing had happened. This creates for mankind, he thinks, a terrible crisis. And in this I agree with him. Mr. Russell, on the other hand, seems to believe that religion has done more harm than good in the world, and that its disappearance will be a blessing. But his picture of the world, and of the modern mind, is the same as that of M. Sartre. He stresses the *purposelessness* of the universe, the facts that man's ideals are his own creations, that the universe outside him in no way supports them, that man is alone and friendless in the world.

Mr. Russell notes that it is science which has produced this situation. There is no doubt that this is correct. But the way in which it has come about is not generally understood. There is a popular belief that some particular scientific discoveries or theories, such as the Darwinian theory of evolution, or the views of geologists about the age of the earth, or a series of such discoveries, have done the damage. It would be foolish to deny that these discoveries have had a great effect in undermining religious dogmas. But this account does not at all go to the root of the matter. Religion can probably outlive any scientific discoveries which could be made. It can accommodate itself to them. The root cause of the decay of faith has not been any particular discovery of science, but rather the general spirit of science and certain basic assumptions upon which modern science, from the seventeenth century onwards, has proceeded.

2

It was Galileo and Newton—notwithstanding that Newton himself was a deeply religious man—who destroyed the old comfortable picture of a friendly universe governed by spiritual values. And this was effected, not by Newton's discovery of the law of gravitation nor by any of Galileo's brilliant investigations, but by the general picture of the world which these men and others of their time made the basis of the science, not only of their own day, but of all succeeding generations down to the present. That is why the century immediately following Newton, the eighteenth century, was notoriously an age of religious skepticism. Skepticism did not have to wait for the discoveries of Darwin and the geologists in the nineteenth century. It flooded the world immediately after the age of the rise of science.

Neither the Copernican hypothesis nor any of Newton's or Galileo's particular discoveries were the real causes. Religious faith might well have accommodated itself to the new astronomy. The real turning point between the medieval age of faith and the modern age of unfaith came when the scientists of the seventeenth century turned their backs upon what used to be called "final causes." The final cause of a thing or event meant the purpose which it was supposed to serve in the universe, its cosmic purpose. What lay back of this was the presupposition that there is a cosmic order or plan and that everything which exists could in the last analysis be explained in terms of its place in this cosmic plan, that is, in terms of its purpose.

Plato and Aristotle believed this, and so did the whole medieval Christian world. For instance, if it were true that the sun and the moon were created and exist for the purpose of giving light to man, then this fact would explain why the sun and the moon exist. We might not be able to discover the purpose of everything, but everything must have a purpose. Belief in final causes thus amounted to a belief that the world is governed by purposes, presumably the purposes of some overruling mind. This belief was not the invention of Christianity. It was basic to the whole of Western civilization, whether in the ancient pagan world or in Christendom, from the time of Socrates to the rise of science in the seventeenth century.

The founders of modern science—for instance, Galileo, Kepler, and Newton—were mostly pious men who did not doubt God's purposes. Nevertheless they took the revolutionary step of consciously and deliberately expelling the idea of purpose as controlling nature from their new science of nature. They did this on the ground that inquiry into purposes is useless for what science aims at: namely, the prediction and control of events. To predict an eclipse, what you have to know is not its purpose but its causes. Hence science from the seventeenth century onwards became exclusively an inquiry into causes. The conception of purpose in the world was ignored and frowned on. This, though silent and almost unnoticed, was the greatest revolution in human history, far outweighing in importance any of the political revolutions whose thunder has reverberated through the world.

For it came about in this way that for the past three hundred years there has been growing up in men's minds, dominated as they are by science, a new imaginative picture of the world. The world, according to this new picture, is purposeless, senseless, meaningless. Nature is nothing but matter in motion. The motions of matter are governed, not by any purpose, but by blind forces and laws. Nature on this view, says Whitehead—to whose writings I am indebted in this part of my paper—is "merely the hurrying of material, endlessly, meaninglessly." You can draw a sharp line across the history of Europe dividing it into two epochs of very unequal length. The line passes through the lifetime of Galileo. European man before Galileo—whether ancient pagan or more recent Christian—thought of the world as controlled by plan and purpose. After Galileo European man thinks of it as utterly purposeless. This is the great revolution of which I spoke.

It is this which has killed religion. Religion could survive the discoveries that the sun, not the earth, is the center; that men are descended from simian ancestors; that the earth is hundreds of millions of years old. These discoveries may render out of date some of the details of older theological dogmas, may force their restatement in new intellectual frameworks. But they do not touch the essence of the religious vision itself, which is the faith that there is plan and purpose in the world, that the world is a moral order, that in the end all things are for the best. This faith may express itself through many different intellectual dogmas, those of Christianity, of Hinduism, of Islam. All and any of these intellectual dogmas may be destroyed without destroying the essential religious spirit. But that spirit cannot survive destruction of belief in a plan and purpose of the world, for that is the very heart of it. Religion can get on with any sort of astronomy, geology, biology, physics. But it cannot get on with a purposeless and meaningless universe.

If the scheme of things is purposeless and meaningless, then the life of man is purposeless and meaningless too. Everything is futile, all effort is in the end worthless. A man may, of course, still pursue disconnected ends, money, fame, art, science, and may gain pleasure from them. But his life is hollow at the center. Hence the dissatisfied, disillusioned, restless, spirit of modern man.

The picture of a meaningless world, and a meaningless human life, is, I think, the basic theme of much modern art and literature. Certainly it is the basic theme of modern philosophy. According to the most characteristic philosophies of the modern period from Hume in the eighteenth century to the so-called positivists of today, the world is just what it is, and that is the end of all inquiry. There is no reason for its being what it is. Everything might just as well have been quite different, and there would have been no reason for that either. When you have stated what things are, what things the world contains, there is nothing more which could be said, even by an omniscient being. To ask any question about *why* things are thus, or what purpose their being so serves, is to ask a senseless question, because they serve no purpose at all. For instance, there is for modern philosophy no such thing as the ancient problem of evil. For this once famous question presupposes that pain and misery, though they seem so inexplicable and irrational to us, must ultimately subserve some rational purpose, must have their places in the cosmic plan. But this is nonsense. There is no such overruling rationality in the universe. Belief in the ultimate irrationality of everything is the quintessence of what is called the modern mind.

It is true that, parallel with these philosophies which are typical of the modern mind, preaching the meaninglessness of the world, there has run a line of idealistic philosophies whose contention is that the world is after all spiritual in nature and that moral ideals and values are inherent in its structure. But most of these idealisms were simply philosophical expressions of romanticism, which was itself no more than an unsuccessful counterattack of the religious against the scientific view of things. They perished, along with romanticism in literature and art, about the beginning of the present century, though of course they still have a few adherents.

At the bottom these idealistic systems of thought were rationalizations of man's wishful thinking. They were born of the refusal of men to admit the cosmic darkness. They were comforting illusions within the warm glow of which the more tender-minded intellectuals sought to shelter themselves from the icy winds of the universe. They lasted a little while. But they are shattered now, and we return once more to the vision of a purposeless world.

3

Along with the ruin of the religious vision there went the ruin of moral principles and indeed of all values. If there is a cosmic purpose, if there is in the nature of things a drive towards goodness, then our moral systems will derive their validity from this. But if our moral rules do not proceed from something outside us in the nature of the universe—whether we say it is God or simply the universe itself—then they must be our own inventions. Thus it came to be believed that moral rules must be merely an expression of our own likes and dislikes. But likes and dislikes are notoriously variable. What pleases one man, people, or culture displeases another. Therefore morals are wholly relative.

This obvious conclusion from the idea of a purposeless world made its appearance in Europe immediately after the rise of science, for instance in the philosophy of Hobbes. Hobbes saw at once that if there is no purpose in the world there are no values either. "Good and evil," he writes, "are names that signify our appetites and aversions; which in different tempers, customs, and doctrines of men are different. . . . Every man calleth that which pleaseth him, good; and that which displeaseth him, evil."

This doctrine of the relativity of morals, though it has recently received an impetus from the studies of anthropologists, was thus really implicit in the whole scientific mentality. It is disastrous for morals because it destroys their entire traditional foundation. That is why philosophers who see the danger signals, from the time at least of Kant, have been trying to give to morals a new foundation, that is, a secular or nonreligious foundation. This attempt may very well be intellectually successful. Such a foundation, independent of the religious view of the world, might well be found. But the question is whether it can ever be a *practical* success, that is, whether apart from its logical validity and its influence with intellectuals, it can ever replace among the masses of men the lost religious foundation. On that question hangs perhaps the future of civilization. But meanwhile disaster is overtaking us.

The widespread belief in "ethical relativity" among philosophers, psychologists, ethnologists, and sociologists is the theoretical counterpart of the repudiation of principle which we see all around us, especially in international affairs, the field in which morals have always had the weakest foothold. No one any longer effectively believes in moral principles except as the private prejudices either of individual men or of nations or cultures. This is the inevitable consequence of the doctrine of ethical relativity, which in turn is the inevitable consequence of believing in a purposeless world.

Another characteristic of our spiritual state is loss of belief in the freedom of the will. This also is a fruit of the scientific spirit, though not of any particular scientific discovery. Science has been built up on the basis of determinism, which is the belief that every event is completely determined by a chain of causes and is therefore theoretically predictable beforehand. It is true that recent physics seems to challenge this. But so far as its practical consequences are concerned, the damage has long ago been done. A man's actions, it was argued, are as much events in the natural world as is an eclipse of the sun. It follows that men's actions are as theoretically predictable as an eclipse. But if it is certain now that John Smith will murder Joseph Jones at 2.15 P.M. on January 1, 1963, what possible meaning can it have to say that when that time comes John Smith will be *free* to choose whether he will commit the murder or not? And if he is not free, how can he be held responsible?

It is true that the whole of this argument can be shown by a competent philosopher to be a tissue of fallacies—or at least I claim that it can. But the point is that the analysis required to show this is much too subtle to be understood by the average entirely unphilosophical man. Because of this, the argument against free will is generally swallowed whole by the unphilosophical. Hence the thought that man is not free, that he is the helpless plaything of forces over which he has no control, has deeply penetrated the modern mind. We hear of economic determinism, cultural determinism, historical determinism. We are not responsible for what we do because our glands control us, or because we are the products of environment or heredity. Not moral self-control, but the doctor, the psychiatrist, the educationist, must save us from doing evil. Pills and injections in the future are to do what Christ and the prophets have failed to do. Of course I do not mean to deny that doctors and educationists can and must help. And I do not mean in any way to belittle their efforts. But I do wish to draw attention to the weakening of moral controls, the greater or less repudiation of personal responsibility which, in the popular thinking of the day, result from these tendencies of thought.

4

What, then, is to be done? Where are we to look for salvation from the evils of our time? All the remedies I have seen suggested so far are, in my opinion, useless. Let us look at some of them.

Philosophers and intellectuals generally can, I believe, genuinely do something to help. But it is extremely little. What philosophers can do is to show that neither the relativity of morals nor the denial of free will really follows from the grounds which have been supposed to support them. They can also try to discover a genuine secular basis for morals to replace the religious basis which has disappeared. Some of us are trying to do these things. But in the first place philosophers unfortunately are not agreed about these matters, and their disputes are utterly confusing to the non-philosophers. And in the second place their influence is practically negligible because their analyses necessarily take place on a level on which the masses are totally unable to follow them.

The bishops, of course, propose as remedy a return to belief in God and in the doctrines of the Christian religion. Others think that a new religion is what is needed. Those who make these proposals fail to realize that the crisis in man's spiritual condition is something unique in history for which there is no sort of analogy in the past. They are thinking perhaps of the collapse of the ancient Greek and Roman religions. The vacuum then created was easily filled by Christianity, and it might have been filled by Mithraism if Christianity had not appeared. By analogy they think that Christianity might now be replaced by a new religion, or even that Christianity itself, if revivified, might bring back health to men's lives.

But I believe that there is no analogy at all between our present state and that of the European peoples at the time of the fall of paganism.

Men had at that time lost their belief only in particular dogmas, particular embodiments of the religious view of the world. It had no doubt become incredible that Zeus and the other gods were living on the top of Mount Olympus. You could go to the top and find no trace of them. But the imaginative picture of a world governed by purpose, a world driving towards the good—which is the inner spirit of religion—had at that time received no serious shock. It had merely to re-embody itself in new dogmas, those of Christianity or some other religion. Religion itself was not dead in the world, only a particular form of it.

But now the situation is quite different. It is not merely that particular dogmas, like that of the virgin birth, are unacceptable to the modern mind. That is true, but it constitutes a very superficial diagnosis of the present situation of religion. Modern skepticism is of a wholly different order from that of the intellectuals of the ancient world. It has attacked and destroyed not merely the outward forms of the religious spirit, its particularized dogmas, but the very essence of that spirit itself, belief in a meaningful and purposeful world. For the founding of a new religion a new Jesus Christ or Buddha would have to appear, in itself a most unlikely event and one for which in any case we cannot afford to sit and wait. But even if a new prophet and a new religion did appear, we may predict that they would fail in the modern world. No one for long would believe in them, for modern men have lost the vision, basic to all religion, of an ordered plan and purpose of the world. They have before their minds the picture of a purposeless universe, and such a world-picture must be fatal to any religion at all, not merely to Christianity.

We must not be misled by occasional appearances of a revival of the religious spirit. Men, we are told, in their disgust and disillusionment at the emptiness of their lives, are turning once more to religion, or are searching for a new message. It may be so. We must expect such wistful yearnings of the spirit. We must expect men to wish back again the light that is gone, and to try to bring it back. But however they may wish and try, the light will not shine again,—not at least in the civilization to which we belong.

Another remedy commonly proposed is that we should turn to science itself, or the scientific spirit, for our salvation. Mr. Russell and Professor Dewey both make this proposal, though in somewhat different ways. Professor Dewey seems to believe that discoveries in sociology, the application of scientific method to social and political problems, will rescue us. This seems to me to be utterly naïve. It is not likely that science, which is basically the cause of our spiritual troubles, is likely also to produce the cure for them. Also it lies in the nature of science that, though it can teach us the best means for achieving our ends, it can never tell us what ends to pursue. It cannot give us any ideals. And our trouble is about ideals and ends, not about the means for reaching them.

5

No civilization can live without ideals, or to put it in another way, without a firm faith in moral ideals. Our ideals and moral ideas have in the past been rooted in religion. But the religious basis of our ideals has been undermined, and the superstructure of ideals is plainly tottering. None of the commonly suggested remedies on examination seems likely to succeed. It would therefore look as if the early death of our civilization were inevitable.

Of course we know that it is perfectly possible for individual men, very highly educated men, philosophers, scientists, intellectuals in general, to live moral lives without any religious convictions. But the question is whether a whole civilization, a whole family of peoples, composed almost entirely of relatively uneducated men and women, can do this.

It follows, of course, that if we could make the vast majority of men as highly educated as the very few are now, we might save the situation. And we are already moving slowly in that direction through the techniques of mass education. But the critical question seems to concern the time-lag. Perhaps in a few hundred years most of the population will, at the present rate, be sufficiently highly educated and civilized to combine high ideals with an absence of religion. But long before we reach any such stage, the collapse of our civilization may have come about. How are we to live through the intervening period?

I am sure that the first thing we have to do is to face the truth, however bleak it may be, and then next we have to learn to live with it. Let me say a word about each of these two points. What I am urging as regards the first is complete honesty. Those who wish to resurrect Christian dogmas are not, of course, consciously dishonest. But they have that kind of unconscious dishonesty which consists in lulling oneself with opiates and dreams. Those who talk of a new religion are merely hoping for a new opiate. Both alike refuse to face the truth that there is, in the universe outside man, no spirituality, no regard for values, no friend in the sky, no help or comfort for man of any sort. To be perfectly honest in the admission of this fact, not to seek shelter in new or old illusions, not to indulge in wishful dreams about this matter, this is the first thing we shall have to do.

I do not urge this course out of any special regard for the sanctity of truth in the abstract. It is not self-evident to me that truth is the supreme value to which all else must be sacrificed. Might not the discoverer of a truth which would be fatal to mankind be justified in suppressing it, even in teaching men a falsehood? Is truth more valuable than goodness and beauty and happiness? To think so is to invent yet another absolute, another religious delusion in which Truth with a capital T is substituted for God. The reason why we must now boldly and honestly face the truth that the universe is non-spiritual and indifferent to goodness, beauty, happiness, or truth is not that it would be wicked to suppress it, but simply that it is too late to do so, so that in the end we cannot do anything else but face it. Yet we stand on the brink, dreading the icy plunge. We need courage. We need honesty.

Now about the other point, the necessity of learning to live with the truth. This means learning to live virtuously and happily, or at least contentedly, without illusions. And this is going to be extremely difficult because what we have now begun dimly to perceive is that human life in the past, or at least human happiness, has almost wholly depended upon illusions. It has been said that man lives by truth, and that the truth will make us free. Nearly the opposite seems to me to be the case. Mankind has managed to live only by means of lies, and the truth may very well destroy us. If one were a Bergsonian one might believe that nature deliberately puts illusions into our souls in order to induce us to go on living.

The illusions by which men have lived seem to be of two kinds. First, there is what one may perhaps call the Great Illusion—I mean the religious illusion that the universe is moral and good, that it follows a wise and noble plan, that it is gradually generating some supreme value, that goodness is bound to triumph in it. Secondly, there is a whole host of minor illusions on which human happiness nourishes itself. How much of human happiness notoriously comes from the illusions of the lover about his beloved? Then again we work and strive because of the illusions connected with fame, glory, power, or money. Banners of all kinds, flags, emblems, insignia, ceremonials, and rituals are invariably symbols of some illusion or other. The British Empire, the connection between mother country and dominions, is partly kept going by illusions surrounding the notion of kingship. Or think of the vast amount of human happiness which is derived from the illusion of supposing that if some nonsense syllable, such as "sir" or "count" or "lord" is pronounced in conjunction with our names, we belong to a superior order of people.

There is plenty of evidence that human happiness is almost wholly based upon illusions of one kind or another. But the scientific spirit, or the spirit of truth, is the enemy of illusions and therefore the enemy of human happiness. That is why it is going to be so difficult to live with the truth.

There is no reason why we should have to give up the host of minor illusions which render life supportable. There is no reason why the lover should be scientific about the loved one. Even the illusions of fame and glory may persist. But without the Great Illusion, the illusion of a good, kindly, and purposeful universe, we shall *have* to learn to live. And to ask this is really no more than to ask that we become genuinely civilized beings and not merely sham civilized beings.

I can best explain the difference by a reminiscence. I remember a fellow student in my college days, an ardent Christian, who told me that if he did not believe in a future life, in heaven and hell, he would rape, murder, steal, and be a drunkard. That is what I call being a sham civilized being. On the other hand, not only could a Huxley, a John Stuart Mill, a David Hume, live great and fine lives without any religion, but a great many others of us, quite obscure persons, can at least live decent lives without it.

To be genuinely civilized means to be able to walk straightly and to live honorably without the props and crutches of one or another of the childish dreams which have so far supported men. That such a life is likely to be ecstatically happy I will not claim. But that it can be lived in quiet content, accepting resignedly what cannot be helped, not expecting the impossible, and thankful for small mercies, this I would maintain. That it will be difficult for men in general to learn this lesson I do not deny. But that it will be impossible I would not admit since so many have learned it already.

Man has not yet grown up. He is not adult. Like a child he cries for the moon and lives in a world of fantasies. And the race as a whole has perhaps reached the great crisis of its life. Can it grow up as a race in the same sense as individual men grow up? Can man put away childish things and adolescent dreams? Can he grasp the real world as it actually is, stark and bleak, without its romantic or religious halo, and still retain his ideals, striving for great ends and noble achievements? If he can, all may yet be well. If he cannot, he will probably sink back into the savagery and brutality from which he came, taking a humble place once more among the lower animals.

Man Out of Darkness:
Religion Has Not Lost Its Power
Theodore M. Greene

1

When Professor Stace says that the question of purpose in the universe is the crucial cultural issue of our times, he is certainly right. He is also right in urging us to face the truth, whatever it is, and to live with it honestly and courageously. The question is, Is "the truth" what he thinks it is? Has science, as Professor Stace claims, given us a new imaginative picture of the world—a picture of a meaningless and purposeless universe indifferent to all human aspiration? This picture in its large outline is certainly not "new"—in our tradition it is at least as old as Democritus and Lucretius. Nor is it correct to say that science has given us a picture of reality *as a whole* which logically *excludes* meaning and purpose. All that can fairly be said is that the scientific account of the "world of nature" does not, at least at present, include moral or religious purpose and meaning. The picture science paints is neutral with respect to such purpose and meaning because the scientific enterprise, in and of itself, simply ignores these issues.

It must be admitted, however, that the concept of a purposeless universe has been judged by many people to have received the endorsement of modern science. We must also grant that this picture, with its prestige thus greatly enhanced, has profoundly influenced the thought and the unconscious attitudes of a lot of people, particularly the intelligentsia, but also the man in the street.

But this is *not* the whole story. Not only has organized Christianity lost no ground during the last decades; it is actually increasing its following in this country, in England, and in some portions of Europe. More people are going to church with, in many cases, a deeper sense of spiritual need. Theological seminaries are crowded with students who are, on the whole, abler than their pre-war predecessors, yet seminaries are unable to satisfy the demand of churches for more clergy. Missionary activity is increasing in scope and improving in quality. Christianity is more widely spread geographically and more deeply rooted among more peoples than it has ever been. The Christian ecumenical movement is making rapid strides: through it Christians are coming together on a world-wide scale as never before.

There is also increasingly evident in various branches of the Church a growing tendency to take stock of their inadequacies and failures, to indulge in contrite self-examination, and to seek to promote a revitalization of Christian belief, thought, and social action.

No less significant is the renewed interest of college students in a faith to live by. Most of these eager inquirers are largely ignorant of the Bible, Christian doctrine, and the Christian tradition. Many of them are highly critical of Christian orthodoxy and traditionalism and are indignant at what they (often justly) regard as self-righteousness, wishful thinking, and cant in organized religion. Few are properly equipped to grapple intelligently with the basic problems of religious faith in our secular society. But they are neither complacent nor dogmatic; they are deeply troubled and sincerely anxious to find whatever light and strength religion can provide. In short, the "spirit of religion" is a vital force in their lives.

Who, then, is the common man who, according to Professor Stace, has absorbed the idea of a purposeless universe so completely that he has lost all belief not only in God but in moral principles, freedom of the will, and moral responsibility, and could not now be persuaded to abandon or modify this idea even if the intellectual and spiritual leaders in his community were convinced that it was erroneous? In so far as he is impervious to philosophy, he will not greatly be affected by naturalism in its modern scientific dress. If, on the other hand, he has been impressed—indeed, very deeply impressed—by the "new world picture," is there any reason why philosophers and scientists, in combination, could not gradually impress another picture of the world upon his mind?

This leaves us with the question, Can we formulate a constructive argument in support of a critical religious faith? I believe we can.

2

The scientific method has amply demonstrated its validity and power in the areas of inquiry, and for the purposes, for which it has been designed. Witness the spectacular advance of science over the past three hundred years, the large measure of agreement among reputable scientists, and the technological achievements of applied science, every one of which is a pragmatic demonstration of the scientist's understanding of natural processes.

Science also invites, and supports, more embracing philosophical accounts of the nature of the physical world, and no responsible interpretation of reality as a whole can ignore, or contradict, careful philosophical generalizations based upon well-established scientific conclusions. The position I would defend is therefore committed to affirmative reliance on scientific evidence and to the full incorporation, at any point in history, of accepted scientifically supported interpretations of nature.

Science, however, in the stricter sense of the term, is not all-inclusive; it addresses itself to a specific type of inquiry into a specific area of reality for a specific purpose. Pure science concerns itself solely with temporal events, both "physical" and "psycho-physical." It studies these to discover and formulate recurrences and uniformities, commonly called "laws of nature"; and it does so partly to satisfy man's native curiosity, partly to facilitate his control of nature for greater human welfare. But, as Professor Stace admits, it is by its very nature unqualified to deal with values; "it can teach us the best means for achieving our ends, it can never tell us what ends to pursue." This fact is enormously important, for it means that science, in its strict sense, simply has nothing to say about God or goodness or beauty.

Hence the "imaginative picture of the world" which science, in and of itself, supports is *of course* a picture of a valueless, meaningless universe. How could it be otherwise? But this doesn't prove that there are no values and no God in the universe; it merely proves that science can't possibly discover these values and this Deity if they do exist.

Furthermore, no scientific conclusions, at any point in history, are final, definitive, or certain. They are *necessarily* hypothetical and tentative. It follows that philosophical extrapolations of science are equally tentative and hypothetical. For example, late-nineteenth-century science supported the philosophical doctrine of strict mechanistic determinism; some qualified philosophers today are not sure that the most recent scientific thinking justifies any such philosophical conclusion. In any case, the farther science advances, the less disposed are first-rate scientists to believe that they have fathomed the mysteries even of the world of nature, let alone the whole of reality. Their attitude is humble and cautious, not dogmatic and assured.

If my analysis is correct thus far, it follows that science cannot properly deny that there *may* be meaning and purpose, or even a God, in the universe, though it cannot itself make any such assertions. Responsible belief in God and in a cosmic purpose is possible, however, only if affirmative evidence can be adduced for its support. Without such evidence, moral and religious belief would have to be wholly blind, and I would condemn blind faith as heartily as does Professor Stace. What kind of evidence, then, would be relevant and coercive? On what kind of experience can an enlightened belief in God and cosmic meaning be based?

The obvious answer would seem to be: on man's moral and religious experiences. Moralists like Socrates and Kant based their beliefs in a meaningful cosmos on man's moral experiences at their best. Christian theologians have based their beliefs on man's Christian experiences, individual and corporate. Is this procedure invalid? Is it wrong to believe that we can achieve reliable knowledge of objective moral values by means of a critical interpretation of man's experience of duty, his respect for his fellow man, his loyalty to moral ideals, or that we can achieve reliable knowledge of God by critical interpretation of man's religious experiences as described, for example, in the New Testament?

It is precisely at this point that we can relate man's search for, and knowledge of, God and moral values to man's scientific study of, and knowledge of, nature. The scientific method is, in essence, the method of rational interpretation of sensory evidence. (I will ignore here the complications raised by psychology.) This means that *both* sensory evidence *and* rational interpretation are essential for scientific knowledge; that sensory data without interpretation are blind, and that reasoning, however consistent, which is not based on sensory evidence is empty of content.

If we can accept the basic scientific assumption that logical interpretation of *sensory* evidence gives us an ever increasing understanding of the world of *nature*, why can we not similarly assume that the logical interpretation of *moral and religious* data, if such exist, can give us an ever increasing understanding of a *spiritual*—that is, a moral and religious—dimension of reality which is related to, but not identical with, the world of nature? If this were possible, it would then be the task of philosophy to try to give an account of reality which does justice *both* to sensory *and* to moral and religious experiences, to science *and* to ethics and theology at their best.

The crucial point in the entire constructive argument is thus the concept of "experience." If the only type of experience which can be taken seriously—that is, accepted as providing contact with reality and clues to its nature—is sensory experience, then Professor Stace's conclusions inevitably follow. But why must experience be so narrowly defined? What is to prevent us from being really empirical and believing that man's moral and religious experiences, which are no less coercive, vivid, sharable, and rationally interpretable than his sensory experiences, provide further contacts with reality and further clues to its nature?

3

Reflective religious faith (in contrast to blind superstition and uncritical faith) rests on precisely this more liberal and inclusive conception of experience. It is always anchored in the primary religious experiences of the individual believer, set in the context of the religious experiences of other individuals in the same and other religious traditions. That is, it rests on the deep conviction of reflective religious believers that only in and through such experiences do we confront a living God. But religious faith, if it is reflective, is never identified with mere experience, however intense, however often repeated, and however widely shared by others. The factor of reasonable interpretation is as essential as the factor of the primary experience itself.

What we actually find in the history of religions, therefore, parallels what we find in the history of science. The earliest attempts in our tradition at a "scientific" understanding of nature were those of the pre-Socratic thinkers who tried to explain the whole of nature in terms of one or more of the four basic "elements"—earth, air, fire, and water. Only very gradually did this attempt grow out of its primitive crudities into the rich pattern of concepts, principles, and methods that constitute modern science. Similarly, primitive religious beliefs and practices were crude, uncritical, and superstitious; it is only gradually that religious experience and belief have developed into what we find them to be, at their best, in the higher religions.

I do not wish to press this analogy between science and religion too hard. Pure science is merely a way of knowing; religion is a way of life based on a way of knowing. Science can use quantitative measurement as theology cannot. And scientists, at least in principle, can hope for a degree of mutual understanding and agreement which theologians have not yet achieved. This disagreement, however, need not invalidate the belief that man can in some measure know God. If God is the infinite and mysterious Being that religious people believe He is, it is to be expected that man, with his finite mind, will have the greatest difficulty in apprehending His nature at all adequately. I must admit that men of religion have had great difficulty in achieving and maintaining an attitude of humble open-minded search, and are tempted to be dogmatic and intolerant towards conflicting beliefs regarding the Deity. I do insist, however, on the validity of the religious quest—the belief that man can and does encounter the Divine, that he can and should reflect upon these encounters, and that such reflection can progressively increase our understanding of God and render our belief in Him less superstitious and more responsible and mature.

Many people feel obliged to repudiate religious belief because they identify religion with one of its cruder, more superstitious forms, or because they interpret more enlightened religious beliefs and practices in a crudely anthropomorphic manner. Anyone who thinks that enlightened Christians believe that God is literally in the sky, or that the phrase in the Nicene Creed "sitteth on the right hand of the Father" literally means that God has a body with a right and a left hand, must of course, as an intelligent man, reject such rubbish. It is true that most professing Christians are deplorably uninformed regarding the language of religious utterance and inclined to a crude anthropomorphism in their thinking about God. But the fact that most people are also scientifically illiterate does not justify us in reading this illiteracy into science and in repudiating science on that score. Similarly, Christianity at its enlightened best should not be identified with its unenlightened distortions.

Let us therefore be fair to religion before we decide to brand all religious faith as the "Great Illusion." We can and should distinguish man's everyday encounters with nature and his unscientific conceptions of physical objects from the scientist's much more precise observations and much more critical interpretations of them. We need not, in making this distinction, condemn the common man's experiences or beliefs as illusory, but we should recognize their limitations. We can say that he possesses "opinions" rather than "knowledge," defining opinions as beliefs which may be valid so far as they go but which a man who cannot rise above opinions cannot rationally refine or test.

Similarly, we can and should distinguish between the common man's coercive religious experiences which he rather crudely interprets in terms of an inadequate theology, and the far deeper experiences of the saint and the far more refined interpretations of the competent theologian and philosopher of religion. This does not mean that the religious beliefs of the common man are necessarily false, or that he fails to find strength and joy in his religious life; it does not mean that Christianity is available only to intellectual and spiritual aristocrats. Far from it—witness Jesus' concern for children and uneducated people. "Come unto me, *all* ye that labor and are heavy laden." But Jesus was also concerned to eradicate inadequate conceptions of God in the minds of his disciples, and for twenty centuries his followers have tried to refine and clarify man's understanding of God—witness the long history of progressive theological clarification. Every honest man must of course make his own final decision as to what he believes and what his ultimate loyalties are to be; but a man is less than honest with himself if he fails to inform himself as best he can what Christianity, or any other religion, is at its *best* before he rejects it as illusory.

I must add a word regarding the vexed problem of authority. The position I have been sketching, most inadequately, might be labeled "Liberal Christian Protestantism." This position, on the question of authority, is at variance with Christian positions which assert the literal truth of every word of the Bible or the infallibility of certain ecclesiastical dogmas. I cannot recognize the "absolute" authority of either a book or a church. I do, however, recognize the impressive authority, in a non-absolutistic sense, of the accumulated wisdom of the Church and of the Bible as a uniquely rich and revealing record of authentic religious experiences and vital beliefs, and I also agree with those who believe that Jesus taught "as one having authority." Such a belief is not only completely credible: it is, to me, quite inescapable.

This authority of the Bible (interpreted in the light of the best available Biblical scholarship), and of the Church (interpreted in the light of the best, religiously informed, historical wisdom) and of Jesus Christ, encountered not only in the New Testament but in Christian devotion through the centuries and today by countless sincere Christians, is an enormously impressive testimony that the venture of Christian faith is not illusory, escapist, or irrational, but is magnificently rooted in the poignant experience of Christian love and helpfully elucidated in enlightened Christian doctrine. This faith is *not*, I believe, to be confused with omniscience or infallibility—it is still faith, not absolute knowledge. But it need not be blind faith, superstitious and irrational; it can become, for each individual and for mankind, a knowledge of God which is more and more deeply rooted in experience, more and more enlightened, more and more productive of that reflective commitment which is the mark of responsible maturity.

4

Where does this leave us with regard to Professor Stace's major thesis? It leaves us, I believe, with a way of approaching reality which he does not seriously envisage and which, if followed out, may lead us to a conception of the universe very different from the one which he offers us as the only possible conception today. Of course I have not been able to describe what Christians accept as crucial experiences of God, any more than he was able to describe the crucial scientific contacts with nature upon which scientists base their scientific theories. Nor have I been able to summarize the interpretations of these religious experiences offered by competent theologians, any more than he was able to summarize the major conclusions of modern science.

Anyone who wishes to verify science at first hand must train himself in the scientific method, participate in scientific experiment, and test scientific theories for belief. And even if he does so he must accept on the authority of other scientists the reports of countless other experiments and vast areas of detailed scientific theory.

Similarly, really to explore the religious approach to reality, a man must submit himself to a spiritual discipline, participate in crucial religious experiences at first hand, and test their theological interpretations for himself. The most deeply religious and thoughtful of men, moreover, must rely on the testimony of other members of the religious community, past and present, since he cannot hope, in a single lifetime, to duplicate all the religious experiences and to explore all the theological interpretations which are to be found in his own and other religious traditions. I have therefore in no sense offered a "proof" of God's existence and nature; I have merely pointed to the empirical method whereby religious beliefs can be generated and tested.

I should not wish to suggest that Christianity is the only religion which should be taken seriously. A responsible philosophy of religion will study all the religions of mankind, the more primitive as well as the higher, in the same sympathetic and critical spirit. Nor would I insist on any exclusive reliance on any, or all, orthodox ecclesiastical approaches to God. "God moves in a mysterious way," and *all* of man's spiritual aspirations, experiments, and reflections deserve encouragement and open-minded scrutiny. It is in this spirit that I should always welcome the secular and humanistic search for whatever can give meaning and purpose to human life. This does not mean that all roads are equally illuminating and promising. Some must certainly be dead-ends and others painfully indirect and tortuous. But no one who wishes to avoid dogmatism can presume to deny categorically that genuine light and strength may be available to those who are searching for a cosmic meaning along some other road than the one he himself is traveling.

I have not been able to demonstrate God's existence; neither have I proved that the universe is meaningful and purposive; nor do I wish to assert that it is with the dogmatic assurance of those who deny cosmic purpose. I can, however, record my own conviction, in company with countless others, that these moral and religious approaches to reality provide evidence which justifies, nay, compels, the conclusion that there is a meaning and purpose at the heart of things. But no one can hope to encounter and comprehend this value-dimension of reality who does not feel a sense of need sufficient to motivate a humble, honest search for what others claim to have found. Philosophers, scientists, and all men capable of sincere idealism can themselves enter upon this search only in this spirit of eager inquiry.

Religion cannot, it is true, "get on with a purposeless and meaningless universe," but it alone—or, at best, its moral equivalent—can reveal to us a universe which has a purpose and a meaning. Only to the man of religion do the "heavens declare the glory of God"; but to him they do declare this glory. Hence the peculiar responsibility of those who feel that the religious spirit is alive in them, and particularly the responsibility of organized religion. The Churches could do far more than they are doing now to educate their clergy and laity, to vitalize the Christian experience of their people, to translate Christian belief into social action, to combat racial prejudice and social privilege within the Christian community, and, above all, to cultivate the tolerance and the humility that should be the first fruits of Christian love. Were the Christian leaven in the Churches purer and more powerful, it would be far more effective in quickening the religious spirit which today, though far from dead, is often dormant and lethargic.

Professor Stace is, I think, quite right in insisting that the vitality of our culture depends essentially upon the vitality of the religious spirit in it. That is why his charges against religion are so serious and his prophecies so ominous. The implication of his argument, and of my counterargument thus far, has been that the chief function of religion is to vitalize a human culture. In any informed religious perspective, however, and certainly in the Christian perspective, this is to put second things first.

The prime motive for religious revival cannot be the saving of our own or any other civilization, for that would involve the attempt to make God simply serve human ends and satisfy human desires. In the Great Commandment of Christianity, the love of God and His worship is man's supreme privilege and duty; the exhortation to love your neighbor as yourself follows as a necessary corollary. A true Christian does believe that only in and through God's love for man, and man's responsive love for God, can individual men, or mankind, be saved, in this world or the next, and the New Testament is eloquent in its condemnation of those who profess to love God but fail to translate this love into charity toward their fellow men. But God alone is holy, not mankind or any human culture. Religion, if valid, is first of all an end in itself, though *also* an essential condition of cultural vitality. Only in this perspective can we hope to avoid a sentimentalized and distorted interpretation of religion.

My final word to Mr. Stace, then, is this. Man finds himself today not in "darkness" but in a cultural and spiritual twilight which T. S. Eliot describes as a "place of disaffection . . . in a dim light," a state of "neither plenitude nor vacancy," "a twittering world." It may be that we must, as Eliot believes we must, "descend lower" into

> Internal darkness, deprivation
> And destitution of all property,
> Desiccation of the world of sense,
> Evacuation of the world of fancy,
> Inoperancy of the world of spirit

before we can hope, as individuals or as a race, to achieve the requisite sense of need and humility. The Christian Gospel directs us not to a

romantic primrose path of comforting illusions, but to the painful road
of suffering and sacrifice, to the way of the Cross. Men have never
really *lived* by illusions: they have merely existed, in some kind of
fool's paradise. Men cannot now *really* live, fully and deeply, on illusions, either the "minor" illusions of "fame, glory, power, or money"
which Professor Stace rather cynically invites us not to give up, or the
Great Illusion which he identifies with religious faith but which should
perhaps rather be identified with Stygian disbelief in God. We are
indeed "standing on the brink." We do indeed need courage and
honesty, *not,* however, to face an inevitable loss of faith, but rather
to search our own hearts and minds to see whether we may not ourselves have generated this "darkness" and inadvertently invented the
myth that the "light will not shine again." May it perchance be true
that "the light shineth in darkness; and the darkness comprehended
it not"?

Each of us must finally assume the responsibility of deciding whether
to believe the grim injunction: Since faith is impossible and civilization doomed, resign yourselves to quiet contentment and be thankful
for small mercies—this is the test of secular maturity; or, alternatively,
the sober but heart-warming injunction to achieve religious maturity
and joy: "These things I have spoken unto you, that in me ye might
have peace. In the world ye shall have tribulation: but be of good
cheer; I have overcome the world."

Celebrating with Dr. Leary
Diana Trilling

Although we had been told on what was presumably sound authority
that the previous Tuesday evening, the opening night of Dr. Leary's
scheduled series of Psychedelic Celebrations, the audience had been
"tough" and that therefore on our evening too we must expect some
element of danger, or at least unpleasantness, actually it would be hard
to imagine a milder scene than awaited us at the Village Barn, the small
theatre in Greenwich Village to which Dr. Leary's show had suddenly
moved from the Village Theatre where it had originally been booked.
Here, surely, was nothing for fear on the score of criminality, menace,
or even bad manners. My husband and I were meeting friends. There
had been confusion about the arrangements because of the change of
theater, so that we arrived almost an hour before the announced curtain time. But the entrance to the Barn was already jammed—no fewer

than two hundred people, probably close to three hundred, were waiting for admission and as time went on the crowd became so dense that it blocked traffic through the street. But the conduct of Dr. Leary's audience was exemplary. There was no sign of impatience about the possibility of not getting seats; no one pushed or showed any of the usual impulse to assert territorial claims. On the other hand I should scarcely describe it as a friendly gathering, and this despite the fact that most of Dr. Leary's audience was of much the same age—under thirty—and of roughly the same situation in life: middle-class dissident, above the average in education.

It was not a crowd that talked or laughed; I saw no exchange of greetings, it was even difficult to particularize couples. The group seemed to be made up of strangely isolate young people who, if they were acquainted with each other, were not concerned to further the connection. The general atmosphere was nevertheless one of virtually palpable benevolence. If one can speak of the face of a gathering, this was the face of an entire, an almost programmatic, goodwill and peaceableness—it reminded me of the mandatory calm of recent converts to Christian Science. At first I was surprised by this prevalence of benignity in young people many of whom might be assumed to be in some degree involved in the subversive world of drug-taking and who, at any rate, were all of them dressed in the rather violent contemporary uniforms of dissent, either harshly black or, at the other extreme, colorful in refusal of middle-class conformities of dress—until I reminded myself that, after all, there lies at the heart of the LSD movement as of most contemporary movements of youthful protest the conviction that it is those who accept, or at least accommodate themselves to, the values of Western society who have lost the knowledge of peace and kindliness. Then, too, LSD would seem to have a gentling effect on the personality. I have observed this curious transformation in all the young people I know who have taken the drug; even after only one or two trips they attain a sort of supra-humanity, as if they had been purged of mortal error; and as far as I can make out, this change persists. But one must be cautious with conclusions drawn only from personal observation. In our present highly-deficient state of scientific understanding of LSD, we know with certainty only that its power to work alterations on the brain is enormous: it is 5,000 times more powerful than mescaline. But the precise nature of the changes it makes and how far they extend or how long they last we do not know—which is of course why those who use it or who for whatever reason do not wish to oppose its use can persuade themselves that all warning of its danger is without scientific foundation.

We were fortunate in having reserved Press seats for the four of us by telephone, otherwise we might never have got into Dr. Leary's show. It was when I was trying to get through the lobby to pick up our tickets that I had the encounter which stays with me as summing up the peculiar quality of transcendence that characterized this audience. A young man blocked my path. I touched his shoulder to ask if I could pass. Although the situation demanded no more than politeness, he turned elaborately, looked down at me from what seemed a divine height and said, "I want you to do anything you want to do." So sublime a response surely had its reference elsewhere than where we stood. Not merely his words but the young man's smile, his bearing, were clearly pointed at some sweeter moral universe than a crowded theater lobby in Greenwich Village, New York. Yet, even at this early moment in my psychedelic evening, I knew it was a mistake to regard this young man as an extraordinary instance of elevation. It was his personal quality, not mine, that appeared to be the norm of the occasion—in a gathering like Dr. Leary's I had already come to feel cumbersomely earthbound, of a graceless and unloving species. Since my night among Dr. Leary's followers—and followers I must suppose the largest part of his audience to have been, judging not only by appearance and manner but by their conduct in the course of the performance and certainly in the question-and-answer period at the end of the ceremonies—I have seen a special LSD issue of the French magazine, *Crapouillot*, with excellent photographs of people at various stages of LSD intoxication. Some of the subjects appear to be having a grievously bad time but none of them, no matter in what agony, is without his smile of fine imperturbability, which bears about the same relation to our usual notions of self-containment that the smile of classical hysteria (*"la belle indifférence"*) bears to our usual imagination of pleasurable emotion.

Is it perhaps straining for consistency that I found in Dr. Leary's prose, written or spoken, a character not unlike that of his audience —the same imperviousness achieved at an equal cost in substantive actuality? For instance, a placard was posted in the lobby to explain the last-minute switch of Dr. Leary's show from the Village Theatre to the Village Barn. Later I copied it out:

> With regard to Dr. Leary's Psychedelic Celebration at the Village Theatre: It is with regret that Dr. Leary has discovered inequities and is experiencing financial problems with the theater. Therefore he is forced to announce that he will no longer appear at the Village Theatre. Instead, Dr. Leary will conduct a psychedelic religious celebration tonight at the Village Barn at 9:00. There will be no admission charge.

Prose like this, at once so plain and "elegant," colloquial and fine, commonplace and yet formal, almost legalistic, is compounded of entirely familiar elements of communication. Certainly it has no shock value. But when we examine it we see that although it is offered in explanation, it explains nothing; it merely seduces one into the belief that one has been addressed with a familiar cogency. And so with Dr. Leary's spoken language. It creates the illusion of coherence, it seems to proceed reasonably enough; it is only when one applies oneself to it that it eludes the grasp. Dr. Leary's impossible plausibility would not seem, however, to be consciously contrived, and in this his verbal style differs from that of more orthodox evangelists. Dr. Leary is nothing if not sincere; his language could not be less ornate or theatrical. In fact, it is precisely from its naturalness and sincerity that its hallucinatory quality derives. Much more than Dr. Leary's speech reminded me of someone like Father Divine, it put me in mind of the mother of Lee Oswald, as Jean Stafford describes her in a remarkable little book, *A Mother in History*, the transcription of a series of interviews between Miss Stafford and Mrs. Oswald. Just as, in the case of Mrs. Oswald, I began to long for some stageprop or costume to assure me that this mistress of the ardently simple and utterly unconnected statement was only acting, not communicating a real-life condition, just so as I put myself to Dr. Leary's "honesty" I came to yearn for the contrivance of theater.

But, more, what particularly struck me when I came back to Dr. Leary's notice in the lobby after I had become better acquainted with his mode of discourse was its premise of innocence. It is of course its innocence that constitutes a chief appeal of Dr. Leary's doctrine to the privileged young who, perhaps because they are the offspring of a parent-generation intent on keeping no knowledge from them, now regard their elders as uniquely impure in motive and behavior. If the audience at the Village Barn was a fair sampling, and I think it was, Dr. Leary's followers are certainly not to be associated with any ordinary image we may have of juvenile delinquency. The class difference, involving as it does not only differences in education but in social assumption, significantly separates the users of LSD from the young world of street gangs and violence. The LSD phenomenon therefore represents a quite separate social problem located, I think, at that special place in society where cultural influences tend to supplant the better-understood social pressures.

Still, nothing I learned in my evening with Dr. Leary proposed the idea that because his young followers make so urgent an option for virtue and purity of motive, they have any special endowment of native goodness, or even any notable sensitivity to ugliness, or inability to sustain it. As to the first, there is no ground for the belief that behind their benevolence there do not lie the usual human angers and aggressions. As to the second, in the course of my evening at the Barn

I came to suspect that if we are going to stay with the "frightened generation" explanation of the LSD phenomenon we need to be precise about what we mean. Far from suggesting any extreme vulnerability to the terrors of life, these young people seemed to me to be unduly armored—and if this is because LSD has reduced their moral alertness, then we must regard the drug as perhaps more dehumanizing than we have yet recognized. My point could not be simpler: at the most alarming moments of the evening, when Dr. Leary announced that he knew no child over the age of seven who was not on drugs, or when his coadjutor, Dr. Alpert, in response to a question about 16-, 17-, or 18-year-olds on LSD, said, "Even if they end up in a hospital or prison for a few months, it doesn't bother me," there was no slightest sign of dismay in their audience. Fearful these young people may be, like the rest of us; they have a fearsome world in which to be young. But fear can show itself in a number of ways, and defines character only by the form it takes and the ends it is made to serve. To express concern for the children of Viet Nam and yet remain unmoved by the idea of submitting 7-year-olds to hallucinogenic drugs is surely to obey the dictates of culture rather than of reliable feeling.

Dr. Leary and Dr. Alpert have both been university teachers, teaching psychologists. I daresay my own response to statements as cruelly irresponsible as these—they were casual remarks, really, spoken with an entire ease—is underscored by the importance I assign, the special importance, to their former profession. In a society as mobile as that of America, the school is more than an institution for teaching the intellectual disciplines, it is the matrix of our ongoing culture, the chief source and guardian of our personal and social morality. What the school establishes today, the home will have absorbed by tomorrow— most of the precepts of our post-Freudian family culture were first formulated in our teacher-training programs. But the problem is that it is exactly because America is so open-ended that youth is valued as it is, beyond its possible emotional and social capacities. And this means that the teacher whose task it is to instruct the young in the complexity of the conditions on which the continuing life of society depends and in the limitations imposed upon the individual by emotional and social reality must himself be able to resist the seductions of rebelliousness for its own youthful sake—which seems to be a difficult demand to make today of anyone of radical spirit and imagination. No one in American public life, certainly no one in government, has the ear of the young like their university instructors, unless it is the advanced social and literary critics, and these are often the same persons, so that if— as now is increasingly happening—the teacher is reluctant to surrender the glamor of youthful rebelliousness and to discover its own grave satisfaction in the exercise of the parental role, he leaves his students in the position of children who have been robbed of the definition they can only achieve when those who train them, and whom they naturally rebel against, have a firm authority of their own; they face emptiness, a world without boundaries. I am not suggesting that the tide of nihilism in which the young appear to be more and more caught up takes its sole or primary force from the school, but only that if anything is to be done to stem it, the salvage will have to be undertaken by the same class of people who did such a successful job of bringing the failure of modern culture to our educated consciousness. Dr. Leary was dismissed, as Dr. Alpert was too, from his Harvard post for engaging his students in his experiments with drugs, but I doubt he would have reached the young as he has were it not for his earlier professional certification.

But, at our evening in the Barn, Dr. Leary was not resting with his pedagogic function. He also made it a religious occasion, and thus drew on the shared fund of recollected church-going his audience, even his young audience, might be supposed to have brought to his celebration. (We keep it in mind, however, that Dr. Leary is under indictment for illegal possession of drugs and if he is to plead freedom of religion under the First Amendment, he does well to put public emphasis on his religious convictions.) His show our night was called "The Incarnation of Christ"; he also does an "Illumination of the Buddha." The ceremonies had been advertised on the theater rather than the religious pages of the papers, with Dr. Leary "IN PERSON" as the leading attraction. His religious purpose was nevertheless kept dominant. In addition to the film-and-dance portion of the program, itself ritualistic, there was a sermon, there were prayers by Dr. Leary, and even a moment of silent prayer on the part of the "congregation." Early in the performance Dr. Leary reminded us that while we were gathered here in New York for our religious ceremonies our opposite numbers in India were enjoying the religious ecstasy on the shores of the Ganges, and our opposite numbers in Mexico attaining their exaltation with peyote. Of ecstasy and exaltation there might actually be none, either in Dr. Leary's program or his audience, but unmistakably a spirit of devoutness permeated the auditorium. The religious emotions of Dr. Leary seemed, however, to be considerably interfered with by the strains and temptations of showmanship. And he was very tired, one saw his fatigue from the start, as soon as he took his place on the platform in the darkened hall; he might have been managing a hangover. This was a weary impresario and performer, a weary pedagogue, a weary Messiah—the multiplication and confusion of roles that Dr. Leary now assumes are his burden as the leader of a movement which even he could not have guessed would grow so fast.

We had been shown to our seats at a Press table; amusingly, not unexpectably, a disproportionate space in this small auditorium had been set aside for those Dr. Leary might hope would give his movement still more of the publicity it has already had in such abundance. Although it was legitimate enough that we should present ourselves as members of the Press, at least for me even this means we had used to procure seats added to the self-consciousness I had felt ever since I had arrived at the hall. It is always uncomfortable to sightsee in other people's emotional universe; and after all it had come only as an afterthought, when we were already seated, that I might some time want to write about the occasion and should therefore take notes. Some days later I was to read a review of our evening in the *New York Times*, by a reporter who apparently spotted us for the tourists we were. She got us by name and described us as "initiates of the older cults of politics and psychoanalysis." We were likened—and this is uncommonly vivid reporting for the *Times*—to "atheists attending a religious ritual out of sociological interest . . . our expressions faintly tinged with boredom and distaste." Well, the sociological posture was unquestionably readiest to hand, but I am afraid I was unprotected by scientific distance from the objects of my study. I looked around the theater at this strangely subdued and isolate audience, and I was painfully aware of the chasm that stretched between the world of these young people and my own at the same age, of the difference between this dedication of theirs and the political dedication of the Marxist '30's in which I had come to maturity. We too, at their age, had pointed to the violence of those in power. My contemporaries, too, had set themselves to make a revolution in consciousness, which would make us "free." But our means had been social and political, and now the very concept of society was inoperative. But if ours had been an ideology of social involvement, not of withdrawal, this could now be no boast— it had led to a blockage of hope which could perhaps never be, certainly had not been, surmounted by a succeeding generation. And for us there had been no atomic bomb. And there had been no such limitlessness in our world, no such vacuum as now passes for the social and personal structure of life. It was not necessary to find any particular emotional vulnerability of even feelingness in Dr. Leary's followers to recognize that they had sufficient ground for confusion and despair, a good bit more even than we had had when we rejected our society as given.

The unease of my situation was much relieved as soon as Allen Ginsberg came to sit at my side, and this is surely not the least interesting aspect of the evening, that by some marvelous transmutation of things as we think them to be, the fact that Ginsberg sat next to me throughout most of the performance was more than a comfort, it provided my chief link with sanity. We had seen him entering the hall and had waved. He had come over to say hello and just then the performance began. To avoid disturbance, Ginsberg sat down at my side. His beard was by far the most lavish in this well-bearded audience; were it still not a blackest black, he should be called the good grey poet of the psychedelic movement, such is his air of venerableness and wisdom, such the authority with which he now seems vested. Time had passed —seven years, eight years?—since I had last seen him. Then, too, it had been a public evening of which I had also tried (not entirely successfully, as it turned out; but, then, one has not the right to ask self-consciousness of one's readers, only of oneself) to report the inevitable reciprocity between the observed and the observer. It was very little later that Dr. Leary mentioned, in all mildness, the presence in the hall of agents from the Narcotics Squad; for a bad instant, as I looked around me and saw no one who met the description, I supposed it might be the four of us Dr. Leary was referring to—except, of course, we had Allen Ginsberg to vouch for us, he was our security in this alien territory. Throughout the ceremonies, speaking in a low steady voice, precise, in firm pedagogic control of knowledge it pleased him to share, this former student of my husband's gave me the assurance I needed of my own identity, unchallenged, in no subtlest degree suborned. The adroitness with which Ginsberg made his aesthetic and critical removal from what was going on onstage while keeping intact his old ties of theoretical and even practical approval of the drug-taking enterprise was something of a triumph. Everything about him indeed, his weight of purpose no less than his canniness, freshly pressed upon me the importance, in the psychedelic universe as elsewhere, of the wish for fame and immortality, the most traditional impulse of the gifted. For what is it, finally, other than the force of this desire, that has sustained Ginsberg, regulated the degree of his involvement in dangerous personal experiment, urged him beyond the anonymousness implicit in the pursuit of selfhood through drugs.

Is Dr. Leary, as well, an exception to the harsh rule of self-eradication in drugs? I doubt it. Certainly drug promotion is now giving Dr. Leary a rare celebrity. And by the evidence of these religious ceremonies he courts immortality in the largest possible way by identification with immortal principles and personages. But succeed as he may in making converts to his religion, as a self he wears the pale but indelible marks of doom: you see it as soon as he takes the microphone in his hand and invites the spotlight. As a self, he has the invincible anonymousness of a television master of ceremonies, than which surely nothing could be more stricken from the immortal rolls. Dr. Leary looks to be in his mid-forties; he is tall, slim, with a suggestion of willowiness. He is, if you will, handsome, with something of the consciousness of the professional charmer, and I should suppose he is especially comfortable in his stage costume of white trousers and open-necked white shirt. The family background seems to be a little vague: apparently it was Irish Catholic, middle-Western; one reads of an Army father and that he himself went to West Point, but this is not the impression he creates—in appearance and voice he is only "sensitive" deteriorated Harvard, throwing away some considerable advantages of birth. He is fair-haired and tousled, wears a necklace, and performs in bare feet. When he takes the microphone in his hand, one feels it is a natural extension of his infatuate ego and that it will more and more become his staff and his rod, his auxiliary drug, his surrogate selfhood. As the evening wore on, with Dr. Leary up there on the platform and Allen Ginsberg at my side, I had the sense of a certain entertaining ambiguity in the relation of these two psychedelic figures. At least before friends like ourselves from an earlier period in his career Ginsberg seemed to me to make a point of his poetic pride, of his superiority to the leader, even of his superior scholarship, but I may have misread him. At any rate, in the course of the ceremonies, he several times alluded to the need for humor in dealing with the LSD subject. For the poverty of Dr. Leary's show as art he was carefully and courteously apologetic.

There was, first, the darkening of the hall and Dr. Leary's entrance into the spotlight, behind him a white and still-empty screen. From the wings of this makeshift theater came the soft strumming of a guitar, and immediately the audience was churchy-still—except that the comparison is absurd: church is where people cough and rustle and squirm and there was no coughing or rustling or squirming in the Barn, unless on the part of four unlicensed sociologists. Through the next two hours (I guess the show lasted) Dr. Leary had his audience in entire control; he could be envied by the professionals.

With his opening remarks Dr. Leary effectively formulated, if one can put it so, the incoherence through which I would try to grope for the remainder of the evening. I have a friend who shares his apartment with a painter; one day my friend's mother (this is a Jewish story) came to see him, examined the paintings on his walls and turned to her son with the question, "Who authorized these pictures?" It was the question I would have put to Dr. Leary: Who, or what, had authorized this particular conglomerate of pageant, preachment, classroom, re-

vival meeting, dance, movie, and off-Broadway amateur night? Where
had this performance come from, what was the source of its inspiration?
How much was it the psychedelic experience itself that was being reproduced for us, how much an "artistic" derivation? How much was
Dr. Leary improvising a gospel, and how much was he bearing witness
to the accepted doctrine? Where did the play end and pedagogy begin,
where did pedagogy end and the play begin? Had Dr. Leary and his
co-performers recently taken LSD and was the drug thus so-to-speak
present in the talk that accompanied the film, or had there been at least
the intention of artistic detachment from the actual drugged state? It
was reported of the movie, *Flaming Creatures,* whether accurately or
not I have no way of knowing, that its actors were all of them under
drugs when it was made; this one could credit from the loose automa-
tism of their movements and their dispersed sexuality. Dr. Leary's
film and the sporadic miming that took place in front of the screen
and the words Dr. Leary himself spoke and those that were intoned
antiphonally by the male pantomimist and a woman at the side of the
stage were certainly all of them sufficiently lifeless to suggest some similar interference with normal process. Still, I realize that an actor has
to be highly skilled to simulate nature unimpeded by human awkward-
ness. What looked like blocked transmission in Dr. Leary's show may
simply have been amateurishness. "You have to go out of your mind
to come to your senses." "We don't pray to anyone up there but to
what is inside ourselves." Even announcing his best-shaped slogans,
Dr. Leary himself, and despite his naturalness and sincerity, failed to
take significant shape except in a form already made iconographic by
nightclub and television "personalities." The essential quality he conveyed was that of a schoolmaster acting the master of ceremonies in
a school show—a good-looking, tired, essentially vulgar, still-boyish
teacher, histrionic, equally pleased with his popularity with his students and with the privileges of office which he could exercise as occasion demanded.

He stayed in the spotlight, quite alone, for rather a while. I had
no sense it was too long for his audience. His lecture-preachment-
patter covered a general territory already well known from repeated
accounts of the doctrine. What one had not been sufficiently prepared
for was the vagrancy of Dr. Leary's thought, its bold (however tired),
bald carelessness of the ordinary rules of reasonableness, of intelligible
discourse. For the occasion of ceremony everything was spoken with
the cadence of ceremony, something between a croon and a subdued
exhortation. *We pray we are not hung up and that you will have a good
trip* (did he mean in our next LSD session, or only metaphorically, here

in the theater?). . . . *The voyage is always the same* (did he mean reliable, or was he remarking the singleness of the indicated path?). . . . *We renew and reenact the ancient myths* (this could refer to the play, but it could also refer to the sacred journey to which we were being urged). . . . *We pass on what we* (an editorialized Dr. Leary, psychologist?) *have learned in ten years of hard work. . . . We* (Dr. Leary and his audience? Dr. Leary and others under the influence of LSD?) *meet in our retinas, we meet on the screen in the vibrating beams of light, also we meet in the liquid canals of the ear; then we move within to resurrect the body, rediscover the timepiece of the universe: the heartbeat . . . Then we breathe together. . . . You should not take a trip without a road map. . . . Myths are cellular. . . . The myth is a blueprint. . . . Tonight we invite you to relive the myth of Jesus Christ. . . . The resurrection of Jesus Christ has been a rough trip for all of us* (Dr. Leary and his co-authors? All of us in the 20th century who are the inheritors of the Christian tradition?). . . .

First we ran into Christian backlash, second the backlash from Jews and atheists. . . . The Christian myth means, once there was a man who took all the guilts, the shoulds and shouldn'ts, on his own shoulders and wiped them out. If you experience this myth (before you take the drug? afterwards?) *you are free. . . . Go back and free the world from good and evil. . . . The tolling of the bell at Millbrook* (here the clanging of a loud bell presumably took us to Dr. Leary's "institute") *takes us on a voyage of discovery. You have to have a guide in the person who has been there before you: an old witch or a frog or a hunchback. Today, your teen-age child. . . . They have the key to the voyage and it always involves a chemical tick.* (Trick?) *This is the Chalice, the Holy Communion, and always the Last Supper: good-bye to all back there. . . . I welcome you in the name of the Father, the Son, and the Holy Ghost. . . . Give thanks as we take the Chalice and let our thanks ascend. Drink. This is my flesh, bone and blood. . . . As often as you do this, do this in memory of me.*

Lights had now begun to flash on the screen and Dr. Leary moved to the side of the stage. His voice rose in intensity. *Open the naked eye, find the center!* Great circles of light appear on the screen, and the show complicates itself:

GIRL'S VOICE: *Can you float through the universe of your body and not lose your way?*

No one directly answers the question. Mushroom-like patterns form on the screen. In front of the screen a man in black trousers, bare above the waist, sways slowly, it would seem painfully, his arms weaving and reaching in the familiar dance-idiom of tortured quest.

GIRL'S VOICE: *What is happening?*

DR. LEARY: *Float to the center.*

MAN'S VOICE: *I am drowning in blood. . . . Help. . . . Please make it stop. . . . No, no, don't make it stop.*

GIRL'S VOICE: *Blood to death. . . . Out. . . . Out. . . . Blood to death. . . . Life. . . . Life. . . . Scarlet. . . .*

MAN'S VOICE: *So warm. . . . Drifting down. . . . Melting. . . . Breathing. . . . Breath of life. . . .*

Here my notes indicate a certain amount of groaning on the stage but not who is the sufferer. Unfortunately, I have no shorthand. But if at first I am troubled by my inability to catch every word being spoken on the stage, soon enough as I catch the drift I realize that the drift is all. It is said of LSD that it taps the unconscious in order to add to the store of the conscious: this is indeed its principal and much-vaunted value, that it is supposed to augment consciousness. But surely to call the LSD experience consciousness-enhancing is to merge two meanings of the word "consciousness"—that which we oppose to *un*-consciousness and by which we mean those activities of the mind which we can take note of as they proceed, and, second, the honorific meaning, that of active and useful awareness. If one is to judge the LSD state by Dr. Leary's representation or adumbration of it in his ceremonies or by anything one has so far read of it, what happens under LSD may very well be a flooding of the mind with images or emotions from which it is otherwise closed off. But what the mind does with this new material speaks not at all of a significantly enhanced mental activity such as we usually adduce in our appreciation of awareness. The problem is, of course, an old one in aesthetics. It is not without interest that the new Coleridge scholarship demonstrates with some persuasiveness that "Kubla Khan" was not actually an opium dream and that Coleridge offered it as such only in polemic, as a defense of the role of nonreason in the writing of poetry. But it is not solely an aesthetic problem, it is also a scientific problem and a vexing one: how define what we mean by consciousness, especially in the creative process?

The dialogue between male and female voice now peters out and Dr. Leary relinquishes the spotlight so that the full attention of the audience can be focused on the screen. The pictures that appear look to me like magnified blood cells or other organic matter. Then gradually they become more complex, "social," sometimes fleetingly identifiable. Also, the background music now rises in volume, becomes more assertive—Ginsberg whispers to me, "The *Missa Luba,* a Congo version of the Catholic Mass," and obediently I hear what could perhaps be the *Kyrie Eleison;* he whispers "Verdi's *Requiem*" and, more reluctantly, I hear that as well. Without my having quite noted, the guitar has eliminated itself, been replaced by a sound-track to accompany what is apparently intended as a representation, or evocation, of the evolutionary process, a kind of psychedelic March of Time. Ginsberg mentions a word that sounds like *Straboscopia,* which I take to derive from the same root as *Strabismus:* "*Med.* A disorder of the eye in which the optic axes cannot be directed to the same object because of incoordination of the muscles of the eyeballs. . . ." In later dictionary consultation I realize he said *Stroboscopic,* pertaining to "an instrument for observing the successive phases of a periodic motion by means of light periodically interrupted." But the difference is only objective. The camera's wish to catch the speed of psychedelic imagery affects me like a sickness of the eye. From my Press table I no longer see Dr. Leary. I assume he is seated stage right. His voice resumes the incantation:

Let's return to the 20th century and reincarnate Jesus Christ. Let's do it every one of us right now. . . . You have to take on all the guilt, sin, and wretchedness of the world. . . . You have to do this for everyone so that there won't be any more. . . . Then we're all through with the good-evil thing and you will be reborn. . . . All-embracing, Dr. Leary invites the police and the narcotics agents to join in the rebirth, and for the first and only time in the evening, his audience is vocally responsive. "You're right," come several voices from the audience, soft, devout.

My notes do not say if Dr. Leary is now once more stage center, in full spotlight, but I recollect him to be. The film has now run its spotty course, from our unicellular origins to our modern metropolitan mediocrity, and we can have the sermon. Certainly it is in fullest stage center that Dr. Leary makes his biggest pitch of the evening, inviting someone to come up from the audience on to the platform, take off his clothes, and be nailed to the cross. *Let's look in the bag. There are some nails here and a crown of thorns.* The audience remains unmoving. Dr. Leary is apparently not surprised, he had expected no volunteers; one wonders, in fact, what he would do if a too-eager listener proffered his services. He repeats: *Will anyone volunteer to be nailed to the cross if we guarantee you there will be no more evil in the world?* He dissipates the reverential hush, or at least lifts it a fraction, with a prepared comment: Dr. Leary confides to us that he had been warned that if he made such a proposal in this setting, "four hundred and ninety-seven exhibitionists, sado-masochists, and faggots would storm the platform." There is no laughter. *No, we must not do it that way, we must do it with our clothes on, or even our uniforms. . . . But let's do it.*

There follows the more formal sermon, wholly Dr. Leary's own show and, like all sermons, lengthy. Its text, Dr. Leary announces, is from William Blake *who had been in our profession a couple of hundred years ago* (sic)*. . . . He who is a fool persists in his folly* (sic)*. . . .* We must start a new religion, says Dr. Leary, and start a new country. *We have been working six years*—it had been ten, I recall, a few minutes back—*to work out a plan to turn on this country and this planet. . . . Starting a new religion is like starting a new business. Or a garden. There are inevitable sequences. . . . A series of ordeals or tests. . . . We have no paranoia or hostility about our opposition, it's a rough business starting a new religion. It's a rough business but highly stylized, more classic than baseball or football. . . . We must turn on, tune in, and drop out. . . . Turn off your mind and go within. . . . You need a sacrament and today it is a chemical. The chemicals we use are ancient. . . . Treat these sacraments with the respect they deserve. Before you turn on you must be in a state of grace. You must look into yourself and see where you have sinned. On your own chessboard. You are the only one who can forgive yourself. You look in your mirror, in your retina is the history. You confess to yourself. If you don't go to confession before you take a sacrament you may writhe, suffer, call for a doctor. . . . Once you turn on, then you tune in, show others what has been shown to you.* Dr. Leary calls on Rudi and Jackie, assistants, to come forward and testify. They have apparently helped to put the show together, now they will help us tune in.

DR. LEARY: *Rudi, where are we now and where are we going?*

RUDI (thinking): *We are working from a core which is a circle of love. A very beautiful and pure thing.*

DR. LEARY: *Jackie, where are we?*

JACKIE (who is a girl): *We are here and happy to be here. And we are going from here out, to turn on the world.*

DR. LEARY: *We have to work with the young, the artists, the underground groups for a new breakthrough. Artists change consciousness and the change lasts. . . . We work to change family life. . . . Encourage husbands and wives to take LSD together. . . . I can't imagine a husband being turned on without wanting to turn on his wife. I can't imagine parents being turned on without wanting to turn on their children. I know no child over the age of seven who hasn't been given drugs and I know many of them. The parents turn on the children.*

Dr. Leary has a practiced device of irony. He echoes his outrages of decency in the voice of outraged respectability:

Imagine turning on children!

There is a pregnant pause, and Dr. Leary recapitulates:

The psychedelic experience is one you want to share with those you care most about. . . . Inconceivable that parents would take LSD and not want their children to share the experience.

The audience continues to be dead still: no one stamps, hisses, rises to object. No one leaves the theater. (And no reporter, to my knowledge, undertakes to report what we all of us at Dr. Leary's Press tables so clearly heard.) From this point forward, the rest of Dr. Leary's sermon is bound to be anti-climax:

We are now in a legal and political phase. . . . Several million Americans are taking LSD, more taking marijuana, for serious purposes. . . . They need an institution. . . . We are working with the courts to license small groups to take LSD. . . . After you tune in you drop out. It happens so gracefully. . . . A detachment from old ambitions and drives. . . . What we meet and work for is what you want and know is possible. . . . We need and invite your comments and questions.

The comments and questions that comprise the remainder of the program may be what Dr. Leary invites, they cannot be what he needs. But then, what speaker ever gets the questions he needs, and these were at least intended neither to provoke nor challenge. Dr. Leary fares better than most public speakers when they finish a talk and discover to whom they have been speaking and what they are thought to have said. A man rises from the audience to say that he has confronted the beast: Is this what Dr. Leary meant by confrontation with the wolf? Myself, I had heard no mention of wolves, singular or plural. I wonder if the questioner has in mind the beast one confronts in the mirror when one confesses to oneself, or merely an encounter on the psychedelic journey. Dr. Leary is perhaps himself confused. At any rate, he chooses this moment to call to the stage "his well-known colleague" Dr. Richard Alpert, recently returned from California. Together, Dr. Leary and Dr. Alpert respond to the question that has been asked by explaining the uterine recapitulation of man's long slow evolution. *Memory cards flash through your brain when you take LSD, so it doesn't fit your tidy 20th-century mind.* I conclude from this that when you take LSD you return to the womb and relive the prenatal development.

The second questioner is a priest; he is recognized by Dr. Leary and Dr. Alpert as a friend. The priest wants to know whether after many trips you could not have the same experience without taking the drug. It is Dr. Alpert who undertakes to reply: *After a trip you get depressed by your new sense of your daily life. After enough of this, you stay high all the time because you have revised your life. . . . LSD is not a substitute for the conscious effort of digging here and now. . . . LSD is a constant reminder of our divinity. We mustn't stop because we are too busy. . . . Find someone not on LSD and find out how he and I are us.* This is the point at which I recall, with a certain syntactical confusion, the priest in Ilf and Petrov's wonderful *The Little Golden Calf* of whom the verb "befuddle" is used as an active verb of expression: "Yes," befuddled the priest—"No," befuddled the priest. But of course this was in another country. . . . The priest sits down; he is apparently satisfied with the answer that has been given him.

And now the master of ceremonies introduces Allen Ginsberg from the audience, calls him to the stage. Ginsberg rises modestly but readily —had he been forewarned?—to join the circle on the platform. While he is threading his way through the audience, Dr. Leary intersperses some remarks on electrons, heightens the scientific authority of the occasion. He also addresses himself to the subject of people killing themselves under the effects of LSD: the percentage is negligible, he assures us, and anyway these are the people who failed to go to confession and expunge their guilts. Dr. Leary gives the nod to the next questioner.

This time the question, although manifestly not intended to give offense, does suggest criticism; it is carefully larded with apology. It seems that although the questioner himself understands the moral nature of the LSD enterprise, there are people of his acquaintance who take the drug just for kicks. Would Dr. Leary comment on this? From the other side of the theater, I have no trouble hearing the question. But Dr. Leary seems to have difficulty; he turns to his coadjutors in appeal but meeting no help he invites his interrogator to the stage. But on his way, this young man is checked by another member of the audience who rises to protest that such a question can only come from someone caught "in the game"—which is to say, someone under the influence of this-worldly, non-psychedelic, values. A moment of tension develops between the two men at the foot of the platform—it represents something of a relief amidst all this benignity—and then Allen Ginsberg intervenes: *You're taking it too seriously, keep some humor.* The questioner addresses the stage in self-defense: *But I want a successful revolution.* To which Leary responds soothingly: *Tell us why, how are we sliding back from the center?* The questioner identifies himself as an instructor in a college in South Jersey. Grievingly he explains that some of his students fail to understand the moral purpose of LSD, they take it for the sensation, they are not *serious.* (He hits the word as I have not heard a word hit since the days when the comrades would accuse each other of being *subjective.*) *And I want you to win, I want a revolution like you do.* The troubled comrade from South Jersey is at last disposed of by Dr. Alpert, judiciously: *It doesn't matter from what motive these kids of 16, 17, or 18 take LSD, if they turn on for 30 seconds the experience is so profound. Even if they end up in a hospital or prison for a few months, it doesn't bother me. . . . The confusion is the greatest kind of confusion for these kids, at any age. It opens the door and makes a mensch of them.* The audience is relieved and ready for the catharsis of humor after such unblessed controversy.

The necessary humorous relief is supplied by a Negro, a solid and comely man who rises at the rear of the hall and announces in a big resonant voice that he has only a single question to ask: *What is LSD?* Although he has produced through the hall the only titter of the evening, he meets a wall of impenetrable silence on the stage. The questioner repeats his question, once, twice, a third time. He becomes insistent: *I'm just asking a single question. I hear you all talking about LSD. What I want to know is, what is LSD?* After what seems forever —the audience is becoming restive—someone onstage has the presence of mind to answer firmly: *It is a chemical.* And the subject is closed; the questioner sits down. Dr. Leary makes a few remarks about his LEAGUE FOR SPIRITUAL DISCOVERY, much in the spirit of a preacher before the plate is passed; no plate is passed, the evening has been an expense to no one. *We in the League are working, at risk, to legalize marijuana and LSD. . . . It is an intimate family thing we're doing.* Allen Ginsberg steps forward and announces an anti-war rally on the following Saturday—no, not an anti-war rally, a "peaceable march, a transcendence over anger." The meeting is at an end.

There is again no elbowing or pressing as the crowd begins to leave the hall. Now, as not before the performance started, I begin to see couples, pairs of boys and girls holding hands, much as married couples leave funerals or weddings with clasped hands, bound in the intimacy of shared deep emotion. (Dr. Leary, incidentally, could not be more pious than he is about coupling: approaching the sexual subject, he speaks only of "making love to your wife.") It also becomes possible, here and there, to particularize other sightseers among the dedicated: the slowed-down man in his late thirties who wears the mark of yearning, of loneliness, of the failed artist; the dykish, tight-lipped girl who belongs at the side of the swimming-pool of a woman's "Y"; the bookkeeper, as I am certain, who stands out in the crowd for her excruciating neatness and spinsterishness not less than for her advanced years —it is she whom I overhear greeting an acquaintance: "What did you think of it? Weren't you *impressed?*" These are the wanderers between worlds.

But for the most part the audience is as one had first perceived it: young, Village but middle-class, good contemporary faces of the kind one wants to trust, the faces of people to whom intellectual leadership might be thought appropriate, except that they had made another choice and the signal of it is in their eyes. The four of us appeal to each other: Is it only the gifted who go in for this sort of thing? Are these the best, the brightest, of their generation? We of course haven't the answer, any more than we have the answer to a corollary question. How can any enlightened person of whatever age take this psychedelic leader with intellectual seriousness, assent in an ideology so barren of ideas? As we move out on to the street, away from the theater—unregenerate, we are looking for a beer—this becomes, in fact, the nub of our anxiety. For us, Dr. Leary's religious ceremony had been ridiculous when it had not been despicable, but we had been surrounded by young people of good education who not only could take Dr. Leary's drug and this celebration of it but had also somehow managed to issue to the whole subject of LSD a safe-conduct which exempted it from rational inspection, creating—or perhaps only responding to?—an atmosphere in which whoever would put it to adverse question is automatically taken to be repressive, retrograde, lacking in imagination, deficient indeed in scientific open-mindedness.

But Dr. Leary's epiphany gave rise to perhaps even bleaker thoughts than these. In the past month I had heard of four more young people, four adolescent children of friends, who had broken down as a result of LSD—two college boys and a college girl who had had to be hospitalized, a high school boy who, on the edge of psychosis, had had to be withdrawn from school. This made, so far, seven LSD casualties within my own small circle of acquaintance. Of course, some or all of them may have been predisposed to mental breakdown. And we had no figures to tell us whether they were in any way representative of what could happen to Dr. Leary's followers. This being so, how long were we to wait for the statistics to accumulate and be got in order?

For Dr. Alpert there were surely no such anxieties. "These kids" were simply casualties of the new dispensation, eggs that had to be broken to make Dr. Leary's omelette. But I could no more shrug off this concern, retreat into "scientific" or ironic detachment, than I could muster "objectivity" to meet the destruction of the young for the sake of some new Jerusalem of the political imagination. The destruction of a person's mental powers is *actual*, like hunger, poverty, death. It happens in actual life; it entails actual anguish. No, the nub of my anxiety as I left Dr. Leary's show was not that his audience could give credence to the nonsense he spoke—clever as so many of his young followers are, they have no doubt already learned to trust the LSD tale rather than its teller—but the recognition that the direction we take from our present-day assumption that the new and dissident are good in themselves, no matter what their form, may very well lose for us the basic and ordinary knowledge of human decency, including the knowledge that the human mind, even in all its weakness and error, is valuable.

The Mystic's Experience of God
Rufus M. Jones

According to those who have been there, the experience that we call mystical is charged with the conviction of real, direct contact and commerce with God. It is the almost universal testimony of those who are mystics that they find God through their experience. John Tauler says that in his best moments of "devout prayer and the uplifting of the mind to God," he experiences "the pure presence of God" in his own soul; but he adds that all he can tell others about the experience is "as poor and unlike it as the point of a needle is to the heavens above us."

There are many different degrees of intensity, concentration, and conviction in the experiences of different individual mystics, and also in the various experiences of the same individual from time to time. There has been a tendency in most studies of mysticism to regard the state of ecstacy as *par excellence* mystical experience. That is, however, a grave mistake. The calmer, more meditative, less emotional, less ecstatic experiences of God possess greater constructive value for life and character than do ecstatic experiences which presuppose a peculiar psychical frame and disposition. The seasoned Quaker, in the corporate hush and stillness of a silent meeting, is far removed from ecstasy, but he is not the less convinced that he is meeting with God.

The more normal, expansive mystical experiences come apparently when the personal self is at its best. Its powers and capacities are raised to an unusual unity and fused together. The whole being, with its accumulated submerged life, *finds itself*. The process of preparing for any high achievement is a severe and laborious one; but nothing seems easier in the moment of success than is the accomplishment for which the life has been prepared. There comes to be formed within the person what Aristotle called "a dexterity of soul," so that the person does with ease what he has become skilled to do. A mystic of the fourteenth century stated the principle in these words: "It is my aim to be to the Eternal God what a man's hand is to a man."

There are many human experiences which carry a man up to levels where he has not usually been before, and where he finds himself possessed of insight and energies that he had hardly suspected were his until that moment. One leaps to his full height when the right inner spring is reached. We are quite familiar with the way in which instinctive tendencies in us, and emotions both egoistic and social, become organized under a group of ideas and ideals into a single system, which we call a sentiment, such as love, or patriotism, or devotion to truth. It forms slowly, and one hardly realizes that it has formed until some occasion unexpectedly brings it into full operation and we find ourselves able with perfect ease to overcome the most powerful inhibitory and opposing instincts and habits, which until then had usually controlled us. Literary and artistic geniuses supply us with many instances in which, in a sudden flash, the crude material at hand is shot through with vision, and the complicated plot of a drama, the full significance of a character, or the complete glory of a statue stands revealed, as if, to use R. L. Stevenson's illustration, a jinni had brought it on a golden tray as a gift from another world. Abraham Lincoln, striking off in a few intense minutes his Gettysburg address, as beautiful in style and perfect in form as anything in human literature, is as good an illustration as we need of the way in which a highly organized person, by a kindling flash, has at his hand all the moral and spiritual gains of a lifetime.

We come now to the central question of our consideration: Do mystical experiences settle anything? Are they purely subjective and one-sided, or do they prove to have objective reference and so to be two-sided? Do they take the experiment across the chasm that separates "self" from "other"?

The most striking effect of such experience is not new fact-knowledge, not new items of empirical information, but new moral energy, heightened conviction, increased caloric quality, enlarged spiritual vision, an unusual radiant power of life. In short, the whole personality, in the case of the constructive mystics, appears to be raised to a new level of life and to have gained from somewhere many calories of life-feeding, spiritual substance. We are quite familiar with the way in which adrenaline suddenly flushes into the physical system and adds a new and incalculable power to brain and muscle. Under its stimulus a man can carry out a piano when the house is on fire. May not, perhaps, some energy, from some Source with which our spirits are allied, flush our inner being with forces and powers by which we can be fortified to stand the universe and more than stand it?

I believe that mystical experiences do, in the long run, expand our knowledge of God, and do succeed in verifying themselves. Mysticism is a sort of spiritual protoplasm, which underlies, as a basic substance, much that is best in religion, in ethics, and in life itself. It has generally been the mystic, the prophet, the seer, who have spotted out new ways forward in the jungle of our world or lifted our race to new spiritual levels. Their experiences have in some way equipped them for unusual tasks, have given supplies of energy to them which their neighbors did not have, and have apparently brought them into vital correspondence with dimensions and regions of reality that others miss. The proof that they have found God, or at least a domain of spiritual reality, is to be seen rather in the moral and spiritual fruits which test out and verify the experience.

Consciousness of beauty or of truth or of goodness baffles analysis as much as consciousness of God does. These values have no objective standing ground in current psychology. They are not things in the world of space. They submit to no adequate causal explanation. They have their ground of being in some other kind of world than that of the mechanical order, a world composed of quantitative masses of matter in motion. These experiences of value, which are as real for experience as stone walls are, make very clear the fact that there are depths and capacities in the nature of the normal human mind which we do not usually recognize, and of which we have scant and imperfect accounts in our textbooks. Our minds taken in their full range, in other words, have some sort of contact and relationship with an eternal nature of things far deeper than atoms and molecules.

Only very slowly and gradually has the race learned, through finite symbols and temporal forms, to interpret beauty and truth and goodness, which, in their essence, are as ineffable and indescribable as is the mystic's experience of God. Plato often speaks as if he had high moments of experience when he rose to the naked vision of beauty—beauty "alone, separate, and eternal," as he says. But, as a matter of fact, however exalted heavenly and enduring beauty may be in its essence, we know *what it is* only as it appears in fair forms of objects, of body, of soul, of actions; in harmonious blending of sounds or colors; in well-ordered or happily combined groupings of many aspects in one unity, which is as it ought to be. Truth and moral goodness always transcend our attainments, and we sometimes feel that the very end and goal of life is the pursuit of that truth or that goodness which eye hath not seen nor ear heard. But whatever truth we do attain, or whatever goodness we do achieve, is always concrete. Truth is just this one more added fact that resists all attempt to doubt it. Goodness is just this simple everyday deed that reveals a heroic spirit and a brave venture of faith in the midst of difficulties.

So, too, the mystic knowledge of God is not some esoteric communication, supplied through trance or ecstasy; it is an intuitive personal touch with God, felt to be the essentially real, the bursting forth of an intense love for Him, which heightens all the capacities and activities of life, followed by the slow laboratory effects which verify it. "All I could never be" now *is*. It seems possible to stand the universe—even to do something toward the transformation of it. And if the experience does not prove that the soul has found God, it at least does this: it makes the soul feel that proofs of God are wholly unnecessary.

Plato and Bacon
Thomas Babington Macaulay

. . . The difference between the philosophy of Bacon and that of his predecessors cannot, we think, be better illustrated than by comparing his views on some important subjects with those of Plato. We select Plato, because we conceive that he did more than any other person towards giving to the minds of speculative men that bent which they retained till they received from Bacon a new impulse in a diametrically opposite direction.

It is curious to observe how differently these great men estimated the value of every kind of knowledge. Take Arithmetic for example. Plato, after speaking slightly of the convenience of being able to reckon and compute in the ordinary transactions of life, passes to what he considers as a far more important advantage. The study of the properties of numbers, he tells us, habituates the mind to the contemplation of pure truth, and raises it above the material universe. He would have his disciples apply themselves to this study,—not that they may be able to buy or sell,—not that they may qualify themselves to be shopkeepers or travelling merchants,—but that they may learn to withdraw their minds from the ever-shifting spectacle of this visible and tangible world, and to fix them on the immutable essence of things.

Bacon on the other hand, valued this branch of knowledge only on account of its uses with reference to that visible and tangible world which Plato so much despised. He speaks with scorn of the mystical arithmetic of the later Platonists; and laments the propensity of mankind to employ, on mere matters of curiosity, powers, the whole exertion of which is required for purposes of solid advantage. He advises arithmeticians to leave these trifles, and to employ themselves in framing convenient expressions, which may be of use in physical researches.

The same reasons which led Plato to recommend the study of arithmetic, led him to recommend also the study of mathematics. The vulgar crowd of geometricians, he says, will not understand him. They have practice always in view. They do not know that the real use of the science is to lead man to the knowledge of abstract, essential, eternal truth. Indeed, if we are to believe Plutarch, Plato carried this feeling so far, that he considered geometry as degraded by being applied to any purpose of vulgar utility. Archytas, it seems, had framed machines of extraordinary power, on mathematical principles. Plato remonstrated with his friend; and declared that this was to degrade a noble intellectual exercise into a low craft, fit only for carpenters and wheelwrights. The office of geometry, he said, was to discipline the mind, not to minister to the base wants of the body. His interference was successful; and from that time, according to Plutarch, the science of mechanics was considered as unworthy of the attention of a philosopher.

Archimedes in a later age imitated and surpassed Archytas. But even Archimedes was not free from the prevailing notion that geometry was degraded by being employed to produce any thing useful. It was with difficulty that he was induced to stoop from speculation to practice. He was half ashamed of those inventions which were the wonder of hostile nations; and always spoke of them slightingly as mere amusements— as trifles in which a mathematician might be suffered to relax his mind after intense application to the higher parts of his science.

The opinion of Bacon on this subject was diametrically opposed to that of the ancient philosophers. He valued geometry chiefly, if not solely, on account of those uses which to Plato appeared so base. And it is remarkable that the longer he lived the stronger this feeling became. When, in 1605, he wrote the two books on the 'Advancement of Learning,' he dwelt on the advantages which mankind derived from mixed mathematics; but he at the same time admitted, that the beneficial effect produced by mathematical study on the intellect, though a collateral advantage, was 'no less worthy than that which was principal and intended.' But it is evident that his views underwent a change. When, nearly twenty years later, he published the *De Augmentis*, which is the treatise on the 'Advancement of Learning,' greatly expanded and carefully corrected, he made important alterations in the part which related to mathematics. He condemned with severity the high pretensions of the mathematicians,—'delicias et fastum mathematicorum.' Assuming the well-being of the human race to be the end of knowledge, he pronounced that mathematical science could claim no higher rank than that of an appendage, or an auxiliary to other sciences. Mathematical science, he says, is the handmaid of natural philosophy—she ought to demean herself as such—and he declares that he cannot conceive by what ill chance it has happened that she presumes to claim precedence over her mistress. He predicts,—a prediction which would have made Plato shudder,—that as more and more discoveries are made in physics, there will be more and more branches of mixed mathematics. Of that collateral advantage, the value of which, twenty years before, he rated so highly, he says not one word. This omission cannot have been the effect of mere inadvertence. His own treatise was before him. From that treatise he deliberately expunged whatever was favorable to the study of pure mathematics, and inserted several keen reflections on the ardent votaries of that study. This fact in our opinion, admits of only one explanation. Bacon's love of those pursuits which directly tend to improve the condition of mankind, and his jealousy of all pursuits merely curious, had grown upon him, and had, it may be, become immoderate. He was afraid of using any expression which might have the effect of inducing any man of talents to employ in speculations, useful only to the mind of the speculator, a single hour which might be employed in extending the empire of man over matter. If Bacon erred here, we must acknowledge that we greatly prefer his error to the opposite error of Plato.—We have no patience with a philosophy which, like those Roman matrons who swallowed abortives in order to preserve their shapes, takes pains to be barren for fear of being homely.

Let us pass to astronomy. This was one of the sciences which Plato exhorted his disciples to learn, but for reasons far removed from common habits of thinking. 'Shall we set down astronomy,' says Socrates, 'among the subjects of study?' 'I think so,' answers his young friend Glaucon: 'to know something about the seasons, about the months and the years is of use for military purposes, as well as for agriculture and navigation.' 'It amuses me,' says Socrates, 'to see how afraid you are lest the common herd of people should accuse you of recommending useless studies.' He then proceeds in that pure and magnificent diction, which, as Cicero said, Jupiter would use if Jupiter spoke Greek, to explain, that the use of astronomy is not to add to the vulgar comforts of life, but to assist in raising the mind to the contemplation of things which are to be perceived by the pure intellect alone. The knowledge of the actual motions of the heavenly bodies he considers as of little value. The appearances which make the sky beautiful at night are, he tells us, like the figures which a geometrician draws on the sand, mere examples, mere helps to feeble minds. We must get beyond them; we must neglect them; we must attain to an astronomy which is as independent of the actual stars as geometrical truth is independent of the lines of an ill-drawn diagram. This is, we imagine, very nearly, if not exactly, the astronomy which Bacon compared to the ox of Prometheus —a sleek, well shaped hide, stuffed with rubbish, goodly to look at, but containing nothing to eat. He complained that astronomy had, to its great injury, been separated from natural philosophy, of which it was one of the noblest provinces, and annexed to the domain of mathematics. The world stood in need, he said, of a very different astronomy —of a *living astronomy*, of an astronomy which should set forth the nature, the motion, and the influences of the heavenly bodies, as they really are.

On the greatest and most useful of all inventions,—the invention of alphabetical writing,—Plato did not look with much complacency. He seems to have thought that the use of letters had operated on the human mind as the use of the go-cart in learning to walk, or of corks in learning to swim, is said to operate on the human body. It was a support which soon became indispensable to those who used it,—which made vigorous exertion first unnecessary, and then impossible. The powers of the intellect would, he conceived, have been more fully developed without this delusive aid. Men would have been compelled to exercise the understanding and the memory; and, by deep and assiduous meditation, to make truth thoroughly their own. Now, on the contrary, much knowledge is traced on paper, but little is engraved in the soul. A man is certain that he can find information at a moment's notice when he wants it. He therefore suffers it to fade from his mind. Such a man cannot in strictness be said to know any thing. He has the show without the reality of wisdom. These opinions Plato has put into the mouth of an ancient King of Egypt. But it is evident from the context that they were his own; and so they were understood to be by Quinctilian. Indeed they are in perfect accordance with the whole Platonic system.

Bacon's views, as may easily be supposed, were widely different. The powers of the memory, he observes, without the help of writing, can do little towards the advancement of any useful science. He acknowledges that the memory may be disciplined to such a point as to be able to perform very extraordinary feats. But on such feats he sets little value. The habits of his mind, he tells us, are such that he is not disposed to rate highly any accomplishment, however rare, which is of no practical use to mankind. As to these prodigious achievements of the memory, he ranks them with the exhibitions of rope-dancers and tumblers. 'The two performances,' he says, 'are of much the same sort. The one is an abuse of the powers of the body; the other is an abuse of the powers of the mind. Both may perhaps excite our wonder; but neither is entitled to our respect.'

To Plato, the science of medicine appeared one of very disputable advantage. He did not indeed object to quick cures for acute disorders, or for injuries produced by accidents. But the art which resists the slow sap of a chronic disease—which repairs frames enervated by lust, swollen by gluttony, or inflamed by wine—which encourages sensuality, by mitigating the natural punishment of the sensualist, and prolongs existence when the intellect has ceased to retain its entire energy—had no share of his esteem. A life protracted by medical skill he pronounced to be a long death. The exercise of the art of medicine ought, he said, to be tolerated so far as that art may serve to cure the occasional distempers of men whose constitutions are good. As to those who have bad constitutions, let them die;—and the sooner the better. Such men are unfit for war, for magistracy, for the management of their domestic affairs. That however is comparatively of little consequence. But they are incapable of study and speculation. If they engage in any severe mental exercise, they are troubled with giddiness and fulness of the head; all which they lay to the account of philosophy. The best thing that can happen to such wretches is to have done with life at once. He quotes mythical authority in support of this doctrine; and reminds his disciples that the practice of the sons of Æsculapius, as described by Homer, extended only to the cure of external injuries.

Far different was the philosophy of Bacon. Of all the sciences, that which he seems to have regarded with the greatest interest was the science which, in Plato's opinion, would not be tolerated in a well regulated community. To make men perfect was no part of Bacon's plan. His humble aim was to make imperfect men comfortable. The beneficence of his philosophy resembled the beneficence of the common Father, whose sun rises on the evil and the good—whose rain descends for the just and the unjust. In Plato's opinion man was made for philosophy; in Bacon's opinion philosophy was made for man; it was a means to an end;—and that end was to increase the pleasures, and to mitigate the pains of millions who are not and cannot be philosophers. That a valetudinarian who took great pleasure in being wheeled along his terrace, who relished his boiled chicken and his weak wine and water, and who enjoyed a hearty laugh over the Queen of Navarre's tales, should be treated as a *caput lupinum* because he could not read the Timæus without a headache, was a notion which the humane spirit of the English school of wisdom altogether rejected. Bacon would not have thought it beneath the dignity of a philosopher to contrive an improved garden chair for such a valetudinarian,—to devise some way of rendering his medicines more palatable,—to invent repasts which he might enjoy, and pillows on which he might sleep soundly; and this though there might not be the smallest hope that the mind of the poor invalid would ever rise to the contemplation of the ideal beautiful and the ideal good. As Plato had cited the religious legends of Greece to justify his contempt for the more recondite parts of the art of healing, Bacon vindicated the dignity of that art by appealing to the example of Christ; and reminded his readers that the great physician of the soul did not disdain to be also the physician of the body.

When we pass from the science of medicine to that of legislation, we find the same difference between the systems of these two great men. Plato, at the commencement of the fine Dialogue on Laws, lays it down as a fundamental principle, that the end of legislation is to make men virtuous. It is unnecessary to point out the extravagant conclusions to which such a proposition leads. Bacon well knew to how great an extent the happiness of every society must depend on the virtue of its members; and he also knew what legislators can, and what they cannot do for the purpose of promoting virtue. The view which he has given of the end of legislation and of the principal means for the attainment of that end, has always seemed to us eminently happy; even among the many happy passages of the same kind with which his works abound. . . . The end is the well-being of the people. The means are the imparting of moral and religious education; the providing of every thing necessary for defence against foreign enemies; the maintaining of internal order; the establishing of a judicial, financial, and commercial system, under which wealth may be rapidly accumulated and securely enjoyed.

Even with respect to the form in which laws ought to be drawn, there is a remarkable difference of opinion between the Greek and the Englishman. Plato thought a preamble essential; Bacon thought it mischievous. Each was consistent with himself. Plato, considering the moral improvement of the people as the end of legislation, justly inferred that a law which commanded and threatened, but which neither convinced the reason nor touched the heart, must be a most imperfect law. He was not content with deterring from theft a man who still continued to be a thief at heart,—with restraining a son who hated his mother from beating his mother. The only obedience on which he set so much value, was the obedience which an enlightened understanding yields to reason, and which a virtuous disposition yields to precepts of virtue. He really seems to have believed that, by prefixing to every law an eloquent and pathetic exhortation, he should, to a great extent, render penal enactments superfluous. Bacon entertained no such romantic hopes; and he well knew the practical inconveniences of the course which Plato recommended. . . .

Had Plato lived to finish the 'Critias,' a comparison between that noble fiction and the 'New Atlantis,' would probably have furnished us with still more striking instances. It is amusing to think with what horror he would have seen such an institution as 'Solomon's House' rising in his republic; with what vehemence he would have ordered the brewhouses, the perfume-houses, and the dispensatories to be pulled down; and with what inexorable rigor he would have driven beyond the frontier all the Fellows of the College, Merchants of [L]ight and Depredators, Lamps and Pioneers.

To sum up the whole: we should say that the aim of the Platonic philosophy was to exalt man into a god. The aim of the Baconian philosophy was to provide man with what he requires while be continues to be man. The aim of the Platonic philosophy was to raise us far above vulgar wants. The aim of the Baconian philosophy was to supply our vulgar wants. The former aim was noble; but the latter was attainable. Plato drew a good bow; but, like Acestes in Virgil, he aimed at the stars; and therefore, though there was no want of strength or skill, the shot was thrown away. His arrow was indeed followed by a track of dazzling radiance, but it struck nothing. . . . Bacon fixed his eye on a mark which was placed on the earth and within bow-shot, and hit it in the white. The philosophy of Plato began in words and ended in words,—noble words indeed,—words such as were to be expected from the finest of human intellects exercising boundless dominion over the finest of human languages. The philosophy of Bacon began in observations and ended in arts.

The boast of the ancient philosophers was, that their doctrine formed the minds of men to a high degree of wisdom and virtue. This was indeed the only practical good which the most celebrated of those teachers even pretended to effect; and undoubtedly if they had effected this, they would have deserved the greatest praise. But the truth is, that in those very matters in which alone they professed to do any good to mankind, in those very matters for the sake of which they neglected all the vulgar interests of mankind, they did nothing, or worse than nothing. They promised what was impracticable; they despised what was practicable; they filled the world with long words and long beards; and they left it as wicked and as ignorant as they found it. . . .

Suggestions for Writing

1. Write an essay on the thesis "Human happiness nourishes itself on a whole host of minor illusions." Pick out four or five of our minor (or major) obsessions, such as dreams of clothes, cars, water skiing, love, fraternities, family life, money. The problem is to arrange your items in an order of ascending interest—humorous or serious. Give each item no less than a paragraph.

2. Attack or defend Stace's assertion about "the real world as it actually is, stark and bleak."

3. Write an essay on the thesis "Contrary to popular belief, ideals are not off in the clouds: we know *what they are* only as they appear in the fair forms of objects, of body, of soul, of actions."

4. Write an essay in which you contrast Stace with Greene or Jones, working from a thesis that supports one against the other. Conduct your comparison as Macaulay does with Plato and Bacon; treat both men under each of your points.

5. Similarly, contrast Trilling with Jones.

6. Write a passage of straight imitation or parody of Macaulay, taking as your opposites two baseball players, two movie actresses, or perhaps two types of person, like the freshman and the sophomore: "To sum up the whole: we should say that the aim of the freshman is to learn everything. The aim of the sophomore is to appear as if he had already learned it."

7. Write an essay in which you clearly favor one side, but in which you contrast your side with its opposite fully and fairly—for instance, baseball as better than football, one team over another, big college over small, or the ideal over the practical (using Macaulay against himself). Again, treat both sides under each of your points, as Macaulay does.

Language and Literature EDWARD SAPIR · *115*
Cervantes GEORGE SANTAYANA · *122*
Nirvana Now DANIEL P. MOYNIHAN · *128*

Paragraphs

Beginning, Middle, End

These three essays show three different writers, with three different subjects, facing the problem of getting started and of concluding, and they suggest how important it is to set the thesis clearly at the beginning and to round it off at the end, usually in a single paragraph for the beginning and another for the conclusion. Sapir clearly says that he will show how the law of a writer's medium will assert its force. Santayana, although a bit more open in structure, nevertheless clearly announces his demonstration of how the writer's environment shaped everything in his book, from characters, to incidents, to ultimate message. Moynihan just as clearly lays down the importance of the modern activist's rejection of the social system itself.

The beginnings, as if shaped like a funnel, start somewhat broadly, then narrow, in varying degrees of concision, to an assertion of thesis. Notice how the endings seem to turn the funnel upside down. Each ending begins with some fresh restatement of thesis, then broadens out briefly to take in wider implications and deeper meanings. Moynihan's is particularly imaginative.

Each of these essays is ably paragraphed. Each writer, as if working from a norm in his head, measures his thoughts into equal paragraphs, occasionally coming short for emphasis, occasionally expanding for clarity. Notice how almost every paragraph begins with its topic sentence, its own small thesis. Each writer discusses a duality, a surface and a depth, showing that one may be more important than the other, but that both depend upon each other for their mutual significance. The essays are thus alike thematically, as they are alike in their structural adroitness, in spite of their quite different subjects.

Language and Literature
Edward Sapir

Languages are more to us than systems of thought-transference. They are invisible garments that drape themselves about our spirit and give a predetermined form to all its symbolic expression. When the expression is of unusual significance, we call it literature.[1] Art is so personal an expression that we do not like to feel that it is bound to predetermined form of any sort. The possibilities of individual expression are infinite, language in particular is the most fluid of mediums. Yet some limitation there must be to this freedom, some resistance of the medium. In great art there is the illusion of absolute freedom. The formal restraints imposed by the material—paint, black and white, marble, piano tones, or whatever it may be—are not perceived; it is as though there were a limitless margin of elbow-room between the artist's fullest utilization of form and the most that the material is innately capable of. The artist has intuitively surrendered to the inescapable tyranny of the material, made its brute nature fuse easily with his

---

[1] I can hardly stop to define just what kind of expression is "significant" enough to be called art or literature. Besides, I do not exactly know. We shall have to take literature for granted. [The footnotes in this essay are Sapir's.]

conception.[2] The material "disappears" precisely because there is nothing in the artist's conception to indicate that any other material exists. For the time being, he, and we with him, move in the artistic medium as a fish moves in the water, oblivious of the existence of an alien atmosphere. No sooner, however, does the artist transgress the law of his medium than we realize with a start that there is a medium to obey.

Language is the medium of literature as marble or bronze or clay are the materials of the sculptor. Since every language has its distinctive peculiarities, the innate formal limitations—and possibilities—of one literature are never quite the same as those of another. The literature fashioned out of the form and substance of a language has the color and the texture of its matrix. The literary artist may never be conscious of just how he is hindered or helped or otherwise guided by the matrix, but when it is a question of translating his work into another language, the nature of the original matrix manifests itself at once. All his effects have been calculated, or intuitively felt, with reference to the formal "genius" of his own language; they cannot be carried over without loss or modification. Croce[3] is therefore perfectly right in saying that a work of literary art can never be translated. Nevertheless literature does get itself translated, sometimes with astonishing adequacy. This brings up the question whether in the art of literature there are not intertwined two distinct kinds or levels of art—a generalized, non-linguistic art, which can be transferred without loss into an alien linguistic medium, and a specifically linguistic art that is not transferable.[4] I believe the distinction is entirely valid, though we never get the two levels pure in practice. Literature moves in language as a medium, but that medium comprises two layers, the latent content of language—our intuitive record of experience—and the particular conformation of a given

---

[2] This "intuitive surrender" has nothing to do with subservience to artistic convention. More than one revolt in modern art has been dominated by the desire to get out of the material just what it is really capable of. The impressionist wants light and color because paint can give him just these; "literature" in painting, the sentimental suggestion of a "story," is offensive to him because he does not want the virtue of his particular form to be dimmed by shadows from another medium. Similarly, the poet, as never before, insists that words mean just what they really mean.

[3] See Benedetto Croce, Æsthetic.

[4] The question of the transferability of art productions seems to me to be of genuine theoretic interest. For all that we speak of the sacrosanct uniqueness of a given art work, we know very well, though we do not always admit it, that not all productions are equally intractable to transference. A Chopin étude is inviolate; it moves altogether in the world of piano tone. A Bach fugue is transferable into another set of musical timbres without serious loss of esthetic significance. Chopin plays with the language of the piano as though no other language existed (the medium "disappears"); Bach speaks the language of the piano as a handy means of giving outward expression to a conception wrought in the generalized language of tone.

language—the specific how of our record of experience. Literature that draws its sustenance mainly—never entirely—from the lower level, say a play of Shakespeare's, is translatable without too great a loss of character. If it moves in the upper rather than in the lower level—a fair example is a lyric of Swinburne's—it is as good as untranslatable. Both types of literary expression may be great or mediocre.

There is really no mystery in the distinction. It can be clarified a little by comparing literature with science. A scientific truth is impersonal, in its essence it is untinctured by the particular linguistic medium in which it finds expression. It can as readily deliver its message in Chinese[5] as in English. Nevertheless it must have some expression, and that expression must needs be a linguistic one. Indeed the apprehension of the scientific truth is itself a linguistic process, for thought is nothing but language denuded of its outward garb. The proper medium of scientific expression is therefore a generalized language that may be defined as a symbolic algebra of which all known languages are translations. One can adequately translate scientific literature because the original scientific expression is itself a translation. Literary expression is personal and concrete, but this does not mean that its significance is altogether bound up with the accidental qualities of the medium. A truly deep symbolism, for instance, does not depend on the verbal associations of a particular language but rests securely on an intuitive basis that underlies all linguistic expression. The artist's "intuition," to use Croce's term, is immediately fashioned out of a generalized human experience—thought and feeling—of which his own individual experience is a highly personalized selection. The thought relations in this deeper level have no specific linguistic vesture; the rhythms are free, not bound, in the first instance, to the traditional rhythms of the artist's language. Certain artists whose spirit moves largely in the non-linguistic (better, in the generalized linguistic) layer even find a certain difficulty in getting themselves expressed in the rigidly set terms of their accepted idiom. One feels that they are unconsciously striving for a generalized art language, a literary algebra, that is related to the sum of all known languages as a perfect mathematical symbolism is related to all the roundabout reports of mathematical relations that normal speech is capable of conveying. Their art expression is frequently strained, it sounds at times like a translation from an unknown original—which, indeed, is precisely what it is. These artists—Whitmans and Brownings—impress us rather by the greatness of their spirit than the felicity of their art. Their relative failure is of the greatest

---

[5] Provided, of course, Chinese is careful to provide itself with the necessary scientific vocabulary. Like any other language, it can do so without serious difficulty if the need arises.

diagnostic value as an index of the pervasive presence in literature of a larger, more intuitive linguistic medium than any particular language.

Nevertheless, human expression being what it is, the greatest—or shall we say the most satisfying—literary artists, the Shakespeares and Heines, are those who have known subconsciously to fit or trim the deeper intuition to the provincial accents of their daily speech. In them there is no effect of strain. Their personal "intuition" appears as a completed synthesis of the absolute art of intuition and the innate, specialized art of the linguistic medium. With Heine, for instance, one is under the illusion that the universe speaks German. The material "disappears."

Every language is itself a collective art of expression. There is concealed in it a particular set of esthetic factors—phonetic, rhythmic, symbolic, morphological—which it does not completely share with any other language. These factors may either merge their potencies with those of that unknown, absolute language to which I have referred—this is the method of Shakespeare and Heine—or they may weave a private, technical art fabric of their own, the innate art of the language intensified or sublimated. The latter type, the more technically "literary" art of Swinburne and of hosts of delicate "minor" poets, is too fragile for endurance. It is built out of spiritualized material, not out of spirit. The successes of the Swinburnes are as valuable for diagnostic purposes as the semi-failures of the Brownings. They show to what extent literary art may lean on the collective art of the language itself. The more extreme technical practitioners may so over-individualize this collective art as to make it almost unendurable. One is not always thankful to have one's flesh and blood frozen to ivory.

An artist must utilize the native esthetic resources of his speech. He may be thankful if the given palette of colors is rich, if the springboard is light. But he deserves no special credit for felicities that are the language's own. We must take for granted this language with all its qualities of flexibility or rigidity and see the artist's work in relation to it. A cathedral on the lowlands is higher than a stick on Mont Blanc. In other words, we must not commit the folly of admiring a French sonnet because the vowels are more sonorous than our own or of condemning Nietzsche's prose because it harbors in its texture combinations of consonants that would affright on English soil. To so judge literature would be tantamount to loving *Tristan und Isolde* because one is fond of the timbre of horns. There are certain things that one language can do supremely well which it would be almost vain for another to attempt. Generally there are compensations. The vocalism of English is an inherently drabber thing than the vowel scale of French, yet English compensates for this drawback by its greater rhythmical alertness. It is even doubtful if the innate sonority of a phonetic system counts for as much, as esthetic determinant, as the relations between the sounds, the total gamut of their similarities and contrasts. As long as the artist has the wherewithal to lay out his sequences and rhythms, it matters little what are the sensuous qualities of the elements of his material.

The phonetic groundwork of a language, however, is only one of the features that give its literature a certain direction. Far more important are its morphological peculiarities. It makes a great deal of difference for the development of style if the language can or cannot create compound words, if its structure is synthetic or analytic, if the words of its sentences have considerable freedom of position or are compelled to fall into a rigidly determined sequence. The major characteristics of style, in so far as style is a technical matter of the building and placing of words, are given by the language itself, quite as inescapably, indeed, as the general acoustic effect of verse is given by the sounds and natural accents of the language. These necessary fundamentals of style are hardly felt by the artist to constrain his individuality of expression. They rather point the way to those stylistic developments that most suit the natural bent of the language. It is not in the least likely that a truly great style can seriously oppose itself to the basic form patterns of the language. It not only incorporates them, it builds on them. The merit of such a style as W. H. Hudson's or George Moore's[6] is that it does with ease and economy what the language is always trying to do. Carlylese, though individual and vigorous, is yet not style; it is a Teutonic mannerism. Nor is the prose of Milton and his contemporaries strictly English; it is semi-Latin done into magnificent English words.

It is strange how long it has taken the European literatures to learn that style is not an absolute, a something that is to be imposed on the language from Greek or Latin models, but merely the language itself, running in its natural grooves, and with enough of an individual accent to allow the artist's personality to be felt as a presence, not as an acrobat. We understand more clearly now that what is effective and beautiful in one language is a vice in another. Latin and Eskimo, with their highly inflected forms, lend themselves to an elaborately periodic structure that would be boring in English. English allows, even demands, a looseness that would be insipid in Chinese. And Chinese, with its unmodified words and rigid sequences, has a compactness of phrase, a terse parallelism, and a silent suggestiveness that would be too tart, too mathematical, for the English genius. While we cannot assimilate the luxurious periods of Latin nor the pointilliste style of the Chinese classics, we can enter sympathetically into the spirit of these alien techniques.

---

[6] Aside from individual peculiarities of diction, the selection and evaluation of particular words as such.

I believe that any English poet of to-day would be thankful for the concision that a Chinese poetaster attains without effort. Here is an example:[7]

> Wu-river[8] stream mouth evening sun sink,
> North look Liao-Tung,[9] not see home.
> Steam whistle several noise, sky-earth boundless,
> Float float one reed out Middle-Kingdom.

These twenty-eight syllables may be clumsily interpreted: "At the mouth of the Yangtsze River, as the sun is about to sink, I look north toward Liao-Tung but do not see my home. The steam-whistle shrills several times on the boundless expanse where meet sky and earth. The steamer, floating gently like a hollow reed, sails out of the Middle Kingdom."[10] But we must not envy Chinese its terseness unduly. Our more sprawling mode of expression is capable of its own beauties, and the more compact luxuriance of Latin style has its loveliness too. There are almost as many natural ideals of literary style as there are languages. Most of these are merely potential, awaiting the hand of artists who will never come. And yet in the recorded texts of primitive tradition and song there are many passages of unique vigor and beauty. The structure of the language often forces an assemblage of concepts that impresses us as a stylistic discovery. Single Algonkin words are like tiny imagist poems. We must be careful not to exaggerate a freshness of content that is at least half due to our freshness of approach, but the possibility is indicated none the less of utterly alien literary styles, each distinctive with its disclosure of the search of the human spirit for beautiful form.

Probably nothing better illustrates the formal dependence of literature on language than the prosodic aspect of poetry. Quantitative verse was entirely natural to the Greeks, not merely because poetry grew up in connection with the chant and the dance,[11] but because alternations of long and short syllables were keenly live facts in the daily economy of the language. The tonal accents, which were only secondarily stress phenomena, helped to give the syllable its quantitative individuality. When the Greek meters were carried over into Latin verse, there was

---

[7] Not by any means a great poem, merely a bit of occasional verse written by a young Chinese friend of mine when he left Shanghai for Canada.

[8] The old name of the country about the mouth of the Yangtsze.

[9] A province of Manchuria.

[10] I.e., China.

[11] Poetry everywhere is inseparable in its origins from the singing voice and the measure of the dance. Yet accentual and syllabic types of verse, rather than quantitative verse, seem to be the prevailing norms.

comparatively little strain, for Latin too was characterized by an acute awareness of quantitative distinctions. However, the Latin accent was more markedly stressed than that of Greek. Probably, therefore, the purely quantitative meters modeled after the Greek were felt as a shade more artificial than in the language of their origin. The attempt to cast English verse into Latin and Greek molds has never been successful. The dynamic basis of English is not quantity,[12] but stress, the alternation of accented and unaccented syllables. This fact gives English verse an entirely different slant and has determined the development of its poetic forms, is still responsible for the evolution of new forms. Neither stress nor syllabic weight is a very keen psychologic factor in the dynamics of French. The syllable has great inherent sonority and does not fluctuate significantly as to quantity and stress. Quantitative or accentual metrics would be as artificial in French as stress metrics in classical Greek or quantitative or purely syllabic metrics in English. French prosody was compelled to develop on the basis of unit syllable-groups. Assonance, later rhyme, could not but prove a welcome, an all but necessary, means of articulating or sectioning the somewhat spineless flow of sonorous syllables. English was hospitable to the French suggestion of rhyme, but did not seriously need it in its rhythmic economy. Hence rhyme has always been strictly subordinated to stress as a somewhat decorative feature and has been frequently dispensed with. It is no psychologic accident that rhyme came later into English than in French and is leaving it sooner.[13] Chinese verse has developed along very much the same lines as French verse. The syllable is an even more integral and sonorous unit than in French, while quantity and stress are too uncertain to form the basis of a metric system. Syllable-groups—so and so many syllables per rhythmic unit—and rhyme are therefore two of the controlling factors in Chinese prosody. The third factor, the alternation of syllables with level tone and syllables with inflected (rising or falling) tone, is peculiar to Chinese.

To summarize, Latin and Greek verse depends on the principle of contrasting weights; English verse, on the principle of contrasting stresses; French verse, on the principles of number and echo; Chinese verse, on the principles of number, echo, and contrasting pitches. Each of these rhythmic systems proceeds from the unconscious dynamic habit of the language, falling from the lips of the folk. Study carefully

---

[12] Quantitative distinctions exist as an objective fact. They have not the same inner, psychological value that they had in Greek.

[13] Verhaeren was no slave to the Alexandrine, yet he remarked to Symons, *à propos* of the translation of *Les Aubes*, that while he approved of the use of rhymeless verse in the English version, he found it "meaningless" in French.

the phonetic system of a language, above all its dynamic features, and you can tell what kind of a verse it has developed—or, if history has played pranks with its psychology, what kind of verse it should have developed and some day will.

Whatever be the sounds, accents, and forms of a language, however these lay hands on the shape of its literature, there is a subtle law of compensations that gives the artist space. If he is squeezed a bit here, he can swing a free arm there. And generally he has rope enough to hang himself with, if he must. It is not strange that this should be so. Language is itself the collective art of expression, a summary of thousands upon thousands of individual intuitions. The individual goes lost in the collective creation, but his personal expression has left some trace in a certain give and flexibility that are inherent in all collective works of the human spirit. The language is ready, or can be quickly made ready, to define the artist's individuality. If no literary artist appears, it is not essentially because the language is too weak an instrument, it is because the culture of the people is not favorable to the growth of such personality as seeks a truly individual verbal expression.

Cervantes
George Santayana

Cervantes is known to the world as the author of *Don Quixote,* and although his other works are numerous and creditable, and his pathetic life is carefully recorded, yet it is as the author of *Don Quixote* alone that he deserves to be generally known or considered. Had his wit not come by chance on the idea of the Ingenious Hidalgo, Cervantes would never have attained his universal renown, even if his other works and the interest of his career should have sufficed to give him a place in the literary history of his country. Here, then, where our task is to present in miniature only what has the greatest and most universal value, we may treat our author as playwrights are advised to treat their heroes, saying of him only what is necessary to the understanding of the single action with which we are concerned. This single action is the writing of *Don Quixote;* and what we shall try to understand is what there was in the life and environment of Cervantes that enabled him to compose that great book, and that remained imbedded in its characters, its episodes, and its moral.

There was in vogue in the Spain of the sixteenth century a species of romance called books of chivalry. They were developments of the legends dealing with King Arthur and the Knights of the Table Round, and their numerous descendants and emulators. These stories had appealed in the first place to what we should still think of as the spirit of chivalry: they were full of tourneys and single combats, desperate adventures and romantic loves. The setting was in the same vague and wonderful region as the Coast of Bohemia, where to the known mountains, seas, and cities that have poetic names, was added a prodigious number of caverns, castles, islands, and forests of the romancer's invention. With time and popularity this kind of story had naturally intensified its characteristics until it had reached the greatest extravagance and absurdity, and combined in a way the unreality of the fairy tale with the bombast of the melodrama.

Cervantes had apparently read these books with avidity, and was not without a great sympathy with the kind of imagination they embodied. His own last and most carefully written book, the *Travails of Persiles and Sigismunda,* is in many respects an imitation of them; it abounds in savage islands, furious tryants, prodigious feats of arms, disguised maidens whose discretion is as marvelous as their beauty, and happy deliverances from intricate and hopeless situations. His first book also, the *Galatea,* was an embodiment of a kind of pastoral idealism: sentimental verses being interspersed with euphuistic prose, the whole describing the lovelorn shepherds and heartless shepherdesses of Arcadia.

But while these books, which were the author's favorites among his own works, expressed perhaps Cervantes's natural taste and ambition, the events of his life and the real bent of his talent, which in time he came himself to recognize, drove him to a very different sort of composition. His family was ancient but impoverished, and he was forced throughout his life to turn his hand to anything that could promise him a livelihood. His existence was a continuous series of experiments, vexations, and disappointments. He adopted at first the profession of arms, and followed his colors as a private soldier upon several foreign expeditions. He was long quartered in Italy; he fought at Lepanto against the Turks, where among other wounds he received one that maimed his left hand, to the greater glory, as he tells us, of his right; he was captured by Barbary pirates and remained for five years a slave in Algiers; he was ransomed, and returned to Spain only to find official favors and recognitions denied him; and finally, at the age of thirty-seven, he abandoned the army for literature.

His first thought as a writer does not seem to have been to make direct use of his rich experience and varied observation; he was rather possessed by an obstinate longing for that poetic gift which, as he confesses in one place, Heaven had denied him. He began with the idyllic romance, the *Galatea,* already mentioned, and at various times during the rest of his life wrote poems, plays, and stories of a romantic and sentimental type. In the course of these labors, however, he struck one vein of much richer promise. It was what the Spanish call the *picaresque;* that is, the description of the life and character of rogues, pickpockets, vagabonds, and all those wretches and sorry wits that might be found about the highways, in the country inns, or in the slums of cities. Of this kind is much of what is best in his collected stories, the *Novelas Exemplares.* The talent and the experience which he betrays in these amusing narratives were to be invaluable to him later as the author of *Don Quixote,* where they enabled him to supply a foil to the fine world of his poor hero's imagination.

We have now mentioned what were perhaps the chief elements of the preparation of Cervantes for his great task. They were a great familiarity with the romances of chivalry, and a natural liking for them; a life of honorable but unrewarded endeavor both in war and in the higher literature; and much experience of Vagabondia, with the art of taking down and reproducing in amusing profusion the typical scenes and languages of low life. Out of these elements a single spark, which we may attribute to genius, to chance, or to inspiration, was enough to produce a new and happy conception: that of a parody on the romances of chivalry, in which the extravagances of the fables of knighthood should be contrasted with the sordid realities of life. This is done by the ingenious device of representing a country gentleman whose naturally generous mind, unhinged by much reading of the books of chivalry, should lead him to undertake the office of knight-errant, and induce him to ride about the country clad in ancient armor, to right wrongs, to succor defenseless maidens, to kill giants, and to win empires at least as vast as that of Alexander.

—This is the subject of *Don Quixote.* But happy as the conception is, it could not have produced a book of enduring charm and well-seasoned wisdom, had it not been filled in with a great number of amusing and lifelike episodes, and verified by two admirable figures, Don Quixote and Sancho Panza, characters at once intimately individual and truly universal.

Don Quixote at first appears to the reader, and probably appeared to the author as well, as primarily a madman,—a thin and gaunt old village squire, whose brain has been turned by the nonsense he has read and taken for gospel truth; and who is punished for his ridiculous mania by an uninterrupted series of beatings, falls, indignities, and insults. But the hero and the author together, with the ingenuity proper to madness and the inevitableness proper to genius, soon begin to disclose the fund of intelligence and ideal passion which underlies this superficial insanity. We see that Don Quixote is only mad north-northwest, when the wind blows from the quarter of his chivalrous preoccupation. At other times he shows himself a man of great goodness and fineness of wit; virtuous, courageous, courteous, and generous, and in fact the perfect ideal of a gentleman. When he takes, for instance, a handful of acorns from the goat-herds' table and begins a grandiloquent discourse upon the Golden Age, we feel how cultivated the man is, how easily the little things of life suggest to him the great things, and with what delight he dwells on what is beautiful and happy. The truth and pathos of the character become all the more compelling when we consider how naturally the hero's madness and calamities flow from this same exquisite sense of what is good.

The contrast to this figure is furnished by that of Sancho Panza, who embodies all that is matter-of-fact, gross, and plebeian. Yet he is willing to become Don Quixote's esquire, and by his credulity and devotion shows what an ascendency a heroic and enthusiastic nature can gain over the most sluggish of men. Sancho has none of the instincts of his master. He never read the books of chivalry or desired to right the wrongs of the world. He is naturally satisfied with his crust and his onions, if they can be washed down with enough bad wine. His good drudge of a wife never transformed herself in his fancy into a peerless Dulcinea. Yet Sancho follows his master into every danger, shares his discomfiture and the many blows that rain down upon him, and hopes to the end for the governorship of that Insula with which Don Quixote is some day to reward his faithful esquire.

As the madness of Don Quixote is humanized by his natural intelligence and courage, so the grossness and credulity of Sancho are relieved by his homely wit. He abounds in proverbs. He never fails to see the reality of a situation, and to protest doggedly against his master's visionary flights. He holds fast as long as he can to the evidence of his senses, and to his little weaknesses of flesh and spirit. But finally he surrenders to the authority of Don Quixote, and of the historians of chivalry, although not without a certain reluctance and some surviving doubts.

The character of Sancho is admirable for the veracity with which its details are drawn. The traits of the boor, the glutton, and the coward come most naturally to the surface upon occasion, yet Sancho remains a patient, good-natured peasant, a devoted servant, and a humble Christian. Under the cover of such lifelike incongruities, and of a pervasive humor, the author has given us a satirical picture of human nature not inferior, perhaps, to that furnished by Don Quixote himself. For instance: Don Quixote, after mending his helmet, tries its strength with a blow that smashes it to pieces. He mends it a second time, but now, without trial, deputes it to be henceforth a strong and perfect helmet. Sancho, when he is sent to bear a letter to Dulcinea, neglects to deliver it, and invents an account of his interview with the imaginary lady for the satisfaction of his master. But before long, by dint of repeating the story, he comes himself to believe his own lies. Thus self-deception in the knight is the ridiculous effect of courage, and in the esquire the not less ridiculous effect of sloth.

The adventures these two heroes encounter are naturally only such as travelers along the Spanish roads would then have been likely to come upon. The point of the story depends on the familiarity and commonness of the situations in which Don Quixote finds himself, so that the absurdity of his pretensions may be overwhelmingly shown. Critics are agreed in blaming the exceptions which Cervantes allowed himself to make to the realism of his scenes, where he introduced romantic tales into the narrative of the first part. The tales are in themselves unworthy of their setting, and contrary to the spirit of the whole book. Cervantes doubtless yielded here partly to his story-telling habits, partly to a fear of monotony in the uninterrupted description of Don Quixote's adventures. He avoided this mistake in the second part, and devised the visit to the Duke's palace, and the intentional sport there made of the hero, to give variety to the story.

More variety and more unity may still, perhaps, seem desirable in the book. The episodes are strung together without much coherence, and without any attempt to develop either the plot or the characters. Sancho, to be sure, at last tastes the governorship of his Insula, and Don Quixote on his death-bed recovers his wits. But this conclusion, appropriate and touching as it is, might have come almost anywhere in the course of the story. The whole book has, in fact, rather the quality of an improvisation. The episodes suggest themselves to the author's fancy as he proceeds; a fact which gives them the same unexpectedness and sometimes the same incompleteness which the events of a journey naturally have. It is in the genius of this kind of narrative to be a sort of imaginary diary, without a general dramatic structure. The interest depends on the characters and the incidents alone; on the fertility of the author's invention, on the ingenuity of the turns he gives to the story, and on the incidental scenes and figures he describes.

When we have once accepted this manner of writing fiction—which might be called that of the novelist before the days of the novel—we can only admire the execution of *Don Quixote* as masterly in its kind. We find here an abundance of fancy that is never at a loss for some probable and interesting incident; we find a graphic power that makes living and unforgettable many a minor character, even if slightly sketched; we find the charm of the country rendered by little touches without any formal descriptions; and we find a humorous and minute reproduction of the manners of the time. All this is rendered in a flowing and easy style, abounding in both characterization and parody of diverse types of speech and composition; and the whole is still but the background for the figures of Don Quixote and Sancho, and for their pleasant discourse, the quality and savor of which is maintained to the end. These excellences unite to make the book one of the most permanently delightful in the world, as well as one of the most diverting. Seldom has laughter been so well justified as that which the reading of *Don Quixote* continually provokes; seldom has it found its causes in such genuine fancy, such profound and real contrast, and such victorious good-humor.

We sometimes wish, perhaps, that our heroes were spared some of their bruises, and that we were not asked to delight so much in promiscuous beatings and floggings. But we must remember that these three hundred years have made the European race much more sensitive to physical suffering. Our ancestors took that doubtful pleasure in the idea of corporal writhings which we still take in the description of the tortures of the spirit. The idea of both evils is naturally distasteful to a refined mind; but we admit more willingly the kind which habit has accustomed us to regard as inevitable, and which personal experience very probably has made an old friend.

Don Quixote has accordingly enjoyed a universal popularity, and has had the singular privilege of accomplishing the object for which it was written, which was to recall fiction from the extravagances of the books of chivalry to the study of real life. This is the simple object which Cervantes had and avowed. He was a literary man with literary interests, and the idea which came to him was to ridicule the absurdities of the prevalent literary mode. The rich vein which he struck in the conception of Don Quixote's madness and topsy-turvy adventures encouraged him to go on. The subject and the characters deepened under his hands, until from a parody of a certain kind of romances the story threatened to become a satire on human idealism. At the same time Cervantes grew fond of his hero, and made him, as we must feel, in some sort a representative of his own chivalrous enthusiasms and constant disappointments.

We need not, however, see in this transformation any deep-laid malice or remote significance. As the tale opened out before the author's fancy and enlisted his closer and more loving attention, he naturally enriched it with all the wealth of his experience. Just as he diversified it with pictures of common life and manners, so he weighted it with the burden of human tragedy. He left upon it an impress of his own nobility and misfortunes side by side with a record of his time and country. But in this there was nothing intentional. He only spoke out of the fullness of his heart. The highest motives and characters had been revealed to him by his own impulses, and the lowest by his daily experience.

There is nothing in the book that suggests a premeditated satire upon faith and enthusiasm in general. The author's evident purpose is to amuse, not to upbraid or to discourage. There is no bitterness in his pathos or despair in his disenchantment; partly because he retains a healthy fondness for this naughty world, and partly because his heart is profoundly and entirely Christian. He would have rejected with indignation an interpretation of his work that would see in it an attack on religion or even on chivalry. His birth and nurture had made him religious and chivalrous from the beginning, and he remained so by conviction to the end. He was still full of plans and hopes when death overtook him, but he greeted it with perfect simplicity, without lamentations over the past or anxiety for the future.

If we could have asked Cervantes what the moral of Don Quixote was to his own mind, he would have told us perhaps that it was this: that the force of idealism is wasted when it does not recognize the reality of things. Neglect of the facts of daily life made the absurdity of the romances of chivalry and of the enterprise of Don Quixote. What is needed is not, of course, that idealism should be surrendered, either in literature or in life; but that in both it should be made efficacious by a better adjustment to the reality it would transform.

Something of this kind would have been, we may believe, Cervantes's own reading of his parable. But when parables are such direct and full transcripts of life as is the story of Don Quixote, they offer almost as much occasion for diversity of interpretation as does the personal experience of men in the world. That the moral of Don Quixote should be doubtful and that each man should be tempted to see in it the expression of his own convictions, is after all the greatest possible encomium of the book. For we may infer that the truth has been rendered in it, and that men may return to it always, as to Nature herself, to renew their theories or to forget them, and to refresh their fancy with the spectacle of a living world.

Nirvana Now
Daniel P. Moynihan

One of the defining qualities of the period of current history that began, roughly, with the assassination of President Kennedy has been the emergence of widespread, radical protest on the part of American youth. As it happens, this development has been congruent, and in some measure associated, with even wider protest against the current course of American foreign policy, but there is a distinction between those who differ with decisions made by the existing system, and those who reject the system itself. There is at this moment a high level of both kinds of protest, but the latter is the more singular, and almost certainly the more significant.

Following a period when college youth in particular were repeatedly accused of quiescent conformism, this development has taken the World War II generation rather by surprise. More than one college president given to deploring "the silent generation" appears in retrospect not half so bold, and considerably less prescient than he would have had his charges suppose. Never to trust anyone under thirty has become almost a first principle of prudence for academic administrators, and not a bad rule for politicians. It is yet to be seen, however, what if anything we shall learn from this surprising and unexpected development.

Of necessity, we tend to interpret present events in terms of past experience, there being, despite the efforts of the American Academy of Arts and Sciences, as yet but little future experience to guide us. I would, however, argue that we have so far been looking to misleading analogues. We have been seeing in the flamboyance of the hippies, the bitterness of the alienated college youth, the outrageousness of the New Left, little more than mutants of the old bohemianism, the never-ending conflict of generations, and perhaps the persistence of neo-Marxist radicalism. We may be wrong. Just possibly, something more important is abroad. We may be witnessing the first heresies of liberalism.

In its familiar setting heresy refers to religious views contrary to the established dogma of a church. It will seem odd to use it to describe such assertively nonreligious phenomena as the Students for a Democratic Society. Some also will object that inasmuch as the doctrines of liberalism are derived from experience, rather than right reason, there can be no final liberal view about anything, and therefore no finally heretical dissent from such views. I suggest, however, that the phenomenon of protest we observe today is more psychological than doctrinal in origin, and that to the youth of this time secular liberalism presents itself as every bit as much a system of "established and commonly received doctrine" as did Christianity, for example, when it was the legally prescribed belief of the Holy Roman Empire, or the Massachusetts Bay Colony. To be sure, the doctrines of liberalism can be elusive. It is a conviction, Learned Hand might say, that is not too sure of itself —save on the point that it is vastly to be preferred to any creed that is. Liberals are not without tracts—hardly—but tend more to look to institutions as repositories of their beliefs, liberalism being in every sense as much a *way* of doing things, as it is a set of propositions as to what is to be done. It is not without its schisms and assuredly not without its confusions. But in all its essentials of an optimistic belief in progress, in toleration, in equality, in the rule of law, and in the possibility of attaining a high and sustained measure of human happiness here on earth, liberalism is the nigh universally accepted creed of the ruling elites of the Western world. Religious faith persists, even grows. But it does so as a private matter: supernatural beliefs have almost no influence on the course of events. Secular liberalism is triumphant. Not surprisingly, then, given especially the great value liberalism places on skepticism and inquiry, liberalism itself is beginning to be questioned.

It is notorious, of course, that among the most eminent of the literary men of this century the liberal values of the larger society have been viewed with a detachment ranging from indifference to detestation. But these were men born in the nineteenth century, and raised in a world that still had, or thought it had, some options with respect to forsaking the traditionalist, hierarchical, Christian past and embracing the new creed. To these writers it had been a mistake to do so; they withheld their own assent. Thus it may have been incongruous, even perhaps unpatriotic, for a St. Louis boy such as Mr. Eliot to show such enthusiasm for the Church of England and the Royal Family, but it was not absurd. American youth today have no such option. The liberal present is the only world they know, and if it is not to their liking, as for many it is not, their only alternative is to consider how it might evolve into something new, there being no possibility of reverting to something old. What follows is very like a spiritual crisis, and in the manner of individuals and communities that have confronted such in the past, some lapse into indifference and quietism, others escape into varied forms of stabilized hysteria, while still others turn to confront doctrine itself, and in mood of intensely felt revelation reject the very foundations of orthodoxy.

What indeed is most striking about the current surge of protest is the degree to which it reenacts in matters of style and structure the great heresies that have assailed the religious establishments of other ages. "The sun shone," Samuel Beckett writes in the opening passage of *Murphy*, "having no alternative, on the nothing new."

The forms of youthful protest at this time are many, and not all, of course, visible. But there are three clusters of behavior that are sufficiently coherent as to suggest a central tendency in each, and to offer the possibility of analogies with earlier phenomena.

The most familiar-seeming, and for that reason possibly the most deceptive of the new tendencies, is that of the New Left itself. It is familiar because it has taken a familiar form: the organization of a group defined by political objectives. Yet in truth something profoundly new may be present here, for the object of the New Left is not to capture the system but to transform it. The older radicalisms were inextricably involved with things-as-they-are, and, owing especially to Marx's view of economic determinism, they largely deprived the radical challenge to liberal capitalism of any *moral* basis: the system had a destiny that was working itself out regardless of any intentions, good or evil, on the part of mortals so innocent of the laws of economics as to suppose they, rather than things, were in the saddle. The Old Left was so utterly "materialistic" and "realistic" as to use those very terms to describe one of its defining dogmas. As Richard Blumenthal, of the Harvard Class of 1967, recently observed in the *Nation*, it is precisely this "crass materialism" that the Students for a Democratic Society reject. It is precisely the "dehumanizing" of modern society that they resent. Society's "main and transcending" concern, Tom Hayden writes, "must be the unfolding and refinement of the moral, aesthetic and logical capacities of men in a manner that creates genuine independence." However that is to be achieved, Blumenthal adds, it is not likely to be by way of "a house in the country and a two-car garage." The movement is purposely "anti-ideological, even anti-intellectual." It is precisely that rational commitment to logic and consistency—of the kind that can lead from game theory at the RAND Corporation to the use of napalm in Vietnam—that these young persons abhor.

Of late they have set about building things called "independent power bases" among the poor (a concept one fears may have been borrowed from the Strategic Air Command), but the striking fact about the famous Port Huron Statement adopted by S.D.S. in 1962 is that it barely, and then only indirectly, touches on problems such as poverty. It is addressed exclusively to middle-class intellectuals and college students: the "people of this generation, bred in at least modest comfort, housed now in universities, looking uncomfortably to the world we inherit." The world about them was so content with material affluence as to suppose it had attained stability, where in truth there was only stagnation. The theme of the Port Huron Statement is that men must *live*, not simply exist. "Some would have us believe that Americans feel contentment amidst prosperity—but might it not better be called a glaze above deeply felt anxieties about their role in the new world?" Man, they declared, had acquired a role of consumer rather than creator. His capacity for love, for creativity, for meaningful relations with others was being lost amidst the machinery of government. S.D.S. proclaimed a social system in which men would not only share one another's fate, but participate, each one, in shaping that destiny: "We believe in generosity of a kind that imprints one's unique individual qualities in the relation to other men, and to all human activity." For such a goal the Gross National Product is indeed a crude indicator of success.

Who are these outrageous young people? I suggest to you they are Christians arrived on the scene of Second Century Rome. The quality of life of that time remains difficult to assess, not least because triumphant Christianity did so much to put an end to it. James Anthony Froude, however, in his great Victorian essay "Origen and Celsus," gives us a glimpse of that world in his reconstruction of the mind of the Epicurean Celsus, a contemporary of Marcus Aurelius, who composed a tract concerning the illogicalities and misstatements of fact in Christian doctrine of such apparent force that Origen himself undertook to refute him. The second century was not unlike the twentieth, and, leaving aside the somewhat gratuitous assumptions of Europeans that they are the Greeks of this age, let there be no doubt that we are the Romans. It was a world, Froude writes, in which "Moral good and moral evil were played with as fancies in the lecture rooms; but they were fancies merely, with no bearing on life. The one practical belief was that pleasure was pleasant. The very memory disappeared that there was any evil except bodily pain. . . ." It was a tolerant world that knew too much about itself to expect words and deeds invariably to conform. "Into the midst of this strange scene of imposture, profligacy, enthusiasm and craving for light," Froude continues, "Christianity emerged out of Palestine with its message of lofty humility."

Who were these Christians? They were first of all outrageous. They were "bad citizens, refusing public employment and avoiding service in the army; and while . . . they claimed toleration for their own creed, they had no toleration for others; every god but their own they openly called a devil. . . ." They had no temples, no altars, no images, and boasted just that. "Fathers and tutors, they say, are mad or blind, unable to understand or do any good thing, given over to vain imaginations. The weavers and cobblers only are wise, they only have the secret of life, they only can show the way to peace and happiness." Of learning they had little and cared less. Nor had they any great interest in respectable people who observed the rules of society and tried to keep it running; they cared only for the outcast and miserable. To be a sinner, they seemed to say, was the one sure way to be saved. They were altogether of a seditious and revolutionary character.

Such people were a bafflement to Celsus. If he spoke bitterly about them, he observed, it was because he was bitter. One can imagine him thinking, if not quite putting to paper: "Do they not see how precarious is the balance of things; how readily it might all be brought down?" He was every bit an admirable, reasonable man. "He considered," Froude writes, "that human affairs could be best ordered by attention and obedience to the teaching of observed facts, and that superstition, however accredited by honorable objects or apparent good effects, could only be mischievous in the long run. Sorcerers, charlatans, enthusiasts were rising thick on all sides, pretending a mission from the invisible world. Of such men and such messages Celsus and his friends were inexorable antagonists." His is the tone of the sensitive, and in ways holy, Inquisitor speaking before the trial of the Maid in Shaw's *Saint Joan:* "If you have seen what I have seen of heresy, you would not think it a light thing even in the most apparently harmless and even lovable and pious origins. Heresy begins with people who are to all appearances better than their neighbors. A gentle and pious girl, or a young man who has obeyed the command of our Lord by giving all his riches to the poor, and putting on the garb of poverty, the life of austerity, and the rule of humility and charity, may be the founder of a heresy that will wreck both Church and Empire if not ruthlessly stamped out in time." The Christians, Celsus declared, were welcome to stay and become part of the commonwealth, but if that was to be their choice, they must live by its rules. Otherwise be gone. Nothing was required that a reasonable man need find objectionable: to salute the sun, or to sing a hymn to Athene did no harm to anyone. Whatever private views one might have on the subject were one's own affair. But society had a right to allegiance.

Point by point Celsus took on Christianity. Point by point he won the intellectual argument, and lost the moral and spiritual one. For he was thinking about the world, and Christians were thinking about the soul. "Most persons," Froude notes, "would now admit that Celsus spoke with wise diffidence when he hesitated at the assumption that the universe and all that it contained was created solely for the sake of man. Origen is perfectly certain that God had no other object. Sun, moon, and stars, and earth and everything living upon it were subordinated to man. In man alone, or in reference to man, the creation had its purpose and meaning." God commanded that the world provide that which is needed by man: as he is weak there must be compassion; as he is sinful there must be the forgiveness of sins; and above all, as he is Godlike, his life must be seen as sacred. If that condition has never been achieved, neither has the Western world ever been the same since first embracing the belief that it should be. Can there be any mistaking that the New Left speaks to the rational, tolerant, reasonable society of the present with the same irrationality, intolerance and unreasonableness, but possibly also the same truth with which the absurd

Christians spoke to Imperial Rome? Even Froude, professed and militant Christian, was not less a product of Imperial Britain, and in his grasp of Celsus' arguments, a certain affinity shows through. One recalls the curious moral judgments on display in his own essay, "The English in Ireland in the Eighteenth Century."

> Among reasonable beings right is forever tending to make might. Inferiority of numbers is compensated by superior cohesiveness, intelligence, and daring. The better sort of men submit willingly to be governed by those who are nobler and wiser than themselves; organization creates superiority of force; and the ignorant and the selfish may be and are justly compelled for their own advantage to obey a rule which rescues them from their natural weakness. . . . And the right of a people to self-government consists and can consist in nothing but their power to defend themselves. No other definition is possible. . . . When resistance has been tried and failed—when the inequality has been proved beyond dispute by long and painful experience—the wisdom, and ultimately the duty, of the weaker party is to accept the benefits which are offered in exchange for submission.

In truth, is there not a touch of this in the liberal doctrines of the American Empire, with its panoply of technical assistance, constitutional conventions, mutual assistance treaties and development loans, accompanied as it seems to be by the untroubled, or at least willing, use of astonishing degrees of violence to help others perceive the value of going along?

The young people of the New Left know what they want; a larger, more diffuse group can best be described as knowing what they do not want, which is what they have. These are so-called alienated students of the present generation. The psychiatrist Seymour L. Halleck recently described them as "existing in a state of chronic identity crisis. . . . [their] constant cries of 'Who am I, I don't know what I believe, I have no self' are accompanied by anxiety which while subdued is nevertheless pervasive and relentless." Affluence means nothing and the increase in personal freedom that comes with growing up is as much as anything a threat to which the individual responds with "a peculiar kind of apathy and withdrawal. . . . Having failed to develop an internalized value system which allows him to determine his direction in life, he is paralyzed when the external world removes its guidelines and restraints." Such persons, Dr. Halleck reports, will occasionally involve themselves in campus protest movements and sustain the interest for a short while, but not long, which is perhaps just as well as "When he does become involved with the activist groups he can be characterized as the most angry and irrational member of that group."

Sex and drugs are outlets, but joyless ones. They have everything, but nothing works.

Have we not seen this person through history, turning away from a religion that was failing him, rejecting its laws and opting instead for standards of conduct derived wholly from internal personal resources? The object of a liberal secular society being to induce human happiness, it more or less follows that those who reject it will choose to be unhappy and evoke their spirituality in despair more than ecstasy, but *mutatis mutandis,* are we not witnessing the emergence of secular antinomianism?

Not a precise, but an interesting parallel is to be seen in Sabbatianism, the mystical Jewish heresy that sprang up in the Holy Land in the seventeenth century and spread through large sections of Sephardic and then Ashkenazic Jewry. Gershom G. Scholem described this heresy in the Hilda Stich Stroock Lectures delivered in New York in 1938. Judaism faced a series of crises at this time: persecution, apostasy and, for some reason, a sudden impatience with the Lord: how long were the Jews to wander in exile? Scholem writes: "Doctrines arose which had one thing in common: That they tried to bridge the gap between the inner experience and the external reality which had ceased to function as its symbol." Sabbatai Zevi, a Cabalistic ascetic, and almost certainly a manic depressive, proclaimed himself the Messiah in Gaza in 1665, and eventually won a great following even though—and seemingly because—he went on to become an apostate! A singular quality of the man was that under the influence of his manic enthusiasms he would commit acts counter to religious law. Harmless enough at first, this practice developed among his radical followers into full-fledged antinomianism. "The Torah," the radical Sabbatians were fond of declaring, "is the seed-corn of Salvation, and just as the seed-corn must rot in the earth in order to sprout and bear fruit, the Torah must be subverted in order to appear in its true Messianic glory." This developed in time into a doctrine of the holiness of sin when committed by an elect who are fundamentally different from the crowd. It was of course a profound affront to Rabbinical Judaism, and in its extreme forms acquired a sinister cast indeed, but Scholem writes, "The religious . . . and moral nihilism of the radicals is after all only the confused and mistaken expression of their urge towards a fundamental regeneration of Jewish life, which under the historic conditions of those times could not find a normal expression." The heresy plagued Jewry for a century or more, and seems to have had some influence in the rise of the openly antireligious doctrines of the French Revolution. Nathan M. Pusey has voiced his own serious doubts about "the idea that the way to advance civilization is to start over," but one cannot deny the attraction of just this view for persons who find themselves inexplicably not getting from society exactly those satisfactions society most confidently promises them.

Of course, far the most visible of the new protestants are those who do not protest at all, who simply smile, wave daffodils, cover the walls of their *quartiers* with graffiti suggesting we "Legalize Living," and wear their own variety of campaign buttons the quintessential of which demands with purest obstinacy, "Nirvana Now." These are the hippies. Lilies of the field. Bearded and sandaled, they live on air, and love and, alas, drugs. They seek not to change our society, but simply to have nothing to do with it. They are in quest of experiences wholly mystical and internal on the one hand, and tribal on the other. The modern American style of the effective individual functioning in a coherent but competitive society is not for them. Hunter S. Thompson in *The New York Times Sunday Magazine* recently reported an interview with such a young woman living in the Haight-Ashbury section of San Francisco: "I love the whole world," she said, "I am the divine mother, part of Buddha, part of God, part of everything." How did she live? "From meal to meal. I have no money, no possessions, money is beautiful only when it's flowing; when it piles up it's a hang-up. We take care of each other." Did she use drugs? Yes: "When I find myself becoming confused I drop out and take a dose of acid. It's a shortcut to reality; it throws you right into it." Did she pray? "Oh yes, I pray in the morning sun. It nourishes me with its energy so I can spread love and beauty and nourish others. I never pray *for* anything; I don't need anything. Whatever turns me on is a sacrament: LSD, sex, my bells, my colors . . . that is the holy communion, you dig?"

Perhaps not. Yet those assertions would have seemed perfectly clear and altogether admirable to a member of the Brethren of the Free Spirit (or the Spiritual Libertines), a mystical Christian heresy that permeated vast areas of medieval Europe, notably the teeming cities of Flanders and the lowlands, from the twelfth century onward almost to our time. Perhaps because its adepts lived in communities within larger polities, and never took over regions for themselves, and also, being clearly heretical, tended at most times to be more or less underground, little attention has been given the Brethren. But they appear to have significantly influenced the political, if not the religious, development of Europe.

In their mystical craving for an immediate experience of God, their antinomianism, and emphasis on ecstasy, the Brethren of the Free Spirit were not unlike the Jewish Sabbatians, or for that matter the early Christians. Indeed a certain correspondence obtains among all these movements. When they took matters to an extreme of public display, the Brethren, like those before and after them, both fascinated and horrified the orthodox. "The core of the heresy," Norman Cohn writes in *The Pursuit of the Millennium*, ". . . lay in the adept's attitude towards himself: he believed that he had attained a perfection so absolute that he was incapable of sin." Sexual promiscuity became a matter of principle, and marriage was denounced as an impure state. Eroticism and ecstasy were valued beyond all things as symbols of having achieved what was in truth a state of self-deification. In an age when wealth suddenly appeared in Europe, these heretics characteristically preached a communism of property, and chose to be utterly penniless: in Cohn's words, an elite of amoral supermen.

As with Celsus, we are forced to learn most about the views of the Brethren from denunciations by their enemies. Documents from Cromwell's England, a time when the Brethren, known as Ranters, were flourishing, leave no doubt, again in Cohn's words, that the " 'Free Spirit' really was exactly what it was said to be: a system of self-exaltation often amounting to self-deification; a pursuit of total emancipation which in practice could result in antinomianism and particularly in anarchic eroticism; often also a revolutionary social doctrine which denounced the institution of private property; and aimed at its abolition." The Quakers at first saw them as kindred spirits—and the two were often lumped together by others—but efforts at rapprochement were unavailing. The saintly George Fox came upon a group of them as fellow prisoners at Charing Cross. He proposed, we cannot doubt, that they meditate together on the love of God. They called instead for beer and tobacco. A comedy of 1651 by Samuel Sheppard describes the "Character of the roaring Ranters of these Times" in terms that are familiar to say the least:

> . . . our women are all in common.
> We drink quite drunk together, share our Oaths,
> If one man's cloak be rent, all their Cloaths.

A chorus goes:

> Come away, make no delay, of mirth we are no scanters,
> Dance and sing all in a Ring, for we are Jovial Ranters

And the verses fearfully so:

> All lie down, as in a swown,
> To have a pleasing vision.
> And then rise with bared thighs,
> Who'd fear such sweet incision?

> About, about, ye Joviall rout,
> Dance antick like Hob-goblins;
> Drink and roar, and swear and whore,
> But yet no brawls or squoblings.

It is said the youth of Haight-Ashbury are not much addicted to scholarship, and they may be pardoned for giving to their service corps the name of "Diggers," after the primitivist community established near Cobham in Surrey in 1649–50. (Such folk have an instinct for agreeable settings.) But they are nonetheless mistaken. Hippies are Ranters.

Supposing all this to be so, does it matter? I believe it does. In the first place these persons matter: they number some of the fine spirits of the age. A liberal must regret the loss of belief in another as much as a decent churchman would. In the second place, these youths are trying to tell us something. It was Chesterton, surely, who described heresy as truth gone astray.

Seen in large terms, it is clear that these protests have been generated by at least three problems facing our society, each one of which can be said to arise from tendencies that are distinctively those of secular liberalism.

The first tendency is that our optimism, belief in progress, and the possibility of achieving human happiness on earth, combined with our considerable achievement in this respect at home, have led us to an increasingly dangerous and costly effort to extend our system abroad. We are in the grip of what Reinhold Niebuhr has called "The Myth of Democratic Universality," the idea that democracy is a "universal option for all nations." The irony, of course, is that it is just because our own history has been so unique that we are led to suppose that the system that has emerged from it can be made worldwide. It is an effort doomed to fail.

No civilization has ever succeeded in doing anything of the kind, and surely none whose qualities are as historically conditioned as ours should even try. But it is not just that we shall fail: something more serious is involved. In his inaugural lecture at the London School of Economics and Political Science, Michael Oakeshott, succeeding Harold Laski, made a remark of some significance here. ". . . To try to do something which is inherently impossible," he said, "is always a corrupting enterprise." That, in a word, is what I believe has happened to us overseas. As our efforts repeatedly fall short of their pronounced goals, we begin covering up, taking shortcuts, and in desperation end up doing things we would never conceivably start out to do. Princes of the Church, modest sons of small-town grocers, begin proclaiming holy wars in Asia, while the man in the street acquires an appallingly troubled vision of those who protest. In the words of a Columbia student, describing the mood of a crowd watching a peace march: "War is virility; love of peace is bohemianism and quite probably a sexual perversion."

Liberals have simply got to restrain their enthusiasm for civilizing others. It is their greatest weakness and ultimate arrogance. Bertrand Russell suggests that the great Albigensian heresy, with its quest for personal holiness and cult of poverty, was due at least in part to "disappointment of the failure of the crusades." Very likely it will be the success rather than the failure of *our* crusades that will most repel youth. Nathan Glazer has suggested that this generation is already marked by the belief that its government is capable of performing abhorrent deeds.

Not the least reason the American commitment to the diffusion of liberal democracy abroad has become a corrupting enterprise is that those values are not yet genuinely secure at home. This is an ugly fact we somehow never finally confront. At just those moments when we seem about to do so, something, somehow, comes along to distract us. Yet there persists in American opinion a powerful component that is illiberal, irrational, intolerant, anti-intellectual, and capable if unleashed of doing the most grievous damage to the fabric of our own society. A century of universal education has not destroyed this tendency, it has only made it more articulate. And it can drive the liberal elite to astonishing distortions. During this past year we have had to begin admitting that during the height of the cold war the United States government began secretly using intelligence funds to support organizations of liberal and even left-leaning students and intellectuals. This was done out of a sincere and almost certainly sound conviction that the activities of these groups would aid in the struggle against totalitarianism. Observe the irony: the liberals running American foreign policy were forced to resort, in effect, to corrupt practices—totalitarian practices if you will—in order to advance liberal causes—*because the popularly elected Congress would never dream of doing so.* The man most commonly blamed, of course, is a decent enough Irish Democrat from Brooklyn: his voting record is impeccably progressive, but neither he nor his constituents share the elite enthusiasm for intellectuals. In the explanations of it all a note even of poignancy enters: can you imagine, writes one former member of the intelligence establishment, trying to get the F.B.I. to grant security clearances to the Boston Symphony Orchestra? The problem goes beyond an affinity for Culture. We have not been able to get rid of racism, or to secure an equal place for Negroes in our society. (An effort in which liberals themselves have not been unfailingly helpful: Woodrow Wilson restored segregation to federal employment policies.) And we begin to perceive that Negroes are not immune to some of the less attractive qualities of their persecutors. We have not been able to get rid of poverty, and begin to perceive that some of our more treasured liberal reforms may have had unanticipated consequences that may even make it more difficult to do so. (Thus, having destroyed the power of the working class political party organization in our cities, we now pour millions of dollars of federal funds into projects designed to overcome the psychic effects of "powerlessness" among the poor.) And we have not rid ourselves of a brutal streak of violence. If the Administration has escalated the conflict in Vietnam, remember that the largest body of opinion in the United States would bomb the yellow bastards into the stone age, and a solid quarter specifically favors using the atom bomb. Cohn reports that the Ranters really began to flourish after the execution of Charles I.

A third problem that has contributed to the rise of youthful protest is, I would suggest, that as the life of the educated elite in America becomes more rational, more dogged of inquiry and fearless of result, the wellsprings of emotion *do* dry up, and in particular the primal sense of community begins to fade. As much for the successful as for the failed, society becomes, in Durkheim's phrase, "a dust of individuals." But to the rational liberal, the tribal attachments of blood and soil appear somehow unseemly and primitive. They repress or conceal them, much as others might a particularly lurid sexual interest. It is for this reason, I would suggest, that the nation has had such difficulties accepting the persistence of ethnicity and group cohesion as a fact both of domestic and of world politics.

Thus it is possible not only to sympathize with the new protest, but to see much that is valid in it. At the same time we are required to note that which is dangerous. The protest movement is likely to grow rather than otherwise, for the educated middle class from which it draws its strength is growing, and will soon be the dominant American social group. Moreover, the forms of protest are likely to have a striking impact for the very reason that their object is not to redirect the system, but to disrupt it, and this is never a difficult thing to do. It is entirely possible that this disruption could bring to power the forces of the right, and this is indeed an avowed strategy. *Nach Hitler uns.* As the traditional radical Tom Kahn wrote recently in *Partisan Review*, it would be silly to blame the 1966 liberal defeat in California on the New Left and the advocates of Black Power, but "it is enough to say that what they could do, they did." In some forms the rejection of existing society is merely confused, and essentially sophomoric. This winter at Harvard, for example, a document was distributed by a left group that brought to light the fact that in certain regions of Alaska community affairs are under the control of "local politicians, a control that in practice has often been responsive to local interests." At another level, it is anything but. This year, also at Harvard, when a member of the Cabinet came as an invited guest, but under arrangements that did not suit them, the students of the New Left took possession of his person. Such tactics in the early days of Fascist Italy appalled civilization. They are not less objectionable on the Harvard campus. Kahn has described the New Left as "panic disguised as moral superiority" and others have noted how that panic subtly induces a fascination with violence—the most grievous of all possible liberal heresies.

To see history as an earnest evolution from the peat bogs to John Stuart Mill, or to the 1964 Democratic platform, is a simplicity that will not much commend itself to anyone any longer. Having read Mill and having helped draft that platform, I am for one aware of greater short-comings than, say, the former's need to read Wordsworth at the onset of middle age. But neither would I reject the theme of J. H. Plumb's new series, *The History of Human Society,* "that the condition of man now is superior to what it was." Things are better, and where they are best is in the liberal industrial democracies of the North Atlantic world. I hold these regimes to be the best accommodation to the human con-dition yet devised, and will demand to know of those who reject it, just what they have in mind as a replacement. By and large the central religious and philosophical traditions of the West have led us to where we are now. Some of the heresies against that tradition have helped, and some indeed have been incorporated into it. But just as many have evidenced ugly and dangerous tendencies, of which a terrible certainty about things is surely the foremost.

The ancient Gnostics were a charming people, and there is much to be learned from their contact between the hidden, benevolent God, and the Old Testament, law-giving one. But as Scholem writes, "The term *Jewish God,* or *God of Israel,* is abusive and meant to be so. The Gnostics regarded the confusion between the two Gods, the higher, loving one, and the lower who is merely just, as a misfortune for reli-gion. It is metaphysical antisemitism in its profoundest and most effec-tive form which has found expression in these ideas and continues to do so." The Brethren of the Free Spirit are nothing if not a lovable folk, but Cohn notes, "They were in fact gnostics intent upon their own individ-ual salvation; but the gnosis at which they arrived was a quasi-mystical anarchism—an affirmation of freedom so reckless and unqualified that it amounted to a total denial of every kind of restraint and limitation." They were in fact the "remote precursers" of Bakunin and of Nietzsche: "Nietzsche's Superman, in however vulgarized a form, certainly obsessed the imagination of many of the 'armed bohemians' who made the National-Socialist revolution; and many a Communist intellectual, whether he knows it or not, owes more to Bakunin than to Marx."

To protect dissent, no matter how noxious, is one thing. To be indifferent to its growth is another. Men who would undo the system may speak: but they must be answered. The less than soul stirring belief of the liberal in due process, in restraint, in the rule of law is something more than a bourgeois *apparat*: it involves, I argue, the most profound perception of the nature of human society that has yet been achieved, and, precisely in its acknowledgment of the frailty of man and the persistence of sin and failure, it is in the deepest harmony with the central tradition of Judeo-Christian theology. It is not a belief to be frittered away in deference to a mystique of youth.

What we must do first of all is listen. Young people are trying to tell us something. They are probably right in much of what they say, however wrong their prescriptions for righting matters. Then we must respond. American liberalism needs to bring its commitments in balance with its resources—overseas and at home. Some years ago Robert Warshaw noted that "So much of 'official' American culture has been cheaply optimistic that we are likely almost by reflex to take pessimism as a measure of seriousness." It is just this unthinking encouragement of bloated expectation that leads young persons to compare forecast with outcome and to conclude that hypocrisy and duplicity are at work. What is asked of us is honesty: and what that requires is a great deal more rigor in matching our performance to our standards. It is now the only way to maintain the credibility of those standards.

If we do this we shall find, of course, that there is altogether too much that is shoddy and derivative, and in a final sense dishonest, about American life. I suspect we will also find that the awareness of this fact is more diffused within the American electorate than it will have suited the mildly dissenting liberal *cognoscenti* to imagine. It is one thing to read in Richard Rovere's "Letter from Washington" in the *New Yorker* that "This city is awash with lies and deceptions . . ." It is another to learn, as Rovere with his unmatched toughness of mind would insist, that two-thirds of the American people believe the assassination of President Kennedy to have been part of a broader conspiracy. The Catholic philosopher Michael Novak, commenting in *Commonweal* on the growing rejection of the American system by the New Left, has suggested:

> Perhaps the rumors that wealthy businessmen hired former CIA agents to assassinate Kennedy are the mythical expression of a growing

perception of reality: a majority of Americans, and certainly a very wealthy and politically powerful minority, do not wish to see a further social or political revolution in America.

These are signs of danger, as much as are the rioting cities and turbulent campuses. The foundations of popular confidence in the American system are proving to be nothing like so solid and enduring as the confident liberal establishment has supposed. The ability to respond to signs of danger is the essential condition of the ability to survive. It is not too much to declare that our ability is now being tested: it is always being tested. If we respond well to these signs of danger—and if we find a meaningful role in helping to transform the system for those who now attack it—we are likely to evolve a society of considerable nobility. But the first requirement is to acknowledge that what we have so far made of our opportunity is very much less than we should have.

The story is told of the building of the great Catholic Shrine of the Immaculate Conception in Washington: generations of truck drivers, coal miners, and cleaning women contributed their pittances to the coffers of the American hierarchy which slowly amassed the fortune required to construct this most fabulous edifice. It was a building that had everything. Nothing was spared of precious metal and lustrous stone. Nothing was spared by way of design: elements of every architectural tradition in the world were skillfully incorporated in the soaring facade and billowing dome. At last it was finished, and there followed a triumphant week of procession and ceremony, chorus and sermon. Then silence fell. The next morning, a child was praying in the crypt when a vision of Our Lady appeared. Smiling that most beatific of all smiles, she looked down and said, "Build a beautiful church on this site."

Suggestions for Writing

1. To get the feel of using your thesis to connect beginning and end, and to see how even the work of experienced writers may sometimes be improved, rephrase the thesis in each of these three essays. As you go, match each of your thesis sentences with a "restated thesis" that would serve to open the ending paragraph. Example:

Wisdom is more precious than rubies.
Wisdom, then, is a great deal more precious and useful than rubies.

2. Write an essay on some point suggested by these three writers, using (or attacking) a thesis like one of these:

    a. Idealism is unrealistic.

    b. Violence is never justified.

    c. The writer is free to choose his language and to express himself.

    d. Some ideas should be excluded from the campus.

    e. Free enterprise is opportunity for all.

3. To see the way an able essayist unfolds his thought paragraph by paragraph, take one of these three essays and draw up a list of topic sentences —one for each of his paragraphs. Use the actual topic sentence when it seems to cover everything in the paragraph; when it seems inadequate, expand and sharpen it in your own words. First, set down the writer's thesis as clearly as you can in your own words. Then put down the topic sentence for each succeeding paragraph, as it announces the paragraph's own little thesis. Be particularly careful in devising the topic sentence of the concluding paragraph; ideally, it should include and reaffirm the central thesis of the whole essay. Had you been an editor, would you have recommended that these authors reparagraph or rephrase their conclusions?

4. Write an essay illustrating from some experience or observation of your own that "The force of idealism is wasted when it does not recognize the reality of things."

I. THE SIMPLE SENTENCE
    from *The True Believer* ERIC HOFFER · *146*
    from *Triple-threat Man* WOLCOTT GIBBS · *147*

II. COORDINATION
    from *The Beautiful Flower* JOSEPH MITCHELL · *148*
    Better Writing HENRY M. SILVER · *149*

III. SUBORDINATION
    from *Death in the Afternoon* ERNEST HEMINGWAY · *150*
    from *Henry James: Symbolic Imagery in the Later Novels*
        AUSTIN WARREN · *151*

IV. PARALLELS AND PERIODIC PROSE
    Of Studies FRANCIS BACON · *152*
    from *Liberal Knowledge* JOHN HENRY NEWMAN · *153*
    from *A Portrait of the Artist as a Young Man* JAMES JOYCE · *154*

V. THE LONG AND SHORT
    from *Point Counter Point* ALDOUS HUXLEY · *155*
    from *Epilogue to Pygmalion* GEORGE BERNARD SHAW · *156*

Sentences

A Notebook of Styles

With writing as with football, you need practice
in doing all kinds of superhuman exercises so that,
put to the test, you can carry your thought in any
slippery field, and catch the concept that seems
beyond all reach. Here, then, are various styles of
sentence to exercise your pen. They run from the
simple to the extremely complex—as the writers'
thoughts and temperaments grow more subtle. In
following the thoughts, try to enjoy each for its
rhythmic handling, keeping your eyes open for

the way the feat is done. You will be asked to imitate them, to limber and stretch your muscles. Once you have tried the extremes of simplicity and complexity, you can find your own middle ground, and hold it too, since you now can cover both extremes. Each author, of course, writes more than one kind of sentence, but each clearly prefers a particular kind, as the following groups show.

Group I. The Simple Sentence. Writers like Hoffer and Gibbs demonstrate how even the simple, straightforward sentence offers wide variety. Hoffer uses it directly and epigrammatically, as if he were writing proverbs: "We cannot hate those we despise." Gibbs, on the other hand, arches the simple sentence into interesting interruptions and extensions: "This intelligence, in addition to serving a useful purpose—there is too little time for a man to waste any of it on lost causes—produced in me a feeling of nearly perfect detachment."

Group II. Coordination. Mitchell and Silver show two kinds of coordination, the "equal ordering" of equivalent clauses (or sentences) by linking them in a straight line with *and*'s or semicolons, or by letting them stand as simple sentences in a row.

Group III. Subordination. Here the writer's thought grows subtle as he adds thoughts of less importance to his main clause, tying them in with prepositions, relative pronouns, or any other subordinating word—*with, in, who, which, when.*

Group IV. Parallels and Periodic Prose. Those writers, demonstrating additional varieties of coordination and subordination, emphasize parallels in their construction; that is, they put equivalent thoughts into identical phrases and repeat the words linking them—as in Bacon's *for*, Newman's *however enlightened* and *however profound*, or Joyce's *that as*. Notice how often their sentences are "periodic," suspending or holding back some part of the meaning until it can be dropped into place at the period.

Group V. The Long and Short. Huxley and Shaw work long and short sentences in rhythmic spans and contrasts. From a simple short sentence, they will move ahead in lengthening strides, only to come short for emphasis and then move on again.

I/THE SIMPLE SENTENCE

FROM *The True Believer*
Eric Hoffer

It is easier to hate an enemy with much good in him than one who is all bad. We cannot hate those we despise. The Japanese had an advantage over us in that they admired us more than we admired them. They could hate us more fervently than we could hate them. The Americans are poor haters in international affairs because of their innate feeling of superiority over all foreigners. An American's hatred for a fellow American (for Hoover or Roosevelt) is far more virulent than any antipathy he can work up against foreigners. It is of interest that the backward South shows more xenophobia than the rest of the country. Should Americans begin to hate foreigners wholeheartedly, it will be an indication that they have lost confidence in their own way of life.

The undercurrent of admiration in hatred manifests itself in the inclination to imitate those we hate. Thus every mass movement shapes itself after its specific devil. Christianity at its height realized the image of the antichrist. The Jacobins practiced all the evils of the tyranny they had risen against. Soviet Russia is realizing the purest and most colossal example of monopolistic capitalism. Hitler took the Protocols of the Wise Men of Zion for his guide and textbook; he followed them "down to the veriest detail."

It is startling to see how the oppressed almost invariably shape themselves in the image of their hated oppressors. That the evil men do lives after them is partly due to the fact that those who have reason to hate the evil most shape themselves after it and thus perpetuate it. It is obvious, therefore, that the influence of the fanatic is bound to be out of all proportion to his abilities. Both by converting and antagonizing, he shapes the world in his own image. Fanatic Christianity put its imprint upon the ancient world both by gaining adherents and by evoking in its pagan opponents a strange fervor and a new ruthlessness. Hitler imposed himself upon the world both by promoting Nazism and by forcing the democracies to become zealous, intolerant and ruthless. Communist Russia shapes both its adherents and its opponents in its own image.

Thus, though hatred is a convenient instrument for mobilizing a community for defense, it does not, in the long run, come cheap. We pay for it by losing all or many of the values we have set out to defend.

FROM *Triple-threat Man*
Wolcott Gibbs

Twice in my life, for reasons that escape me now, though I'm sure they were discreditable, I allowed myself to be persuaded that I ought to take a hand in turning out a musical comedy. Both these ventures reached Broadway, though my connection with them had ceased long before that, and both closed with inconceivable rapidity. A writer, I suppose, discovers the limits of his talent only through a system of trial and error, and, whatever else I may have learned from these two fiascoes, I came away from them knowing surely and forever that this particular form of art was not for me. This intelligence, in addition to serving a useful purpose—there is too little time for a man to waste any of it on lost causes—produced in me a feeling of nearly perfect detachment. It is an embarrassing fact that I seldom see a straight play, either a comedy or a drama, without the conviction that if I had been asked, I could have provided the author with several very valuable suggestions. A musical, however, is quite another matter. I have no idea how the damn things get there in the first place—by what weird midnight prodigies of collaboration—and I certainly have no coherent advice to offer anyone about fixing things up, being comparatively accomplished only in the construction of English sentences, a knack approximately as useful in these entertainments as the ability to knit.

This lack of the writer's habitual nagging instinct to improve, coupled with an indifference to the form as a means of personal expression, makes me, of course, the practically ideal (or totally disembodied) critic of all musical comedies, and we will proceed immediately to the one called "The Music Man," which is now turning thousands away from the box office at the Majestic. This piece, the all but unassisted work of Meredith Willson, who contrived the book, the music, and the lyrics, received about the most remarkable set of notices in my memory, being greeted by one stunned worshipper as one of the three most exhilarating experiences he had undergone in the theatre in twenty-six years, and by his colleagues as an offering comparing very favorably with "Oklahoma!," "Guys and Dolls," "My Fair Lady," and almost anything else you care to name. I myself have nothing against "The Music Man," regarding it, in fact, as an exceptionally cheerful offering, but it is not as good as all that.

II / COORDINATION

FROM *The Beautiful Flower*
Joseph Mitchell

In the early thirties, I covered Police Headquarters at night for a newspaper, and I often ate in a restaurant named the Grotta Azzurra, which is only a block over, at the southwest corner of Broome and Mulberry, and stays open until two. I still go down there every now and then. The Grotta Azzurra is a classical downtown New York South Italian restaurant: it is a family enterprise, it is in the basement of a tenement, it has marble steps, it displays in a row of bowls propped up on a table dry samples of all the kinds of *pasta* it serves, its kitchen is open to view through an arch, and it has scenes of the Bay of Naples painted on its walls. Among its specialties is striped bass cooked in clam broth with clams, mussels, shrimp, and squid, and it may be possible to find a better fish-and-shellfish dish in one of the great restaurants of the world, but I doubt it. I had a late dinner in the Grotta Azzurra one Sunday night recently, and then sat and talked for a while with two of the waiters at a table in back. We talked about the upheavals in the Police Department under Commissioner Adams; a good many police officials eat in the Grotta Azzurra, and the waiters take an interest in police affairs. I left around midnight and walked west on Broome, heading for the subway. At the northeast corner of Broome and Cleveland Place, just across Broome from Headquarters, there is an eight-story brick building that is called Police Headquarters Annex. It is a dingy old box of a building; it was originally a factory, a Loft candy factory. It houses the Narcotics Squad, the Pickpocket and Confidence Squad, the Missing Persons Bureau, the Bureau of Criminal Information, and a number of other specialized squads and bureaus. I was about halfway up the block when a middle-aged man carrying a briefcase came out of the Annex and started across the street, and as he passed under a street lamp I saw that he was a detective I used to know quite well named Daniel J. Campion. I was surprised that he should be coming out of the Annex at that hour, particularly on a Sunday night, for some months earlier I had heard in the Grotta Azzurra that he had retired from the Police Department on a pension of thirty-five hundred dollars a year and had gone to work for the Pinkertons, the big private-detective agency. He was an Acting Captain when he retired, and the commanding officer of the Pickpocket and Confidence Squad. He had been a member of this squad for over twenty-five years, and had long been considered the best authority in the United States on pickpockets, confidence-game operators, and swindlers. He was also the Department's expert on gypsies. . . .

Better Writing
Henry M. Silver

There is one, but one, certain way to reduce the cost of printing, and that is to sell more copies of what you print. This needs no demonstration; it is in the axiom class. Similarly there is only one way to sell more copies, and that is to write so that more people can understand what you have to say and are attracted by the way you say it. This applies even to specialized books. The marginal sales achieved by clarity and order may not numerically be great but they have their effect. A book which costs $3.38 per copy in an edition of 500 will cost $1.97 in an edition of 1,000—if all are sold.

This matter of improving the writing of scholarship is approached too often on tiptoe or hurried by. It must be faced. At a recent session on scholarly communication there was more time devoted to television than to books. One graduate dean and one commercial publisher made concrete appeals for better writing. Discreet pauses followed; then the discussion hastened on to other matters.

The reason for this discretion must be a feeling that better writing is not achieved but is inherited, through one's genes; you have it or you don't. This is contrary to available testimony. Better writing is self-discipline and a willingness to take pains. Was it not Pascal who apologized for writing a long letter by saying he did not have time to write a shorter? Better scholarly writing is a willingness to do it all over again, striking out redundancies, making two sentences out of one, pausing at each multicellular expression to see if a plain word will not do instead. Those who will not take the time to do these things belong to the "adumbrate" school of writing. The books produced by the members of this flourishing academy do not circulate widely. Perhaps they gain distinction from scarcity. Certainly they achieve higher printing cost.

Better writing is not the ornament of scholarship; it is an element essential to the reduction of printing expense.

III/SUBORDINATION

FROM *Death in the Afternoon*
Ernest Hemingway

Cagancho is a gypsy, subject to fits of cowardice, altogether without integrity, who violates all the rules, written and unwritten, for the conduct of a matador but who, when he receives a bull that he has confidence in, and he has confidence in them very rarely, can do things which all bullfighters do in a way they have never been done before and sometimes standing absolutely straight with his feet still, planted as though he were a tree, with the arrogance and grace that gypsies have and of which all other arrogance and grace seems an imitation, moves the cape spread full as the pulling jib of a yacht before the bull's muzzle so slowly that the art of bullfighting, which is only kept from being one of the major arts because it is impermanent, in the arrogant slowness of his veronicas becomes, for the seeming minutes that they endure, permanent. That is the worst sort of flowery writing, but it is necessary to try to give the feeling, and to some one who has never seen it a simple statement of the method does not convey the feeling. Any one who has seen bullfights can skip such flowerishness and read the facts which are much more difficult to isolate and state. The fact is that the gypsy, Cagancho, can sometimes, through the marvellous wrists that he has, perform the usual movements of bullfighting so slowly that they become, to oldtime bullfighting, as the slow motion picture is to the ordinary motion picture. It is as though a diver could control his speed in the air and prolong the vision of a swan dive, which is a jerk in actual life, although in photographs it seems a long glide, to make it a long glide like the dives and leaps we sometimes take in dreams. Other bullfighters who have or have had this ability with their wrists are Juan Belmonte and, occasionally with the cape, Enrique Torres and Felix Rodriguez.

FROM *Henry James: Symbolic Imagery in the Later Novels*
Austin Warren

The general occasions of the "last period" are tolerably clear, if scarcely of the same order of being. There is, first, the gradual loss of the larger audience reached by *Daisy Miller* and the novels of Howells; then, the judgment that country-house week ends and the "season" in London had already provided saturation; then, the shift, in compositional method, from writing to dictation; then, the impetus of admiration from sympathetic younger writers and the allied, induced, partial participation in the new literary movement of the nineties, the "aesthetic" movement associated with the names of Pater, Wilde, Harland, the *Yellow Book*, and—by extension—of Stevenson, Conrad, Crane, Ford Madox Ford; then, the just completed period of writing for the theater, which produced not only *Guy Domville* but also a conception of the novel as drama; last, the influence, through Maeterlinck and, especially, the later Ibsen, of *symbolisme,* and the return thereby to Hawthorne and a deeper psychology.

The retirement to Rye, which occurred in 1897 when James was fifty-four, distinguished between his life of experience and his life from "past accumulations" (as he once called it). His peregrinations over, he set himself, masterwise, to producing a world compact of all that he had been able, coherently, to think and feel.

Then the process of dictation, beginning with *The Spoils of Poynton*, had its psychological and stylistic consequences. A timid, slow-speaking, stammering boy, Henry had rarely been able to make himself heard at the parental breakfast table. Dictation offered dictatorship: his own voice, uninterrupted by those of more rapid speakers, enabled him to have his oral say in a style which is nearer to his father's than to William's, but slower than his father's. Henry's later manner is an allegro slowed down to a largo, the conversational in apotheosis. "Literary" as, all sprinkled with its commas of parenthesis, it looks on paper, it is an oral style; and, verifiably, it becomes clear, almost luminous, if recommitted to the voice.

IV/PARALLELS AND PERIODIC PROSE

Of Studies
Francis Bacon

Studies serve for delight, for ornament, and for ability. Their chief use for delight, is in privateness and retiring; for ornament, is in discourse; and for ability, is in the judgment and disposition of business. For expert men can execute, and perhaps judge of particulars, one by one; but the general counsels, and the plots and marshalling of affairs, come best from those that are learned. To spend too much time in studies is sloth; to use them too much for ornament is affectation; to make judgment wholly by their rules, is the humour of a scholar. They perfect nature, and are perfected by experience: for natural abilities are like natural plants, that need pruning by study; and studies themselves do give forth directions too much at large, except they be bounded in by experience. Crafty men contemn studies, simple men admire them, and wise men use them; for they teach not their own use; but that is a wisdom without them, and above them, won by observation. Read not to contradict and confute; nor to believe and take for granted; nor to find talk and discourse; but to weigh and consider. Some books are to be tasted, others to be swallowed, and some few to be chewed, and digested; that is, some books are to be read only in parts; others to be read, but not curiously; and some few to be read wholly, and with diligence and attention. Some books also may be read by deputy, and extracts made of them by others; but that would be only in the less important arguments, and the meaner sort of books; else distilled books are like common distilled waters, flashy things. Reading maketh a full man; conference a ready man; and writing an exact man. And therefore, if a man write little, he had need have a great memory; if he confer little, he had need have a present wit; and if he read little, he had need have much cunning, to seem to know that he doth not. Histories make men wise; poets witty; the mathematics subtle; natural philosophy deep; moral grave; logic and rhetoric able to contend. *Abeunt studia in mores.* Nay, there is no stond or impediment in the wit, but may be wrought out by fit studies: like as diseases of the body may have appropriate exercises. Bowling is good for the stone and reins; shooting for the lungs and breast; gentle walking for the stomach; riding for the head, and the like. So if a man's wit be wandering, let him study the mathematics; for in demonstrations, if his wit be called away ever so little, he must begin again. If his wit be not apt to distinguish and find diffcrences, let him study the schoolmen, for they are *cymini sectores.* If he be not apt to beat over matters, and to call up one thing to prove and illustrate another, let him study the lawyers' cases. So every defect of the mind may have a special receipt.

FROM *Liberal Knowledge*
John Henry Newman

. . . Knowledge is one thing, virtue is another; good sense is not conscience, refinement is not humility, nor is largeness and justness of view faith. Philosophy, however enlightened, however profound, gives no command over the passions, no influential motives, no vivifying principles. Liberal Education makes not the Christian, not the Catholic, but the gentleman. It is well to be a gentleman, it is well to have a cultivated intellect, a delicate taste, a candid, equitable, dispassionate mind, a noble and courteous bearing in the conduct of life;—these are the connatural qualities of a large knowledge; they are the objects of a University; I am advocating, I shall illustrate and insist upon them; but still, I repeat, they are no guarantee for sanctity or even for conscientiousness, they may attach to the man of the world, to the profligate, to the heartless,—pleasant, alas, and attractive as he shows when decked out in them. Taken by themselves, they do but seem to be what they are not; they look like virtue at a distance, but they are detected by close observers, and on the long run; and hence it is that they are popularly accused of pretence and hypocrisy, not, I repeat, from their own fault, but because their professors and their admirers persist in taking them for what they are not, and are officious in arrogating for them a praise to which they have no claim. Quarry the granite rock with razors, or moor the vessel with a thread of silk; then may you hope with such keen and delicate instruments as human knowledge and human reason to contend against those giants, the passion and the pride of man.

Surely we are not driven to theories of this kind, in order to vindicate the value and dignity of Liberal Knowledge. Surely the real grounds on which its pretensions rest are not so very subtle or abstruse, so very strange or improbable. Surely it is very intelligible to say, and that is what I say here, that Liberal Education, viewed in itself, is simply the cultivation of the intellect, as such, and its object is nothing more or less than intellectual excellence. . . .

FROM *A Portrait of the Artist as a Young Man*
James Joyce

He drew forth a phrase from his treasure and spoke it softly to himself:
—A day of dappled seaborne clouds.—
The phrase and the day and the scene harmonised in a chord. Words. Was it their colours? He allowed them to glow and fade, hue after hue: sunrise gold, the russet and green of apple orchards, azure of waves, the grey-fringed fleece of clouds. No, it was not their colours: it was the poise and balance of the period itself. Did he then love the rhythmic rise and fall of words better than their associations of legend and colour? Or was it that, being as weak of sight as he was shy of mind, he drew less pleasure from the reflection of the glowing sensible world through the prism of a language many-coloured and richly storied than from the contemplation of an inner world of individual emotions mirrored perfectly in a lucid supple periodic prose?

.   .   .   .   .

. . . . His father's whistle, his mother's mutterings, the screech of an unseen maniac were to him now so many voices of offending and threatening to humble the pride of his youth. He drove their echoes even out of his heart with an execration: but, as he walked down the avenue and felt the grey morning light falling about him through the dripping trees and smelt the strange wild smell of the wet leaves and bark, his soul was loosed of her miseries.

The rain laden trees of the avenue evoked in him, as always, memories of the girls and women in the plays of Gerhart Hauptmann; and the memory of their pale sorrows and the fragrance falling from the wet branches mingled in a mood of quiet joy. His morning walk across the city had begun; and he foreknew that as he passed the sloblands of Fairview he would think of the cloistral silverveined prose of Newman; that as he walked along the North Strand Road, glancing idly at the windows of the provision shops, he would recall the dark humour of Guido Cavalcanti and smile; that as he went by Baird's stone cutting works in Talbot Place the spirit of Ibsen would blow through him like a keen wind, a spirit of wayward boyish beauty; and that passing a grimy marine dealer's shop beyond the Liffey he would repeat the song by Ben Jonson which begins:

> I was not wearier where I lay.

V/THE LONG AND SHORT

FROM *Point Counter Point*
Aldous Huxley

Meanwhile the music played on—Bach's Suite in B minor, for flute and strings. Young Tolley conducted with his usual inimitable grace, bending in swan-like undulations from the loins and tracing luscious arabesques on the air with his waving arms, as though he were dancing to the music. A dozen anonymous fiddlers and cellists scraped at his bidding. And the great Pongileoni glueily kissed his flute. He blew across the mouth hole and a cylindrical air column vibrated; Bach's meditations filled the Roman quadrangle. In the opening *largo* John Sebastian had, with the help of Pongileoni's snout and the air column, made a statement: There are grand things in the world, noble things; there are men born kingly; there are real conquerors, intrinsic lords of the earth. But of an earth that is, oh! complex and multitudinous, he had gone on to reflect in the fugal *allegro*. You seem to have found the truth; clear, definite, unmistakable, it is announced by the violins; you have it, you triumphantly hold it. But it slips out of your grasp to present itself in a new aspect among the cellos and yet again in terms of Pongileoni's vibrating air column. The parts live their separate lives; they touch, their paths cross, they combine for a moment to create a seemingly final and perfected harmony, only to break apart again.

Each is always alone and separate and individual. "I am I," asserts the violin; "the world revolves round me." "Round me," calls the cello. "Round me," the flute insists. And all are equally right and equally wrong; and none of them will listen to the others.

In the human fugue there are eighteen hundred million parts. The resultant noise means something perhaps to the statistician, nothing to the artist. It is only by considering one or two parts at a time that the artist can understand anything. Here, for example, is one particular part; and John Sebastian puts the case. The Rondeau begins, exquisitely and simply melodious, almost a folk song. It is a young girl singing to herself of love, in solitude, tenderly mournful. A young girl singing among the hills, with the clouds drifting overhead. But solitary as one of the floating clouds, a poet had been listening to her song. The thoughts that it provoked in him are the Sarabande that follows the Rondeau. His is a slow and lovely meditation on the beauty (in spite of squalor and stupidity), the profound goodness (in spite of all the evil), the oneness (in spite of such bewildering diversity) of the world. It is a beauty, a goodness, a unity that no intellectual research can discover, that analysis dispels, but of whose reality the spirit is from time to time suddenly and overwhelmingly convinced. A girl singing to herself under the clouds suffices to create the certitude. Even a fine morning is enough. Is it illusion or the revelation of profoundest truth? Who knows? Pongileoni blew, the fiddlers drew their rosined horsehair across the stretched intestines of lambs; through the long Sarabande the poet slowly meditated his lovely and consoling certitude.

FROM *Epilogue to Pygmalion*
George Bernard Shaw

[Clara] was, in short, an utter failure, an ignorant, incompetent, pretentious, unwelcome, penniless, useless little snob; and though she did not admit these disqualifications (for nobody ever faces unpleasant truths of this kind until the possibility of a way out dawns on them) she felt their effects too keenly to be satisfied with her position.

Clara had a startling eyeopener when, on being suddenly wakened to enthusiasm by a girl of her own age who dazzled her and produced in her a gushing desire to take her for a model, and gain her friendship, she discovered that this exquisite apparition had graduated from the gutter in a few months time. It shook her so violently, that when Mr. H. G. Wells lifted her on the point of his puissant pen, and placed her at the angle of view from which the life she was leading and the society to which she clung appeared in its true relation to real human needs and worthy social structure, he effected a conversion and a conviction of sin comparable to the most sensational feats of General Booth or Gypsy Smith. Clara's snobbery went bang. Life suddenly began to move with her. Without knowing how or why, she began to make friends and enemies. Some of the acquaintances to whom she had been a tedious or indifferent or ridiculous affliction, dropped her: others became cordial. To her amazement she found that some "quite nice" people were saturated with Wells, and that this accessibility to ideas was the secret of their niceness. People she had thought deeply religious, and had tried to conciliate on that tack with disastrous results, suddenly took an interest in her, and revealed a hostility to conventional religion which she had never conceived possible except among the most desperate characters. They made her read Galsworthy; and Galsworthy exposed the vanity of Largelady Park and finished her. It exasperated her to think that the dungeon in which she had languished for so many unhappy years had been unlocked all the time, and that the impulses she had so carefully struggled with and stifled for the sake of keeping well with society, were precisely those by which alone she could have come into any sort of sincere human contact. In the radiance of these discoveries, and the tumult of their reaction, she made a fool of herself as freely and conspicuously as when she so rashly adopted Eliza's expletive in Mrs. Higgins's drawing room; for the newborn Wellsian had to find her bearings almost as ridiculously as a baby; but nobody hates a baby for its ineptitudes, or thinks the worse of it for trying to eat the matches; and Clara lost no friends by her follies. They laughed at her to her face this time; and she had to defend herself and fight it out as best she could.

Suggestions for Writing

1. Now, to stretch those muscles, imitate or parody each of the authors in this chapter, two or three sentences for each passage.

2. Write a 100-word sentence, in which you subordinate everything to one, and only one, main clause. You might look at Warren's second sentence (140 words); or you might start with a series of parallel clauses—"When I sit down to write, when I try to think of something to say, when no ideas seem to come at all . . ."—and—who knows?—you may end with a cloistral silver-veined period worthy of Newman.

3. Write four or five epigrammatic sentences like Hoffer's "We cannot hate those we despise" or ". . . every mass movement shapes itself after its specific devil."

4. Now take these same sentences and see if you can enhance them by springing them apart with interruptive phrases and clauses, and by extending them with further subordination: "We cannot—even if we wish—hate those we despise, because we despise only those beneath our contempt."

5. Write a page or so, attempting as wide a variety of short and long sentences as you can manage. Follow a long one with one extremely short; then lengthen your steps to long again, as with "Clara's snobbery went bang" and its successors in Shaw's passage.

The Evolution of Ethics ALBERT SCHWEITZER · *160*
The Real Secret of Piltdown LOREN EISELEY · *169*
Science and the Savages G. K. CHESTERTON · *177*
Sentence Maker HENRY SEIDEL CANBY · *181*

Sentences in Exposition

Here is style in pursuit of clarity, as the author measures out his thought to persuade his reader. Each writer is explaining something he believes highly significant. Of his essay, Schweitzer wrote Mrs. Carleton Smith, who translated it from the French: "This is something very important to me, as it expresses the dominating idea in my thinking." Schweitzer's sentences, skillfully reproduced by Mrs. Smith, are simple and unadorned. His thinking is straightforward and gen-

159

erally "coordinate." Eiseley, also pursuing the clear statement, nevertheless runs to subordination, as in the second sentences of his first two paragraphs. The simple question that he raises draws a multiple explanation, thoughtfully ranked and balanced; and his subordination swells in grander segments as, toward the end, he marvels at the galaxy overhead. Chesterton, like Schweitzer, is basically coordinate: "The answer to the riddle is in England; it is in London; nay, it is in his own heart." But like an orator, he runs his coordinates in parallel and contrasts them epigrammatically: "student of nature" against "student of human nature," for instance. He also can subordinate—as with "man of science" in his second paragraph—and play off short against long.

Canby's essay on Thoreau may serve to summarize the evidence of this section: a writer's sentences—his style—are the writer's very *self*, engaging his particular subject and trying to engage his general reader. To some extent the subject, to some extent the audience, conditions the style; but the author chooses the subject and the word, and his disposition moves his sentences as he develops his style somewhere between the need to express and the need to communicate. Thoreau is mostly concerned with expression— with getting the inside out—and certainly this is the deeper side; for true expression will communicate, but pure communication may be untrue.

To heighten your sense that style may be the man, and that writing shows character, try to form an idea of each writer's personality as you read. Keep an eye on the play of length in his sentences, and be on watch for things from the physical world—sticks, stones, apples, trees. Which writer's sentences have the highest physical contents? When does a man seem to reach for metaphor?

The Evolution of Ethics
Albert Schweitzer

In a very general sense, ethics is the name we give to our concern for good behavior. We feel an obligation to consider not only our own personal well-being but also that of others and of human society as a whole, and it is in the extension of this notion of solidarity with others that the first evolution of ethics is to be seen.

For the primitive man the circle of solidarity is limited to those whom he can look upon as his blood relatives—that is to say, the members of his tribe, who are to him his family. I am speaking from experience. In my hospital I have primitives. When I happen to ask a hospitalized tribesman, who is not himself bedridden, to render little services to a bedridden patient, he will consent only if the latter belongs to his tribe. If not, he will answer me candidly: "This, no brother for me," and neither attempts to persuade him nor threats will make him do this favor for a stranger.

However, as man starts reflecting upon himself and his behavior toward others, he gradually realizes that all men are his brothers and neighbors. Slowly he reaches a point where he sees the circle of his responsibilities enlarged to comprise all human beings with whom he is in contact.

In the history of man, this idea of responsibility toward others has been wholly or partially formulated in various cultures at various times. It was reached by the Chinese thinkers: Lao-tse, born in 604 B.C.; Kung Fu-tse (Confucius), 551–479 B.C.; Meng-tse, 372–289 B.C.; Tchou-ang-tse, fourth century B.C. It was also proclaimed by the Israelite prophets of the eighth century B.C.: Amos, Hosea, and Isaiah. As proclaimed by Jesus and Saint Paul, the idea that man obligates himself to all human beings became an integral part of the Christian system of ethics.

For the great thinkers of India, too, whether they belonged to Brahmanism, Buddhism, or Hinduism, the idea of the brotherhood of man was included in their metaphysical notion of existence, but they had difficulty giving it the proper importance in their ethics because they could not abolish the barriers erected between men in India by the different castes sanctioned by tradition.

Zarathustra, who lived in about the seventh century B.C., was also prevented from reaching the notion of the full brotherhood of man because he had to differentiate between those who believed in Ormuzd, the god of Light and Good, and the nonbelievers who remained in the power of devils. This forced the believers to fight for the coming of the reign of Ormuzd and to consider the nonbelievers as enemies and treat them as such. To understand this, one must remember that the believers were Bactrian tribes who had become sedentary and aspired to live as honest and peaceful families, while the nonbelievers were nomadic tribes who dwelt in the desert and lived from pillage.

Plato and Aristotle and the other thinkers of the classic period of Greek philosophy limited their consideration to the Greek freeman, who did not have to earn his subsistence. All those who did not belong to this aristocracy were dismissed as men of inferior quality in whom there was no need to be concerned.

It was not until the second epoch of Greek thought, when the simultaneous blossoming of Stoicism and Epicureanism occurred, that the idea of the equality of men and of the sympathy which attaches us to all human beings was recognized by these two schools. The most remarkable protagonist of this new conception was the Stoic Panaetius, who lived in the second century B.C. He was the prophet of humanism, and even though the idea of the brotherhood of man never became popular in antiquity, the very fact that philosophy had proclaimed it as a concept dictated by reason was of great importance for its future.

However, this concept has never enjoyed the full authority which it deserves. Down to our time, it has ceaselessly been compromised by the stressing of differences—differences of race, of religious beliefs, and of nationalities—which turn our fellow man into a stranger to whom we owe nothing but indifference, if not contempt.

As we trace the evolution of ethics, we are aware of the influence exerted by the various concepts of the material world. There are the affirmative concepts which insist that interest must be taken in material matters and in the existence we lead on this earth. Others, on the contrary, advocate a negative attitude, urging that we detach ourselves from whatever has to do with the world, including our own existence on earth. Affirmation conforms with our natural feeling. Negation contradicts it. Affirmation invites us to be at home in this world and to throw ourselves voluntarily into action; negation requires that we live in the world as strangers and that we choose a passive role. By its very nature, ethics is affiliated with affirmation. One must be active if one is to serve the ideal of Good. An affirmative concept of the world produces a favorable climate for the development of ethics, while negation, on the contrary, hampers it. Negation of the world was professed by the thinkers of India and by the Christians of antiquity and of the Middle Ages; affirmation by the Chinese thinkers, the Israelite prophets, Zarathustra, and the European thinkers of the Renaissance and of the modern day.

In the thinkers of India, this negative concept of the world was the result of their conviction that true existence is immaterial, immutable, and external and that the worldly existence is fictitious, deceitful, and transient. The world that we consider as real was for them but a mirage of the immaterial world in time and space. By taking interest in this phantasmagoria and in the part he plays in it, they argued, man made a mistake. The only behavior compatible with the true knowledge of the nature of existence is nonactivity.

To a degree, nonactivity does have ethical characteristics. By detaching himself from worldly matters, man renounces the egotism that material interests and mere covetousness arouse in him. Furthermore, an essential aspect of nonactivity is nonviolence.

The thinkers of Brahmanism, of Samkhya, of Jainism, as well as of Buddhism, exalt nonviolence, which they call ahimsa; indeed, they consider it as the sublime principle. However, it is imperfect and incomplete because it concedes to man the egotism to be preoccupied entirely with his salvation. It does not command him in the name of compassion but in the name of metaphysical theories. It demands merely abstention from evil, rather than the positive activity inspired by the notion of Good.

Only a system of ethics affiliated with the affirmation of the world can be natural and complete. Buddha, who rises against the cold Brahmanic doctrine by preaching pity, cannot completely resist the temptation to forgo the principle of nonactivity. He gives in, more than once, unable to keep himself from accomplishing acts of charity or from recommending them to his disciples. Under the cover of ethics the affirmation of the world carries on, in India, a persistent struggle against the principle of nonactivity. In Hinduism, which is a religious movement against the exigencies of Brahmanism, affirmation is recognized as the equal of nonactivity. The reconciliation of the two is set forth in the *Bhagavad Gita.*

Man can believe that he is authorized to take part in the material world only as a spectator. But likewise he has the right to believe that he is called to play an active part. Activity, then, is justified by the spirit which guides it. The man who practices it with the intention of accomplishing the will of God is as right as he who raises the question of nonactivity. Nowadays, the thinkers of India make great concessions to the principle of activity, claiming that it is found in the Upanishads. This is true. The explanation is that the Aryans of India in ancient times, as we learn it from the Veda, had an existence penetrated with naïve *joie de vivre*. The Brahmanic doctrine of negation of the world appears side by side with the concept of affirmation only in the Upanishads, the sacred texts of the first thousand years B.C.

Christianity in early times and in the Middle Ages professed negation of the world without, however, reaching the extremes of nonactivity. Its denial of the world was of a different nature from that of the thinkers of India: to the early Christians the world was not a phantasmagoria, it was an imperfect world destined to be transformed into the perfect world of the kingdom of God. The idea of the kingdom of God was created by the Israelite prophets of the eighth century B.C.

In announcing the imminence of the transformation of the material world into the kingdom of God, Jesus exhorted men to seek the perfection required for participation in the new world. He asked man to detach himself from this world, the better to be preoccupied by the practice of Good. He allowed man to detach himself from material things, but not from his duties toward other men. In Jesus' ethics, activity kept all its rights and all its obligations. This is where Christianity differs from Buddha's religion, with which it shares the idea of compassion. Because it is animated by the spirit of activity, Christian ethics has a certain affinity with the affirmation of the world.

The transformation of the world into the kingdom of God was what the early Christians were looking for immediately, but it never occurred. During antiquity and the Middle Ages, Christianity remained in a situation of having to lose hope in this world, without the compensating hope, which had sustained the early Christians, of seeing the new world at hand. In the Middle Ages there was no enthusiastic affirmation of the world; actually this did not take place until the Renaissance. Christianity identified itself with this new enthusiastic affirmation of the world during the sixteenth and seventeenth centuries. Renaissance ethics—apart from the ideal of perfecting oneself, which came from Jesus—attempted subsequently to create new and better material and spiritual conditions for the existence of human society. From then on, Christian ethics found a goal for its activity and so reached its full bloom. From the union of the Christian and the Renaissance enthusiasm for the world is born the civilization in which we live and which we have to maintain and improve.

In the first century of the Christian era, thinkers of Stoicism—Seneca, Epictetus, and the emperor Marcus Aurelius—following the steps of Panaetius, the creator of the idea of humanism, came to consider Love as the virtue of virtues. Their system of ethics is about the same as that of the great Chinese thinkers. They have in common not only the principle of Love, but also the conviction that it proceeds from reason and is thoroughly reasonable.

During the first and second centuries of the Christian era, the Greco-Roman philosophy seemed to profess the same ethical ideal as that of Christianity. The possibility of agreement between the ancient and Christian worlds existed, but it did not happen. Ethical Stoicism did not become popular. Moreover, it accused Christianity of being a superstition because Christianity claimed that a divine revelation had taken place in Jesus Christ, and was awaiting the miraculous coming of a new world. Christianity, on the other hand, scorned philosophy as a guiding wisdom for this world. What separated Christianity and Stoicism was the fact that the Greco-Roman philosophy adhered to the idea of the affirmation of the world, whereas Christianity adhered to the idea of its negation. No agreement was possible.

Agreement did occur, but only after centuries. When Christianity became more familiar with the enthusiastic affirmation of the world, which the Renaissance had bequeathed to European thought; it at the same time became acquainted with ethical Stoicism and noted with surprise that Jesus' principle of Love had also been stated as a rational truth. Thus it was deduced that the fundamental ideas of religion were revealed truths, confirmed afterwards by reason. Among the thinkers who felt that they belonged to both Christianity and Stoicism were Erasmus and Hugo Grotius.

Under the influence of Christianity, philosophy's ethics acquired an enthusiasm that it had not possessed earlier. Under the influence of philosophy, Christian ethics, on the other hand, started reflecting upon what it owed itself and upon what it should accomplish in this world. Thus was born a spirit which did not allow the ethics of Love any longer to tolerate injustice, cruelties, and superstitions. Torture was abolished, the scourge of the witchcraft trials ceased. Inhuman laws gave way to others more human. A reform without precedent in the previous history of humanity had begun and was accomplished in the first enthusiasm of the discovery that the principle of Love is also taught by reason.

To demonstrate the rationality of altruism, philosophers of the eighteenth century, among whom are Hartley, Baron Holbach, Helvetius, and Bentham, thought that it was enough to show that love of others had a utility value. The Chinese thinkers and the representatives of ethical Stoicism admitted the utility value, but also insisted on other values. According to the eighteenth-century thinkers, altruism would be a well-understood egotism, taking into account the fact that the well-being of the individual and of society can be guaranteed only by the self-sacrifice which men make for their fellow men.

Kant and David Hume refuted this superficial thesis. Kant, in order to defend the dignity of ethics, went so far as to pretend that its utility ought not to be taken into consideration. Obvious as it is, it must not be admitted as a motive of ethics. Ethics, according to the doctrine of the categorical imperative, rules absolutely. It is our conscience which reveals to us what is Good and what is evil. We have but to obey the moral law that we carry within ourselves to gain the certitude that we not only belong to the world as it appears to us in time and space, but that we are at the same time citizens of the spiritual world.

Hume, in order to refute the utilitarian thesis, proceeded in an empirical way. He analyzed the motives of ethics and came to the conclusion that ethics is primarily a matter of feeling. Nature, he argued, endowed us with the faculty of sympathy, which permits and obliges us to feel the joy, apprehensions, and sufferings of others as if they were our own. We are, after an image employed by Hume, like strings vibrating in unison with others. It is this sympathy which leads us to devotion toward others and to the desire to contribute to their well-being and to the well-being of society.

After Hume, philosophy—if we set aside the enterprise of Nietzsche —did not dare seriously to doubt the fact that ethics is primarily a matter of compassion.

But, if this is the case, is ethics capable of defining and setting a limit to the obligations of self-sacrifice, and thereby placing egoism and altruism in accord, as was attempted by the utilitarian theories?

Hume is not much preoccupied by this question. The philosophers who followed him likewise did not think it necessary to take into consideration the consequences of the principle of self-sacrifice through compassion. It is as if they had the presentiment that these consequences might prove to be a little disturbing.

They are indeed. The ethic of self-sacrifice by compassion no longer has the characteristic of a law. It no longer comprises any clearly established and clearly formulated commandments. It is thoroughly subjective, because it leaves to each one the responsibility of deciding how much he will sacrifice himself.

And not only does it cease to give precise commandments: it is no longer satisfied, as the law must be, by the limitations of the possible. It constantly forces us to attempt the impossible, to carry devotion to others so far as to endanger our own existence. In the horrible times we have lived through, there were many of these perilous situations and many persons who sacrificed themselves for others. Even in daily life, the ethic of self-sacrifice asks from each of us that we abdicate selfish interests and renounce advantages for the sake of others. Alas, we too often succeed in silencing our conscience, the guardian of our feeling of responsibility.

How many are the struggles in which the ethic of self-sacrifice abandons us to ourselves! It is seldom that the heads of firms give a job, through compassion, to the man who needs it most, rather than to the man who is most qualified. But evil unto them who think themselves authorized, by such experiences, *never* to take into account the principle of compassion.

A final consequence is to be drawn from the principle of self-sacrifice: it does not allow us to be preoccupied only by human beings, but obliges us to have the same behavior toward all living beings whose fate may be influenced by us. They also are our fellows, for they, too, aspire to happiness. They know fear and suffering, and they dread annihilation.

The man who has kept intact his sensibility finds it quite natural to have pity on all living beings. Why does not philosophy at long last recognize that our behavior toward all life should be an integral part of the ethics which it teaches?

The reason is very simple. Philosophy fears, and rightly so, that this huge enlargement of the circle of our responsibilities will take away from ethics the small hope which it still has to formulate reasonable and satisfactory commandments.

In fact, if we are preoccupied by the fate of all living beings with whom we come in contact, we face conflicts more numerous and more disturbing than those of devotion toward human beings. We are constantly in situations which compel us to harm other creatures or affect their lives. The farmer cannot let all his animals survive. He can keep only those he can feed and the breeding of which assures him necessary income. In many instances, there is the obligation of sacrificing some lives to save others. Whoever shelters a crippled bird finds it necessary to kill insects to feed him. In so doing, he makes an arbitrary decision. By what right does he sacrifice a multitude of lives in order to save a single life? He must also make an arbitrary choice when he exterminates animals which he thinks are harmful, in order to protect others.

It is then incumbent upon each of us to judge whether we must harm or kill, and thus become, by necessity, guilty. We should seek forgiveness by never missing an occasion to rescue living creatures.

What an advance it would be if men started to reflect upon the kindness due all creatures and refrained from harming them by carelessness! We must intensify the struggle against inhuman traditions and feelings remaining in our time if our civilization is to keep any respect for itself. Among inhuman customs which our civilization should no longer tolerate, I must name two: bullfights with their inevitable death, and hunting for sport.

It is finally the exigency of compassion with all beings which makes ethics as complete as it should be.

There is another great change in the evolution of ethics: today it cannot expect help from a concept of the world which justifies what it teaches.

In the past, ethics seemed convinced that it was only requiring a behavior in harmony with the knowledge of the true nature of the world. On this conviction are based not only the religions, but also the rationalist philosophy of the seventeenth and eighteenth centuries.

But it happens that the concept of the world that ethics called upon was the result of the optimistic interpretation of this very world which ethics gave and is still giving. It loaned to the universal will qualities and intentions which gave satisfaction to its own way of feeling and judging.

But in the course of the nineteenth century, research which seeks only objective truth was obliged to face the evidence that ethics had nothing to expect from an ever-closer knowledge of the world. The progress of science consisted in a more precise ascertainment of the processes of nature. It allowed us to use the energies of the universe. But, at the same time, it obliged us to renounce an understanding of the intentions of the universe. The world offers us the disconcerting spectacle of the will to live in conflict with itself. One life maintains itself at the cost of another. The world is horror within magnificence, absurdity within intelligibility, suffering within joy.

How can the ethic of self-sacrifice maintain itself without being justified by an adequate concept of the world? It seems doomed to sink into skepticism. This, however, will not be its fate.

In the beginning, ethics needed to call upon a concept of the world which gave it satisfaction. Having reached the knowledge that the fundamental principle is devotion to others, it becomes fully aware of itself, and thereby self-sufficient.

We are now able to understand its origins and its foundation by meditating upon the world and upon ourselves. We lack a complete and satisfactory knowledge of the world. We are reduced to merely ascertaining that everything in it is living, as we ourselves are, and that all life is a mystery. Our true knowledge of the world consists in being penetrated by the mystery of existence and of life. This mystery becomes ever more mysterious by the progress of scientific research. To be penetrated by the mystery of life corresponds to what is called in the language of the mystic "learned ignorance."

The fundamental idea in our conscience, to which we come back each time we want to reach comprehension of ourselves and of our situation in the world, is: I am life wanting to live, surrounded by life wanting to live. Meditating upon life, I feel the obligation to respect any will-to-live around me as equal to mine and as having a mysterious value.

A fundamental idea of Good then consists in preserving life, in favoring it, in wanting to raise it to its highest value, and evil consists in annihilating life, injuring it, and impeding its growth.

The principle of this veneration of life corresponds to the one of Love, which has been discovered by religion and philosophy seeking an understanding of the fundamental notion of Good.

The term Reverence for Life is larger and at the same time dimmer than the term Love. But it bears within itself the same potentialities. The essentially philosophical notion of Good has the advantage of being more complete than the notion of Love. Love comprises only our obligations toward other beings, but not toward ourselves. It is, for instance, impossible to deduce from it the notion of veracity, the primary quality of the ethical personality in addition to the one of Love. The respect which man owes to his own life obliges him to be faithful to himself by renouncing any self-deceit and by becoming himself in the noblest and deepest way.

By having reverence for life, we enter into a spiritual relation with the world. The absolute is so abstract that we can have no communion with it. It is not given to us to serve the creative will, infinite and unfathomable, by comprehending its nature and its intentions. But we come into spiritual contact with it by the feeling of the mystery of life and by devoting ourselves to all the living beings whom we are able to serve.

The ethics which obliges us to be concerned only with men and with society cannot have this same significance. Only a universal ethics which obliges us to be occupied with all beings puts us in a complete relation with the universe and the will manifested in it.

In the world, the will to live is in conflict with itself. In us it wants, by a mystery that we do not understand, to be at peace with itself. In the world it manifests itself; in us it reveals itself. To be other than the world is our spiritual destiny. By conforming to it we live our existence instead of submitting to it. By practicing reverence for life we become good, deep, and alive.

The Real Secret of Piltdown
Loren Eiseley

How did man get his brain? Many years ago Charles Darwin's great contemporary, and co-discover with him of the principle of natural selection, Alfred Russel Wallace, propounded that simple question. It is a question which has bothered evolutionists ever since, and when Darwin received his copy of an article Wallace had written on this subject he was obviously shaken. It is recorded that he wrote in anguish across the paper, "No!" and underlined the "No" three times heavily in a rising fervor of objection.

Today the question asked by Wallace and never satisfactorily answered by Darwin has returned to haunt us. A skull, a supposedly very ancient skull, long used as one of the most powerful pieces of evidence documenting the Darwinian position upon human evolution, has been proven to be a forgery, a hoax perpetrated by an unscrupulous but learned amateur. In the fall of 1953 the famous Piltdown cranium, known in scientific circles all over the world since its discovery in a gravel pit on the Sussex Downs in 1911, was jocularly dismissed by the world's press as the skull that had "made monkeys out of the anthropologists." Nobody remembered in 1953 that Wallace, the great evolutionist, had protested to a friend in 1913, "The Piltdown skull does not prove much, if anything!"

Why had Wallace made that remark? Why, almost alone among the English scientists of his time, had he chosen to regard with a dubious eye a fossil specimen that seemed to substantiate the theory to which he and Darwin had devoted their lives? He did so for one reason: he did not believe what the Piltdown skull appeared to reveal as to the nature of the process by which the human brain had been evolved. He did not believe in a skull which had a modern brain box attached to an apparently primitive face and given, in the original estimates, an antiquity of something over a million years.

Today we know that the elimination of the Piltdown skull from the growing list of valid human fossils in no way affects the scientific acceptance of the theory of evolution. In fact, only the circumstance that Piltdown had been discovered early, before we had a clear knowledge of the nature of human fossils and the techniques of dating them, made the long survival of this extraordinary hoax possible. Yet in the end it has been the press, absorbed in a piece of clever scientific detection, which has missed the real secret of Piltdown. Darwin saw in the rise of man, with his unique, time-spanning brain, only the undirected play of such natural forces as had created the rest of the living world of plants and animals. Wallace, by contrast, in the case of man, totally abandoned this point of view and turned instead toward a theory of a divinely directed control of the evolutionary process. The issue can be made clear only by a rapid comparison of the views of both men.

As everyone who has studied evolution knows, Darwin propounded the theory that since the reproductive powers of plants and animals potentially far outpace the available food supply, there is in nature a constant struggle for existence on the part of every living thing. Since animals vary individually, the most cleverly adapted will survive and leave offspring which will inherit, and in their turn enhance, the genetic endowment they have received from their ancestors. Because the struggle for life is incessant, this unceasing process promotes endless slow changes in bodily form, as living creatures are subjected to different natural environments, different enemies, and all the vicissitudes against which life has struggled down the ages.

Darwin, however, laid just one stricture on his theory: it could, he maintained, "render each organized being only as perfect or a little more perfect than other inhabitants of the same country." It could allow any animal only a relative superiority, never an absolute perfection— otherwise selection and the struggle for existence would cease to operate. To explain the rise of man through the slow, incremental gains of natural selection, Darwin had to assume a long struggle of man with man and tribe with tribe.

He had to make this assumption because man had far outpaced his animal associates. Since Darwin's theory of the evolutionary process is based upon the practical value of all physical and mental characters in the life struggle, to ignore the human struggle of man with man would have left no explanation as to how humanity by natural selection alone managed to attain an intellectual status so far beyond that of any of the animals with which it had begun its competition for survival.

To most of the thinkers of Darwin's day this seemed a reasonable explanation. It was a time of colonial expansion and ruthless business competition. Peoples of primitive cultures, small societies lost on the world's margins, seemed destined to be destroyed. It was thought that Victorian civilization was the apex of human achievement and that other races with different customs and ways of life must be biologically inferior to Western man. Some of them were even described as only slightly superior to apes. The Darwinians, in a time when there were no satisfactory fossils by which to demonstrate human evolution, were unconsciously minimizing the abyss which yawned between man and ape. In their anxiety to demonstrate our lowly origins they were throwing modern natives into the gap as representing living "missing links" in the chain of human ascent.

It was just at this time that Wallace lifted a voice of lonely protest. The episode is a strange one in the history of science, for Wallace had, independently of Darwin, originally arrived at the same general conclusion as to the nature of the evolutionary process. Nevertheless, only a few years after the publication of Darwin's work, *The Origin of Species,* Wallace had come to entertain a point of view which astounded and troubled Darwin. Wallace, who had had years of experience with natives of the tropical archipelagoes, abandoned the idea that they were of mentally inferior cast. He did more. He committed the Darwinian heresy of maintaining that their mental powers were far in excess of what they really needed to carry on the simple food-gathering techniques by which they survived.

"How, then," Wallace insisted, "was an organ developed so far beyond the needs of its possessor? Natural selection could only have endowed the savage with a brain a little superior to that of an ape, whereas he actually possesses one but little inferior to that of the average member of our learned societies."

At a time when many primitive people were erroneously assumed to speak only in grunts or to chatter like monkeys, Wallace maintained his view of the high intellectual powers of natives by insisting that "the capacity of uttering a variety of distinct articulate sounds and of applying to them an almost infinite amount of modulation . . . is not in any way inferior to that of the higher races. An instrument has been developed in advance of the needs of its possessor."

Finally, Wallace challenged the whole Darwinian position on man by insisting that artistic, mathematical, and musical abilities could not be explained on the basis of natural selection and the struggle for existence. Something else, he contended, some unknown spiritual element, must have been at work in the elaboration of the human brain. Why else would men of simple cultures possess the same basic intellectual powers which the Darwinists maintained could be elaborated only by competitive struggle?

"If you had not told me you had made these remarks," Darwin said, "I should have thought they had been added by someone else. I differ grievously from you and am very sorry for it." He did not, however, supply a valid answer to Wallace's queries. Outside of murmuring about the inherited effects of habit—a contention without scientific validity today—Darwin clung to his original position. Slowly Wallace's challenge was forgotten and a great complacency settled down upon the scientific world.

For seventy years after the publication of *The Origin of Species* in 1859, there were only two finds of fossil human skulls which seemed to throw any light upon the Darwin-Wallace controversy. One was the discovery of the small-brained Java Ape Man, the other was the famous Piltdown or "dawn man." Both were originally dated as lying at the very beginning of the Ice Age, and, though these dates were later to be modified, the skulls, for a very long time, were regarded as roughly contemporaneous and very old.

Two more unlike "missing links" could hardly be imagined. Though they were supposed to share a million-year antiquity, the one was indeed quite primitive and small-brained; the other, Piltdown, in spite of what seemed a primitive lower face, was surprisingly modern in brain. Which of these forms told the true story of human development? Was a large brain old? Had ages upon ages of slow, incremental, Darwinian increase produced it? The Piltdown skull seemed to suggest such a development.

Many were flattered to find their anthropoid ancestry seemingly removed to an increasingly remote past. If one looked at the Java Ape Man, one was forced to contemplate an ancestor, not terribly remote in time, who still had a face and a brain which hinted strongly of the ape. Yet, when by geological evidence this "erect walking ape-man" was finally assigned to a middle Ice Age antiquity, there arose the immediate possibility that Wallace could be right in his suspicion that the human brain might have had a surprisingly rapid development. By contrast, the Piltdown remains seemed to suggest a far more ancient and slow-paced evolution of man. The Piltdown hoaxer, in attaching an ape jaw to a human skull fragment, had, perhaps unwittingly, created a creature which supported the Darwinian idea of man, not too unlike the man of today, extending far back into pre-Ice Age times.

Which story was the right one? Until the exposé of Piltdown in 1953, both theories had to be considered possible and the two hopelessly unlike fossils had to be solemnly weighed in the same balance. Today Piltdown is gone. In its place we are confronted with the blunt statement of two modern scientists, M. R. A. Chance and A. P. Mead.

"No adequate explanation," they confess over eighty years after Darwin scrawled his vigorous "No!" upon Wallace's paper, "has been put forward to account for so large a cerebrum as that found in man."

We have been so busy tracing the tangible aspects of evolution in the *forms of animals* that our heads, the little globes which hold the midnight sky and the shining, invisible universes of thought, have been taken about as much for granted as the growth of a yellow pumpkin in the fall.

Now a part of this mystery as it is seen by the anthropologists of today lies in the relation of the brain to time. "If," Wallace had said, "researches in all parts of Europe and Asia fail to bring to light any proofs of man's presence far back in the Age of Mammals, *it will be at least a presumption that he came into existence at a much later date and by a more rapid process of development.*" If human evolution should prove to be comparatively rapid, "explosive" in other words, Wallace felt that his position would be vindicated, because such a rapid development of the brain would, he thought, imply a divinely directed force at work in man. In the 1870's when he wrote, however, human prehistory was largely an unknown blank. Today we can make a partial answer to Wallace's question. Since the exposure of the Piltdown hoax all of the evidence at our command—and it is considerable—points to man, in his present form, as being one of the youngest and newest of all earth's swarming inhabitants.

The Ice Age extends behind us in time for, at most, a million years. Though this may seem long to one who confines his studies to the written history of man, it is, in reality, a very short period as the student of evolution measures time. It is a period marked more by the extinction of some of the last huge land animals, like the hairy mammoth and the saber-toothed tiger, than it is by the appearance of new forms of life. To this there is only one apparent exception: the rise and spread of man over the Old World land mass.

Most of our knowledge of him—even in his massive-faced, beetle-browed stage—is now confined, since the loss of Piltdown, to the last half of the Ice Age. If we pass backward beyond this point we can find traces of crude tools, stone implements which hint that some earlier form of man was present here and there in Europe, Asia, and particularly Africa in the earlier half of Ice Age time, but to the scientist it is like peering into the mists floating over an unknown landscape. Here and there through the swirling vapor one catches a glimpse of a shambling figure, or a half-wild primordial face stares back at one from some momentary opening in the fog. Then, just as one grasps at a clue, the long gray twilight settles in and the wraiths and the half-heard voices pass away.

Nevertheless, particularly in Africa, a remarkable group of human-like apes have been discovered: creatures with small brains and teeth of a remarkably human cast. Prominent scientists are still debating whether they are on the direct line of ascent to man or are merely near relatives of ours. Some, it is now obvious, existed too late in time to be our true ancestors, though this does not mean that their bodily characters may not tell us what the earliest anthropoids who took the human turn of the road were like.

These apes are not all similar in type or appearance. They are men and yet not men. Some are frailer-bodied, some have great, bone-cracking jaws and massive gorilloid crests atop their skulls. This fact leads us to another of Wallace's remarkable perceptions of long ago. With the rise of the truly human brain, Wallace saw that man had transferred to his machines and tools many of the alterations of parts that in animals take place through evolution of the body. Unwittingly, man had assigned to his machines the selective evolution which in the animal changes the nature of its bodily structure through the ages. Man of today, the atomic manipulator, the aeronaut who flies faster than sound, has precisely the same brain and body as his ancestors of twenty thousand years ago who painted the last Ice Age mammoths on the walls of caves in France.

To put it another way, it is man's ideas that have evolved and changed the world about him. Now, confronted by the lethal radiations of open space and the fantastic speeds of his machines, he has to invent new electronic controls that operate faster than his nerves, and he must shield his naked body against atomic radiation by the use of protective metals. Already he is physically antique in this robot world he has created. All that sustains him is that small globe of gray matter through which spin his ever-changing conceptions of the universe.

Yet, as Wallace, almost a hundred years ago, glimpsed this timeless element in man, he uttered one more prophecy. When we come to trace our history into the past, he contended, sooner or later we will come to a time when the body of man begins to differ and diverge more extravagantly in its appearance. Then, he wrote, we shall know that we stand close to the starting point of the human family. In the twilight before the dawn of the human mind, man will not have been able to protect his body from change and his remains will bear the marks of all the forces that play upon the rest of life. He will be different in his form. He will be, in other words, as variable in body as we know the South African man-apes to be.

Today, with the solution of the Piltdown enigma, we must settle the question of the time involved in human evolution in favor of Wallace, not Darwin; we need not, however, pursue the mystical aspects of

Wallace's thought—since other factors yet to be examined may well account for the rise of man. The rapid fading out of archaeological evidence of tools in lower Ice Age times—along with the discovery of man-apes of human aspect but with ape-sized brains, yet possessing a diverse array of bodily characters—suggests that the evolution of the human brain was far more rapid than that conceived of in early Darwinian circles. At that time it was possible to hear the Eskimos spoken of as possible survivals of Miocene men of several million years ago. By contrast to this point of view, man and his rise now appear short in time—explosively short. There is every reason to believe that whatever the nature of the forces involved in the production of the human brain, a long slow competition of human group with human group or race with race would not have resulted in such similar mental potentialities among all peoples everywhere. Something—some other factor —has escaped our scientific attention.

There are certain strange bodily characters which mark man as being more than the product of a dog-eat-dog competition with his fellows. He possesses a peculiar larval nakedness, difficult to explain on survival principles; his periods of helpless infancy and childhood are prolonged; he has aesthetic impulses which, though they vary in intensity from individual to individual, appear in varying manifestations among all peoples. He is totally dependent, in the achievement of human status, upon the careful training he receives in human society.

Unlike a solitary species of animal, he cannot develop alone. He has suffered a major loss of precise instinctive controls of behavior. To make up for this biological lack, society and parents condition the infant, supply his motivations, and promote his long-drawn training at the difficult task of becoming a normal human being. Even today some individuals fail to make this adjustment and have to be excluded from society.

We are now in a position to see the wonder and terror of the human predicament: man is totally dependent on society. Creature of dream, he has created an invisible world of ideas, beliefs, habits, and customs which buttress him about and replace for him the precise instincts of the lower creatures. In this invisible universe he takes refuge, but just as instinct may fail an animal under some shift of environmental conditions, so man's cultural beliefs may prove inadequate to meet a new situation, or, on an individual level, the confused mind may substitute, by some terrible alchemy, cruelty for love.

The profound shock of the leap from animal to human status is echoing still in the depths of our subconscious minds. It is a transition which would seem to have demanded considerable rapidity of adjustment in order for human beings to have survived, and it also involved the growth of prolonged bonds of affection in the sub-human family, because otherwise its naked, helpless offspring would have perished.

It is not beyond the range of possibility that this strange reduction of instincts in man in some manner forced a precipitous brain growth as a compensation—something that had to be hurried for survival purposes. Man's competition, it would thus appear, may have been much less with his own kind than with the dire necessity of building about him a world of ideas to replace his lost animal environment. As we will show later, he is a pedomorph, a creature with an extended childhood.

Modern science would go on to add that many of the characters of man, such as his lack of fur, thin skull, and globular head, suggest mysterious changes in growth rates which preserve, far into human maturity, foetal or infantile characters which hint that the forces creating man drew him fantastically out of the very childhood of his brutal forerunners. Once more the words of Wallace come back to haunt us: "We may safely infer that the savage possesses a brain capable, if cultivated and developed, of performing work of a kind and degree far beyond what he ever requires it to do."

As a modern man, I have sat in concert halls and watched huge audiences floating dazed on the voice of a great singer. Alone in the dark box I have heard far off as if ascending out of some black stairwell the guttural whisperings and bestial coughings out of which that voice arose. Again, I have sat under the slit dome of a mountain observatory and marveled, as the great wheel of the galaxy turned in all its midnight splendor, that the mind in the course of three centuries has been capable of drawing into its strange, nonspatial interior that world of infinite distance and multitudinous dimensions.

Ironically enough, science, which can show us the flints and the broken skulls of our dead fathers, has yet to explain how we have come so far so fast, nor has it any completely satisfactory answer to the question asked by Wallace long ago. Those who would revile us by pointing to an ape at the foot of our family tree grasp little of the awe with which the modern scientist now puzzles over man's lonely and supreme ascent. As one great student of paleoneurology, Dr. Tilly Edinger, recently remarked, "If man has passed through a Pithecanthropus phase, the evolution of his brain has been unique, not only in its result but also in its tempo. . . . Enlargement of the cerebral hemispheres by 50 per cent seems to have taken place, speaking geologically, within an instant, and without having been accompanied by any major increase in body size."

The true secret of Piltdown, though thought by the public to be merely the revelation of an unscrupulous forgery, lies in the fact that it has forced science to reexamine carefully the history of the most remarkable creation in the world—the human brain.

Science and the Savages
G. K. Chesterton

A permanent disadvantage of the study of folk-lore and kindred subjects is that the man of science can hardly be in the nature of things very frequently a man of the world. He is a student of nature; he is scarcely ever a student of human nature. And even where this difficulty is overcome, and he is in some sense a student of human nature, this is only a very faint beginning of the painful progress towards being human. For the study of primitive race and religion stands apart in one important respect from all, or nearly all, the ordinary scientific studies. A man can understand astronomy only by being an astronomer; he can understand entomology only by being an entomologist (or, perhaps, an insect); but he can understand a great deal of anthropology merely by being a man. He is himself the animal which he studies. Hence arises the fact which strikes the eye everywhere in the records of ethnology and folk-lore—the fact that the same frigid and detached spirit which leads to success in the study of astronomy or botany leads to disaster in the study of mythology or human origins. It is necessary to cease to be a man in order to do justice to a microbe; it is not necessary to cease to be a man in order to do justice to men. That same suppression of sympathies, that same waving away of intuitions or guess-work which make a man preternaturally clever in dealing with the stomach of a spider, will make him preternaturally stupid in dealing with the heart of man. He is making himself inhuman in order to understand humanity. An ignorance of the other world is boasted by many men of science; but in this matter their defect arises, not from ignorance of the other world, but from ignorance of this world. For the secrets about which anthropologists concern themselves can be best learnt, not from books or voyages, but from the ordinary commerce of man with man. The secret of why some savage tribe worships monkeys or the moon is not to be found even by travelling among those savages and taking down their answers in a note-book, although the cleverest man may pursue this course. The answer to the riddle is in England; it is in London; nay, it is in his own heart. When a man has discovered why men in Bond Street wear black hats he will at the same moment have discovered why men in Timbuctoo wear red feathers. The mystery in the heart of some savage war-dance should not be studied in books of scientific travel; it should be studied at a subscription ball. If a man desires to find out the origins of religions, let him not go to the Sandwich Islands; let him go to church. If a man wishes to know the origin of human society, to know what society, philosophically speaking, really is, let him not go into the British Museum; let him go into society.

This total misunderstanding of the real nature of ceremonial gives rise to the most awkward and dehumanized versions of the conduct of men in rude lands or ages. The man of science, not realizing that ceremonial is essentially a thing which is done without a reason, has to find a reason for every sort of ceremonial, and, as might be supposed, the reason is generally a very absurd one—absurd because it originates not in the simple mind of the barbarian, but in the sophisticated mind of the professor. The learned man will say, for instance, "The natives of Mumbojumbo Land believe that the dead man can eat, and will require food upon his journey to the other world. This is attested by the fact that they place food in the grave, and that any family not complying with this rite is the object of the anger of the priests and the tribe." To any one acquainted with humanity this way of talking is topsy-turvy. It is like saying, "The English in the twentieth century believed that a dead man could smell. This is attested by the fact that they always covered his grave with lilies, violets, or other flowers. Some priestly and tribal terrors were evidently attached to the neglect of this action, as we have records of several old ladies who were very much disturbed in mind because their wreaths had not arrived in time for the funeral." It may be of course that savages put food with a dead man because they think that a dead man can eat, or weapons with a dead man because they think that a dead man can fight. But personally I do not believe that they think anything of the kind. I believe they put food or weapons on the dead for the same reason that we put flowers, because it is an exceedingly natural and obvious thing to do. We do not understand, it is true, the emotion which makes us think it obvious and natural; but that is because, like all the important emotions of human existence, it is essentially irrational. We do not understand the savage for the same reason that the savage does not understand himself. And the savage does not understand himself for the same reason that we do not understand ourselves either.

The obvious truth is that the moment any matter has passed through the human mind it is finally and for ever spoilt for all purposes of science. It has become a thing incurably mysterious and infinite; this mortal has put on immortality. Even what we call our material desires are spiritual, because they are human. Science can analyse a pork-chop, and say how much of it is phosphorus and how much is protein; but science cannot analyse any man's wish for a pork-chop, and say how much of it is hunger, how much custom, how much nervous fancy, how much a haunting love of the beautiful. The man's desire for the pork-chop remains literally as mystical and ethereal as his desire for heaven. All attempts, therefore, at a science of any human things, at a science of history, a science of folk-lore, a science of sociology, are by their nature not merely hopeless, but crazy. You can no more be certain in economic history that a man's desire for money was merely a desire for money than you can be certain in hagiology that a saint's desire for God was merely a desire for God. And this kind of vagueness in the primary phenomena of the study is an absolutely final blow to anything in the nature of a science. Men can construct a science with very few instruments, or with very plain instruments; but no one on earth could construct a science with unreliable instruments. A man might work out the whole of mathematics with a handful of pebbles, but not with a handful of clay which was always falling apart into new fragments, and falling together into new combinations. A man might measure heaven and earth with a reed, but not with a growing reed.

As one of the enormous follies of folk-lore, let us take the case of the transmigration of stories, and the alleged unity of their source. Story after story the scientific mythologists have cut out of its place in history, and pinned side by side with similar stories in their museum of fables. The process is industrious, it is fascinating, and the whole of it rests on one of the plainest fallacies in the world. That a story has been told all over the place at some time or other, not only does not prove that it never really happened; it does not even faintly indicate or make slightly more probable that it never happened. That a large number of fishermen have falsely asserted that they have caught a pike two feet long, does not in the least affect the question of whether any one ever really did so. That numberless journalists announce a Franco-German war merely for money is no evidence one way or the other upon the dark question of whether such a war ever occurred. Doubtless in a few hundred years the innumerable Franco-German wars that did not happen will have cleared the scientific mind of any belief in the legendary war of '70 which did. But that will be because if folk-lore students remain at all, their nature will be unchanged; and their services to folk-lore will be still as they are at present, greater than they know. For in truth these men do something far more godlike than studying legends; they create them.

There are two kinds of stories which the scientists say cannot be true, because everybody tells them. The first class consists of the stories which are told everywhere, because they are somewhat odd or clever; there is nothing in the world to prevent their having happened to somebody as an adventure any more than there is anything to prevent their having occurred, as they certainly did occur, to somebody as an idea. But they are not likely to have happened to many people. The second class of their "myths" consist of the stories that are told everywhere for the simple reason that they happen everywhere. Of the first class, for instance, we might take such an example as the story of William Tell, now generally ranked among legends upon the sole ground that it is found in the tales of other peoples. Now, it is obvious that this was told everywhere because whether true or fictitious it is what is called "a good story"; it is odd, exciting, and it has a climax. But to suggest that some such eccentric incident can never have happened in the whole history of archery, or that it did not happen to any particular person of whom it is told, is stark impudence. The idea of shooting at a mark attached to some valuable or beloved person is an idea doubtless that might easily have occurred to any inventive poet. But it is also an idea that might easily occur to any boastful archer. It might be one of the fantastic caprices of some story-teller. It might equally well be one of the fantastic caprices of some tyrant. It might occur first in real life and afterwards occur in legends. Or it might just as well occur first in legends and afterwards occur in real life. If no apple has ever been shot off a boy's head from the beginning of the world, it may be done to-morrow morning, and by somebody who has never heard of William Tell.

This type of tale, indeed, may be pretty fairly paralleled with the ordinary anecdote terminating in a repartee or an Irish bull. Such a retort as the famous "Je ne vois pas la necessité" we have all seen attributed to Talleyrand, to Voltaire, to Henri Quatre, to an anonymous judge, and so on. But this variety does not in any way make it more likely that the thing was never said at all. It is highly likely that it was really said by somebody unknown. It is highly likely that it was really said by Talleyrand. In any case, it is not any more difficult to believe that the *mot* might have occurred to a man in conversation than to a man writing memoirs. It might have occurred to any of the men I have mentioned. But there is this point of distinction about it, that it is not likely to have occurred to all of them. And this is where the first class of so-called myth differs from the second to which I have previously referred. For there is a second class of incident found to be common to the stories of five or six heroes, say to Sigurd, to Hercules, to Rustem, to the Cid, and so on. And the peculiarity of this myth is that not only is it highly reasonable to imagine that it really happened to one hero, but it is highly reasonable to imagine that it really happened to all of them. Such a story, for instance, is that of a great man having his strength swayed or thwarted by the mysterious weakness of a woman. The anecdotal story, the story of William Tell, is as I have said, popular, because it is peculiar. But this kind of story, the story of Samson and Delilah, of Arthur and Guinevere, is obviously popular because it is not peculiar. It is popular as good, quiet fiction is popular, because it tells the truth about people. If the ruin of Samson by a woman, and the ruin of Hercules by a woman, have a common legendary origin, it is gratifying to know that we can also explain, as a fable, the ruin of Nelson by a woman and the ruin of Parnell by a woman. And, indeed, I have no doubt whatever that, some centuries hence, the students of folk-lore will refuse altogether to believe that Elizabeth Barrett eloped with Robert Browning, and will prove their point up to the hilt by the unquestionable fact that the whole fiction of the period was full of such elopements from end to end.

Possibly the most pathetic of all the delusions of the modern students of primitive belief is the notion they have about the thing they call anthropomorphism. They believe that primitive men attributed phenomena to a god in human form in order to explain them, because his mind in its sullen limitation could not reach any further than his own clownish existence. The thunder was called the voice of a man, the lightning the eyes of a man, because by this explanation they were made more reasonable and comfortable. The final cure for all this kind of philosophy is to walk down a lane at night. Any one who does so will discover very quickly that men pictured something semi-human at the back of all things, not because such a thought was natural, but because it was supernatural; not because it made things more comprehensible, but because it made them a hundred times more incomprehensible and mysterious. For a man walking down a lane at night can see the conspicuous fact that as long as nature keeps to her own course, she has no power with us at all. As long as a tree is a tree, it is a top-heavy monster with a hundred arms, a thousand tongues, and only one leg. But so long as a tree is a tree, it does not frighten us at all. It begins to be something alien, to be something strange, only when it looks like ourselves. When a tree really looks like a man our knees knock under us. And when the whole universe looks like a man we fall on our faces.

Sentence Maker
Henry Seidel Canby

Thoreau's writing was to an unusual extent a by-product of his experience. His profession was living, yet, as with all those born to be men of letters, his life seemed incomplete until he had got it described satisfactorily in words. "You . . . have the best of me in my books," he wrote to an admirer in Michigan, Calvin H. Greene, and of course he was right. Therefore, as was natural, he took his writing seriously, and was rich in self-criticism as all writers should be, but are not.

It took him most of the 1840's to get rid of Carlyle's religio-mystical view of literature, which made preachers of the young men of Thoreau's generation. When, in the fifties, his reading swung from literature toward science, he shrugged off this stale generalizing, for there was neither time nor inclination for it. It is only rarely that, after 1850, he writes about a literary masterpiece, for he was no longer studying in that school. Yet it is precisely in this last decade of his life that he makes the shrewdest comments on the art of writing—which is natural, for he had then matured his own. And here he is worth listening to, as is any first-rate writer who tries to analyze his own processes. Not the most philosophic perhaps, but certainly the most valuable, criticism we have is the occasional comment of a good writer on how to write— which means almost invariably how he writes himself.

It was a decade, as we have already seen, of crowded experiences for him with men, women, nature, and the state. There was plenty to write about, so that his Journal sometimes has sudden expansions for a day's thought and adventure which must have taken hours to set in order and express. The whole into which he hoped to fit his parts eluded his grasp, but his faith was firm that if he could reduce his observations to perfect sentences, somehow they would see the light, reach their mark, accomplish their destiny. This optimism has been justified, but only by the labor of many editors, and the enthusiasm of readers searching the trackless Journal for his best.

It was the sentence—a *sententia*—that most occupied his thought. The sentence was his medium—whatever he does and writes about, however often he rewrites or enriches, the fruit of it can be found ripened in a sentence. In the revision of *Walden* for the press, it was doubtful sentences that he threw out, then looked them over, and took back the good ones. They smelled right, as he says, using quaintly his keenest sense as if it could extend itself to words. Naturally he writes best about writing when he is writing about sentences, and these remarks have a biographical value, for they describe as no one else can do the man's mind at work. Only in those deeply impassioned pages about his Sister [the wife of his friend Emerson], so strongly felt as to be scarcely articulate, does he fail to get sentences equal to the emotional intensity or the intellectual insight of his experience. And these, of course, were not meant for publication. With Bacon, Shakespeare, Pope, Doctor Johnson, the makers of the English Bible, and Benjamin Franklin, he belongs among the great makers of the English sentence. Therefore his account of his own practice is interesting.

Two principles, especially, guided him in his writing as, sitting under a pasture oak, he set down his things seen or thought about, or, upstairs in the house on Main Street, worked his notes into his Journal. The first principle might be called intuition made articulate, a favorite idea with all the romantic Transcendentalists [a group of New England writers devoted to a philosophy stressing the importance of the individual]:

> APRIL 1. SUNDAY. 1860 . . . The fruit a thinker bears is *sentences*, —statements or opinions. He seeks to affirm something as true. I am surprised that my affirmations or utterances come to me ready-made,— not fore-thought,—so that I occasionally awake in the night simply to let fall ripe a statement which I had never consciously considered before, and as surprising and novel and agreeable to me as anything can be. As if we only thought by sympathy with the universal mind, which thought while we were asleep. There is such a necessity [to] make a definite statement that our minds at length do it without our consciousness, just as we carry our food to our mouths. This occurred to me last night, but I was so surprised by the fact which I have just endeavored to report that I have entirely forgotten what the particular observation was.

That is the difficulty, of course, with these flashes from a mind in which the heat of long brooding turns to light—if they are not recorded on some sensitive film they are lost and gone, often irrevocably. [It was Thoreau's practice to wait for the flash and then anxiously develop the impression until a sentence was made that was true to the original inspiration, yet communicable to the reader. "There is no more Herculean task than to think a thought about this life and then get it expressed." To write that way is dangerous, since the flow of thought is checked while expression is made perfect; yet it is hard not to believe that here is the secret of Thoreau's durability. [The rifle is more penetrating than the shotgun; the line is remembered when the poem is forgot.]

But these sudden luminosities of thought or irradiations of experience were seldom made articulate at the first trial:

> JAN. 26. 1852 . . . Whatever wit has been produced on the spur of the moment will bear to be reconsidered and reformed with phlegm. The arrow had best not be loosely shot. The most transient and passing remark must be . . . made sure and warranted, as if the earth had rested on its axle to back it, and all the natural forces lay behind it. The writer must direct his sentences as carefully and leisurely as the marksman his rifle. . . . If you foresee that a part of your essay will topple down after the lapse of time, throw it down now yourself.

[margin handwritten note:] change of diction / vividness

Inspiration pricking him on, he writes several such sentences as these lines describe: "I feel the spur of the moment thrust deep into my side. The present is an inexorable rider." Then, with a shift of theme: "The truest account of heaven is the fairest, and I will accept none which disappoints expectation." Here are other comments:

> Nov. 12. 1851 . . . Those sentences are good and well discharged which are like so many little resiliences from the spring floor of our life. . . . Sentences uttered with your back to the wall. . . . Sentences in which there is no strain.

> Aug. 22. 1851 . . . It is the fault of some excellent writers—De Quincey's first impressions on seeing London suggest it to me—that they express themselves with too great fullness and detail. They . . . lack moderation and sententiousness. They . . . say all they mean. Their sentences are not concentrated and nutty. Sentences which suggest far more than they say, which have an atmosphere about them, which do not merely report an old, but make a new, impression . . . to frame these, that is the *art* of writing. Sentences which are expensive, towards which so many volumes, so much life, went; which lie like boulders on the page, up and down or across; which contain the seed of other sentences, not mere repetition, but creation; which a man might sell his grounds and castles to build. If De Quincey had suggested each of his pages in a sentence and passed on, it would have been far more excellent writing. His style is nowhere kinked and knotted up into something hard and significant, which you could swallow like a diamond, without digesting.

That last sentence describes the way Thoreau wrote, and the reason for reading him deliberately. To skim his pages, except in parts of *Cape Cod* or in *The Maine Woods* or in some of the *Excursions,* is like walking rapidly down a gallery of fine paintings. Even with every assistance from theme and narrative, as in *Walden,* Thoreau's work reads slowly—which is not always a virtue, but often a fault, like the faults of paradox and exaggeration, of which he accused himself. He favored his best sentences at the expense of his chapters and paragraphs. They contained the most of him.

His second principle of writing was native to a man who put the art of life ahead of the art of literature. It was, to be vital:

> Sept. 2. 1851 . . . We cannot write well or truly but what we write with gusto. The body, the senses, must conspire with the mind. Expression is the act of the whole man, that our speech may be vascular. The intellect is powerless to express thought without the aid of the heart and liver and of every member.

JAN. 30. FRIDAY. 1852 . . . It is in vain to write on chosen themes. We must wait till they have kindled a flame in our minds. There must be the copulating and generating force of love behind every effort destined to be successful. The cold resolve gives birth to, begets, nothing. . . . Obey, report.

JULY 14. 1852. A writer who does not speak out of a full experience uses torpid words, wooden or lifeless words, such words as "humanitary," which have a paralysis in their tails.

And finally, by way of warning, the original of Barrett Wendell's often quoted phrase, "a diarrhoea of words and constipation of thought":

DEC. 31. 1851 . . . The . . . creative moment . . . in the case of some too easy poets . . . becomes mere diarrhoea, mud and clay relaxed. The poet must not have something pass his bowels merely; that is women's poetry. He must have something pass his brain and heart and bowels, too. . . . So he gets delivered.

The rhetorical quality that many feel, even in Thoreau's best writing, is sometimes only a tone and attitude which he sustains, like a good lecturer, through all of such a book as the *Week* or *Walden*. Yet I think that the difficulty which the modern reader finds in what seems to him the stylized writing of *Walden*, or even of the *Excursions*, has a more important source in this habit of the packed and intensely expressive sentence. Our education in science, or its derivatives, has made us more inductive in our mental processes than were our immediate ancestors. We are accustomed to the kind of writing—especially in newspapers and magazines—that assembles facts, which we call news. The packed statement, which is a deduction handed over for our thinking, is unfamiliar and inspires distrust. Our writing escapes the dogmatic by being dilute and often inconclusive. It is easy to abbreviate, as the success of such magazines as *The Reader's Digest* has shown. We write, not by sentences, not even by paragraphs, but in a stream directed at one outlet. The reading of poetry has decreased in proportion to the increase of this homeopathic way of writing, for the effectiveness of poetry is an effectiveness of charged words and lines. If it is not to have high specific gravity, it would be better to write it in prose. Thoreau suffers from this changed habit of reading, since his sentences, with their backs to the wall, and their feet on Mother Earth, differ from poetry in this respect only in a freer rhythm.

Yet there is no intentional obscurity. "I am thinking," he wrote one day, "by what long discipline and at what cost a man learns to speak simply at last." Nor was there any literary affectation in his creed, although it cannot be denied that, like his contemporaries, he let his words strut and crow now and then with the *Walden* cock. "Why, the roots of *letters*," he says aptly, "are *things*. Natural objects and phenomena are the original symbols or types which express our thoughts and feelings, and yet American scholars, having little or no root in the soil, commonly strive with all their might to confine themselves to the imported symbols alone. All the true growth and experience, the living speech, they would fain reject as 'Americanisms'." "It is a great art in the writer to improve from day to day just that soil and fertility which he has. . . ." "Your mind must not perspire,"—which last, if said of walking out-of-doors, was surely meant for writing indoors also.

The art of writing is much broader and more complex than Thoreau's remarks on sentence-making imply. There is no doubt, however, that his particular art has a survival value much greater than any novelty in his ideas. But, inevitably, it became a perfectionist art, and so a curb upon free writing. Whoever writes by sentences writes slowly, and will often follow his own nose instead of his theme. And being perfectionist, this art made the completion of any whole exceedingly difficult, because each sentence had to be a finished production. He used the spot light instead of the flood. No wonder, then, that, as a student of nature trying to put between the covers of a book an account of that age-old Concord scene in which man had found a new home, Thoreau's work was left half done. Nevertheless, he mopped up his trenches as he crossed them, and left a noble sentence for each significant experience.

Suggestions for Writing

1. Using two or three of the writers in this section, write an essay on the thesis "A writer's style reveals his personality." Make it as imaginative as you can, something on the order of "Lewis Carroll has a great deal of the witch in him, inviting us into his gingerbread house only to fatten us for the oven." Make your portraits extensive, and illustrate with quotations to show your reader what you mean.

2. Sum up Schweitzer's description of the way ethics evolved; then use your summary in support of a thesis about some ethical point suggested by one of the following: the Peace Corps, foreign aid, charity that begins at home, getting tough with Russia, fraternities and sororities, laboratory experiments with living animals, vegetarianism, euthanasia, hunting, giving the job to the man most qualified. You may find an excellent essay in the time you were faced with having to kill, let us say, a mouse, or a fish.

3. Write out a brief explanation of how Piltdown supported Darwin, and of why Darwin hated Wallace's hypothesis. Now, having the thinking straight, and perhaps using Schweitzer's assertion that scientific research has made the mystery of life more mysterious (and perhaps also including Chesterton's thoughts on the same line), write an essay on the subject "My No (or Yes) to Evolution." Your purpose in the exercise is to engage with your own thinking and experience the big questions raised by Schweitzer and Eiseley—to find your own emphatic "No!" or "Yes!" as Darwin did, and then to find persuasive reasons to back it. In other words, bring these big ideas into your own life, and then try them out for size on someone else, that is, on your own hypothetical readers. Somewhere in your essay try to use, as Eiseley does, an experience of your own: "As a modern man, I have sat in concert halls. . . ."

4. If you have any knowledge of experiments in human reactions, as in polls of opinion, or in psychological or sociological experimentation, attack or support Chesterton's suggestion that "the same frigid and detached spirit which leads to success in the study of astronomy or botany leads to disaster" in the study of human affairs.

5. Write an essay on some subject like "the tribal taboos of the sophomore prom."

6. Write an essay attacking or developing Chesterton's idea that scientific investigation of things human is impossible because the basic matter, having passed through the human mind, is "incurably mysterious and infinite." Consider what he says about motives, about anthropomorphic belief. Use what you know of psychology, history, sociology, or literary criticism.

7. Try to write five sentences of the Thoreauvian kind, *sententia* with their roots in natural objects. Sit under an oak and see what sentences your intuition can sprout for you. Write with gusto, the body and senses conspiring. Try something like Thoreau's "The fruit a thinker bears is sentences," or Canby's "The rifle is more penetrating than the shotgun; the line is remembered when the poem is forgot"—sentences that lie like boulders on the page.

8. Write an essay on the following theme: "It is in vain to write on chosen themes."

Where I Lived, and What I Lived For HENRY DAVID THOREAU · *190*
A Slight Sound at Evening E. B. WHITE · *201*
The Importance of Nietzsche ERICH HELLER · *209*

Words
The
Figurative
Dimension

Thoreau, the sentence-smith, knew what every
good writer knows: that words are like seeds,
common and unnoticed, just waiting to be waked
up. Thoreau knew how to pun, to turn our common abstractions back into their original metaphors. In his opening passage, playing with the
idea of buying a farm, playing with the fact that
one can possess a thing only in one's consciousness
and imagination, we find the imaginative pun-
ster at work. *Season* takes on a strong agricultural

climate; *survey* means both to look over (its basic meaning inherited from Latin) and to measure for building; *price* means a cost not only financial but spiritual. The dynamics in *deed* you may trace for yourself. Go through Thoreau thoroughly, with a pencil sharpened for a pun. No other writer can teach you so well the figurative potency in common words, and the way to release it with a play of mind and language that is, indeed, a kind of inspired punning.

White, too, is a master of the sentence—see his second sentence, for example—but his gift, again, comes down to words themselves. He learned from Thoreau the best that anyone can learn from him, the wonder and the simple freedom of being alive in one's own spirit; and he must also have learned something of Thoreau's craft in writing: the potency of individual words. White's pulse is different from Thoreau's, but he has much the same ability to keep his language freshened with metaphor. Both men, you will notice, imply that all language is a metaphor, a kind of perpetual *as if*, expressing the eternal idiom of nature and spirit.

Like Thoreau, White is a playful alluder, slipping in phrases from other writers on the assumption that you are so well read you will recognize and enjoy them. As you read White, mark whatever allusions and echoes you can catch from Thoreau's piece (the second and most famous chapter of *Walden*), not things already marked as quotations, but those appropriated without quotation marks and reapplied in White's own words. (Some of White's allusions are to other chapters, of course, such as his reworking of Thoreau's famous—and ungrammatical—"The mass of men lead lives of quiet desperation," or of Thoreau's notion that the man who inherits a barn is stuck with pushing it ahead of him all the way down the road of life.) Mark all distinctive phrases, like *inspirational puffballs* (notice the effect of coupling the abstract Latin adjective with the concrete Anglo-Saxon noun). Mark also White's colloquial and slangy words—*Nature Boy, whack, show-off, ruckus*—and his words from commercial Americana—*vitamin-enriched, in-town location.* You may learn something of White's marvelous melodies in chiming the formal with the colloquial, as he keeps himself pleasantly in tune with the reader.

Heller, too, is a figurative wordster, though quieter than Thoreau and White. He awakens words by applying them in unexpected contexts—*inspired diatribe* or *national heretic,* for instance. He will assert, to our surprise, that the modern mind "speaks German," and show us exactly the surprising truth in that figuratively extreme statement. Or he will extend the metaphor of the sick-bed in a phrase about Nietzsche's interpreting the temperatures of his own mind. In short, Heller is much less playful than the other two, but his words frequently glow from the same intelligent play. And he seems also to have acquired a certain metaphorical boldness from the man whom he interprets and translates for us, as in Nietzsche's own astonishing metaphors: "Who gave us the sponge with which to wipe out the horizon? How did we set about unchaining our earth from her sun?" Notice Nietzsche's remarkable passage about "the Guest of Stone" on p. 222.

Where I Lived, and What I Lived For
Henry David Thoreau

At a certain season of our life we are accustomed to consider every spot
as the possible site of a house. I have thus surveyed the country on
every side within a dozen miles of where I live. In imagination I have
bought all the farms in succession, for all were to be bought, and I knew
their price. I walked over each farmer's premises, tasted his wild
apples, discoursed on husbandry with him, took his farm at his price,
at any price, mortgaging it to him in my mind; even put a higher price
on it,—took every thing but a deed of it,—took his word for his deed,
for I dearly love to talk,—cultivated it, and him too to some extent, I
trust, and withdrew when I had enjoyed it long enough, leaving him to
carry it on. This experience entitled me to be regarded as a sort of
real-estate broker by my friends. Wherever I sat, there I might live, and
the landscape radiated from me accordingly. What is a house but a
sedes, a seat?—better if a country seat. I discovered many a site for a
house not likely to be soon improved, which some might have thought
too far from the village, but to my eyes the village was too far from
it. Well, there I might live, I said; and there I did live, for an hour,
a summer and a winter life; saw how I could let the years run off,
buffet the winter through, and see the spring come in. The future inhabitants of this region, wherever they may place their houses, may
be sure that they have been anticipated. An afternoon sufficed to lay
out the land into orchard, woodlot, and pasture, and to decide what
fine oaks or pines should be left to stand before the door, and whence
each blasted tree could be seen to the best advantage; and then I let
it lie, fallow perchance, for a man is rich in proportion to the number
of things which he can afford to let alone.

My imagination carried me so far that I even had the refusal of
several farms,—the refusal was all I wanted,—but I never got my
fingers burned by actual possession. The nearest that I came to actual
possession was when I bought the Hollowell place, and had begun to
sort my seeds, and collected materials with which to make a wheelbarrow to carry it on or off with; but before the owner gave me a deed
of it, his wife—every man has such a wife—changed her mind and
wished to keep it, and he offered me ten dollars to release him. Now,
to speak the truth, I had but ten cents in the world, and it surpassed
my arithmetic to tell, if I was that man who had ten cents, or who had
a farm, or ten dollars, or all together. However, I let him keep the

ten dollars and the farm too, for I had carried it far enough; or rather, to be generous, I sold him the farm for just what I gave for it, and, as he was not a rich man, made him a present of ten dollars, and still had my ten cents, and seeds, and materials for a wheelbarrow left. I found thus that I had been a rich man without any damage to my poverty. But I retained the landscape, and I have since annually carried off what it yielded without a wheelbarrow. With respect to landscapes,—

> I am monarch of all I *survey*,
> My right there is none to dispute.

I have frequently seen a poet withdraw, having enjoyed the most valuable part of a farm, while the crusty farmer supposed that he had got a few wild apples only. Why, the owner does not know it for many years when a poet has put his farm in rhyme, the most admirable kind of invisible fence, has fairly impounded it, milked it, skimmed it, and got all the cream, and left the farmer only the skimmed milk.

The real attractions of the Hollowell farm, to me, were: its complete retirement, being about two miles from the village, half a mile from the nearest neighbor, and separated from the highway by a broad field; its bounding on the river, which the owner said protected it by its fogs from frosts in the spring, though that was nothing to me; the gray color and ruinous state of the house and barn, and the dilapidated fences, which put such an interval between me and the last occupant; the hollow and lichen-covered apple trees, gnawed by rabbits, showing what kind of neighbors I should have; but above all, the recollection I had of it from my earliest voyages up the river, when the house was concealed behind a dense grove of red maples, through which I heard the house-dog bark. I was in haste to buy it, before the proprietor finished getting out some rocks, cutting down the hollow apple trees, and grubbing up some young birches which had sprung up in the pasture, or, in short, had made any more of his improvements. To enjoy these advantages I was ready to carry it on; like Atlas, to take the world on my shoulders,—I never heard what compensation he received for that,—and do all those things which had no other motive or excuse but that I might pay for it and be unmolested in my possession of it; for I knew all the while that it would yield the most abundant crop of the kind I wanted if I could only afford to let it alone. But it turned out as I have said.

All that I could say, then, with respect to farming on a large scale (I have always cultivated a garden) was, that I had had my seeds ready. Many think that seeds improve with age. I have no doubt that time discriminates between the good and the bad; and when at last I shall plant, I shall be less likely to be disappointed. But I would say to my fellows, once for all, As long as possible live free and uncommitted. It makes but little difference whether you are committed to a farm or the county jail.

Old Cato, whose "De Re Rusticâ" is my "Cultivator," says,—and the only translation I have seen makes sheer nonsense of the passage,— "When you think of getting a farm, turn it thus in your mind, not to buy greedily; nor spare your pains to look at it, and do not think it enough to go round it once. The oftener you go there the more it will please you, if it is good." I think I shall not buy greedily, but go round and round it as long as I live, and be buried in it first, that it may please me the more at last.

The present was my next experiment of this kind, which I purpose to describe more at length, for convenience, putting the experience of two years into one. As I have said, I do not propose to write an ode to dejection, but to brag as lustily as chanticleer in the morning, standing on his roost, if only to wake my neighbors up.

When first I took up my abode in the woods, that is, began to spend my nights as well as days there, which, by accident, was on Independence day, or the fourth of July, 1845, my house was not finished for winter, but was merely a defence against the rain, without plastering or chimney, the walls being of rough, weather-stained boards, with wide chinks, which made it cool at night. The upright white hewn studs and freshly planed door and window casings gave it a clean and airy look, especially in the morning, when its timbers were saturated with dew, so that I fancied that by noon some sweet gum would exude from them. To my imagination it retained throughout the day more or less of this auroral character, reminding me of a certain house on a mountain which I had visited the year before. This was an airy and unplastered cabin, fit to entertain a travelling god, and where a goddess might trail her garments. The winds which passed over my dwelling were such as sweep over the ridges of mountains, bearing the broken strains, or celestial parts only, of terrestrial music. The morning wind forever blows, the poem of creation is uninterrupted; but few are the ears that hear it. Olympus is but the outside of the earth everywhere.

The only house I had been the owner of before, if I except a boat, was a tent, which I used occasionally when making excursions in the summer, and this is still rolled up in my garret; but the boat, after passing from hand to hand, has gone down the stream of time. With this more substantial shelter about me, I had made some progress toward settling in the world. This frame, so slightly clad, was a sort of crystallization around me, and reacted on the builder. It was suggestive somewhat as a picture in outlines. I did not need to go out-doors to take the air, for the atmosphere within had lost none of its freshness. It was not so much within-doors as behind a door where I sat, even in the rainiest weather. The Harivansa says, "An abode without birds is like a meat without seasoning." Such was not my abode, for I found myself suddenly neighbor to the birds; not by having imprisoned one, but having caged myself near them. I was not only nearer to some of those which commonly frequent the garden and the orchard, but to those wilder and more thrilling songsters of the forest which never, or rarely, serenade a villager,—the wood-thrush, the veery, the scarlet tanager, the field-sparrow, the whippoorwill, and many others.

I was seated by the shore of a small pond, about a mile and a half south of the village of Concord and somewhat higher than it, in the midst of an extensive wood between that town and Lincoln, and about two miles south of that our only field known to fame, Concord Battle Ground; but I was so low in the woods that the opposite shore, half a mile off, like the rest, covered with wood, was my most distant horizon. For the first week, whenever I looked out on the pond it impressed me like a tarn high up on the side of a mountain, its bottom far above the surface of other lakes, and, as the sun arose, I saw it throwing off its nightly clothing of mist, and here and there, by degrees, its soft ripples or its smooth reflecting surface was revealed, while the mists, like ghosts, were stealthily withdrawing in every direction into the woods, as at the breaking up of some nocturnal conventicle. The very dew seemed to hang upon the trees later into the day than usual, as on the sides of mountains.

This small lake was of most value as a neighbor in the intervals of a gentle rain storm in August, when, both air and water being perfectly still, but the sky overcast, mid-afternoon had all the serenity of evening, and the wood-thrush sang around, and was heard from shore to shore. A lake like this is never smoother than at such a time; and the clear portion of the air above it being shallow and darkened by clouds, the water, full of light and reflections, becomes a lower heaven itself so much the more important. From a hill top near by, where the wood had been recently cut off, there was a pleasing vista southward across the pond, through a wide indentation in the hills which form the shore there, where their opposite sides sloping toward each other suggested a stream flowing out in that direction through a wooded valley, but stream there was none. That way I looked between and over the near green hills to some distant and higher ones in the horizon, tinged with blue. Indeed, by standing on tiptoe I could catch a glimpse of some of the peaks of the still bluer and more distant mountain ranges in the north-west, those true-blue coins from heaven's own mint, and also of some portion of the village. But in other directions, even from this point, I could not see over or beyond the woods which surrounded me. It is well to have some water in your neighborhood, to give buoyancy to and float the earth. One value even of the smallest well is, that when you look into it you see that earth is not continent but insular. This is as important as that it keeps butter cool. When I looked across the pond from this peak toward the Sudbury meadows, which in time of flood I distinguished elevated perhaps by a mirage in their seething valley, like a coin in a basin, all the earth beyond the pond appeared like a thin crust insulated and floated even by this small sheet of intervening water, and I was reminded that this on which I dwelt was but *dry land*.

Though the view from my door was still more contracted, I did not feel crowded or confined in the least. There was pasture enough for my imagination. The low shrub-oak plateau to which the opposite shore arose, stretched away toward the prairies of the West and the steppes of Tartary, affording ample room for all the roving families of men. "There are none happy in the world but beings who enjoy freely a vast horizon,"—said Damodara, when his herds required new and larger pastures.

Both place and time were changed, and I dwelt nearer to those parts of the universe and to those eras in history which had most attracted me. Where I lived was as far off as many a region viewed nightly by astronomers. We are wont to imagine rare and delectable places in some remote and more celestial corner of the system, behind the constellation of Cassiopeia's Chair, far from noise and disturbance. I discovered that my house actually had its site in such a withdrawn, but forever new and unprofaned, part of the universe. If it were worth the while to settle in those parts near to the Pleiades or the Hyades, to Aldebaran or Altair, then I was really there, or at an equal remoteness from the life which I had left behind, dwindled and twinkling with as fine a ray to my nearest neighbor, and to be seen only in moonless nights by him. Such was that part of creation where I had squatted;—

> There was a shepherd that did live,
>   And held his thoughts as high
> As were the mounts whereon his flocks
>   Did hourly feed him by.

What should we think of the shepherd's life if his flocks always wandered to higher pastures than his thoughts?

Every morning was a cheerful invitation to make my life of equal simplicity, and I may say innocence, with Nature herself. I have been as sincere a worshipper of Aurora as the Greeks. I got up early and bathed in the pond; that was a religious exercise, and one of the best things which I did. They say that characters were engraven on the bathing tub of king Tching-thang to this effect: "Renew thyself completely each day; do it again, and again, and forever again." I can understand that. Morning brings back the heroic ages. I was as much affected by the faint hum of a mosquito making its invisible and unimaginable tour through my apartment at earliest dawn, when I was sitting with door and windows open, as I could be by any trumpet that ever sang of fame. It was Homer's requiem; itself an Illiad and Odyssey in the air, singing its own wrath and wanderings. There was something cosmical about it; a standing advertisement, till forbidden, of the everlasting vigor and fertility of the world. The morning, which is the most memorable season of the day, is the awakening hour. Then there is least somnolence in us; and for an hour, at least, some part of us awakes which slumbers all the rest of the day and night. [Little is to be expected of that day, if it can be called a day, to which we are not awakened by our Genius, but by the mechanical nudgings of some servitor, are not awakened by our own newly-acquired force and aspirations from within, accompanied by the undulations of celestial music, instead of factory bells, and a fragrance filling the air—to a higher life than we fell asleep from; and thus the darkness bear its fruit, and prove itself to be good, no less than the light. That man who does not believe that each day contains an earlier, more sacred, and auroral hour than he has yet profaned, has despaired of life, and is pursuing a descending and darkening way. After a partial cessation of his sensuous life, the soul of man, or its organs rather, are reinvigorated each day, and his Genius tries again what noble life it can make. All memorable events, I should say, transpire in morning time and in a morning atmosphere. The Vedas say, "All intelligences awake with the morning." Poetry and art, and the fairest and most memorable of the actions of men, date from such an hour. All poets and heroes, like Memnon, are the children of Aurora, and emit their music at sunrise. To him whose elastic and vigorous thought keeps pace with the sun, the day is a perpetual morning. It matters not what the clocks say or the attitudes and labors of men. Morning is when I am awake and there is a dawn in me. Moral reform is the effort to throw off sleep. Why is it that men give so poor an account of their day if they have not been slumbering? They are not such poor calculators. If they had not been overcome with drowsiness they would have performed something. The millions are awake enough for physical labor; but only one in a million is awake enough for effective intellectual exertion, only one in a hundred millions to a poetic or divine life. To be awake is to be alive. I have never yet met a man who was quite awake. How could I have looked him in the face?

We must learn to reawaken and keep ourselves awake, not by mechanical aids, but by an infinite expectation of the dawn, which does not forsake us in our soundest sleep. I know of no more encouraging fact than the unquestionable ability of man to elevate his life by a conscious endeavor. It is something to be able to paint a particular picture, or to carve a statue, and so to make a few objects beautiful; but it is far more glorious to carve and paint the very atmosphere and medium through which we look, which morally we can do. To affect the quality of the day, that is the highest of arts. Every man is tasked to make his life, even in its details, worthy of the contemplation of his most elevated and critical hour. If we refused, or rather used up, such paltry information as we get, the oracles would distinctly inform us how this might be done.

I went to the woods because I wished to live deliberately, to front only the essential facts of life, and see if I could not learn what it had to teach, and not, when I came to die, discover that I had not lived. I did not wish to live what was not life, living is so dear; nor did I wish to practice resignation, unless it was quite necessary. I wanted to live deep and suck out all the marrow of life, to live so sturdily and Spartan-like as to put to rout all that was not life, to cut a broad swath and shave close, to drive life into a corner, and reduce it to its lowest terms, and, if it proved to be mean, why then to get the whole and genuine meanness of it, and publish its meanness to the world; or if it were sublime, to know it by experience, and be able to give a true account of it in my next excursion. For most men, it appears to me, are in a strange uncertainty about it, whether it is of the devil or of God, and have *somewhat hastily* concluded that it is the chief end of man here to "glorify God and enjoy him forever."

Still we live meanly, like ants; though the fable tells us that we were long ago changed into men; like pygmies we fight with cranes; it is error upon error, and clout upon clout, and our best virtue has for its occasion a superfluous and evitable wretchedness. Our life is frittered away by detail. An honest man has hardly need to count more than his ten fingers, or in extreme cases he may add his ten toes, and lump the rest. Simplicity, simplicity, simplicity! I say, let your affairs be as two or three, and not a hundred or a thousand; instead of a million count half a dozen, and keep your accounts on your thumb nail. In the midst of this chopping sea of civilized life, such are the clouds and storms and quicksands and thousand-and-one items to be allowed for, that a man has to live, if he would not founder and go to the bottom and not make his port at all, by dead reckoning, and he must be a great calculator indeed who succeeds. Simplify, simplify. Instead of three meals a day, if it be necessary eat but one; instead of a hundred dishes, five; and reduce other things in proportion. Our life is like a German Confederacy, made up of petty states, with its boundary forever fluctuating, so that even a German cannot tell you how it is bounded at any moment. The nation itself, with all its so-called internal improvements, which, by the way, are all external and superficial, is just such an unwieldy and overgrown establishment, cluttered with furniture and tripped up by its own traps, ruined by luxury and heedless expense, by want of calculation and a worthy aim, as the million households in the land; and the only cure for it as for them is in a rigid economy, a stern and more than Spartan simplicity of life and elevation of purpose. It lives too fast. Men think that it is essential that the *Nation* have commerce, and export ice, and talk through a telegraph, and ride thirty miles an hour, without a doubt, whether *they* do or not; but whether we should live like baboons or like men, is a little uncertain. If we do not get our sleepers, and forge rails, and devote days and nights to the work, but go to tinkering upon our *lives* to improve *them,* who will build railroads? And if railroads are not built, how shall we get to heaven in season? But if we stay at home and mind our business, who will want railroads? We do not ride on the railroad; it rides upon us. Did you ever think what those sleepers are that underlie the railroad? Each one is a man, an Irishman, or a Yankee man. The rails are laid on them, and they are covered with sand, and the cars run smoothly over them. They are sound sleepers, I assure you. And every few years a new lot is laid down and run over; so that, if some have the pleasure of riding on a rail, others have the misfortune to be ridden upon. And when they run over a man that is walking in his sleep, a supernumerary sleeper in the wrong position, and wake him up, they suddenly stop the cars, and make a hue and cry about it, as if this were an exception. I am glad to know that it takes a gang of men for every five miles to keep the sleepers down and level in their beds as it is, for this is a sign that they may sometime get up again.

Why should we live with such hurry and waste of life? We are determined to be starved before we are hungry. Men say that a stitch in time saves nine, and so they take a thousand stitches to-day to save nine tomorrow. As for *work,* we haven't any of any consequence. We have the Saint Vitus' dance, and cannot possibly keep our heads still. If I should only give a few pulls at the parish bellrope, as for a fire, that is, without setting the bell, there is hardly a man on his farm in the outskirts of Concord, notwithstanding that press of engagements which was his excuse so many times this morning, nor a boy, nor a woman, I might almost say, but would forsake all and follow that sound, not mainly to save property from the flames, but, if we will confess the truth, much more to see it burn, since burn it must, and we, be it known, did not set it on fire,—or to see it put out, and have a hand in it, if that is done as handsomely; yes, even if it were the parish church itself. Hardly a man takes a half hour's nap after dinner, but when he wakes he holds up his head and asks, "What's the news?" as if the rest of mankind had stood his sentinels. Some give directions to be waked every half hour, doubtless for no other purpose; and then, to pay for it, they tell what they have dreamed. After a night's sleep the news is as indispensable as the breakfast. "Pray tell me any thing new that has happened to a man anywhere on this globe,"—and he reads it over his coffee and rolls, that a man has had his eyes gouged out this morning on the Wachito River; never dreaming the while that he lives in the dark unfathomed mammoth cave of this world, and has but the rudiment of an eye himself.

For my part, I could easily do without the post-office. I think that there are very few important communications made through it. To speak critically, I never received more than one or two letters in my life—I wrote this some years ago—that were worth the postage. The penny-post is, commonly, an institution through which you seriously offer a man that penny for his thoughts which is so often safely offered in jest. And I am sure that I never read any memorable news in a newspaper. If we read of one man robbed, or murdered, or killed by accident, or one house burned, or one vessel wrecked, or one steamboat blown up, or one cow run over on the Western Railroad, or one mad dog killed, or one lot of grasshoppers in the winter,—we never need read of another. One is enough. If you are acquainted with the principle, what do you care for a myriad instances and applications? To a philosopher all *news*, as it is called, is gossip, and they who edit and read it are old women over their tea. Yet not a few are greedy after this gossip. There was such a rush, as I hear, the other day at one of the offices to learn the foreign news by the last arrival, that several large squares of plate glass belonging to the establishment were broken by the pressure,—news which I seriously think a ready wit might write a twelve-month or twelve years beforehand with sufficient accuracy. As for Spain, for instance, if you know how to throw in Don Carlos and the Infanta, and Don Pedro and Seville and Granada, from time to time in the right proportions,—they may have changed the names a little since I saw the papers,—and serve up a bull-fight when other entertainments fail, it will be true to the letter, and give us as good an idea of the exact state or ruin of things in Spain as the most succinct and lucid reports under this head in the newspapers: and as for England, almost the last significant scrap of news from that quarter was the revolution of 1649; and if you have learned the history of her crops for an average year, you never need attend to that thing again, unless your speculations are of a merely pecuniary character. If one may judge who rarely looks into the newspapers, nothing new does ever happen in foreign parts, a French revolution not excepted.

What news! how much more important to know what that is which was never old! "Kieou-he-yu (great dignitary of the state of Wei) sent a man to Khoung-tseu to know his news. Khoung-tseu caused the messenger to be seated near him, and questioned him in these terms: What is your master doing? The messenger answered with respect: My master desires to diminish the number of his faults, but he cannot come to the end of thém. The messenger being gone, the philosopher remarked: What a worthy messenger! What a worthy messenger!" The preacher, instead of vexing the ears of drowsy farmers on their day of rest at the end of the week,—for Sunday is the fit conclusion of an ill-spent week, and not the fresh and brave beginning of a new one, —with this one other draggle-tail of a sermon, should shout with thundering voice,—"Pause! Avast! Why so seeming fast, but deadly slow?"

Shams and delusions are esteemed for soundest truths, while reality is fabulous. If men would steadily observe realities only, and not allow themselves to be deluded, life, to compare it with such things as we know, would be like a fairy tale and the Arabian Nights' Entertainments. If we respected only what is inevitable and has a right to be, music and poetry would resound along the streets. When we are unhurried and wise, we perceive that only great and worthy things have any permanent and absolute existence,—that petty fears and petty pleasures are but the shadow of the reality. This is always exhilarating and sublime. By closing the eyes and slumbering, and consenting to be deceived by shows, men establish and confirm their daily life of routine and habit everywhere, which still is built on purely illusory foundations. Children, who play life, discern its true law and relations more clearly than men, who fail to live it worthily, but who think that they are wiser by experience, that is, by failure. I have read in a Hindoo book, that "there was a king's son, who, being expelled in infancy from his native city, was brought up by a forester, and, growing up to maturity in that state, imagined himself to belong to the barbarous race with which he lived. One of his father's ministers having discovered him, revealed to him what he was, and the misconception of his character was removed, and he knew himself to be a prince. So soul," continues the Hindoo philosopher, "from the circumstances in which it is placed, mistakes its own character, until the truth is revealed to it by some holy teacher, and then it knows itself to be *Brahme*." I perceive that we inhabitants of New England live this mean life that we do because our vision does not penetrate the surface of things. We think that that *is* which *appears* to be. If a man should walk through this town and see only the reality, where, think you, would the "Mill-dam" go to? If he should give us an account of the realities he beheld there, we should not recognize the place in his description. Look at a meeting-house, or a courthouse, or a jail, or a shop, or a dwelling-house, and say what that thing really is before a true gaze, and they would all go to pieces in your account of them. Men esteem truth remote, in the outskirts of the system, behind the farthest star, before Adam and after the last man. In eternity there is indeed something true and sublime. But all these times and places and occasions are now and here. God himself culminates in the present moment, and will never be more divine in the lapse of all the ages. And we are enabled to apprehend at all what is sublime and noble only by the perpetual instilling and drenching of the reality that surrounds us. The universe constantly and obediently answers to our conceptions; whether we travel fast or slow, the track is laid for us. Let us spend our lives in conceiving then. The poet or the artist never yet had so fair and noble a design but some of his posterity at least could accomplish it.

Let us spend one day as deliberately as Nature, and not be thrown off the track by every nutshell and mosquito's wing that falls on the rails. Let us rise early and fast, or break fast, gently and without perturbation; let company come and let company go, let the bells ring and the children cry,—determined to make a day of it. Why should we knock under and go with the stream? Let us not be upset and overwhelmed in that terrible rapid and whirlpool called a dinner, situated in the meridian shallows. Weather this danger and you are safe, for the rest of the way is down hill. With unrelaxed nerves, with morning vigor, sail by it, looking another way, tied to the mast like Ulysses. If the engine whistles, let it whistle till it is hoarse for its pains. If the bell rings, why should we run? We will consider what kind of music they are like. Let us settle ourselves, and work and wedge our feet downward through the mud and slush of opinion, and prejudice, and tradition, and delusion, and appearance, that alluvion which covers the globe, through Paris and London, through New York and Boston and Concord, through church and state, through poetry and philosophy and religion, till we come to a hard bottom and rocks in place, which we can call *reality*, and say, This is, and no mistake; and then begin, having a *point d'appui*, below freshet and frost and fire, a place where you might found a wall or a state, or set a lamp-post safely, or perhaps a gauge, not a Nilometer, but a Realometer, that future ages might know how deep a freshet of shams and appearances had gathered from time to time. If you stand right fronting and face to face to a fact, you will see the sun glimmer on both its surfaces, as if it were a cimeter, and feel its sweet edge dividing you through the heart and marrow, and so you will happily conclude your mortal career. Be it life or death, we crave only reality. If we are really dying, let us hear the rattle in our throats and feel cold in the extremities; if we are alive, let us go about our business.

Time is but the stream I go a-fishing in. I drink at it; but while I drink I see the sandy bottom and detect how shallow it is. Its thin current slides away, but eternity remains. I would drink deeper; fish in the sky, whose bottom is pebbly with stars. I cannot count one. I know not the first letter of the alphabet. I have always been regretting that I was not as wise as the day I was born. The intellect is a cleaver; it discerns and rifts its way into the secret of things. I do not wish to be any more busy with my hands than is necessary. My head is hands and feet. I feel all my best faculties concentrated in it. My instinct tells me that my head is an organ for burrowing, as some creatures use their snout and fore-paws, and with it I would mine and burrow my way through these hills. I think that the richest vein is somewhere hereabouts; so by the divining rod and thin rising vapors I judge; and here I will begin to mine.

A Slight Sound at Evening
E. B. White

In his journal for July 10–12, 1841, Thoreau wrote: "A slight sound at evening lifts me up by the ears, and makes life seem inexpressibly serene and grand. It may be in Uranus, or it may be in the shutter." The book into which he later managed to pack both Uranus and the shutter was published in 1854, and now, a hundred years having gone by, *Walden*, its serenity and grandeur unimpaired, still lifts us up by the ears, still translates for us that language we are in danger of forgetting, "which all things and events speak without metaphor, which alone is copious and standard."

Walden is an oddity in American letters. It may very well be the oddest of our distinguished oddities. For many it is a great deal too odd, and for many it is a particular bore. I have not found it to be a well-liked book among my acquaintances, although usually spoken of with respect, and one literary critic for whom I have the highest regard can find no reason why anyone gives *Walden* a second thought. To admire the book is, in fact, something of an embarrassment, for the mass of men have an indistinct notion that its author was a sort of Nature Boy.

I think it is of some advantage to encounter the book at a period in one's life when the normal anxieties and enthusiasms and rebellions of youth closely resemble those of Thoreau in that spring of 1845 when he borrowed an axe, went out to the woods, and began to whack down some trees for timber. Received at such a juncture, the book is like an invitation to life's dance, assuring the troubled recipient that no matter what befalls him in the way of success or failure he will always be welcome at the party—that the music is played for him, too, if he will but listen and move his feet. In effect, that is what the book is—an invitation, unengraved; and it stirs one as a young girl is stirred by her first big party bid. Many think it a sermon; many set it down as an attempt to rearrange society; some think it an exercise in nature-loving; some find it a rather irritating collection of inspirational puffballs by an eccentric show-off. I think it none of these. It still seems to me the best youth's companion yet written by an American, for it carries a solemn warning against the loss of one's valuables, it advances a good argument for traveling light and trying new adventures, it rings with the power of positive adoration, it contains religious feeling without religious images, and it steadfastly refuses to record bad news. Even its pantheistic note is so pure as to be noncorrupting—pure as the flute-note blown across the pond on those faraway summer nights. If our colleges and universities were alert, they would present a cheap pocket edition of the book to every senior upon graduating, along with his sheepskin, or instead of it. Even if some senior were to take it literally and start felling trees, there could be worse mishaps: the axe is older than the Dictaphone and it is just as well for a young man to see what kind of chips he leaves before listening to the sound of his own voice. And even if some were to get no farther than the table of contents, they would learn how to name eighteen chapters by the use of only thirty-nine words and would see how sweet are the uses of brevity.

If Thoreau had merely left us an account of a man's life in the woods, or if he had simply retreated to the woods and there recorded his complaints about society, or even if he had contrived to include both records in one essay, *Walden* would probably not have lived a hundred years. As things turned out, Thoreau, very likely without knowing quite what he was up to, took man's relation to nature and man's dilemma in society and man's capacity for elevating his spirit and he beat all these matters together, in a wild free interval of self-justification and delight, and produced an original omelette from which people can draw nourishment in a hungry day. *Walden* is one of the first of the vitamin-enriched American dishes. If it were a little less good than it is, or even a little less queer, it would be an abominable book. Even as it is, it will continue to baffle and annoy the literal mind and all those who are unable to stomach its caprices and imbibe its theme. Certainly the plodding economist will continue to have rough going if he hopes to emerge from the book with a clear system of economic thought. Thoreau's assault on the Concord society of the mid-nineteenth century has the quality of a modern Western: he rides into the subject at top speed, shooting in all directions. Many of his shots ricochet and nick him on the rebound, and throughout the melee there is a horrendous cloud of inconsistencies and contradictions, and when the shooting dies down and the air clears, one is impressed chiefly by the courage of the rider and by how splendid it was that somebody should have ridden in there and raised all that ruckus.

When he went to the pond, Thoreau struck an attitude and did so deliberately, but his posturing was not to draw the attention of others to him but rather to draw his own attention more closely to himself. "I learned this at least by my experiment: that if one advances confidently in the direction of his dreams, and endeavors to live the life which he has imagined, he will meet with a success unexpected in common hours." The sentence has the power to resuscitate the youth drowning in his sea of doubt. I recall my exhilaration upon reading it, many years ago, in a time of hesitation and despair. It restored me to health. And now in 1954 when I salute Henry Thoreau on the hundredth birthday of his book, I am merely paying off an old score—or an installment on it.

In his journal for May 3–4, 1838—Boston to Portland—he wrote: "Midnight—head over the boat's side—between sleeping and waking—with glimpses of one or more lights in the vicinity of Cape Ann. Bright moonlight—the effect heightened by seasickness." The entry illuminates the man, as the moon the sea on that night in May. In Thoreau the natural scene was heightened, not depressed, by a disturbance of the stomach, and nausea met its match at last. There was a steadiness in at least one passenger if there was none in the boat. Such steadiness (which in some would be called intoxication) is at the heart of *Walden* —confidence, faith, the discipline of looking always at what is to be seen, undeviating gratitude for the life-everlasting that he found growing in his front yard. "There is nowhere recorded a simple and irrepressible satisfaction with the gift of life, any memorable praise of God." He worked to correct that deficiency. *Walden* is his acknowledgment of the gift of life. It is the testament of a man in a high state of indignation because (it seemed to him) so few ears heard the uninterrupted poem of creation, the morning wind that forever blows. If the man sometimes wrote as though all his readers were male, unmarried, and well-connected, it is because he gave his testimony during the callow years, and, for that matter, never really grew up. To reject the book because of the immaturity of the author and the bugs in the logic is to throw away a bottle of good wine because it contains bits of the cork.

Thoreau said he required of every writer, first and last, a simple and sincere account of his own life. Having delivered himself of this chesty dictum, he proceeded to ignore it. In his books and even in his enormous journal, he withheld or disguised most of the facts from which an understanding of his life could be drawn. *Walden,* subtitled "Life in the Woods," is not a simple and sincere account of a man's life, either in or out of the woods; it is an account of a man's journey into the mind, a toot on the trumpet to alert the neighbors. Thoreau was well aware that no one can alert his neighbors who is not wide awake himself, and he went to the woods (among other reasons) to make sure that he would stay awake during his broadcast. What actually took place during the years 1845–47 is largely unrecorded, and the reader is excluded from the private life of the author, who supplies almost no gossip about himself, a great deal about his neighbors and about the universe.

As for me, I cannot in this short ramble give a simple and sincere account of my own life, but I think Thoreau might find it instructive to know that this memorial essay is being written in a house that, through no intent on my part, is the same size and shape as his own domicile on the pond—about ten by fifteen, tight, plainly finished, and at a little distance from my Concord. The house in which I sit this morning was built to accommodate a boat, not a man, but by long experience I have learned that in most respects it shelters me better than the larger dwelling where my bed is, and which, by design, is a man-house not a boathouse. Here in the boathouse I am a wilder and, it would appear, a healthier man, by a safe margin. I have a chair, a bench, a table, and I can walk into the water if I tire of the land. My house fronts a cove. Two fishermen have just arrived to spot fish from the air—an osprey and a man in a small yellow plane who works for the fish company. The man, I have noticed, is less well equipped than the hawk, who can dive directly on his fish and carry it away, without telephoning. A mouse and a squirrel share the house with me. The building is, in fact, a multiple dwelling, a semidetached affair. It is because I am semidetached while here that I find it possible to transact this private business with the fewest obstacles.

There is also a woodchuck here, living forty feet away under the wharf. When the wind is right, he can smell my house; and when the wind is contrary, I can smell his. We both use the wharf for sunning, taking turns, each adjusting his schedule to the other's convenience. Thoreau once ate a woodchuck. I think he felt he owed it to his readers, and that it was little enough, considering the indignities they were suffering at his hands and the dressing-down they were taking. (Parts of *Walden* are pure scold.) Or perhaps he ate the woodchuck because he believed every man should acquire strict business habits, and the woodchuck was destroying his market beans. I do not know. Thoreau had a strong experimental streak in him. It is probably no harder to eat a woodchuck than to construct a sentence that lasts a hundred years. At any rate, Thoreau is the only writer I know who prepared himself for his great ordeal by eating a woodchuck; also the only one who got a hangover from drinking too much water. (He was drunk the whole time, though he seldom touched wine or coffee or tea.)

Here in this compact house where I would spend one day as deliberately as Nature if I were not being pressed by *The Yale Review*, and with a woodchuck (as yet uneaten) for neighbor, I can feel the companionship of the occupant of the pondside cabin in Walden woods, a mile from the village, near the Fitchburg right of way. Even my immediate business is no barrier between us: Thoreau occasionally batted out a magazine piece, but was always suspicious of any sort of purposeful work that cut into his time. A man, he said, should take care not to be thrown off the track by every nutshell and mosquito's wing that falls on the rails.

There has been much guessing as to why he went to the pond. To set it down to escapism is, of course, to misconstrue what happened. Henry went forth to battle when he took to the woods, and *Walden* is the report of a man torn by two powerful and opposing drives —the desire to enjoy the world (and not be derailed by a mosquito wing) and the urge to set the world straight. One cannot join these two successfully, but sometimes, in rare cases, something good or even great results from the attempt of the tormented spirit to reconcile them. Henry went forth to battle, and if he set the stage himself, if he fought on his own terms and with his own weapons, it was because it was his nature to do things differently from most men, and to act in a cocky fashion. If the pond and the woods seemed a more plausible site for a house than an in-town location, it was because a cowbell made for him a sweeter sound than a churchbell. *Walden*, the book, makes the sound of the cowbell, more than a churchbell, and proves the point, although both sounds are in it, and both remarkably clear and sweet. He simply preferred his churchbell at a little distance.

I think one reason he went to the woods was a perfectly simple and commonplace one—and apparently he thought so, too. "At a certain season of our life," he wrote, "we are accustomed to consider every spot as the possible site of a house." There spoke the young man, a few years out of college, who had not yet broken away from home. He hadn't married, and he had found no job that measured up to his rigid standards of employment, and like any young man, or young animal, he felt uneasy and on the defensive until he had fixed himself a den. Most young men, of course, casting about for a site, are content merely to draw apart from their kinfolks. Thoreau, convinced that the greater part of what his neighbors called good was bad, withdrew from a great deal more than family: he pulled out of everything for a while, to serve everybody right for being so stuffy, and to try his own prejudices on the dog.

The house-hunting sentence above, which starts the Chapter called "Where I Lived, and What I Lived For," is followed by another passage that is worth quoting here because it so beautifully illustrates the off-beat prose that Thoreau was master of, a prose at once strictly disciplined and wildly abandoned. "I have surveyed the country on every side within a dozen miles of where I live," continued this delirious young man. "In imagination I have bought all the farms in succession, for all were to be bought, and I knew their price. I walked over each farmer's premises, tasted his wild apples, discoursed on husbandry with him, took his farm at his price, at any price, mortgaging it to him in my mind; even put a higher price on it—took everything but a deed of it—took his word for his deed, for I dearly love to talk—cultivated it, and him too to some extent, I trust, and withdrew when I had enjoyed it long enough, leaving him to carry it on." A copydesk man would get a double hernia trying to clean up that sentence for the management, but the sentence needs no fixing, for it perfectly captures the meaning of the writer and the quality of the ramble.

"Wherever I sat, there might I live, and the landscape radiated from me accordingly." Thoreau, the home-seeker, sitting on his hummock with the entire State of Massachusetts radiating from him, is to me the most humorous of the New England figures, and *Walden* the most humorous of the books, though its humor is almost continuously sub-surface and there is nothing funny anywhere, except a few weak jokes and bad puns that rise to the surface like a perch in the pond that rose to the sound of the maestro's flute. Thoreau tended to write in sentences, a feat not every writer is capable of, and *Walden* is, rhetorically speaking, a collection of certified sentences, some of them, it would now appear, as indestructible as they are errant. The book is distilled from the vast journals, and this accounts for its intensity: he picked out bright particles that pleased his eye, whirled them in the kaleidoscope of his content, and produced the pattern that has endured—the color, the form, the light.

On this its hundredth birthday, Thoreau's *Walden* is pertinent and timely. In our uneasy season, when all men unconsciously seek a retreat from a world that has got almost completely out of hand, his house in the Concord woods is a haven. In our culture of gadgetry and the multiplicity of convenience, his cry "Simplicity, simplicity, simplicity!" has the insistence of a fire alarm. In the brooding atmosphere of war and the gathering radioactive storm, the innocence and serenity of his summer afternoons are enough to burst the remembering heart, and one gazes back upon that pleasing interlude—its confidence, its purity, its deliberateness—with awe and wonder, as one would look upon the face of a child asleep.

"This small lake was of most value as a neighbor in the intervals of a gentle rain-storm in August, when, both air and water being perfectly still, but the sky overcast, midafternoon had all the serenity of evening, and the wood-thrush sang around, and was heard from shore to shore." Now, in the perpetual overcast in which our days are spent, we hear with extra perception and deep gratitude that song, tying century to century.

I sometimes amuse myself by bringing Henry Thoreau back to life and showing him the sights. I escort him into a phone booth and let him dial Weather. "This is a delicious evening," the girl's voice says, "when the whole body is one sense, and imbibes delight through every pore." I show him the spot in the Pacific where an island used to be, before some magician made it vanish. "We know not where we are," I murmur. "The light which puts out our eyes is darkness to us. Only that day dawns to which we are awake." I thumb through the latest copy of *Vogue* with him. "Of two patterns which differ only by a few threads more or less of a particular color," I read, "the one will be sold readily, the other lie on the shelf, though it frequently happens that, after the lapse of a season, the latter becomes the most fashionable." Together we go outboarding on the Assabet, looking for what we've lost—a hound, a bay horse, a turtledove. I show him a distracted farmer who is trying to repair a hay baler before the thunder shower breaks. "This farmer," I remark, "is endeavoring to solve the problem of a livelihood by a formula more complicated than the problem itself. To get his shoe strings he speculates in herds of cattle."

I take the celebrated author to Twenty-One for lunch, so the waiters may study his shoes. The proprietor welcomes us. "The gross feeder," remarks the proprietor, sweeping the room with his arm, "is a man in the larva stage." After lunch we visit a classroom in one of those schools conducted by big corporations to teach their superannuated executives how to retire from business without serious injury to their health. (The shock to men's systems these days when relieved of the exacting routine of amassing wealth is very great and must be cushioned.) "It is not necessary," says the teacher to his pupils, "that a man should earn his living by the sweat of his brow, unless he sweats easier than I do. We are determined to be starved before we are hungry."

I turn on the radio and let Thoreau hear Winchell beat the red hand around the clock. "Time is but the stream I go a-fishing in," shouts Mr. Winchell, rattling his telegraph key. "Hardly a man takes a half hour's nap after dinner, but when he wakes he holds up his head and asks, 'What's the news?' If we read of one man robbed, or murdered, or killed by accident, or one house burned, or one vessel wrecked, or one steamboat blown up, or one cow run over on the Western Railroad, or one mad dog killed, or one lot of grasshoppers in the winter—we need never read of another. One is enough."

I doubt that Thoreau would be thrown off balance by the fantastic sights and sounds of the twentieth century. "The Concord nights," he once wrote, "are stranger than the Arabian nights." A four-engined air liner would merely serve to confirm his early views on travel. Everywhere he would observe, in new shapes and sizes, the old predicaments and follies of men—the desperation, the impedimenta, the meanness—along with the visible capacity for elevation of the mind and soul. "This curious world which we inhabit is more wonderful than it is convenient; more beautiful than it is useful; it is more to be admired and enjoyed than used." He would see that today ten thousand engineers are busy making sure that the world shall be convenient if they bust doing it, and others are determined to increase its usefulness even though its beauty is lost somewhere along the way.

At any rate, I'd like to stroll about the countryside in Thoreau's company for a day, observing the modern scene, inspecting today's snowstorm, pointing out the sights, and offering belated apologies for my sins. Thoreau is unique among writers in that those who admire him find him uncomfortable to live with—a regular hairshirt of a man. A little band of dedicated Thoreauvians would be a sorry sight indeed: fellows who hate compromise and have compromised, fellows who love wildness and have lived tamely, and at their side, censuring them and chiding them, the ghostly figure of this upright man, who long ago gave corroboration to impulses they perceived were right and issued warnings against the things they instinctively knew to be their enemies. I should hate to be called a Thoreauvian, yet I wince every time I walk into the barn I'm pushing before me, seventy-five feet by forty, and the author of *Walden* has served as my conscience through the long stretches of my trivial days.

Hairshirt or no, he is a better companion than most, and I would not swap him for a soberer or more reasonable friend even if I could. I can reread his famous invitation with undiminished excitement. The sad thing is that not more acceptances have been received, that so many decline for one reason or another, pleading some previous engagement or ill health. But the invitation stands. It will beckon as long as this remarkable book stays in print—which will be as long as there are August afternoons in the intervals of a gentle rainstorm, as long as there are ears to catch the faint sounds of the orchestra. I find it agreeable to sit here this morning, in a house of correct proportions, and hear across a century of time his flute, his frogs, and his seductive summons to the wildest revels of them all.

The Importance of Nietzsche
Erich Heller

1

In 1873, two years after Bismarck's Prussia had defeated France, a young German who happened to live in Switzerland and taught classical philology in the University of Basle, wrote a treatise concerned with "the German mind." It was an inspired diatribe against, above all, the German notion of *Kultur* and against the philistine readiness to believe that military victory proved cultural superiority. This was, he said, a disastrous superstition, symptomatic in itself of the absence of any true culture. According to him, the opposite was true: the civilization of the vanquished French was bound more and more to dominate the victorious German people that had wasted its spirit upon the chimera of political power.[1]

This national heretic's name, rather obscure at the time, was Friedrich Nietzsche. What, almost a century ago, he wrote about the perverse relationship between military success and intellectual dominance proved true: not then, perhaps, but now. Defeated in two wars, Germany appears to have invaded vast territories of the world's mind, with Nietzsche himself as no mean conqueror. For his was the vision of things to come. Among all the thinkers of the nineteenth century he is, with the possible exceptions of Dostoevsky and Kierkegaard, the only one who would not be too amazed by the amazing scene upon which we now move in sad, pathetic, heroic, stoic, or ludicrous bewilderment. Much, too much, would strike him as *déjà vu:* yes, he had foreseen it; and he would understand: for the "Modern Mind" speaks German, not always good German, but fluent German nonetheless. It was, alas, forced to learn the idiom of Karl Marx, and was delighted to be introduced to itself in the language of Sigmund Freud; taught by Ranke

---

[1] I have omitted Heller's footnotes, which merely cite the German sources.—S.B.

and, later, Max Weber, it acquired its historical and sociological self-consciousness, moved out of its tidy Newtonian universe on the instruction of Einstein, and followed a design of Oswald Spengler's in sending from the depth of its spiritual depression most ingeniously engineered objects higher than the moon. Whether it discovers, with Heidegger, the true habitation of its *Existenz* on the frontiers of Nothing, or mediates, with Sartre and Camus, *le Néant* or the Absurd; whether—to pass to its less serious moods—it is nihilistically young and profitably angry in London or rebelliously debauched and buddhistic in San Francisco—*man spricht deutsch*. It is all part of a story told by Nietzsche.

As for modern German literature and thought, it is hardly an exaggeration to say that they would not be what they are if Nietzsche had never lived. Name almost any poet, man of letters, philosopher, who wrote in German during the twentieth century and attained to stature and influence—Rilke, George, Kafka, Thomas Mann, Ernst Jünger, Musil, Benn, Heidegger, or Jaspers—and you name at the same time Friedrich Nietzsche. He is to them all—whether or not they know and acknowledge it (and most of them do)—what St. Thomas Aquinas was to Dante: the categorical interpreter of a world which they contemplate poetically or philosophically without ever radically upsetting its Nietzschean structure.

Nietzsche died in 1900, after twelve years of a total eclipse of his intellect, insane—and on the threshold of this century. Thinking and writing to the very edge of insanity, and with some of his last pages even going over it, he read and interpreted the temperatures of his own mind; but by doing so, he has drawn the fever-chart of an epoch. Indeed, much of his work reads like the self-diagnosis of a desperate physician who, suffering the disease on our behalf, comes to prescribe as a cure that we should form a new idea of health, and live by it.

He was convinced that it would take at least fifty years before a few men would understand what he had accomplished; and he feared that even then his teaching would be misinterpreted and misapplied. "I am terrified," he wrote, "by the thought of the sort of people who may one day invoke my authority." But is this not, he added, the anguish of every great teacher? He knows that he may prove a disaster as much as a blessing. The conviction that he was a great teacher never left him after he had passed through that period of sustained inspiration in which he wrote the first part of *Zarathustra*. After this, all his utterances convey the disquieting self-confidence and the terror of a man who has reached the culmination of that paradox which he embodies, a paradox which we shall try to name and which ever since has cast its dangerous spell over some of the finest and some of the coarsest minds.

Are we then, at the remove of two generations, in a better position to probe Nietzsche's mind and to avoid, as he hoped some might, the misunderstanding that he was merely concerned with the religious, philosophical, or political controversies fashionable in his day? And if this be a misinterpretation, can we put anything more valid in its place? What is the knowledge which he claims to have, raising him in his own opinion far above the contemporary level of thought? What the discovery which serves him as a lever to unhinge the whole fabric of traditional values?

It is the knowledge that God is dead.

The death of God he calls the greatest event in modern history and the cause of extreme danger. Note well the paradox contained in these words. He never said that there was no God, but that the Eternal had been vanquished by Time and that the Immortal suffered death at the hands of mortals: God is dead. It is like a cry mingled of despair and triumph, reducing, by comparison, the whole story of atheism and agnosticism before and after him to the level of respectable mediocrity and making it sound like a collection of announcements by bankers who regret they are unable to invest in an unsafe proposition. Nietzsche, for the nineteenth century, brings to its *perverse* conclusion a line of religious thought and experience linked with the names of St. Paul, St. Augustine, Pascal, Kierkegaard, and Dostoevsky, minds for whom God was not simply the creator of an order of nature within which man has his clearly defined place, but to whom He came rather in order to challenge their natural being, making demands which appeared absurd in the light of natural reason. These men are of the family of Jacob: having wrestled with God for His blessing, they ever after limp through life with the framework of Nature incurably out of joint. Nietzsche is just such a wrestler; except that in him the shadow of Jacob merges with the shadow of Prometheus. Like Jacob, Nietzsche too believed that he prevailed against God in that struggle, and won a new name for himself, the name of Zarathustra. But the words *he* spoke on his mountain to the angel of the Lord were: "I will not let thee go, except thou curse me." Or, in words which Nietzsche did in fact speak: "I have on purpose devoted my life to exploring the whole contrast to a truly religious nature. I know the Devil and all his visions of God."

"God is dead"—this is the very core of Nietzsche's spiritual existence, and what follows is despair, *and* hope in a new greatness of man, visions of catastrophe *and* glory, the icy brilliance of analytical reason, fathoming with affected irreverence those depths hitherto hidden by awe and fear, and, side-by-side with it, the ecstatic invocations of a ritual healer. Probably inspired by Hölderlin's dramatic poem *Empedocles*, the young Nietzsche, who loved what he knew of Hölderlin's poetry, at the age of twenty planned to write a drama with Empedocles as its hero. His notes show that he saw the Greek philosopher as the tragic personification of his age, as a man in whom the latent conflicts of his epoch attained to consciousness, as one who suffered and died as the victim of an unresolvable tension: born with the soul of a *homo religiosus,* a seer, a prophet, and poet, he yet had the mind of a radical skeptic; and defending his soul against his mind and, in turn, his mind against his soul, he made his soul lose its spontaneity, and finally his mind its rationality. Had Nietzsche ever written the drama *Empedocles,* it might have become, in uncanny anticipation, his *own* tragedy.

It is a passage from Nietzsche's *Gaya Scienza,* his *Cheerful Science,* which conveys best the substance and quality of the mind, indeed the whole spiritual situation, from which the pronouncement of the death of God sprang. The passage is prophetically entitled "The Madman" and might have been called "The New Diogenes." Here is a brief extract from it:

> Have you not heard of that madman who, in the broad light of the forenoon, lit a lantern and ran into the market-place, crying incessantly: "I am looking for God!" . . . As it happened, many were standing there who did not believe in God, and so he aroused great laughter . . . The madman leapt right among them . . . "Where is God?" he cried. "Well, I will tell you. *We have murdered him*—you and I . . . But how did we do this deed? . . . Who gave us the sponge with which to wipe out the whole horizon? How did we set about unchaining our earth from her sun? Whither is it moving now? Whither are we moving? . . . Are we not falling incessantly? . . . Is night not approaching, and more and more night? Must we not light lanterns in the forenoon? Behold the noise of the gravediggers, busy to bury God . . . And we have killed him! What possible comfort is there for us? . . . Is not the greatness of this deed too great for us? To appear worthy of it, must not we ourselves become gods?"—At this point the madman fell silent and looked once more at those around him: "Oh," he said, "I am too early. My time has not yet come. The news of this tremendous event is still on its way . . . Lightning and thunder take time, the light of the stars takes time to get to us, deeds take time to be seen and heard . . . and *this* deed is still farther from them than the farthest stars—*and yet it was they themselves who did it!*"

And elsewhere, in a more prosaic mood, Nietzsche says: "People have no notion yet that from now onwards they exist on the mere pittance of inherited and decaying values"—soon to be overtaken by an enormous bankruptcy.

The story of the Madman, written two years before *Zarathustra* and containing *in nuce* the whole message of the Superman, shows the distance that divides Nietzsche from the conventional attitudes of atheism. He is the madman, breaking with his sinister news into the marketplace complacency of the pharisees of unbelief. They have done away with God, and yet the report of their own deed has not yet reached them. They know not what they have done, but He who could forgive them is no more. Much of Nietzsche's work ever after is the prophecy of their fate: "The story I have to tell is the history of the next two centuries . . . For a long time now our whole civilization has been driving, with a tortured intensity growing from decade to decade, as if towards a catastrophe: restlessly, violently, tempestuously, like a mighty river desiring the end of its journey, without pausing to reflect, indeed fearful of reflection. . . . Where we live, soon nobody will be able to exist." For men become enemies, and each his own enemy. From now onward they will *hate*, Nietzsche believes, however many *comforts* they will lavish upon themselves, and hate *themselves* with a new hatred, unconsciously at work in the depths of their souls. True, there will be ever better reformers of society, ever better socialists, and ever better hospitals, and an ever increasing intolerance of pain and poverty and suffering and death, and an ever more fanatical craving for the greatest happiness of the greatest numbers. Yet the deepest impulse informing their striving will not be love and will not be compassion. Its true source will be the panic-struck determination not to have to ask the question "What is the meaning of our lives?"—the question which will remind them of the death of God, the uncomfortable question inscribed on the features of those who are uncomfortable, and asked above all by pain and poverty and suffering and death. Rather than allowing that question to be asked, they will do everything to smooth it away from the face of humanity. For they cannot endure it. And yet they will despise themselves for not enduring it, and for their guilt-ridden inability to answer it; and their self-hatred will betray them behind the back of their apparent charity and humanitarian concern. For *there* they will assiduously construct the tools for the annihilation of human kind. "There will be wars," Nietzsche writes, "such as have never been waged on earth." And he says: "I foresee something terrible. Chaos everywhere. Nothing left which is of any value; nothing which commands: Thou shalt!" This would have been the inspiration of the final work which Nietzsche often said he would write and never wrote: *The Will to Power*, or, as he sometimes wanted to call it, *The Transvaluation of All Values*. It might have given his full diagnosis of what he termed nihilism, the state of human beings and societies faced with a total eclipse of all values.

It is in defining and examining the (for him *historical*) phenomenon of nihilism that Nietzsche's attack on Christianity sets in (and it has remained the only truly subtle point which, within the whole range of his more and more unrestrained argumentativeness, this Antichrist makes against Christianity). For it is at this point that Nietzsche asks (and asks the same question in countless variations throughout his works): What are the *specific* qualities which the Christian tradition has instilled and cultivated in the minds of men? They are, he thinks, twofold: on the one hand, a more refined sense of truth than any other civilization has known, an almost uncontrollable desire for absolute spiritual and intellectual certainties; and, on the other hand, the ever-present suspicion that life on this earth is not in itself a supreme value, but in need of a higher, a transcendental justification. This, Nietzsche believes, is a destructive, and even self-destructive alliance, which is bound finally to corrode the very Christian beliefs on which it rests. For the mind, exercised and guided in its search for knowledge by the most sophisticated and comprehensive theology the world has ever known—a theology which through St. Thomas Aquinas has assimilated into its grand system the genius of Aristotle—was at the same time fashioned and directed by the indelible Christian distrust of the ways of the world. Thus it had to follow, with the utmost logical precision and determination, a course of systematically "devaluing" the knowably real. This mind, Nietzsche predicts, will eventually, in a frenzy of intellectual honesty, unmask as humbug and "meaningless" that which it began by regarding as the finer things in life. The boundless faith in truth, the joint legacy of Christ and Greek, will in the end dislodge every possible belief in the truth of any faith. Souls, long disciplined in a school of unworldliness and humility, will insist upon knowing the worst about themselves, indeed will only be able to grasp what is humiliating. Psychology will denigrate the creations of beauty, laying bare the tangle of unworthy desires of which they are "mere" sublimations. History will undermine the accumulated reputation of the human race by exhuming from beneath the splendid monuments the dead body of the past, revealing everywhere the spuriousness of motives, the human, all-too-human. And science itself will rejoice in exposing this long-suspected world as a mechanical contraption of calculable pulls and pushes, as a self-sufficient agglomeration of senseless energy, until finally, in a surfeit of knowledge, the scientific mind will perform the somersault of self-annihilation.

"The nihilistic consequences of our natural sciences"—this is one of Nietzsche's fragmentary jottings—"from its pursuits there follows ultimately a self-decomposition, a turning against itself," which—and this is one of his most amazingly precise predictions—would first show itself in the impossibility, within science itself, of comprehending the very object of its inquiry within *one* logically coherent system, and would lead to extreme scientific pessimism, to an inclination to embrace a kind of analytical, abstract mysticism by which man would shift himself and his world to where, Nietzsche thinks, they were driving "ever since Copernicus: from the center towards an unknown X."

2

It is the tremendous paradox of Nietzsche that he himself follows, and indeed consciously wishes to hasten, this course of "devaluation"—particularly as a psychologist: and at the onset of megalomania he called himself the first psychologist in the world—"there was no psychology before me," a self-compliment which Sigmund Freud all but endorsed when, surprisingly late in his life, he came to know Nietzsche's writings. He had good reason to do so. Consider, for instance, the following passage from Nietzsche's *Beyond Good and Evil:*

> The world of historical values is dominated by forgery. These great poets, like Byron, Musset, Poe, Leopardi, Kleist, Gogol (I dare not mention greater names, but I mean them)—all endowed with souls wishing to conceal a break; often avenging themselves with their works upon some inner desecration, often seeking oblivion in their lofty flights from their all-too-faithful memories, often lost in mud and almost in love with it until they become like will-o-the-wisps of the morasses and simulate the stars . . . oh what a torture are all these great artists and altogether these higher beings, what a torture to him who has guessed their true nature.

This does indeed anticipate many a more recent speculation on traumata and compensations, on lusts and sublimations, on wounds and bows. Yet the extraordinary Nietzsche—incomprehensible in his contradictions except as the common strategist of two opposing armies who plans for the victory of a mysterious third—a few pages later takes back the guessing, not without insulting himself in the process: "From which it follows that it is the sign of a finer humanity to respect 'the mask' and not, in the wrong places, indulge in psychology and psychological curiosity." And furthermore: "He who does not *wish* to see what is great in a man, has the sharpest eye for that which is low and superficial in him, and so gives away—himself."

If Nietzsche is not the first psychologist of Europe, he is certainly a great psychologist—and perhaps really the first who comprehended what his more methodical successors, "strictly scientific" in their approach, did not see: *the psychology and the ethics of knowledge itself;* and both the psychology and the ethics of knowledge are of particular relevance when the knowledge in question purports to be knowledge of the human psyche. It was, strangely enough, Nietzsche's amoral metaphysics, his doubtful but immensely fruitful intuition of the Will to Power as being the ultimate reality of the world, that made him into the first *moralist of knowledge* in his century and long after. While all his scientific and scholarly contemporaries throve on the comfortable assumptions that, firstly, there was such a thing as "objective," and therefore morally neutral, knowledge, and that, secondly, everything that *can* be known "objectively" is therefore also *worth knowing,* he realized that knowledge, or at least the mode of knowledge predominant at his time and ours, is the subtlest guise of the Will to Power; and that *as a manifestation of the will it is liable to be judged morally.* For him, there can be no knowledge without a compelling urge to acquire it; and he knew that the knowledge thus acquired invariably reflects the nature of the impulse by which the mind was prompted. It is this impulse which *creatively* partakes in the making of the knowledge, and its share in it is truly immeasurable when the knowledge is about the very source of the impulse: the soul. This is why all interpretations of the soul must to a high degree be self-interpretations: the sick interpret the sick, and the dreamers interpret dreams. Or, as the Viennese satirist Karl Kraus—with that calculated injustice which is the prerogative of satire—once said of a certain psychological theory: "Psychoanalysis is the disease of which it pretends to be the cure."

Psychology is bad psychology if it disregards its own psychology. Nietzsche knew this. He was, as we have seen from his passage about "those great men," a most suspicious psychologist, but he was at the same time suspicious of the suspicion which was the father of his thought. Homer, to be sure, did not suspect his heroes, but Stendhal did. Does this mean that Homer knew less about the heroic than Stendhal? Does it make sense to say that Flaubert's Emma Bovary is the product of an imagination more profoundly initiated into the psychology of women than that which created Dante's Beatrice? Is Benjamin Constant, who created the dubious lover Adolphe, on more intimate terms with the nature of a young man's erotic passion than is Shakespeare, the begetter of Romeo? Certainly, Homer's Achilles and Stendhal's Julien Sorel are different heroes, Dante's Beatrice and Flaubert's Emma Bovary are different women, Shakespeare's Romeo and Constant's Adolphe are different lovers, but it would be naïve to believe that they simply differ "in actual fact." Actual facts hardly exist in either art or psychology: both interpret and both claim universality for the meticulously presented particular. Those creatures made by creative imaginations can indeed not be compared; yet if they differ as, in life, one person differs from another, at the same time, because they have their existence not "in life" but in art, they are incommensurable above all by virtue of their author's incommensurable *wills* to know the human person, to know the hero, the woman, the lover. It is not better and more knowing minds that have created the suspect hero, the unlovable woman, the disingenuous lover, but minds possessed by different desires for a different knowledge, a knowledge uninformed with the wonder and pride that know Achilles, the love that knows Beatrice, the passion and compassion that know Romeo. When Hamlet has come to know the frailty of woman, he knows Ophelia not better than when he was "unknowingly" in love with her; he only knows her differently and he knows her worse.

All *new* knowledge about the soul is knowledge about a *different* soul. For can it ever happen that the freely discovering mind says to the soul: "This is what you are!"? Is it not rather as if the mind said to the soul: "This is how I *wish* you to see yourself! This is the image after which I create you! This is my secret about you: I shock you with it and, shockingly, at once wrest it from you"? And worse: having thus received *and* revealed its secret, the soul is no longer what it was when it lived in secrecy. For there are secrets which are *created* in the process of their revelation. And worse still: having been told its secrets, the soul may cease to be a soul. The step from modern psychology to soul-lessness is as imperceptible as that from modern physics to the dissolution of the concept "matter."

It is this disturbing state of affairs which made Nietzsche deplore "the torture" of psychologically "guessing the true nature of those higher beings" and, at the same time, recommend "respect for the mask" as a condition of "finer humanity." (A great pity he never wrote what, if we are to trust his notes, he planned to say in the abortive *Will to Power* about the literature of the nineteenth century. For no literary critic of the age has had a more penetrating insight into the "nihilistic" character of that "absolute aestheticism" that, from Baudelaire onward, has been the dominant inspiration of European poetry. Respectfully, and sometimes not so respectfully, Nietzsche recognized that behind the aesthetic "mask" there was a face distorted by the loathing of "reality." And it was the realistic and psychological novel that revealed to him that epoch's utterly pessimistic idea of its world. How intimately he knew those aesthetic Furies, or furious Muses, that haunted the mind of Flaubert, inspiring him to produce an *œuvre* in which absolute pessimism, radical psychology, and extreme aestheticism are so intriguingly fused.)

For Nietzsche, however, *all* the activities of human consciousness share the predicament of psychology. There can be, for him, no "pure" knowledge, only satisfactions, however sophisticated, of the ever-varying intellectual needs of the *will* to know. He therefore demands that man should accept *moral responsibility* for the kind of questions he asks, and that he should realize what *values* are implied in the answers he seeks—and in this he was more Christian than all our post-Faustian Fausts of truth and scholarship. "The desire for truth," he says, "is itself in need of critique. Let this be the definition of my philosophical task. By way of experiment, I shall question for once the value of truth." And does he not! And he protests that, in an age which is as uncertain of its values as is his and ours, the search for truth will issue in either trivialities or—catastrophe. We may well wonder how he would react to the pious hopes of our day that the intelligence and moral conscience of politicians will save the world from the disastrous products of our scientific explorations and engineering skills. It is perhaps not too difficult to guess; for he knew that there was a fatal link between the moral resolution of scientists to follow the scientific search *wherever,* by its own momentum, it will take us, and the moral debility of societies not altogether disinclined to "apply" the results, however catastrophic. Believing that there was a hidden identity between *all* the expressions of the Will to Power, he saw the element of moral nihilism in the ethics of our science: its determination not to let "higher values" interfere with its highest value—Truth (as it conceives it). Thus he said that the goal of knowledge pursued by the natural sciences means perdition.

3

"God is dead"—and man, in his heart of hearts, is incapable of forgiving himself for having done away with Him: he is bent upon punishing himself for this, his "greatest deed." For the time being, however, he will take refuge in many an evasive action. With the instinct of a born hunter, Nietzsche pursues him into all his hiding places, cornering him in each of them. Morality without religion? Indeed not: "All purely moral demands without their religious basis," he says, "must needs end in nihilism." What is there left? Intoxication. "Intoxication with music, with cruelty, with hero-worship, or with hatred . . . Some sort of mysticism . . . Art for Art's sake, Truth for Truth's sake, as a narcotic against self-disgust; some kind of routine, *any* silly little fanaticism. . . ." But none of these drugs can have any lasting effect. The time, Nietzsche predicts, is fast approaching when secular crusaders, tools of man's collective suicide, will devastate the world with their rival claims to compensate for the lost Kingdom of Heaven by setting up on earth the ideological rules of Love and Justice which, by the very force of the spiritual derangement involved, will lead to the rules of cruelty and slavery; and he prophesies that the war for global domination will be fought on behalf of philosophical doctrines.

In one of his notes written at the time of *Zarathustra* Nietzsche says: "He who no longer finds what is great in God, will find it nowhere. He must either deny or create it." These words take us to the heart of that paradox that enwraps Nietzsche's whole existence. He is, by the very texture of his soul and mind, one of the most radically religious natures that the nineteenth century brought forth, but is endowed with an intellect which guards, with the aggressive jealousy of a watchdog, all the approaches to the temple. For such a man, what, after the *denial* of God, is there left to *create?* Souls, not only strong enough to endure Hell, but to transmute its agonies into superhuman delight —in fact: the Superman. Nothing short of the transvaluation of all values can save us. Man has to be made immune from the effects of his second Fall and final separation from God: he must learn to see in his second expulsion the promise of a new paradise. For "the Devil may become envious of him who suffers so deeply, and throw him out— into Heaven."

Is there, then, any cure? Yes, says Nietzsche: a new kind of psychic health. And what is Nietzsche's conception of it? How is it to be brought about? By perfect self-knowledge *and* perfect self-transcendence. But to explain this, we should have to adopt an idiom disturbingly compounded of the language of Freudian psychology and tragic heroism. For the self-knowledge which Nietzsche expects all but requires a course in depth-analysis; but the self-transcendence he means lies not in the practice of virtue as a sublimation of natural meanness; it can only be found in a kind of unconditional and almost supranatural sublimity. If there were a Christian virtue, be it goodness, innocence, chastity, saintliness, or self-sacrifice, that could not, however much he tried, be interpreted as a compensatory maneuver of the mind to "transvalue" weakness and frustration, Nietzsche might affirm it (as he is constantly tempted to praise Pascal). The trouble is that there cannot be such a virtue. For virtues are reflected upon by minds; and even the purest virtue will be suspect to a mind filled with suspicion. To think thoughts so immaculate that they must command the trust of even the most untrusting imagination, and to act from motives so pure that they are out of reach of even the most cunning psychology, this is the unattainable ideal, it would seem, of this first psychologist of Europe. "Caesar—with the heart of Christ!" he once exclaimed in the secrecy of his notebook. Was this perhaps a definition of the Superman, this darling child of his imagination? It may well be; but this lofty idea meant, alas, that he had to think the meanest thought: he saw in the real Christ an illegitimate son of the Will to Power, a frustrated rabbi who set out to save himself and the underdog humanity from the intolerable strain of impotently resenting the Caesars: *not* to be Caesar was now proclaimed a spiritual distinction—a newly invented form of power, the power of the powerless.

Nietzsche had to fail, and fail tragically, in his determination to create a new man from the clay of negation. Almost with the same breath with which he gave the life of his imagination to the Superman, he blew the flame out again. For Zarathustra who preaches the Superman also teaches the doctrine of the Eternal Recurrence of All Things; and according to this doctrine nothing can ever come into being that had not existed at some time before—and, Zarathustra says, "never yet has there been a Superman." Thus the expectation of the Superman, this majestic new departure of life, indeed the possibility of any novel development, seems frustrated from the outset, and the world, caught forever in a cycle of gloomily repeated constellations of energy, stands condemned to a most dismal eternity.

Yet the metaphysical nonsense of these contradictory doctrines is not entirely lacking in poetic and didactic method. The Eternal Recurrence of All Things is Nietzsche's mythic formula of a meaningless world, the universe of nihilism, and the Superman stands for its transcendence, for the miraculous resurrection of meaning from its total negation. All Nietzsche's miracles are paradoxes designed to jerk man out of his false beliefs—in time before they bring about his spiritual destruction in an ecstasy of disillusionment and frustration. The Eternal Recurrence is the high school meant to teach strength through despair. The Superman graduates from it *summa cum laude et gloria*. He is the prototype of health, the man who has learned to live without belief and without truth, and, superhumanly delighting in life "as such," actually *wills* the Eternal Recurrence: Live in such a way that you desire nothing more than to live this very same life again and again! The Superman, having attained to this manner of existence which is exemplary and alluring into all eternity, despises his former self for craving moral sanctions, for satisfying his will to power in neurotic sublimation, for deceiving himself about the "meaning" of life. What will he be then, this man who at last knows what life *really* is? Recalling Nietzsche's own accounts of all-too-human nature, and his analysis of the threadbare fabric of traditional values and truths, may he not be the very monster of nihilism, a barbarian, not necessarily blond, but perhaps a conqueror of the world, shrieking bad German from under his dark mustache? Yes, Nietzsche feared his approach in history: the vulgar caricature of the Superman. And because he also feared that the liberally decadent and agnostically disbelieving heirs to Christian morality would be too feeble to meet the challenge, having enfeebled the idea of civilized existence and rendered powerless the good, he sent forth from his imagination the Superman to defeat the defeat of man.

Did Nietzsche himself *believe* in the truth of his doctrines of the Superman and the Eternal Recurrence? In one of his posthumously published notes he says of the Eternal Recurrence: "We have produced the hardest possible thought—the Eternal Recurrence of All Things— now let us create the creature who will accept it lightheartedly and joy-fully!" Clearly, there must have been times when he thought of the Eternal Recurrence not as a "Truth" but as a kind of spiritual Dar-winian test to select for survival the spiritually fittest. There is a note of his which suggests precisely this: "I perform the great experiment: Who can bear the idea of the Eternal Recurrence?" This is a measure of Nietzsche's own unhappiness: the nightmare of nightmares was to him the idea that he might have to live his identical life again and again and again; and an ever deeper insight into the anatomy of despair we gain from this note: "Let us consider this idea in its most terrifying form: existence, as it is, without meaning or goal, but inescapably re-current, without a final into nothingness. . . . Those who cannot bear the sentence, There is no salvation, *ought* to perish!" Indeed, Nietzsche's Superman is the creature strong enough to live forever a cursed exis-tence and even to transmute it into the Dionysian rapture of tragic acceptance. Schopenhauer called man the *animal metaphysicum*. It is certainly true of Nietzsche, the renegade *homo religiosus*. Therefore, if God was dead, then for Nietzsche man was an eternally cheated misfit, the diseased animal, as he called him, plagued by a metaphysical hun-ger which it was now impossible to feed even if all the Heavens were to be ransacked. Such a creature was doomed: he had to die out, giving way to the Superman who would miraculously feed on barren fields and finally conquer the metaphysical hunger itself without any detriment to the glory of life.

Did Nietzsche himself *believe* in the Superman? In the manner in which a poet believes in the truth of his creations. Did Nietzsche believe in the truth of poetic creations? Once upon a time when, as a young man, he wrote *The Birth of Tragedy*, Nietzsche did believe in the power of art to transfigure life by creating lasting images of true beauty out of the meaningless chaos. It had seemed credible enough as long as his gaze was enraptured by the distant prospect of classical Greece and the enthusiastic vicinity of Richard Wagner's Tribschen. Soon, however, his deeply Romantic belief in art turned to skepticism and scorn; and his unphilosophical anger was provoked by those "metaphysical counterfeiters," as he called them, who en-throned the trinity of beauty, goodness, and truth. "One should beat them," he said. Poetic beauty *and* truth? No, "we have *Art* in order not to perish of Truth"; and, says Zarathustra, "poets lie too much"—and adds dejectedly: "But Zarathustra too is a poet . . . *We* lie too much." And he did: while Zarathustra preached the Eternal Recurrence, his author confided to his diary: "I do not wish to live *again.* How have I borne life? By creating. What has made me endure? The vision of the Superman who affirms life. I have tried to affirm life *myself*—but ah!"

Was he, having lost God, capable of truly believing in anything? "He who no longer finds what is great in God will find it nowhere—he must either deny it or create it." Only the "either-or" does not apply. All his life Nietzsche tried to do both. He had the passion for truth and no belief in it. He had the love of life and despaired of it. This is the stuff from which demons are made—perhaps the most powerful secret demon eating the heart out of the modern mind. To have written and enacted the extremest story of this mind is Nietzsche's true claim to greatness. "The Don Juan of the Mind" he once called, in a "fable" he wrote, a figure whose identity is hardly in doubt:

> The Don Juan of the Mind: no philosopher or poet has yet discovered him. What he lacks is the love of the things he knows, what he possesses is *esprit,* the itch and delight in the chase and intrigue of knowledge—knowledge as far and high as the most distant stars. Until in the end there is nothing left for him to chase except the knowledge which hurts most, just as a drunkard in the end drinks absinthe and methylated spirits. And in the very end he craves for Hell—it is the only knowledge which can still seduce him. Perhaps it too will disappoint, as everything that he knows. And if so, he will have to stand transfixed through all eternity, nailed to disillusion, having himself become the Guest of Stone, longing for a last supper of knowledge which he will never receive. For in the whole world of things there is nothing left to feed his hunger.

It is a German Don Juan, this Don Juan of the Mind; and it is amazing that Nietzsche should not have recognized his features: the features of Goethe's Faust at the point at which he has succeeded at last in defeating the plan of salvation.

And yet Nietzsche's work, wrapped in paradox after paradox, taking us to the limits of what is still comprehensible and often beyond, carries elements which issue from a center of sanity. No doubt, this core is in perpetual danger of being crushed, and was in fact destroyed in the end. But it is there, and is made of the stuff of which goodness is made. A few years before he went mad, he wrote: "My life is now comprised in the wish that the truth about all things be different from my way of seeing it: if only someone would convince me of the improbability of my truths!" And he said: "Lonely and deeply suspicious of myself as I was, I took, not without secret spite, sides *against* myself and *for* anything that happened to hurt me and was hard for me." Why? Because he was terrified by the prospect that all the better things in life, all honesty of mind, integrity of character, generosity of heart, fineness of aesthetic perception, would be corrupted and finally cast away by the new barbarians, unless the mildest and gentlest hardened themselves for the war which was about to be waged against them: "Caesar —with the heart of Christ!"

Time and again we come to a point in Nietzsche's writings where the shrill tones of the rebel are hushed by the still voice of the autumn of a world waiting in calm serenity for the storms to break. Then this tormented mind relaxes in what he once called the *Rosengeruch des Unwiederbringlichen*—an untranslatably beautiful lyricism of which the closest equivalent in English is perhaps Yeats' lines:

> Man is in love and loves what vanishes.
> What more is there to say?

In such moments the music of Bach brings tears to his eyes and he brushes aside the noise and turmoil of Wagner; or he is, having deserted Zarathustra's cave in the mountains, enchanted by the gentle grace of a Mediterranean coastline. Rejoicing in the quiet lucidity of Claude Lorrain, or seeking the company of Goethe in conversation with Eckermann, or comforted by the composure of Stifter's *Nachsommer*, a Nietzsche emerges, very different from the one who used to inhabit the fancies of Teutonic schoolboys and, alas, schoolmasters, a Nietzsche who is a traditionalist at heart, a desperate lover who castigates what he loves because he knows it will abandon him and the world. It is the Nietzsche who can with one sentence cross out all the dissonances of his apocalyptic voices: "I once saw a storm raging over the sea, and a clear blue sky above it; it was then that I came to dislike all sunless, cloudy passions which know no light, except the lightning." And this was written by the same man who said that his tool for philosophizing was the hammer, and of himself that he was not human but dynamite.

In these regions of his mind dwells the terror that he may have helped to bring about the very opposite of what he desired. When this terror comes to the fore, he is much afraid of the consequences of his teaching. Perhaps the best will be driven to despair by it, the very worst accept it? And once he put into the mouth of some imaginary titanic genius what is his most terrible prophetic utterance: "Oh grant madness, you heavenly powers! Madness that at last I may believe in myself . . . I am consumed by doubts, for I have killed the Law. . . . If I am not more than the Law, then I am the most abject of all men."

What, then, is the final importance of Nietzsche? For one of his readers it lies in his example which is so strange, profound, confounded, alluring, and forbidding that it can hardly be looked upon as exemplary. But it cannot be ignored either. For it has something to do with living lucidly in the dark age of which he so creatively despaired.

Suggestions for Writing

1. Write five or six sentences, each containing a pun that awakens a sleeping metaphor, as Thoreau does with "spur of the moment" (see Canby, p. 184). Try something like "The apple of Jones's eye seemed a little over-ripe," or "And there she planted her feet: you could almost see them take root."

2. To familiarize yourself with figurative writing, take several of Thoreau's figures of speech and analyze each one according to the three principal levels of figurative subtlety: the simile, the metaphor, the implied metaphor. The *simile* makes its figurative comparison openly, using *like, as,* or *as if:*

> She was *like* a cow.
>
> She walked *as* a cow walks.
>
> She chewed *as if* she were some thoughtful cow.

The *metaphor* exaggerates further by pretending that "She *is* a cow." (In other words, drop the *like* from a simile and you have a metaphor.) The *implied metaphor* hints at the pretended identity without naming it, implying "cow" by using only a cowlike attribute or two: "She chewed her cud thoughtfully."

Now, pick up one of your selections from Thoreau's figures of speech, put it in whichever of the three levels it belongs, and fill in the other two levels, rephrasing the figure to suit them. For instance, the following figure of Thoreau's is an implied metaphor: "a poet has put his farm in rhyme, . . . milked it, skimmed it, and got all the cream." Now, what would the figure be, stated plainly as a simile and as a metaphor? Your answer would look like this:

> SIMILE: The farm is like a cow.
>
> METAPHOR: The farm is the cow.
>
> IMPLIED METAPHOR: (Thoreau) "a poet . . . milked it, skimmed it, and got all the cream."

Here is another example, with Thoreau giving the metaphor, and leaving you the simile and implied metaphor to make:

SIMILE: The distant mountain ranges are like coins.
METAPHOR: (Thoreau) "distant mountain ranges . . . , those true-blue coins from heaven's own mint."
IMPLIED METAPHOR: The distant mountain ranges seemed fresh and newly minted.

3. Write five phrases that mix formal and informal diction, as in the following of White's: "the immaturity of the author and the *bugs* in the logic"; "so beautifully illustrates the *offbeat* prose"; "It was his nature to do things differently from most men, and to act in a *cocky* fashion"; "perfectly captures the meaning of the writer and the quality of the *ramble*."

4. Write an essay illustrating from your own experience one of Thoreau's assertions: "A man is rich in proportion to the number of things he can afford to let alone"; "To be awake is to be alive"; "Let us spend one day as deliberately as Nature" (this last might be a wonderful opening for humor, the shoes full of water, the sandwiches full of ants).

5. Illustrate from your own experience, and with references and allusions to Thoreau, the Thoreauvian satisfaction in building a tree house, spending the night in the woods, planting a watermelon patch, turning a boathouse (just the size of Thoreau's cabin) into a studio for rumination, or knowing a woodchuck (as yet uneaten).

6. Write about some book that has changed the direction of your life.

7. Try a passage in parody or imitation of Thoreau. Now try one imitating White, attempting to catch a prose that can echo Shakespeare's "Sweet are the uses of adversity," that can add an eggbeater and a Western, that can follow a *plodding economist* with a *rough going*, and that still can pay a hairshirt of a man a praise so high it almost bursts the remembering heart.

8. Write five couples of words not usually found together, as in Heller's *inspired diatribe* (this is known as *oxymoron*—a "pointed stupidity," *oxy* meaning "point" and *moron* meaning what it says), where the apparent contradiction of the terms sharpens the underlying point: *mad genius, beautifully ugly, a wicked virtue,* and so forth. Write another five in which the two words come from different areas of activity or thought, as when Heller transplants *heretic* from the religious to the political area by adding *national,* when he calls Nietzsche a *national heretic.* Try something like *political wallflower, academic shortstop, athletic thinker,* and so forth.

9. Write a metaphor that extends through several sentences, as in Heller's extension of "he read and interpreted the temperatures of his own mind."

10. Try three or four Nietzschean paradoxes, attained by playing on different forms of the same word: "Nothing short of the *transvaluation* of all *values* can save us"—"even the purest virtue will be *suspect* to a mind filled with *suspicion*"—"the *power* of the *powerless*."

Shooting an Elephant GEORGE ORWELL · *227*
Fifth Avenue Uptown: A Letter from Harlem JAMES BALDWIN · *233*

The Auto-biographical Essay

Orwell's famous essay is a classic example of personal anecdote used to illustrate a general expository point—imperialism is evil—a thesis that might have been developed at length in a conventional essay, with illustrations from history and testimony from other observers. As you read, notice how Orwell's language keeps the picture before your eyes, and how, when his impressions grow vivid, he moves into metaphor to tell you more clearly how it was—"as neatly as one skins a rabbit." Ask yourself what the difference in force is between the simile and the metaphor, between "like a huge rock toppling" and "grandmotherly air." Notice also how Orwell's stringent honesty about his feelings enforces his thesis, that which he knows to be right.

Baldwin also writes from intense personal experience to illuminate his thesis—"Negroes want to be treated like men, not like poor fish on a hook, nor enemies caught on the barbed wire of an entrenchment." But he draws from a much broader mixture of memory and reportorial observation than does Orwell. He, too, writes with metaphorical power, as he catches his thesis in that barbed phrase about the struggle on upper Fifth Avenue, or sees his stunted trees snarling. His language, like Orwell's, grows vivid from his intensely immediate feeling, a kind of sad indignation now objectified to enforce a general point, as he remembers his childhood, or looks at the present scene so hopelessly unchanged, or draws on what he has learned of facts and attitudes in the meantime.

Shooting an Elephant
George Orwell

In Moulmein, in Lower Burma, I was hated by large numbers of people —the only time in my life that I have been important enough for this to happen to me. I was sub-divisional police officer of the town, and in an aimless, petty kind of way anti-European feeling was very bitter. No one had the guts to raise a riot, but if a European woman went through the bazaars alone somebody would probably spit betel juice over her dress. As a police officer I was an obvious target and was baited whenever it seemed safe to do so. When a nimble Burman tripped me up on the football field and the referee (another Burman) looked the other way, the crowd yelled with hideous laughter. This happened more than once. In the end the sneering yellow faces of young men that met me everywhere, the insults hooted after me when I was at a safe distance, got badly on my nerves. The young Buddhist priests were the worst of all. There were several thousands of them in the town and none of them seemed to have anything to do except stand on street corners and jeer at Europeans.

All this was perplexing and upsetting. For at that time I had already made up my mind that imperialism was an evil thing and the sooner I chucked up my job and got out of it the better. Theoretically—and secretly, of course—I was all for the Burmese and all against their oppressors, the British. As for the job I was doing, I hated it more bitterly than I can perhaps make clear. In a job like that you see the dirty work of Empire at close quarters. The wretched prisoners hud-dling in the stinking cages of the lockups, the grey, cowed faces of the long-term convicts, the scarred buttocks of the men who had been flogged with bamboos—all these oppressed me with an intolerable sense of guilt. But I could get nothing into perspective. I was young and ill-educated and I had had to think out my problems in the utter silence that is imposed on every Englishman in the East. I did not even know that the British Empire is dying, still less did I know that it is a great deal better than the younger empires that are going to supplant it. All I knew was that I was stuck between my hatred of the empire I served and my rage against the evil-spirited little beasts who tried to make my job impossible. With one part of my mind I thought of the British Raj as an unbreakable tyranny, as something clamped down, in *saecula saeculorum,* upon the will of prostrate peoples; with another part I thought that the greatest joy in the world would be to drive a bayonet into a Buddhist priest's guts. Feelings like these are the normal by-products of imperialism; ask any Anglo-Indian official, if you can catch him off duty.

One day something happened which in a roundabout way was en-lightening. It was a tiny incident in itself, but it gave me a better glimpse than I had had before of the real nature of imperialism—the real motives for which despotic governments act. Early one morning the sub-inspector at a police station the other end of the town rang me up on the 'phone and said that an elephant was ravaging the bazaar. Would I please come and do something about it? I did not know what I could do, but I wanted to see what was happening and I got on to a pony and started out. I took my rifle, an old .44 Winchester and much too small to kill an elephant, but I thought the noise might be useful *in terrorem.* Various Burmans stopped me on the way and told me about the elephant's doings. It was not, of course, a wild elephant, but a tame one which had gone "must." It had been chained up, as tame elephants always are when their attack of "must" is due, but on the previous night it had broken its chain and escaped. Its mahout, the only person who could manage it when it was in that state, had set out in pursuit, but had taken the wrong direction and was now twelve hours' journey away, and in the morning the elephant had suddenly reappeared in the town. The Burmese population had no weapons and were quite helpless against it. It had already destroyed somebody's bamboo hut, killed a cow and raided some fruit-stalls and devoured the stock; also it had met the municipal rubbish van and, when the driver jumped out and took to his heels, had turned the van over and in-flicted violences upon it.

The Burmese sub-inspector and some Indian constables were waiting for me in the quarter where the elephant had been seen. It was a very poor quarter, a labyrinth of squalid bamboo huts, thatched with palm-leaf, winding all over a steep hillside. I remember that it was a cloudy, stuffy morning at the beginning of the rains. We began questioning the people as to where the elephant had gone and, as usual, failed to get any definite information. That is invariably the case in the East; a story always sounds clear enough at a distance, but the nearer you get to the scene of events the vaguer it becomes. Some of the people said that the elephant had gone in one direction, some said that he had gone in another, some professed not even to have heard of any elephant. I had almost made up my mind that the whole story was a pack of lies, when we heard yells a little distance away. There was a loud, scandalized cry of "Go away, child! Go away this instant!" and an old woman with a switch in her hand came round the corner of a hut, violently shooing away a crowd of naked children. Some more women followed, clicking their tongues and exclaiming; evidently there was something that the children ought not to have seen. I rounded the hut and saw a man's dead body sprawling in the mud. He was an Indian, a black Dravidian coolie, almost naked, and he could not have been dead many minutes. The people said that the elephant had come suddenly upon him round the corner of the hut, caught him with its trunk, put its foot on his back and ground him into the earth. This was the rainy season and the ground was soft, and his face had scored a trench a foot deep and a couple of yards long. He was lying on his belly with arms crucified and head sharply twisted to one side. His face was coated with mud, the eyes wide open, the teeth bared and grinning with an expression of unendurable agony. (Never tell me, by the way, that the dead look peaceful. Most of the corpses I have seen looked devilish.) The friction of the great beast's foot had stripped the skin from his back as neatly as one skins a rabbit. As soon as I saw the dead man I sent an orderly to a friend's house nearby to borrow an elephant rifle. I had already sent back the pony, not wanting it to go mad with fright and throw me if it smelt the elephant.

The orderly came back in a few minutes with a rifle and five cartridges, and meanwhile some Burmans had arrived and told us that the elephant was in the paddy fields below, only a few hundred yards away. As I started forward practically the whole population of the quarter flocked out of the houses and followed me. They had seen the rifle and were all shouting excitedly that I was going to shoot the elephant. They had not shown much interest in the elephant when he was merely ravaging their homes, but it was different now that he was going to be shot. It was a bit of fun to them, as it would be to an English crowd; besides they wanted the meat. It made me vaguely uneasy. I had no intention of shooting the elephant—I had merely sent for the rifle to defend myself if necessary— and it is always unnerving to have a crowd following you. I marched down the hill, looking and feeling a fool, with the rifle over my shoulder and an ever-growing army of people jostling at my heels. At the bottom, when you got away from the huts, there was a metalled road and beyond that a miry waste of paddy fields a thousand yards across, not yet ploughed but soggy from the first rains and dotted with coarse grass. The elephant was standing eight yards from the road, his left side towards us. He took not the slightest notice of the crowd's approach. He was tearing up bunches of grass, beating them against his knees to clean them and stuffing them into his mouth.

I had halted on the road. As soon as I saw the elephant I knew with perfect certainty that I ought not to shoot him. It is a serious matter to shoot a working elephant—it is comparable to destroying a huge and costly piece of machinery—and obviously one ought not to do it if it can possibly be avoided. And at that distance, peacefully eating, the elephant looked no more dangerous than a cow. I thought then and I think now that his attack of "must" was already passing off; in which case he would merely wander harmlessly about until the mahout came back and caught him. Moreover, I did not in the least want to shoot him. I decided that I would watch him for a little while to make sure that he did not turn savage again, and then go home.

But at that moment I glanced round at the crowd that had followed me. It was an immense crowd, two thousand at the least and growing every minute. It blocked the road for a long distance on either side. I looked at the sea of yellow faces above the garish clothes—faces all happy and excited over this bit of fun, all certain that the elephant was going to be shot. They were watching me as they would watch a conjurer about to perform a trick. They did not like me, but with the magical rifle in my hands I was momentarily worth watching. And suddenly I realized that I should have to shoot the elephant after all. The people expected it of me and I had got to do it; I could feel their two thousand wills pressing me forward, irresistibly. And it was at this moment, as I stood there with the rifle in my hands, that I first grasped the hollowness, the futility of the white man's dominion in the East. Here was I, the white man with his gun, standing in front of the un-armed native crowd—seemingly the leading actor of the piece; but in reality I was only an absurd puppet pushed to and fro by the will of those yellow faces behind. I perceived in this moment that when the white man turns tyrant it is his own freedom that he destroys. He becomes a sort of hollow, posing dummy, the conventionalized figure of a sahib. For it is the condition of his rule that he shall spend his life in trying to impress the "natives," and so in every crisis he has got to do what the "natives" expect of him. He wears a mask, and his face grows to fit it. I had got to shoot the elephant. I had committed myself to doing it when I sent for the rifle. A sahib has got to act like a sahib; he has got to appear resolute, to know his own mind and do definite things. To come all that way, rifle in hand, with two thousand people marching at my heels, and then to trail feebly away, having done nothing—no, that was impossible. The crowd would laugh at me. And my whole life, every white man's life in the East, was one long struggle not to be laughed at.

But I did not want to shoot the elephant. I watched him beating his bunch of grass against his knees, with that preoccupied grandmotherly air that elephants have. It seemed to me that it would be murder to shoot him. At that age I was not squeamish about killing animals, but I had never shot an elephant and never wanted to. (Somehow it always seems worse to kill a *large* animal.) Besides, there was the beast's owner to be considered. Alive, the elephant was worth at least a hundred pounds; dead, he would only be worth the value of his tusks, five pounds, possibly. But I had got to act quickly. I turned to some experienced-looking Burmans who had been there when we arrived, and asked them how the elephant had been behaving. They all said the same thing: he took no notice of you if you left him alone, but he might charge if you went too close to him.

It was perfectly clear to me what I ought to do. I ought to walk up to within, say, twenty-five yards of the elephant and test his behavior. If he charged, I could shoot; if he took no notice of me, it would be safe to leave him until the mahout came back. But also I knew that I was going to do no such thing. I was a poor shot with a rifle and the ground was soft mud into which one would sink at every step. If the elephant charged and I missed him, I should have about as much chance as a toad under a steamroller. But even then I was not thinking particularly of my own skin, only of the watchful yellow faces behind. For at that moment, with the crowd watching me, I was not afraid in the ordinary sense, as I would have been if I had been alone. A white man mustn't be frightened in front of "natives"; and so, in general, he isn't frightened. The sole thought in my mind was that if anything went wrong those two thousand Burmans would see me pursued, caught, trampled on and reduced to a grinning corpse like that Indian up the hill. And if that happened it was quite probable that some of them would laugh. That would never do. There was only one alternative. I shoved the cartridges into the magazine and lay down on the road to get a better aim.

The crowd grew very still, and a deep, low, happy sigh, as of people who see the theatre curtain go up at last, breathed from innumerable throats. They were going to have their bit of fun after all. The rifle was a beautiful German thing with cross-hair sights. I did not then know that in shooting an elephant one would shoot to cut an imaginary bar running from ear-hole to ear-hole. I ought therefore, as the elephant was sideways on, to have aimed straight at his ear-hole; actually I aimed several inches in front of this, thinking the brain would be further forward.

When I pulled the trigger I did not hear the bang or feel the kick—one never does when a shot goes home—but I heard the devilish roar of glee that went up from the crowd. In that instant, in too short a time, one would have thought, even for the bullet to get there, a mysterious, terrible change had come over the elephant. He neither stirred nor fell, but every line of his body had altered. He looked suddenly stricken, shrunken, immensely old, as though the frightful impact of the bullet had paralysed him without knocking him down. At last, after what seemed a long time—it might have been five seconds, I dare say —he sagged flabbily to his knees. His mouth slobbered. An enormous senility seemed to have settled upon him. One could have imagined him thousands of years old. I fired again into the same spot. At the second shot he did not collapse but climbed with desperate slowness to his feet and stood weakly upright, with legs sagging and head drooping. I fired a third time. That was the shot that did for him. You could see the agony of it jolt his whole body and knock the last remnant of strength from his legs. But in falling he seemed for a moment to rise, for as his hind legs collapsed beneath him he seemed to tower upwards like a huge rock toppling, his trunk reaching skywards like a tree. He trumpeted, for the first and only time. And then down he came, his belly towards me, with a crash that seemed to shake the ground even where I lay.

I got up. The Burmans were already racing past me across the mud. It was obvious that the elephant would never rise again, but he was not dead. He was breathing very rhythmically with long rattling gasps, his great mound of a side painfully rising and falling. His mouth was wide open—I could see far down into caverns of pale pink throat. I waited a long time for him to die, but his breathing did not weaken. Finally I fired my two remaining shots into the spot where I thought his heart must be. The thick blood welled out of him like red velvet, but still he did not die. His body did not even jerk when the shots hit him, the tortured breathing continued without a pause. He was dying, very slowly and in great agony, but in some world remote from me where not even a bullet could damage him further. I felt that I had got to put an end to that dreadful noise. It seemed dreadful to see the great beast lying there, powerless to move and yet powerless to die, and not even to be able to finish him. I sent back for my small rifle and poured shot after shot into his heart and down his throat. They seemed to make no impression. The tortured gasps continued as steadily as the ticking of a clock.

In the end I could not stand it any longer and went away. I heard later that it took him half an hour to die. Burmans were bringing dahs and baskets even before I left, and I was told they had stripped his body almost to the bones by the afternoon.

Afterwards, of course, there were endless discussions about the shooting of the elephant. The owner was furious, but he was only an Indian and could do nothing. Besides, legally I had done the right thing, for a mad elephant has to be killed, like a mad dog, if its owner fails to control it. Among the Europeans opinion was divided. The older men said I was right, the younger men said it was a damn shame to shoot an elephant for killing a coolie, because an elephant was worth more than any damn Coringhee coolie. And afterwards I was very glad that the coolie had been killed; it put me legally in the right and it gave me a sufficient pretext for shooting the elephant. I often wondered whether any of the others grasped that I had done it solely to avoid looking a fool.

Fifth Avenue Uptown: A Letter from Harlem
James Baldwin

There is a housing project standing now where the house in which we grew up once stood, and one of those stunted city trees is snarling where our doorway used to be. This is on the rehabilitated side of the avenue. The other side of the avenue—for progress takes time—has not been rehabilitated yet and it looks exactly as it looked in the days when we sat with our noses pressed against the windowpane, longing to be allowed to go "across the street." The grocery store which gave us credit is still there, and there can be no doubt that it is still giving credit. The people in the project certainly need it—far more, indeed, than they ever needed the project. The last time I passed by, the Jewish proprietor was still standing among his shelves, looking sadder and heavier but scarcely any older. Farther down the block stands the shoe-repair store in which our shoes were repaired until reparation became impossible and in which, then, we bought all our "new" ones. The Negro proprietor is still in the window, head down, working at the leather.

These two, I imagine, could tell a long tale if they would (perhaps they would be glad to if they could), having watched so many, for so long, struggling in the fishhooks, the barbed wire, of this avenue.

The avenue is elsewhere the renowned and elegant Fifth. The area I am describing, which, in today's gang parlance, would be called "the turf," is bounded by Lenox Avenue on the west, the Harlem River on the east, 135th Street on the north, and 130th Street on the south. We never lived beyond these boundaries; this is where we grew up. Walking along 145th Street—for example—familiar as it is, and similar, does not have the same impact because I do not know any of the people on the block. But when I turn east on 131st Street and Lenox Avenue, there is first a soda-pop joint, then a shoeshine "parlor," then a grocery store, then a dry cleaners', then the houses. All along the street there are people who watched me grow up, people who grew up with me, people I watched grow up along with my brothers and sisters; and, sometimes in my arms, sometimes underfoot, sometimes at my shoulder—or on it—their children, a riot, a forest of children, who include my nieces and nephews.

When we reach the end of this long block, we find ourselves on wide, filthy, hostile Fifth Avenue, facing that project which hangs over the avenue like a monument to the folly, and the cowardice, of good intentions. All along the block, for anyone who knows it, are immense human gaps, like craters. These gaps are not created merely by those who have moved away, inevitably into some other ghetto; or by those who have risen, almost always into a greater capacity for self-loathing and self-delusion; or yet by those who, by whatever means—World War II, the Korean war, a policeman's gun or billy, a gang war, a brawl, madness, an overdose of heroin, or, simply, unnatural exhaustion—are dead. I am talking about those who are left, and I am talking principally about the young. What are they doing? Well, some, a minority, are fanatical churchgoers, members of the more extreme of the Holy Roller sects. Many, many more are "moslems," by affiliation or sympathy, that is to say that they are united by nothing more—and nothing less—than a hatred of the white world and all its works. They are present, for example, at every Buy Black street-corner meeting—meetings in which the speaker urges his hearers to cease trading with white men and establish a separate economy. Neither the speaker nor his hearers can possibly do this, of course, since Negroes do not own General Motors or RCA or the A & P, nor, indeed, do they own more than a wholly insufficient fraction of anything else in Harlem (those who *do* own anything are more interested in their profits than in their fellows). But these meetings nevertheless keep alive in the participators a certain pride of bitterness without which, however futile this bitterness may be, they could scarcely remain alive at all. Many have given up. They stay home and watch the TV screen, living on the earnings of their parents, cousins, brothers, or uncles, and only leave the house to go to the movies or to the nearest bar. "How're you making it?" one may ask, running into them along the block, or in the bar. "Oh, I'm TV-ing it"; with the saddest, sweetest, most shamefaced of smiles, and from a great distance. This distance one is compelled to respect; anyone who has traveled so far will not easily be dragged again into the world. There are further retreats, of course, than the TV screen or the bar. There are those who are simply sitting on their stoops, "stoned," animated for a moment only, and hideously, by the approach of someone who may lend them the money for a "fix." Or by the approach of someone from whom they can purchase it, one of the shrewd ones, on the way to prison or just coming out.

And the others, who have avoided all of these deaths, get up in the morning and go downtown to meet "the man." They work in the white man's world all day and come home in the evening to this fetid block. They struggle to instill in their children some private sense of honor or dignity which will help the child to survive. This means, of course, that they must struggle, stolidly, incessantly, to keep this sense alive in themselves, in spite of the insults, the indifference, and the cruelty they are certain to encounter in their working day. They patiently browbeat the landlord into fixing the heat, the plaster, the plumbing; this demands prodigious patience; nor is patience usually enough. In trying to make their hovels habitable, they are perpetually throwing good money after bad. Such frustration, so long endured, is driving many strong, admirable men and women whose only crime is color to the very gates of paranoia.

One remembers them from another time—playing handball in the playground, going to church, wondering if they were going to be promoted at school. One remembers them going off to war—gladly, to escape this block. One remembers their return. Perhaps one remembers their wedding day. And one sees where the girl is now—vainly looking for salvation from some other embittered, trussed, and struggling boy —and sees the all-but-abandoned children in the streets.

Now I am perfectly aware that there are other slums in which white men are fighting for their lives, and mainly losing. I know that blood is also flowing through those streets and that the human damage there is incalculable. People are continually pointing out to me the wretchedness of white people in order to console me for the wretchedness of blacks. But an itemized account of the American failure does not console me and it should not console anyone else. That hundreds of thousands of white people are living, in effect, no better than the "niggers" is not a fact to be regarded with complacency. The social and moral bankruptcy suggested by this fact is of the bitterest, most terrifying kind.

The people, however, who believe that this democratic anguish has some consoling value are always pointing out that So-and-So, white, and So-and-So, black, rose from the slums into the big time. The existence—the public existence—of, say, Frank Sinatra and Sammy Davis, Jr., proves to them that America is still the land of opportunity and that inequalities vanish before the determined will. It proves nothing of the sort. The determined will is rare—at the moment, in this country, it is unspeakably rare—and the inequalities suffered by the many are in no way justified by the rise of a few. A few have always risen—in every country, every era, and in the teeth of regimes which can by no stretch of the imagination be thought of as free. Not all of these people, it is worth remembering, left the world better than they found it. The determined will is rare, but it is not invariably benevolent. Furthermore, the American equation of success with the big time reveals an awful disrespect for human life and human achievement. This equation has placed our cities among the most dangerous in the world and has placed our youth among the most empty and most bewildered. The situation of our youth is not mysterious. Children have never been very good at listening to their elders, but they have never failed to imitate them. They must, they have no other models. That is exactly what our children are doing. They are imitating our immorality, our disrespect for the pain of others.

All other slum dwellers, when the bank account permits it, can move out of the slum and vanish altogether from the eye of persecution. No Negro in this country has ever made that much money and it will be a long time before any Negro does. The Negroes in Harlem, who have no money, spend what they have on such gimcracks as they are sold. These include "wider" TV screens, more "faithful" hi-fi sets, more "powerful" cars, all of which, of course, are obsolete long before they are paid for. Anyone who has ever struggled with poverty knows how extremely expensive it is to be poor; and if one is a member of a captive population, economically speaking, one's feet have simply been placed on the treadmill forever. One is victimized, economically, in a thousand ways—rent, for example, or car insurance. Go shopping one day in Harlem—for anything—and compare Harlem prices and quality with those downtown.

The people who have managed to get off this block have only got as far as a more respectable ghetto. This respectable ghetto does not even have the advantages of the disreputable one—friends, neighbors, a familiar church, and friendly tradesmen; and it is not, moreover, in the nature of any ghetto to remain respectable long. Every Sunday, people who have left the block take the lonely ride back, dragging their increasingly discontented children with them. They spend the day talking, not always with words, about the trouble they've seen and the trouble—one must watch their eyes as they watch their children—they are only too likely to see. For children do not like ghettos. It takes them nearly no time to discover exactly why they are there.

The projects in Harlem are hated. They are hated almost as much as policemen, and this is saying a great deal. And they are hated for the same reason: both reveal, unbearably, the real attitude of the white world, no matter how many liberal speeches are made, no matter how many lofty editorials are written, no matter how many civil-rights commissions are set up.

The projects are hideous, of course, there being a law, apparently respected throughout the world, that popular housing shall be as cheerless as a prison. They are lumped all over Harlem, colorless, bleak, high, and revolting. The wide windows look out on Harlem's invincible and indescribable squalor: the Park Avenue railroad tracks, around which, about forty years ago, the present dark community began; the unrehabilitated houses, bowed down, it would seem, under the great weight of frustration and bitterness they contain; the dark, the ominous schoolhouses from which the child may emerge maimed, blinded, hooked, or enraged for life; and the churches, churches, block upon block of churches, niched in the walls like cannon in the walls of a fortress. Even if the administration of the projects were not so insanely humiliating (for example: one must report raises in salary to the management, which will then eat up the profit by raising one's rent; the management has the right to know who is staying in your apartment; the management can ask you to leave, at their discretion), the projects would still be hated because they are an insult to the meanest intelligence.

Harlem got its first private project, Riverton*—which is now, naturally, a slum—about twelve years ago because at that time Negroes were not allowed to live in Stuyvesant Town. Harlem watched Riverton go up, therefore, in the most violent bitterness of spirit, and hated it long before the builders arrived. They began hating it at about the time people began moving out of their condemned houses to make room for this additional proof of how thoroughly the white world despised them.

---

* The inhabitants of Riverton were much embittered by this description; they have, apparently, forgotten how their project came into being; and have repeatedly informed me that I cannot possibly be referring to Riverton, but to another housing project which is directly across the street. It is quite clear, I think, that I have no interest in accusing any individuals or families of the depredations herein described: but neither can I deny the evidence of my own eyes. Nor do I blame anyone in Harlem for making the best of a dreadful bargain. But anyone who lives in Harlem and imagines that he has not struck this bargain, or that what he takes to be his status (in whose eyes?) protects him against the common pain, demoralization, and danger, is simply self-deluded.

And they had scarcely moved in, naturally, before they began smashing windows, defacing walls, urinating in the elevators, and fornicating in the playgrounds. Liberals, both white and black, were appalled at the spectacle. I was appalled by the liberal innocence—or cynicism, which comes out in practice as much the same thing. Other people were delighted to be able to point to proof positive that nothing could be done to better the lot of the colored people. They were, and are, right in one respect: that nothing can be done as long as they are treated like colored people. The people in Harlem know they are living there because white people do not think they are good enough to live anywhere else. No amount of "improvement" can sweeten this fact. Whatever money is now being earmarked to improve this, or any other ghetto, might as well be burnt. A ghetto can be improved in one way only: out of existence.

Similarly, the only way to police a ghetto is to be oppressive. None of the Police Commissioner's men, even with the best will in the world, have any way of understanding the lives led by the people they swagger about in twos and threes controlling. Their very presence is an insult, and it would be, even if they spent their entire day feeding gumdrops to children. They represent the force of the white world, and that world's real intentions are, simply, for that world's criminal profit and ease, to keep the black man corraled up here, in his place. The badge, the gun in the holster, and the swinging club make vivid what will happen should his rebellion become overt. Rare, indeed, is the Harlem citizen, from the most circumspect church member to the most shiftless adolescent, who does not have a long tale to tell of police incompetence, injustice, or brutality. I myself have witnessed and endured it more than once. The businessmen and racketeers also have a story. And so do the prostitutes. (And this is not, perhaps, the place to discuss Harlem's very complex attitude toward black policemen, nor the reasons, according to Harlem, that they are nearly all downtown.)

It is hard, on the other hand, to blame the policeman, blank, good-natured, thoughtless, and insuperably innocent, for being such a perfect representative of the people he serves. He, too, believes in good intentions and is astounded and offended when they are not taken for the deed. He has never, himself, done anything for which to be hated —which of us has?—and yet he is facing, daily and nightly, people who would gladly see him dead, and he knows it. There is no way for him not to know it: there are few things under heaven more unnerving than the silent, accumulating contempt and hatred of a people. He moves through Harlem, therefore, like an occupying soldier in a bitterly hostile country; which is precisely what, and where, he is, and is the reason he walks in twos and threes. And he is not the only one who knows why he is always in company: the people who are watching him know why, too. Any street meeting, sacred or secular, which he and his colleagues uneasily cover has as its explicit or implicit burden the cruelty and injustice of the white domination. And these days, of course, in terms increasingly vivid and jubilant, it speaks of the end of that domination. The white policeman standing on a Harlem street corner finds himself at the very center of the revolution now occurring in the world. He is not prepared for it—naturally, nobody is—and, what is possibly much more to the point, he is exposed, as few white people are, to the anguish of the black people around him. Even if he is gifted with the merest mustard grain of imagination, something must seep in. He cannot avoid observing that some of the children, in spite of their color, remind him of children he has known and loved, perhaps even of his own children. He knows that he certainly does not want *his* children living this way. He can retreat from his uneasiness in only one direction: into a callousness which very shortly becomes second nature. He becomes more callous, the population becomes more hostile, the situation grows more tense, and the police force is increased. One day, to everyone's astonishment, someone drops a match in the powder keg and everything blows up. Before the dust has settled or the blood congealed, editorials, speeches, and civil-rights commissions are loud in the land, demanding to know what happened. What happened is that Negroes want to be treated like men.

Negroes want to be treated like men: a perfectly straightforward statement, containing only seven words. People who have mastered Kant, Hegel, Shakespeare, Marx, Freud, and the Bible find this statement utterly impenetrable. The idea seems to threaten profound, barely conscious assumptions. A kind of panic paralyzes their features, as though they found themselves trapped on the edge of a steep place. I once tried to describe to a very well-known American intellectual the conditions among Negroes in the South. My recital disturbed him and made him indignant; and he asked me in perfect innocence, "Why don't all the Negroes in the South move North?" I tried to explain what *has* happened, unfailingly, whenever a significant body of Negroes move North. They do not escape Jim Crow: they merely encounter another, not-less-deadly variety. They do not move to Chicago, they move to the South Side; they do not move to New York, they move to Harlem. The pressure within the ghetto causes the ghetto walls to expand, and this expansion is always violent. White people hold the line as long as they can, and in as many ways as they can, from verbal intimidation to physical violence. But inevitably the border which has divided the ghetto from the rest of the world falls into the hands of the ghetto. The white people fall back bitterly before the black horde; the landlords make a tidy profit by raising the rent, chopping up the rooms, and all but dispensing with the upkeep; and what has once been a neighborhood turns into a "turf." This is precisely what happened when the Puerto Ricans arrived in their thousands—and the bitterness thus caused is, as I write, being fought out all up and down those streets.

Northerners indulge in an extremely dangerous luxury. They seem to feel that because they fought on the right side during the Civil War, and won, they have earned the right merely to deplore what is going on in the South, without taking any responsibility for it; and that they can ignore what is happening in Northern cities because what is happening in Little Rock or Birmingham is worse. Well, in the first place, it is not possible for anyone who has not endured both to know which is "worse." I know Negroes who prefer the South and white Southerners, because "At least there, you haven't got to play any guessing games!" The guessing games referred to have driven more than one Negro into the narcotics ward, the madhouse, or the river. I know another Negro, a man very dear to me, who says, with conviction and with truth, "The spirit of the South is the spirit of America." He was born in the North and did his military training in the South. He did not, as far as I can gather, find the South "worse"; he found it, if anything, all too familiar. In the second place, though, even if Birmingham *is* worse, no doubt Johannesburg, South Africa, beats it by several miles, and Buchenwald was one of the worst things that ever happened in the entire history of the world. The world has never lacked for horrifying examples; but I do not believe that these examples are meant to be used as justification for our own crimes. This perpetual justification empties the heart of all human feeling. The emptier our hearts become, the greater will be our crimes. Thirdly, the South is not merely an embarrassingly backward region, but a part of this country, and what happens there concerns every one of us.

As far as the color problem is concerned, there is but one great difference between the Southern white and the Northerner: the Southerner remembers, historically and in his own psyche, a kind of Eden in which he loved black people and they loved him. Historically, the flaming sword laid across this Eden is the Civil War. Personally, it is the Southerner's sexual coming of age, when, without any warning, unbreakable taboos are set up between himself and his past. Everything, thereafter, is permitted him except the love he remembers and has never ceased to need. The resulting, indescribable torment affects every Southern mind and is the basis of the Southern hysteria.

None of this is true for the Northerner. Negroes represent nothing to him personally, except, perhaps, the dangers of carnality. He never sees Negroes. Southerners see them all the time. Northerners never think about them whereas Southerners are never really thinking of anything else. Negroes are, therefore, ignored in the North and are under surveillance in the South, and suffer hideously in both places. Neither the Southerner nor the Northerner is able to look on the Negro simply as a man. It seems to be indispensable to the national self-esteem that the Negro be considered either as a kind of ward (in which case we are told how many Negroes, comparatively, bought Cadillacs last year and how few, comparatively, were lynched), or as a victim (in which case we are promised that he will never vote in our assemblies or go to school with our kids). They are two sides of the same coin and the South will not change—*cannot* change—until the North changes. The country will not change until it reexamines itself and discovers what it really means by freedom. In the meantime, generations keep being born, bitterness is increased by incompetence, pride, and folly, and the world shrinks around us.

It is a terrible, an inexorable, law that one cannot deny the humanity of another without diminishing one's own: in the face of one's victim, one sees oneself. Walk through the streets of Harlem and see what we, this nation, have become.

Suggestions for Writing

1. Find an experience that once taught you some general truth about man and the universe, or one in which you now can see some such significance, though it seemed unimportant at the time. Very few students have shot an elephant, but perhaps you were in an automobile accident, or stole your best friend's storybook doll, or broke a promise. The incident may be small; the lesson may be obvious. The point is that in this incident you learned the lesson for the first time, first realized that the abstract truths actually operate in daily scrapes and quibbles. Your aim in doing the exercise is to make your readers, through vivid and figurative detail after detail, see and feel exactly how it was. To keep yourself within the expository traces, write out a clear thesis—"One day something happened that taught me the real nature of robbery: that you really steal more from yourself than from others"—and then set it clearly at the end of a good beginning paragraph, or at least after a reasonable introduction that sets the scene and lets the reader know where he is going.

2. Write an essay about your own neighborhood, following Baldwin in mixing childhood memories with present observations and broader pertinent sociological facts, and similarly keeping your language vivid with sharp figurative detail.

An Experimental Investigation LOIS Z. SMITH · *243*

Get-Out-If-You-Can! AMERICAN TRADITIONS PROJECT · *252*

The Horrors of Exposition

Too Much or Too Little

Your subject may so strongly dictate your style that what comes out bears no trace of human intervention. Or you may so far intrude upon your subject that all is false and folksy. One way is too impersonal; the other, too personal. And both obscure your message.

The first essay in this section does about as creditable a job as one can expect from the slender inch of knowledge its elaborate rigging produces, and from a tradition encouraging the

242

utmost in wordiness and repetition. The writing could have been much weaker. I have, in fact, chosen both of these essays for their strengths as well as their weaknesses, to exercise us in the rigors of writing. As you read the first essay (which I have already abridged for convenience), ask yourself how, given such subject matter, you might have used simpler phrases and further condensed the entire report.

The second essay tries, unworthily, to sell a worthy subject. This is, of course, an advertisement. As you go, underline words and phrases that seem to show the author thinking a little too well of himself, and not well enough of his subject or his audience.

no style

An Experimental Investigation of Young Children's Interest and Expressive Behavior Responses to Single Statement, Verbal Repetition, and Ideational Repetition of Content in Animal Stories
Lois Z. Smith

The aim of this study was to develop an experimental technique for measuring and comparing the interest and expressive behavior responses which two-, three-, and four-year-old children give to single statement, verbal repetition, and ideational repetition of content in animal stories.

The study involved (1) the writing of stories containing these three elements, (2) the training of observers and the establishing of reliability in the use of the observer's blanks, and (3) conducting the experimental story groups.

The subjects used in the establishing of the reliability of the observers were 14 four- and five-year-old children who were attending the preschool laboratories of the Iowa Child Welfare Research Station. The subjects of the experimental story groups were 33 two-, and three,- and four-year-old children. The average chronological age of the group used for establishing the reliability of the observers was 42.5 months with a standard deviation of 7.21, the average mental age 50.0 months with a standard deviation of 8.87. The average chronological age of 27 children in the main experimental group given the Stanford revision of the Binet scale was 50.9 months with a standard deviation of 6.25, and an average mental age of 59.3 with a standard deviation of 9.96. The 6 children given the Kuhlmann revision of the Binet scale had an average chronological age of 36 months with a standard deviation of 2.52 and an average mental age of 43.2 with a standard deviation of 5.46.

Preparation of the Stories

The stories for the experiment were written so that they would contain certain general characteristics recommended by educators and writers of young children's stories. The following were used as guiding principles in the construction of the stories:

1. A single incident told in chronological sequence was to be used as a plot.
2. The story must be within the child's experience.
3. The vocabulary must be understandable to children.
4. The units whether words, phrases, or sentences must be simple.
5. Young children are fond of animal stories in which the animals talk and act like people.

An incident was borrowed from a story for older children. It supplied the necessary chronological sequence of events within the experience of the young child. The story *Two Little Geese* was taken from a story called *Mrs. Goose's Rubbers*. The story was about a goose who had lost her rubbers and the sequence of events consisted of her attempt to find them. Some parts of the original story were incorporated in the experimental story while other parts were re-written. . . .

As a guide in choosing a vocabulary for the stories which children of these ages would understand, all of the words of each story were listed and their occurrence in children's vocabularies checked. The studies of Bateman, Beyer, Brandenburg, Bush, and Gale and Gale were used. . . . Only those words which occurred in five or more of the vocabularies were used.

In order to make the story simple, short declarative sentences were used as often as possible. The average number of words in the sentences used in the stories was six.

The stories were written in 3 forms. Form A was told in single statements. The 2 similar characters were treated as a unit by means of a plural or compound subject. For example:

Mr. Goose and Mrs. Goose had lost their rubbers.
They said, "We must have them to go down town."

Form B was told with a verbal repetition of content. In this form *too* each of 2 animal characters responded individually. The words used *much* to describe the behavior of the first character were repeated in describ- *detail* ing the behavior of the second except that the pronouns were varied in sex and number to agree with their respective antecedents and the verbs were changed in form to agree in number with their respective subjects. For example:

Mr. Goose had lost his rubbers.
He said, "I must have them to go down town."
Mrs. Goose had lost her rubbers.
She said, "I must have them to go down town."

In Form C the stories were characterized by ideational repetition. Each one of the two similar characters responded individually. The first character acted and spoke. The same words were used to describe this action as those used in Form A and in Form B in the repeated statements about both characters. In describing the behavior of the second character in Form C the idea is repeated but the words are different. For example:

Mr. Goose had lost his rubbers.
He said, "I must have them to go down town."
Mrs. Goose's rubbers were lost. "I cannot go to the store without them," she said.

From observation of story groups in the preschool laboratories it was decided that a story requiring three minutes would come well within the period during which even the youngest child could give attention to the story. The reading of Form A required 1½ minutes, and Form B and Form C each required 3 minutes. The stories were written in one-half minute units so that each item of expressive behavior or interest could be checked on the basis of occurrence within half minutes. Each unit of a story was typed in the story book on the space between two leaves so that turning a page indicated to the observers the end of a half minute unit.

Three comparable stories were written for the experiment, one for use as a trial story in establishing reliability; the others for use in the experiment proper. The story *Two Little Geese* is reported on pages [246–247].

Two Little Geese

FORM A	FORM B	FORM C
Mr. and Mrs. Goose could not find their red rubbers.	Mr. Goose could not find his red rubbers.	Mr. Goose could not find his red rubbers.
"We need them to go down town," they said.	"I need them to go down town," he said.	He said, "I need them to go down town."
They had peeked into every corner of the little dark closet under the stairs.	Mrs. Goose could not find her red rubbers.	Mrs. Goose's rubbers were lost.
Their red rubbers were not there.	"I need them to go down town," she said.	She said, "I cannot go to the store without them."
Mr. and Mrs. Goose looked under the bed.	Mr. Goose peeked into every corner of the little dark closet under the stairs.	Mr. Goose peeked into every corner of the little dark closet under the stairs.
They opened the ice box and looked into it.	His red rubbers were not there.	His red rubbers were not there.
Their red rubbers were lost.	Mrs. Goose peeked into every corner of the little dark closet under the stairs.	From top to bottom of the dark closet Mrs. Goose looked for her red rubbers. She did not find them.
	Her red rubbers were not there.	
Mr. and Mrs. Goose rolled up the rug and looked under it.	Mr. Goose looked under the bed.	Mr. Goose looked under the bed.
They saw no red rubbers.	Mrs. Goose looked under the bed.	Down under the bed Mrs. Goose crawled to look.
They heard the rain drops hitting the roof of their house.	Mr. Goose opened the ice box and looked into it.	Mr. Goose opened the ice box and looked into it. His red rubbers were lost.
They put on their coats and hats.	His red rubbers were lost.	
They picked up their baskets and very green umbrellas.	Mrs. Goose opened the ice box and looked into it.	Mrs. Goose could not find her rubbers in the ice box. They were gone.
They went out the door.	Her red rubbers were lost.	
Mr. and Mrs. Goose closed the door.		
They opened their big green umbrellas.	Mr. Goose rolled up the rug and looked under it. He saw no red rubbers.	Mr. Goose rolled up the rug and looked under it. He saw no red rubbers.
Plop! Four big somethings fell on their heads nearly knocking their hats off.	Mrs. Goose rolled up the rug and looked under it. She saw no red rubbers.	Mrs. Goose's red rubbers were not under the rug. She lifted it to look.
Mr. and Mrs. Goose looked to see what had dropped.	Mr. Goose heard the rain drops hitting the roof of the house.	Mr. Goose heard the rain drops hitting the roof of his house.
There were their red rubbers.	Mrs. Goose heard the rain drops hitting the roof of the house.	The rain was falling on the top of the house. Mrs. Goose listened.
They put on their red rubbers.		
They walked in the water on their way down town.		

Two Little Geese—*Concluded*

FORM A	FORM B	FORM C
	Mr. Goose put on his coat and hat.	Mr. Goose put on his coat and hat.
	Mrs. Goose put on her coat and hat.	Mrs. Goose had her wraps on.
	Mr. Goose picked up his basket and green umbrella.	Mr. Goose picked up his basket and green umbrella.
	Mrs. Goose picked up her basket and green umbrella.	Mrs. Goose was carrying her basket and green umbrella.
	Mr. Goose went out on the porch.	Mr. Goose went out on the porch.
	Mr. Goose closed the door.	Mr. Goose closed the door.
	Mrs. Goose went out on the porch.	Mrs. Goose shut the door behind her.
	Mrs. Goose closed the door.	
	Mr. Goose opened his big green umbrella.	Mr. Goose opened his big green umbrella.
	Plop! Two big somethings fell on his head.	Plop! Two big somethings fell on his head. They nearly knocked his hat off.
	They nearly knocked his hat off.	
	Mrs. Goose opened her big green umbrella.	Mrs. Goose put up her umbrella.
	Plop! Two big somethings fell on her head.	Out of it dropped something that put her bonnet over one of her eyes.
	They nearly knocked her hat off.	
	Mr. Goose looked to see what had dropped.	Mr. Goose looked to see what had dropped.
	There were his little red rubbers.	There were his little red rubbers.
	Mrs. Goose looked to see what had dropped.	Mrs. Goose saw that her two little red rubbers had fallen out of her umbrella.
	There were her little red rubbers.	
	Mr. Goose put on his red rubbers.	Mr. Goose put on his red rubbers.
	He walked through the water on his way down town.	He walked in the water on his way down town.
	Mrs. Goose put on her red rubbers.	With her red rubbers on her little feet, Mrs. Goose went through the rain to the store.
	She walked through the water on her way down town.	

Training of the Story-teller

The story-teller made special preparation for the telling of the stories in order that the telling would be as uniform as possible. Each form of each story was memorized. A careful study was made of the enunciation, pronunciation, expression, and voice used in telling the stories. The story was timed so that the story-teller always took the same amount of time in telling it. Persons trained in telling children's stories criticized the story-teller's presentation of the story. A small story book which lay on the lap of the story-teller served as a guide and aided in maintaining uniformity.

The personality of the story-teller as manifested by dramatic pause, voice quality, inflection, and facial expression was evidenced only enough to insure the children's interest and was made uniform for all forms of stories.

At the end of the experiment the story-teller asked the observers to report on her uniformity in manner and time of presentation of the stories. . . .

Training the Observers and Establishing the Reliability of the Observer's Blank

Following the preparation of the stories, the next problem was the development of a technique for recording the interest and expressive behavior of the children in the story situations. The observer's blank as used in this study lists 5 types of expressive behavior (1) laughs, (2) smiles, (3) claps hands, nods approval, etc. (4) annoyed, (5) neutral; and 3 types of interest (1) watches, (2) any combination of watching or not watching, (3) does not watch.

The experimenter in weighing the observations of expressive behavior assumed that greater amounts of expressiveness in enjoyment or disapproval of the story should be given the higher positive or negative scores while less expressiveness should be given scores falling between the extremes. Thus the scale of expressive behavior ranges from −1 to 3 and 1 as the midpoint for neutral expressiveness.

Expressive Behavior Items	Score
1. Laughs—the child's amusement is expressed by a chuckle, giggle, or snort.	3
2. Smiles—the child's mouth is drawn up into a smile.	3
3. Claps hands, or nods approval.	3
4. Annoyed—the child scowls or watches the door.	2
5. There is an absence of 1, 2, 3, and 4. The child has a neutral expression.	1

A scale for interest values was chosen which ranged from 0 to 2. The score of 1 served as a midpoint from which differences were judged. The folowing are definitions of interest items:

Interest Items	Score
1. Watches—the child's eyes are focused on the story-teller all of the time except possibly for a glance.	2
2. Any variation between 1 and 3.	1
3. Does not watch—his eyes are focused on other things—not on the story-teller except for a possible glance.	0

All three of the observers were college graduates and two were graduate students with special training in child psychology. Twelve hours during a period of two weeks were spent in training the observers for the experiment. This period of training was characterized by the experimenter's telling of stories to groups of children and the observers checking on the observation blank the behavior responses of the same 2 children. Disagreements were noted and discussed. Definitions were agreed upon and examples of the types of behavior cited. This procedure was repeated until the number of disagreements became so few as to indicate that the observers were sufficiently trained. . . .

Experimental Story Groups

The next problem of the study was the division of the two-, three-, and four-year-old children into story groups. Since it was hoped that the influence arising from the individual reactions of the children would be similar for all the groups, the 6 groups were made fairly comparable on the basis of mental age and extroversion-introversion ratings. Thirty-three children served as subjects.

One story was presented to each of the experimental story groups previous to the experiment. This was done for the training of the observers and for the purpose of permitting the children to become accustomed to the experimental story group situation. The story, *Two Little Kittens,* was used for establishing reliability, and the stories *Two Little Dogs* and *Two Little Geese* were used in the experiment proper.

The experimental story groups were conducted each week over a period of 6 weeks. The order was arranged so that 3 of the groups received the *Two Little Geese* story first and 3 of the groups the *Two Little Dogs* story first. The forms of each story were presented in 3 different orders so that the influence of position in the series was equalized for each form. . . .

The first time the child was taken for a story group, the teacher in charge of the preschool group said, "Mrs. . . . would like to tell you

useless details
can't tell what is important
no sense of organization
no personality behind facts

a story." The experimenter said nothing to the children, merely waited for them at the door. The 6 children were brought into the testing room and seated in little chairs grouped around the story-teller. The 3 observers sat facing the children in positions closest to the children whom they were to observe. The story-teller began by saying, "I am Mrs. . . . I am going to tell you a story about (giving the name of the story)." She started a stop-watch which she had in the pocket of her smock at the instant she began the story. At the completion of the reading material she had between the pages of the small green-covered story book on her lap, she turned the page. This movement was a signal to the observers that a half minute had elapsed. At the close of the story, the stop-watch was stopped. The experimenter said, "That is all. Perhaps some other day I shall tell you another story." The length of time used in telling the story was recorded and the children were taken back to play.

Analysis of the Experimental Results

The interest and expressive behavior scores and the means, standard deviations, and coefficients of variation of the score from Forms A, B, and C of the *Two Little Geese* story and of the *Two Little Dogs* story are shown.

. . . . .

Another table gives the means and standard deviations of the interest scores and the expressive behavior scores from Forms A and B, Forms A and C, Forms B and C, arranged for comparison of the different forms of the *Two Little Dogs* story.

. . . . .

Summary and Conclusions

The aim of the present study was to develop an experimental technique for measuring and comparing the interest and expressive behavior responses which two-, three-, and four-year-old children derive from single statement, verbal repetition, and ideational repetition of content in animal stories. The solution of the problems arising in the study required 3 procedures; the first of which was the writing of 3 stories containing single statement, verbal repetition, and ideational repetition of content; second, the training of observers and establishing of reliability on the use of the observer's blank; third, the conducting of the experimental story groups.

The 3 observers were trained and their reliability was established on the use of an observer's blank.

The subjects of the investigation were 33 children who were enrolled in the preschool laboratories of the Iowa Child Welfare Research Station. These subjects were arranged in 6 comparable groups to which the forms of the stories were presented in 3 different orders. The specific findings of this study are:

1. The observation and observer's blank used in this experiment are a reliable technique for the measurement and comparison of the interest and expressive behavior responses of two-, three- and four-year-old children to single statement, verbal repetition, and ideational repetition of content in animal stories. This is revealed by the correlation of .96 ±.011 which is the average of 6 correlations between scores made by the 3 observers on the same children.

2. The coefficients of variability of the interest and expressive behavior scores from all forms of the *Two Little Dogs* story were slightly higher than those from the corresponding forms of the *Two Little Geese* story.

3. The significant differences between the interest of the 33 children in Form A, Form B, and Form C of the *Two Little Dogs* story as shown by the means of their scores seemed to indicate that Form B, with verbal repetition of content, was more interesting than either Form A with single statement or Form C with ideational repetition of content. The significant differences between the means of scores for expressive behavior showed a significantly greater response to Form B, characterized by verbal repetition of content, than to Form A or Form C.

4. There appeared to be no relationship between chronological age and the children's interest and expressive behavior responses to Form A and Form B. However, there was a positive relationship between Form C, characterized by ideational repetition of content, and chronological age. This meant that the older children were more interested and showed greater expressive responses to Form C of the stories than did the younger children.

5. Although the mental age of the 33 children showed no relationship to the expressive behavior scores made on Form A and Form B of the story, there was a positive relationship between the children's expressive behavior scores from Form C of the story and mental age. This relationship indicated that the mentally older children tended to give the more expressive responses to Form C which was characterized by ideational repetition of content than did the younger children.

6. A partial correlation between expressive behavior scores from Form C and mental age with chronological age held constant approached significance while a correlation between expressive behavior

scores from Form C and chronological age with mental age held constant did not approach significance. These correlations indicate that the expressive behavior arising from the ideational repetition in Form C may have been related to those factors peculiar to mental age, and not to those factors peculiar to chronological age.

7. Correlations of the interest scores from the different forms of the *Two Little Dogs* story showed a positive relationship between only Form A, single statement, and Form C, ideational repetition of content. This showed that those children who were interested in stories which were characterized by single statement also tended to be interested in stories which were characterized by ideational repetition of content.

8. Correlations revealed no relationship between the expressive behavior responses on these 3 forms of the stories, single statement, verbal repetition, and ideational repetition of content.

9. There was no relationship between extroversion rating and the children's interest and expressive behavior responses to the forms of the story.

a lot of vividness.

questions left unanswered
where, how did people
organize, how did area
take to idea

wrong style

Get-Out-If-You-Can!
American Traditions Project

It was only an ordinary street light, but the enchanted people of the dark slum gazed upon it with joy and wonderment, for they had put it there . . .

But that was later. The town and its people had been there a long time.

A town really *is* its people.

The people had rolling, rhythmic names . . . like Juan, Diego, Fernando. Some of their ancestors, illustriously stealing a march on the Pilgrims, had found Mexico and founded California. And their poetic names bedeck landmarks throughout the State.

But the town was a rathole. It wasn't really a town, only an isolated ghetto section on the east side of a central California city, rat-ridden, disease-prone, captured by dirt and poverty. Its residents—the modern inheritors of the rhythmic names—had a sardonic name for their community. They called it *Sal-Si-Puedes!* Which means "Get-Out-If-You-Can!"

In the lovelier sections of the city, some had an explanation for this. They were apt to sigh and regret that Mexican-Americans "just didn't care how they lived." As one leading citizen said: "Give those people a thousand dollars and they would still live like that."

But Fred Ross was convinced that nobody could actually enjoy living in a slum. The tall, scholarly director of the California Federation for Civic Unity couldn't give anyone a thousand dollars—not on his modest subsidy from the American Friends Service Committee. Nevertheless, like a good neighbor, he came calling on the folks in Get-Out-If-You-Can! And he brought something much more important than money—an active faith in the American tradition.

His was not a quick or easy way. Alone at first, fighting against fear, distrust, apathy, Fred Ross trudged along the pitiful rows of shabby houses and lean-tos, talking, talking, talking . . .

"Take a look. Rats running through your yards and homes. Unpaved roads. Dangerously poor sewage disposal. A garbage situation that's unbelievable. Why?"

A young lumber worker at last provided an opening for the answer Ross was bursting to give. "Once," the lumber worker recalled, "I took a bunch of petitions down to the Courthouse for paved streets, street lights, gas, storm drains, all that stuff. They didn't take it seriously."

Ross pounced. "I also went to the Courthouse. I counted the Spanish names on the voters' registration list. Sixteen hundred of a possible 21,000. Do you know that in America the government governs only with the consent—and desires—of the governed? Suppose we all got busy and registered three or four times that many to vote? Suppose—?"

It didn't happen all at once. But soon Ross found himself the catalyst that activated a Catholic priest, a Mexican-American nurse, two laborers and others. There was a memorable mass meeting, resulting in formation of the non-profit, non-partisan Community Service Organization. Its goal—to get out the vote, develop a civic identity and purpose, to form a community in the American tradition.

Sociologists had politely complicated names for the problems of *Sal-Si-Puedes*—depressed income, cultural lags, lingual barriers, inter-cultural tensions, social apathy, inter-group hostility and lots more.

The self-help pioneers of the CSO in *Sal-Si-Puedes* pitched in with a small vocabulary and a whale of a lot of enthusiasm. In ten weeks, working evenings, spending 3,000 man-hours, wondering, hoping, they registered 4,000 voters to put little, lost *Sal-Si-Puedes* on the political map at City Hall and the Courthouse.

The magic of getting results didn't happen all at once. But it started even during the door-to-door voter registration drive. Ditchdiggers ended perennial flood hazards by repairing Silver Creek, and factory *did the people do it, passive voice defeats purpose*

refuse dumping in the creek was forbidden. Paving crews made miles of muddy roads passable. Playgrounds sprouted on shabby sand lots. Traffic control signs appeared. Newspapers began to report happenings in *Sal-Si Puedes;* and its leaders were invited to join the PTA, to speak before clubs across the tracks.

Then one day, providing assurance for the women who had to be out after dark, cutting the mortality rate for children crossing the street, pushing back the grim shadows of a century, the first street light came.

And the enchanted people of the dark slum gazed upon it with joy and wonderment, for they had put it there.

Suggestions for Writing

1. So that you may learn about, and clear your own prose of, that worst of modern expository horrors—the preference for modifying nouns with nouns instead of adjectives—change the title and opening paragraph of the first selection into as oppressive a noun-noun passage as possible, as follows: "An Experiment Investigation of Young Children Interest and Expression Behavior. . . ."

2. Rewrite the title and first three paragraphs of the first selection, eliminating unnecessary words and pointless distinctions. What is the difference, for instance, between an *experimental investigation* and an *experiment?* Does the writer need to distinguish between *interest* and *responses* (does she really do so in the experiment)? What is the difference between *content in animal stories* and *animal stories?* Underline every *of* in the passage, and then try to eliminate as many as possible by rephrasing. Eliminate the passive voice (notice the omnipresent *used*) by substituting *I.* For example, change "the subjects used in the establishing of" to "I established."

3. In clean and simple prose (about 500 words), describe the experiment and the findings reported in the first selection.

4. Write an essay analyzing the difficulties of pinning down the evidence in experiments, like Miss Smith's, that deal with human emotions or with language. The following excerpt from William K. Wimsatt's *Philosophic Words* (New Haven, 1948, p. 24) may be helpful:

> It is beyond the scope of an analysis of style to *prove* that any qualities of style *exist* in writing. A writing cannot be proved to have more or less meaning than is understood on reading it. Where a certain quality is recognized as a part of style, statistics may give a numerical ratio between the frequency of the quality in one writing and that in another. But the process of making statistics is one of gathering items under a

head, and only according to a definition may the items be gathered. Only by the definition have they any relevance. It is the formulating of the definition, not the counting after that, which is the work of studying style.*

When a critic is conscious of quality X in a writing, no accumulation of statistics will increase his consciousness of it. But if he simply announces that the writing has X, he may be challenged. If he says that it has X because he has found X in fifteen examples of fifteen hundred words each, he is less likely to be challenged; if he adds that the average is a hundred occurrences in each example, even less likely. This, however, is not proof, but something more like persuasion, for logically the whole matter rests on the definition with which he began, and statistical details are taken, no less than a blanket statement, on faith.

---

* Professor L. A. Sherman counted the number of words per sentence for the *whole* of Macaulay's *History of England* and found that the average was 23.43. "Here, then, in this 23.43," he wrote, "was the resultant of the forces which had made Macaulay's literary character" ("On Certain Facts and Principles in the Development of Form in Literature," *The University Studies of the University of Nebraska*, I [No. 4, 1892], 350–3). Such, and only such, can be the conclusion reached by counting items chosen without reference to meaning. Cf. Abraham Wolf, *Textbook of Logic* (London, 1930), pp. 231, 236. [Wimsatt's footnote]

5. In a burlesque of ponderous scholarship, write the worst essay you can contrive, with everything noun-to-noun, everything passively voiced and wordy. Choose some subject like "An Experiment-type Woman Student Investigation Study of Pencil, Pen, and Pen-and-Pencil Tapping in a Control Situation of the Fourth Table of the Second Study Hall of the Library of the College."

6. After you have decided exactly where the overpersonal and emotional language falsifies "Get-Out-If-You-Can!," write a sober, honest essay on the same subject, with the same data. (The faults are largely the opposite of those in the first selection, but notice *factory refuse dumping*, noun-noun-noun.)

A Modest Proposal JONATHAN SWIFT · *257*
Coleridge THOMAS CARLYLE · *264*
After the Population Explosion HARRISON BROWN · *271*

The Ironic Essay

Nothing teaches the connotations of words more surely than trying to write irony—because in irony some words say the opposite of what they mean and some say exactly what they mean, and others speak subtleties in between. The three quite different essays in this section show how this ironic blending of straight and veiled statement works. You will see how the ironist takes a fictitious pose, a pretense he shares in secret with his reader. You will see how the blend of straight

10

and veiled statement varies with the pose taken, and how irony may enter a perfectly straight essay for a time, tongue in cheek.

Swift's pose is the most thoroughly assumed, and his irony is the most thorough: most of his words say the opposite of his true message. To bring home the abominations of eighteenth-century Ireland, Swift pretends to be a man of logical but weirdly limited mind, as he makes his most immodest proposal. Carlyle ironically poses as an admirer of Coleridge, a cloudy Zeus and *guru* snuffling among his worshipers, but the claims of biographical accuracy and fair play continually break through the ironic clouds. Harrison Brown, on the other hand, constructs an ironic illustration from real scientific facts to illustrate an otherwise completely straight essay. He is so close to the facts, indeed, that you may miss his ironic shift—"To those who feel that life in such circumstances might be rather crowded . . ."—from which he brings you back to the straight line with his confession of writing nonsense.

A Modest Proposal for Preventing the Children of Ireland from Being a Burden to Their Parents or Country
Jonathan Swift

It is a melancholy object to those who walk through this great town [Dublin], or travel in the country, when they see the streets, the roads, and cabin-doors, crowded with beggars of the female sex, followed by three, four, or six children, all in rags, and importuning every passenger for an alms. These mothers, instead of being able to work for their honest livelihood, are forced to employ all their time in strolling to beg sustenance for their helpless infants; who, as they grow up, either turn thieves for want of work, or leave their dear native country to fight for the Pretender in Spain, or sell themselves to the Barbadoes.

I think it is agreed by all parties, that this prodigious number of children in the arms, or on the backs, or at the heels of their mothers, and frequently of their fathers, is, in the present deplorable state of the kingdom, a very great additional grievance; and, therefore, whoever could find out a fair, cheap, and easy method of making these children sound, useful members of the commonwealth, would deserve so well of the public, as to have his statue set up for a preserver of the nation.

But my intention is very far from being confined to provide only for the children of professed beggars; it is of a much greater extent, and shall take in the whole number of infants at a certain age, who are born of parents in effect as little able to support them, as those who demand our charity in the streets.

As to my own part, having turned my thoughts for many years upon this important subject, and maturely weighed the several schemes of our projectors, I have always found them grossly mistaken in their computation. It is true, a child, just dropped from its dam, may be supported by her milk for a solar year, with little other nourishment; at most, not above the value of two shillings, which the mother may certainly get, or the value in scraps, by her lawful occupation of begging; and it is exactly at one year old that I proposed to provide for them in such a manner, as, instead of being a charge upon their parents, or the parish, or wanting food and raiment for the rest of their lives, they shall, on the contrary, contribute to the feeding and partly to the clothing, of many thousands.

There is likewise another great advantage in my scheme, that it will prevent those voluntary abortions, and that horrid practice of women murdering their bastard children, alas, too frequent among us! sacrificing the poor innocent babes, I doubt more to avoid the expense than the shame, which would move tears and pity in the most savage and inhuman breast.

The number of souls in this kingdom being usually reckoned one million and a half, of these I calculate there may be about two hundred thousand couple whose wives are breeders; from which number I subtract thirty thousand couple, who are able to maintain their own children, (although I apprehend there cannot be so many, under the present distresses of the kingdom;) but this being granted, there will remain a hundred and seventy thousand breeders. I again subtract fifty thousand, for those women who miscarry, or whose children die by accident or disease within the year. There only remain a hundred and twenty thousand children of poor parents annually born. The question therefore is, How this number shall be reared and provided for? which, as I have already said, under the present situation of affairs, is utterly impossible by all the methods hitherto proposed. For we can neither employ them in handicraft or agriculture; we neither build houses (I mean in the country,) nor cultivate land: they can very seldom pick up a livelihood by stealing, till they arrive at six years old, except where they are of towardly parts; although I confess they learn the rudiments much earlier; during which time they can, however, be properly looked upon only as probationers; as I have been informed by a principal gentleman in the county of Cavan, who protested to me, that he never knew above one or two instances under the age of six, even in a part of the kingdom so renowned for the quickest proficiency in that art.

I am assured by our merchants, that a boy or a girl before twelve years old is no saleable commodity; and even when they come to this age they will not yield above three pounds, or three pounds and half-a-crown at most, on the exchange; which cannot turn to account either to the parents or kingdom, the charge of nutriment and rags having been at least four times that value.

I shall now, therefore, humbly propose my own thoughts, which I hope will not be liable to the least objection.

I have been assured by a very knowing American of my acquaintance in London, that a young healthy child, well nursed, is, at a year old, a most delicious, nourishing, and wholesome food, whether stewed, roasted, baked, or boiled; and I make no doubt that it will equally serve in a fricassee or a ragout.

I do therefore humbly offer it to public consideration, that of the hundred and twenty thousand children already computed, twenty thousand may be reserved for breed, whereof only one-fourth part to be males; which is more than we allow to sheep, black-cattle, or swine; and my reason is, that these children are seldom the fruits of marriage, a circumstance not much regarded by our savages, therefore one male will be sufficient to serve four females. That the remaining hundred thousand may, at a year old, be offered in sale to the persons of quality and fortune through the kingdom; always advising the mother to let them suck plentifully in the last month, so as to render them plump and fat for a good table. A child will make two dishes at an entertainment for friends; and when the family dines alone, the fore or hind quarter will make a reasonable dish, and, seasoned with a little pepper or salt, will be very good boiled on the fourth day, especially in winter.

I have reckoned, upon a medium, that a child just born will weigh twelve pounds, and in a solar year, if tolerably nursed, will increase to twenty-eight pounds.

I grant this food will be somewhat dear, and therefore very proper for landlords, who, as they have already devoured most of the parents, seem to have the best title to the children.

Infant's flesh will be in season throughout the year, but more plentifully in March, and a little before and after: for we are told by a grave author, an eminent French physician, that fish being a prolific diet, there are more children born in Roman Catholic countries about nine months after Lent, than at any other season; therefore, reckoning a year after Lent, the markets will be more glutted than usual, because the number of Popish infants is at least three to one in this kingdom; and therefore it will have one other collateral advantage, by lessening the Papists among us.

I have already computed the charge of nursing a beggar's child (in which list I reckon all cottagers, labourers, and four-fifths of the farmers) to be about two shillings per annum, rags included; and I believe no gentleman would repine to give ten shillings for the carcass of a good fat child, which, as I have said, will make four dishes of excellent nutritive meat, when he has only some particular friend, or his own family, to dine with him. Thus the squire will learn to be a good landlord, and grow popular among his tenants; the mother will have eight shillings net profit, and be fit for work till she produces another child.

Those who are more thrifty (as I must confess the times require) may flay the carcass; the skin of which, artificially dressed, will make admirable gloves for ladies, and summer-boots for fine gentlemen.

As to our city of Dublin, shambles [slaughter houses] may be appointed for this purpose in the most convenient parts of it, and butchers, we may be assured, will not be wanting; although I rather recommend buying the children alive, then dressing them hot from the knife, as we do roasting pigs.

A very worthy person, a true lover of his country, and whose virtues I highly esteem, was lately pleased, in discoursing on this matter, to offer a refinement upon my scheme. He said, that many gentlemen of this kingdom, having of late destroyed their deer, he conceived that the want of venison might be well supplied by the bodies of young lads and maidens, not exceeding fourteen years of age, nor under twelve; so great a number of both sexes in every country being now ready to starve for want of work and service; and these to be disposed of by their parents, if alive, or otherwise by their nearest relations. But, with due deference to so excellent a friend, and so deserving a patriot, I cannot be altogether in his sentiments; for as to the males, my American acquaintance assured me, from frequent experience, that their flesh was generally tough and lean, like that of our schoolboys, by continual exercise, and their taste disagreeable; and to fatten them would not answer the charge. Then as to the females, it would, I think, with humble submission, be a loss to the public, because they soon would become breeders themselves: and besides, it is not improbable that some scrupulous people might be apt to censure such a practice, (although indeed very unjustly,) as a little bordering upon cruelty; which, I confess, has always been with me the strongest objection against any project, how well soever intended.

But in order to justify my friend, he confessed that this expedient was put into his head by the famous Psalmanazar, a native of the island Formosa, who came from thence to London above twenty years ago; and in conversation told my friend, that in his country, when any young person happened to be put to death, the executioner sold the carcass to persons of quality as a prime dainty; and that in his time the body of a plump girl of fifteen, who was crucified for an attempt to poison the emperor, was sold to his imperial majesty's prime minister of state, and other great mandarins of the court, in joints from the gibbet, at four hundred crowns. Neither indeed can I deny, that, if the same use were made of several plump young girls in this town, who, without one single groat to their fortunes, cannot stir abroad without a chair, and appear at playhouse and assemblies in foreign fineries which they never will pay for, the kingdom would not be the worse.

Some persons of a desponding spirit are in great concern about that vast number of poor people, who are aged, diseased, or maimed; and I have been desired to employ my thoughts, what course may be taken to ease the nation of so grievous an encumbrance. But I am not in the least pain upon that matter, because it is very well known, that they are every day dying, and rotting, by cold and famine, and filth and vermin, as fast as can be reasonably expected. And as to the young labourers, they are now in almost as hopeful a condition: they cannot get work, and consequently pine away for want of nourishment, to a degree, that if at any time they are accidentally hired to common labour, they have not strength to perform it; and thus the country and themselves are happily delivered from the evils to come.

I have too long digressed, and therefore shall return to my subject. I think the advantages by the proposal which I have made are obvious and many, as well as of the highest importance.

For first, as I have already observed, it would greatly lessen the number of Papists, with whom we are yearly over-run, being the principal breeders of the nation, as well as our most dangerous enemies; and who stay at home on purpose to deliver the kingdom to the Pretender, hoping to take their advantage by the absence of so many good Protestants, who have chosen rather to leave their country than stay at home and pay tithes against their conscience to an Episcopal curate.

Secondly, The poorer tenants will have something valuable of their own, which by law may be made liable to distress, and help to pay their landlord's rent; their corn and cattle being already seized, and money a thing unknown.

Thirdly, Whereas the maintenance of a hundred thousand children, from two years old and upwards, cannot be computed at less than ten shillings a piece per annum, the nation's stock will be thereby increased fifty thousand pounds per annum, beside the profit of a new dish introduced to the tables of all gentlemen of fortune in the kingdom, who have any refinement in taste. And the money will circulate among ourselves, the goods being entirely of our own growth and manufacture.

Fourthly, The constant breeders, beside the gain of eight shillings sterling per annum by the sale of their children, will be rid of the charge of maintaining them after the first year.

Fifthly, This food would likewise bring great custom to taverns; where the vintners will certainly be so prudent as to procure the best receipts for dressing it to perfection, and, consequently, have their houses frequented by all the fine gentlemen, who justly value themselves upon their knowledge in good eating: and a skilful cook, who understands how to oblige his guests, will contrive to make it as expensive as they please.

Sixthly, This would be a great inducement to marriage, which all wise nations have either encouraged by rewards, or enforced by laws and penalties. It would increase the care and tenderness of mothers toward their children, when they were sure of a settlement for life to the poor babes, provided in some sort by the public, to their annual profit or expense. We should see an honest emulation among the married women, which of them could bring the fattest child to the market. Men would become as fond of their wives during the time of their pregnancy as they are now of their mares in foal, their cows in calf, their sows when they are ready to farrow; nor offer to beat or kick them (as is too frequent a practice) for fear of a miscarriage.

Many other advantages might be enumerated. For instance, the addition of some thousand carcasses in our exportation of barrelled beef; the propagation of swine's flesh, and improvement in the art of making good bacon, so much wanted among us by the great destruction of pigs, too frequent at our table; which are no way comparable in taste or magnificence to a well-grown, fat, yearling child, which, roasted whole, will make a considerable figure at a lord mayor's feast, or any other public entertainment. But this, and many others, I omit, being studious of brevity.

Supposing that one thousand families in this city would be constant customers for infants' flesh, beside others who might have it at merry-meetings, particularly at weddings and christenings, I compute that Dublin would take off annually about twenty thousand carcasses; and the rest of the kingdom (where probably they will be sold somewhat cheaper) the remaining eighty thousand.

I can think of no one objection, that will possibly be raised against this proposal, unless it should be urged, that the number of people will be thereby much lessened in the kingdom. This I freely own, and it was indeed one principal design in offering it to the world. I desire the reader will observe, that I calculate my remedy for this one individual kingdom of Ireland, and for no other that ever was, is, or I think ever can be, upon earth. Therefore let no man talk to me of other expedients:

true meaning

of taxing our absentees at five shillings a pound: of using neither clothes, nor household furniture, except what is our own growth and manufacture: of utterly rejecting the materials and instruments that promote foreign luxury: of curing the expensiveness of pride, vanity, idleness, and gaming in our women: of introducing a vein of parsimony, prudence, and temperance: of learning to love our country, in the want of which we differ even from LAPLANDERS, and the inhabitants of To-PINAMBOO: of quitting our animosities and factions, nor acting any longer like the Jews, who were murdering one another at the very moment their city was taken: of being a little cautious not to sell our country and conscience for nothing: of teaching landlords to have at least one degree of mercy toward their tenants: lastly, of putting a spirit of honesty, industry, and skill into our shopkeepers; who, if a resolution could now be taken to buy only our native goods, would immediately unite to cheat and exact upon us in the price, the measure, and the goodness, nor could ever yet be brought to make one fair proposal of just dealing, though often and earnestly invited to it.

Therefore I repeat, let no man talk to me of these and the like expedients, till he has at least some glimpse of hope, that there will be ever some hearty and sincere attempt to put them in practice.

But, as to myself, having been wearied out for many years with offering vain, idle, visionary thoughts, and at length utterly despairing of success, I fortunately fell upon this proposal; which, as it is wholly new, so it has something solid and real, of no expense and little trouble, full in our own power, and whereby we can incur no danger in disobliging ENGLAND. For this kind of commodity will not bear exportation, the flesh being of too tender a consistence to admit a long continuance in salt, although perhaps I could name a country, which would be glad to eat up our whole nation without it.

After all, I am not so violently bent upon my own opinion as to reject any offer proposed by wise men, which shall be found equally innocent, cheap, easy, and effectual. But before something of that kind shall be advanced in contradiction to my scheme, and offering a better, I desire the author, or authors, will be pleased maturely to consider two points. First, as things now stand, how they will be able to find food and raiment for a hundred thousand useless mouths and backs. And, secondly, there being a round million of creatures in human figure throughout this kingdom, whose whole subsistence put into a common stock would leave them in debt two millions of pounds sterling, adding those who are beggars by profession, to the bulk of farmers, cottagers, and labourers, with the wives and children who are beggars in effect; I desire those politicians who dislike my overture, and may perhaps be so bold as to attempt an answer, that they will first ask the parents of these mortals, whether they would not at this day think it a great happiness to have been sold for food at a year old, in the manner I prescribe, and thereby have avoided such a perpetual scene of misfortunes, as they have since gone through, by the oppression of landlords, the impossibility of paying rent without money or trade, the want of common sustenance, with neither house nor clothes to cover them from the inclemencies of the weather, and the most inevitable prospect of entailing the like, or greater miseries, upon their breed for ever.

I profess, in the sincerity of my heart, that I have not the least personal interest in endeavouring to promote this necessary work, having no other motive than the public good of my country, by advancing our trade, providing for infants, relieving the poor, and giving some pleasure to the rich. I have no children by which I can propose to get a single penny; the youngest being nine years old, and my wife past child-bearing.

Coleridge[1]
Thomas Carlyle

Coleridge sat on the brow of Highgate Hill, in those years, looking down on London and its smoke-tumult, like a sage escaped from the inanity of life's battle; attracting towards him the thoughts of innumerable brave souls still engaged there. His express contributions to poetry, philosophy, or any specific province of human literature or enlightenment, had been small and sadly intermittent; but he had, especially among young inquiring men, a higher than literary, a kind of prophetic or magician character. He was thought to hold, he alone in England, the key of German and other Transcendentalisms; knew the sublime secret of believing by 'the reason' what 'the understanding' had been obliged to fling out as incredible; and could still, after Hume and Voltaire had done their best and worst with him, profess himself an orthodox Christian, and say and print to the Church of England, with its singular old rubics and surplices at Allhallowtide, *Esto perpetua*.[2]

---

[1] From Carlyle's *The Life of John Sterling* (London, 1851), Part I, Ch. VIII. John Sterling (1806–44) was a British author most renowned for his critical works. He is remembered today primarily as the subject of Carlyle's biography. I have added the numbered footnotes.—S.B.

[2] "Be everlasting."

A sublime man; who, alone in those dark days, had saved his crown of spiritual manhood; escaping from the black materialisms, and revolutionary deluges, with 'God, Freedom, Immortality' still his: a king of men. The practical intellects of the world did not much heed him, or carelessly reckoned him a metaphysical dreamer: but to the rising spirits of the young generation he had this dusky sublime character; and sat there as a kind of *Magus,* girt in mystery and enigma; his Dodona oak-grove[3] (Mr. Gilman's house at Highgate) whispering strange things, uncertain whether oracles or jargon.

The Gilmans did not encourage much company, or excitation of any sort, round their sage; nevertheless access to him, if a youth did reverently wish it, was not difficult. He would stroll about the pleasant garden with you, sit in the pleasant rooms of the place—perhaps take you to his own peculiar room, high up, with a rearward view, which was the chief view of all. A really charming outlook, in fine weather. Close at hand, wide sweep of flowery leafy gardens, their few houses mostly hidden, the very chimney-pots veiled under blossomy umbrage, flowed gloriously down hill, gloriously issuing in wide-tufted undulating plain-country, rich in all charms of field and town. Waving blooming country of the brightest green; dotted all over with handsome villas, handsome groves; crossed by roads and human traffic, here inaudible or heard only as a musical hum; and behind all swam, under olive-tinted haze, the illimitable limitary ocean of London, with its domes and steeples definite in the sun, big Paul's and the many memories attached to it hanging high over all. Nowhere, of its kind, could you see a grander prospect on a bright summer day, with the set of the air going southward,—southward, and so draping with the city-smoke not *you* but the city. Here for hours would Coleridge talk, concerning all conceivable or inconceivable things; and liked nothing better than to have an intelligent, or failing that, even a silent and patient human listener. He distinguished himself to all that ever heard him as at least the most surprising talker extant in this world,—and to some small minority, by no means to all, as the most excellent.

The good man, he was now getting old, towards sixty perhaps; and gave you the idea of a life that had been full of sufferings; a life heavy-laden, half-vanquished, still swimming painfully in seas of manifold physical and other bewilderment. Brow and head were round, and of massive weight, but the face was flabby and irresolute. The deep eyes, of a light hazel, were as full of sorrow as of inspiration; confused

---

[3] The oak grove at the town of Dodona, in northern Greece, contained the temple of a famous oracle of Zeus. A Magus was a Persian (and Median) "Wise Man," a Zoroastrian priest or astrologer.

pain looked mildly from them, as in a kind of mild astonishment. The whole figure and air, good and amiable otherwise, might be called flabby and irresolute; expressive of weakness under possibility of strength. He hung loosely on his limbs, with knees bent, and stooping attitude; in walking, he rather shuffled than decisively stept; and a lady once remarked, he never could fix which side of the garden walk would suit him best, but continually shifted, in corkscrew fashion, and kept trying both. A heavy-laden, high-aspiring and surely much-suffering man. His voice, naturally soft and good, had contracted itself into a plaintive snuffle and sing-song; he spoke as if preaching,—you would have said, preaching earnestly and also hopelessly the weightiest things. I still recollect his "object" and "subject," terms of continual recurrence in the Kantean province; and how he sang and snuffled them into "om-m-mject" and "sum-m-mject," with a kind of solemn shake or quaver, as he rolled along. No talk, in his century or in any other, could be more surprising.

Sterling, who assiduously attended him, with profound reverence, and was often with him by himself, for a good many months, gives a record of their first colloquy.* Their colloquies were numerous, and he had taken note of many; but they are all gone to the fire, except this first, which Mr. Hare has printed,—unluckily without date. It contains a number of ingenious, true and half-true observations, and is of course a faithful epitome of the things said; but it gives small idea of Coleridge's way of talking;—this one feature is perhaps the most recognisable, "Our interview lasted for three hours, during which he talked two hours and three quarters." Nothing could be more copious than his talk; and furthermore it was always, virtually or literally, of the nature of a monologue; suffering no interruption, however reverent; hastily putting aside all foreign additions, annotations, or most ingenuous desires for elucidation, as well-meant superfluities which would never do. Besides, it was talk not flowing anywhither like a river, but spreading everywhither in inextricable currents and regurgitations like a lake or sea; terribly deficient in definite goal or aim, nay often in logical intelligibility; *what* you were to believe or do, on any earthly or heavenly thing, obstinately refusing to appear from it. So that, most times, you felt logically lost; swamped near to drowning in this tide of ingenious vocables, spreading out boundless as if to submerge the world.

To sit as a passive bucket and be pumped into, whether you consent or not, can in the long-run be exhilarating to no creature; how eloquent soever the flood of utterance that is descending. But if it be withal a confused unintelligible flood of utterance, threatening to submerge

---

* *Biography,* by Hare, pp. xvi.–xxvi.

all known landmarks of thought, and drown the world and you!—I have heard Coleridge talk, with eager musical energy, two stricken hours, his face radiant and moist, and communicate no meaning whatsoever to any individual of his hearers,—certain of whom, I for one, still kept eagerly listening in hope; the most had long before given up, and formed (if the room were large enough) secondary humming groups of their own. He began anywhere: you put some question to him, made some suggestive observation: instead of answering this, or decidedly setting out towards answer of it, he would accumulate formidable apparatus, logical swim-bladders, transcendental life-preservers and other precautionary and vehiculatory gear, for setting out; perhaps did at last get under way,—but was swiftly solicited, turned aside by the glance of some radiant new game on this hand or that, into new courses; and ever into new; and before long into all the Universe, where it was uncertain what game you would catch, or whether any.

His talk, alas, was distinguished, like himself, by irresolution: it disliked to be troubled with conditions, abstinences, definite fulfillments;—loved to wander at its own sweet will, and make its auditor and its claims and humble wishes a mere passive bucket for itself! He had knowledge about many things and topics, much curious reading; but generally all topics led him, after a pass or two, into the high seas of theosophic philosophy, the hazy infinitude of Kantean transcendentalism, with its "sum-m-mjects" and "om-m-mjects." Sad enough; for with such indolent impatience of the claims and ignorances of others, he had not the least talent for explaining this or anything unknown to them; and you swam and fluttered in the mistiest wide unintelligible deluge of things, for the most part in a rather profitless uncomfortable manner.

Glorious islets, too, I have seen rise out of the haze; but they were few, and soon swallowed in the general element again. Balmy sunny islets, islets of the blest and the intelligible:—on which occasions those secondary humming groups would all cease humming, and hang breathless upon the eloquent words; till once your islet got wrapt in the mist again, and they could recommence humming. Eloquent artistically expressive words you always had; piercing radiances of a most subtle insight came at intervals; tones of noble pious sympathy, recognisable as pious though strangely coloured, were never wanting long: but in general you could not call this aimless, cloudcapt, cloud-based, lawlessly meandering human discourse of reason by the name of "excellent talk," but only of "surprising"; and were reminded bitterly of Hazlitt's account of it: "Excellent talker, very,—if you let him start from no premises and come to no conclusion." Coleridge was not without what talkers call wit, and there were touches of prickly sarcasm in him, contemptuous enough of the world and its idols and popular dignitaries; he had traits even of poetic humour: but in general he seemed deficient in laughter; or indeed in sympathy for concrete human things either on the sunny or on the stormy side. One right peal of concrete laughter at some convicted flesh-and-blood absurdity, one burst of noble indignation at some injustice or depravity, rubbing elbows with us on this solid Earth, how strange would it have been in that Kantean haze-world, and how infinitely cheering amid its vacant air-castles and dim-melting ghosts and shadows! None such ever came. His life had been an abstract thinking and dreaming, idealistic, passed amid the ghosts of defunct bodies and of unborn ones. The moaning singsong of that theo-sophico-metaphysical monotony left on you, at last, a very dreary feeling.

In close colloquy, flowing within narrower banks, I suppose he was more definite and apprehensible; Sterling in aftertimes did not complain of his unintelligibility, or imputed it only to the abstruse high nature of the topics handled. Let us hope so, let us try to believe so! There is no doubt but Coleridge could speak plain words on things plain: his observations and responses on the trivial matters that occurred were as simple as the commonest man's, or were even distinguished by superior simplicity as well as pertinency. "Ah, your tea is too cold, Mr. Coleridge!" mourned the good Mrs. Gilman once, in her kind, reverential and yet protective manner, handing him a very tolerable though belated cup.—"It's better than I deserve!" snuffled he, in a low hoarse murmur, partly courteous, chiefly pious, the tone of which still abides with me: "It's better than I deserve!"

But indeed, to the young ardent mind, instinct with pious nobleness, yet driven to the grim deserts of Radicalism for a faith, his speculations had a charm much more than literary, a charm almost religious and prophetic. The constant gist of his discourse was lamentation over the sunk condition of the world; which he recognised to be given-up to Atheism and Materialism, full of mere sordid misbeliefs, mispursuits and misresults. All Science had become mechanical; the science not of men, but of a kind of human beavers. Churches themselves had died away into a godless mechanical condition; and stood there as mere Cases of Articles, mere Forms of Churches; like the dried carcasses of once-swift camels, which you find left withering in the thirst of the universal desert,—ghastly portents for the present, beneficent ships of the desert no more. Men's souls were blinded, hebetated; and sunk under the influence of Atheism and Materialism, and Hume and Voltaire: the world for the present was as an extinct world, deserted of God, and incapable of welldoing till it changed its heart and spirit. This, expressed I think with less of indignation and with more of long-drawn querulousness, was always recognisable as the ground-tone:—in which truly a pious young heart, driven into Radicalism and the opposition party, could not but recognise a too sorrowful truth; and ask of the Oracle, with all earnestness, What remedy, then?

The remedy, though Coleridge himself professed to see it as in sunbeams, could not, except by processes unspeakably difficult, be described to you at all. On the whole, those dead Churches, this dead English Church especially, must be brought to life again. Why not? It was not dead; the soul of it, in this parched-up body, was tragically asleep only. Atheistic Philosophy was true on its side, and Hume and Voltaire could on their own ground speak irrefragably for themselves against any Church: but lift the Church and them into a higher sphere of argument, *they* died into inanition, the Church revivified itself into pristine florid vigour,—became once more a living ship of the desert, and invincibly bore you over stock and stone. But how, but how! By attending to the "reason" of man, said Coleridge, and duly chaining-up the "understanding" of man: the *Vernunft* (Reason) and *Verstand* (Understanding) of the Germans, it all turned upon these, if you could well understand them,—which you couldn't. For the rest, Mr. Coleridge had on the anvil various Books, especially was about to write one grand Book *On the Logos,* which would help to bridge the chasm for us. So much appeared, however: Churches, though proved false (as you had imagined), were still true (as you were to imagine): here was an Artist who could burn you up an old Church, root and branch; and then as the Alchymists professed to do with organic substances in general, distil you an "Astral Spirit" from the ashes, which was the very image of the old burnt article, its airdrawn counterpart,—this you still had, or might get, and draw use from if you could. Wait till the Book on the Logos were done;—alas, till your own terrene eyes, blind with conceit and the dust of logic, were purged, subtilised and spiritualised into the sharpness of vision requisite for discerning such an "om-m-mject."—The ingenuous young English head, of those days, stood strangely puzzled by such revelations; uncertain whether it were getting inspired, or getting infatuated into flat imbecility; and strange effulgence, of new day or else of deeper meteoric night, coloured the horizon of the future for it.

Let me not be unjust to this memorable man. Surely there was here, in his pious, ever-labouring, subtle mind, a precious truth, or prefigurement of truth; and yet a fatal delusion withal. Prefigurement that, in spite of beaver sciences and temporary spiritual hebetude and cecity, man and his Universe were eternally divine; and that no past nobleness, or revelation of the divine, could or would ever be lost to him. Most true, surely, and worthy of all acceptance. Good also to do what you can with old Churches and practical Symbols of the Noble: nay, quit not the burnt ruins of them while you find there is still gold to be dug there. But, on the whole, do not think you can, by logical alchymy, distil astral spirits from them; or if you could, that said astral spirits, or defunct logical phantasms, could serve you in anything. What the light of your mind, which is the direct inspiration of the Almighty, pronounces incredible,—that, in God's name, leave uncredited; at your peril do not try believing that. No subtlest hocus-pocus of "reason" *versus* "understanding" will avail for that feat;—and it is terribly perilous to try it in these provinces!

The truth is, I now see, Coleridge's talk and speculation was the emblem of himself: in it, as in him, a ray of heavenly inspiration struggled, in a tragically ineffectual degree, with the weakness of flesh and blood. He says once, he "had skirted the howling deserts of Infidelity"; this was evident enough: but he had not had the courage, in defiance of pain and terror, to press resolutely across said deserts to the new firm lands of Faith beyond; he preferred to create logical fatamorganas for himself on this hither side, and laboriously solace himself with these.

To the man himself Nature had given, in high measure, the seeds of a noble endowment; and to unfold it had been forbidden him. A subtle lynx-eyed intellect, tremulous pious sensibility to all good and all beautiful; truly a ray of empyrean light;—but imbedded in such weak laxity of character, in such indolences and esuriences as had made strange work with it. Once more, the tragic story of a high endowment with an insufficient will. An eye to discern to divineness of the Heaven's splendours and lightnings, the insatiable wish to revel in their godlike radiances and brilliances; but no heart to front the scathing terrors of them, which is the first condition of your conquering an abiding place there. The courage necessary for him, above all things, had been denied this man. His life, with such ray of the empyrean in it, was great and terrible to him; and he had not valiantly grappled with it, he had fled from it; sought refuge in vague day-dreams, hollow compromises, in opium, in theosophic metaphysics. Harsh pain, danger, necessity, slavish harnessed toil, were of all things abhorrent to him. And so the empyrean element, lying smothered under the terrene, and yet inextinguishable there, made sad writhings. For pain, danger, difficulty, steady slaving toil, and other highly disagreeable behests of destiny, shall in no wise be shirked by any brightest mortal that will approve himself loyal to his mission in this world; nay, precisely the higher he is, the deeper will be the disagreeableness, and the detestability to flesh and blood, of the tasks laid on him; and the heavier too, and more tragic, his penalties, if he neglect them.

For the old Eternal Powers do live forever; nor do their laws know any change, however we in our poor wigs and church-tippets may attempt to read their laws. To *steal* into Heaven,—by the modern method, of sticking ostrich-like your head into fallacies on Earth, equally as by the ancient and by all conceivable methods,—is forever forbidden. High-treason is the name of that attempt; and it continues to be punished as such. Strange enough: here once more was a kind of Heaven-scaling Ixion[4]; and to him, as to the old one, the just gods were very stern! The ever-revolving, never-advancing Wheel (of a kind) was his, through life; and from his Cloud Juno did not he too procreate strange Centaurs, spectral Puseyisms,[5] monstrous illusory Hybrids, and ecclesiastical Chimeras,—which now roam the earth in a very lamentable manner.

After the Population Explosion
Harrison Brown

At one time or another almost all of us have been asked: How many human beings can the Earth support? When this question is put to me, I find it necessary to respond with another question: In what kind of world are you willing to live? In the eyes of those who care about their environment, we have perhaps already passed the limits of growth. In the eyes of those who don't care how they live or what dangers they create for posterity, the limits of growth lie far ahead.

The populations of all biological species are limited by environmental factors, and man's is no exception. Food supplies and the presence of predators are of prime importance. When two rabbits of opposite sex are placed in a fenced-in field of grass, they will go forth and multiply, but the population will eventually be limited by the grass supply. If predators are placed in the field, the rabbit population will either stabilize at a new level or possibly become extinct. Given no predators and no restrictions on food, but circumscribed space, the

---

[4] A Greek king admitted into Olympus as a guest by Zeus. He attempted to seduce Hera (Juno), Zeus's wife, but she substituted a cloud for herself, by which he became the father of the Centaurs. For his offence, Zeus bound him to a fiery wheel forever turning in the river Tartarus in Hades.

[5] Edward Pusey, English clergyman, started a movement at Oxford, running from 1833 to 1841 (also called the Tractarian movement), which aimed to bring the English church back toward simple, primitive Christianity.

number of rabbits will still be limited, either by the psychological and biological effects of overcrowding or by being buried in their own refuse.

When man, endowed with the power of conceptual thought, appeared upon the Earth scene, something new was introduced into the evolutionary process. Biological evolution, which had dominated all living species for billions of years, gave way to cultural evolution. As man gradually learned how to control various elements of his environment, he succeeded in modifying a number of the factors that limited his population. Clothing, fire, and crude shelters extended the range of habitable climate. Tools of increasing sophistication helped man gather edible vegetation, hunt animals more effectively, and protect himself from predators.

But no matter how effective the tools, there is a limit to the number of food gatherers who can inhabit a given area of land. One cannot kill more animals than are born or pick more fruit than trees bear. The maximum population of a worldwide food-gathering society was about ten million persons. Once that level was reached, numerous cultural patterns emerged that caused worldwide birth rates and death rates to become equal. In some societies, the natural death rate was elevated by malnutrition and disease; in others, the death rate was increased artificially by such practices as infanticide or the waging of war. In some cases, certain sex taboos and rituals appear to have lowered the birth rate. But, however birth and death rates came into balance, we can be confident that for a long time prior to the agricultural revolution the human population remained virtually constant.

With the introduction of agriculture about 10,000 years ago, the levels of population that had been imposed by limited supplies of food were raised significantly. Even in the earliest agricultural societies, several hundred times as much food could be produced from a given area of fertile land than could be collected by food gatherers. As the technology of agriculture spread, population grew rapidly. This new technology dramatically affected the entire fabric of human culture. Man gave up the nomad life and settled in villages, some of which became cities. Sufficient food could be grown to make it possible for about 10 per cent of the population to engage in activities other than farming.

The development of iron technology and improved transportation accelerated the spread of this peasant-village culture. Indeed, had new technological developments ceased to appear after 1700, it is nevertheless likely that the peasant-village culture would have spread to all inhabitable parts of the Earth, eventually to reach a level of roughly five billion persons, some 500 million of whom would live in cities. But long before the population had reached anything close to that level, the emergence of new technologies leading up to the Industrial Revolution markedly changed the course of history. The steam engine for the first time gave man a means of concentrating enormous quantities of in-animate mechanical energy, and the newly found power was quickly applied.

During the nineteenth century in western Europe, improved transportation, increased food supplies, and a generally improved environment decreased the morbidity of a number of infectious diseases and virtually eliminated the large fluctuations in mortality rates that had been so characteristic of the seventeenth and eighteenth centuries. As mortality rates declined and the birth rate remained unchanged, populations in these areas increased rapidly. But as industrialization spread, a multiplicity of factors combined to lessen the desirability of large families. After about 1870, the size of families decreased, at first slowly and then more rapidly; eventually, the rate of population growth declined.

During the nineteenth and early twentieth centuries, some of the new technologies were gradually transplanted to the non-industrialized parts of the world, but in a very one-sided manner. Death rates were reduced appreciably, and, with birth rates unchanged, populations in these poorer countries increased rapidly and are still growing.

In spite of the fact that the annual rate of population growth in the industrialized countries has dropped to less than 1 percent, the world-wide rate is now close to 2 percent, the highest it has ever been. This rate represents a doubling of population about every thirty-five years. The human population is now 3.5 billion and at the present rate of increase is destined to reach 6.5 billion by the turn of the century and ten billion fifty years from now. Beyond that point, how much further can population grow?

An analysis of modern technology's potential makes it clear that from a long-range, theoretical point of view, food supplies need no longer be the primary factor limiting population growth. Today nearly 10 per cent of the land area of the Earth, or about 3.5 billion acres, is under cultivation. It is estimated that with sufficient effort about fifteen billion acres of land could be placed under cultivation—some four times the present area. Such a move would require prodigious effort and investment and would necessitate the use of substantial quantities of desalinated water reclaimed from the sea. Given abundant energy resources, however, it now appears that in principle this can be done economically.

Large as the potential is for increasing the area of agricultural land, the increases in yield that can be obtained through fertilizers, application of supplementary water, and the use of new high-yielding varieties of cereals are even more impressive. Whereas in the past the growth of plants was circumscribed by the availability of nutrients and water, this need no longer be true. Using our new agricultural technology, solar energy can be converted into food with a high degree of efficiency, and even on the world's presently cultivated lands several times as much food can be produced each year than is now being grown.

To accomplish these objectives, however, an enormous amount of industrialization will be required. Fertilizers must be produced; thus, phosphate rock must be mined and processed, and nitrogen fixation plants must be built. Pesticides and herbicides are needed; thus, chemical plants must be built. All this requires steel and concrete, highways, railroads, and trucks. To be sure, the people of India, for example, might not need to attain Japan's level of industrialization in order to obtain Japanese levels of crop yield (which are about the highest in the world), but they will nevertheless need a level of industrialization that turns out to be surprisingly high.

Colin Clark, the director of the Agricultural Economics Research Institute of Oxford and a noted enthusiast for large populations, estimates that, given this new agricultural land and a level of industrialization sufficiently high to apply Japanese standards of farming, close to thirty billion persons could be supported on a Western European diet. Were people to content themselves with a Japanese diet, which contains little animal protein, he estimates that 100 billion persons could be supported.

To those who feel that life under such circumstances might be rather crowded, I should like to point out that even at the higher population level, the mean density of human beings over the land areas of the Earth would be no more than that which exists today in the belt along the Eastern Seaboard between Boston and Washington, D.C., where the average density is now 2,000 persons per square mile and where many people live quite comfortably. After all, Hong Kong has a population density of about 13,000 persons per square mile (nearly six times greater), and I understand that there are numerous happy people there.

Of course, such a society would need to expend a great deal of energy in order to manufacture, transport, and distribute the fertilizers, pesticides, herbicides, water, foodstuffs, and countless associated raw materials and products that would be necessary.

In the United States we currently consume energy equivalent to the burning of twelve-and-a-half short tons of coal per person per year. This quantity is bound to increase in the future as we find it necessary to process lower-grade ores, as we expend greater effort on controlling pollution (which would otherwise increase enormously), and as we recover additional quantities of potable water from the sea. Dr. Alvin

Weinberg, director of the Oak Ridge National Laboratory, and his associates estimate that such activities will cost several additional tons of coal per person per year, and they suggest that for safety we budget twenty-five tons of coal per person per year in order to maintain our present material standard of living. Since we are a magnanimous people, we would not tolerate a double standard of living (a rich one for us and a poor one for others); so I will assume that this per capita level of energy expenditure will be characteristic of the world as a whole.

It has been estimated that the world's total usable coal reserve is on the order of 7,600 billion tons. This amount would last a population of thirty billion persons only ten years and a population of 100 billion only three years. Clearly, long before such population levels are reached, man must look elsewhere for his energy supplies.

Fortunately, technology once again gets us out of our difficulty, for nuclear fuels are available to us in virtually limitless quantities in the form of uranium and thorium for fission, and possibly in the form of deuterium for fusion. The Conway granite in New Hampshire could alone provide fuel for a population of twenty billion persons for 200 years. When we run out of high-grade granites, we can move on to process low-grade granites. Waste rock can be dumped into the holes from which it came and can be used to create new land areas on bays and on the continental shelf. Waste fission products can be stored in old salt mines.

Actually, a major shift to nuclear fuel might well be necessary long before our supplies of fossil fuels are exhausted. The carbon dioxide concentration in our atmosphere is rapidly increasing as a result of our burning of coal, petroleum, and natural gas, and it is destined to increase still more rapidly in the future. More than likely, any such increase will have a deleterious effect upon our climate, and if this turns out to be the case, use of those fuels will probably be restricted.

Thus, we see that in theory there should be little difficulty in feeding a world population of thirty billion or even 100 billion persons and in providing it with the necessities of life. But can we go even further?

With respect to food, once again technology can come to our rescue, for we have vast areas of the seas to fertilize and farm. Even more important, we will be able to produce synthetic foods in quantity. The constituents of our common oils and fats can already be manufactured on a substantial scale for human consumption and animal feeds. In the not too distant future, we should be able to synthetically produce complete, wholesome foods, thus bypassing the rather cumbersome process of photosynthesis.

Far more difficult than the task of feeding people will be that of cooling the Earth, of dissipating the heat generated by nuclear power plants. It has been suggested that if we were to limit our total energy generation to no more than 5 per cent of the incident solar radiation, little harm would be done. The mean surface temperature of the Earth would rise by about 6 degrees F. A temperature rise much greater than this could be extremely dangerous and should not be permitted until we have learned more about the behavior of our ocean/atmosphere system.

Of course, there will be local heating problems in the vicinity of the power stations. Dr. Weinberg suggests a system of "nuclear parks," each producing about forty million kilowatts of electricity and located on the coast or offshore. A population of 333 billion persons would require 65,000 such parks. The continental United States, with a projected population of close to twenty-five billion persons, would require nearly 5,000 parks spaced at twenty-mile intervals along its coastline.

Again, I want to allay the fears of those who worry about crowding. A population of 333 billion spread uniformly over the land areas of the Earth would give us a population density of only 6,000 persons per square mile, which, after all, is only somewhat greater than the population density in the city of Los Angeles. Just imagine the thrill of flying from Los Angeles to New York and having the landscape look like Los Angeles all the way. Imagine the excitement of driving from Los Angeles to New York on a Santa Monica Freeway 2,800 miles long.

A few years ago Dr. J. H. Fremlin of the University of Birmingham analyzed the problem of population density and concluded that several stages of development might be possible beyond the several-hundred-billion-person level of population. He conceives of hermetically sealing the outer surface of the planet and of using pumps to transfer heat to the solid outer skin from which it would be radiated directly into space. Combining this with a roof over the oceans to prevent excessive evaporation of water and to provide additional living space, he feels it would be possible to accommodate about 100 persons per square yard, thus giving a total population of about sixty million billion persons. But, frankly, I consider this proposal visionary. Being basically conservative, I doubt that the human population will ever get much above the 333-billion-person level.

Now some readers might be thinking that I am writing nonsense, and they are right. My facts are correct; the conclusions I have drawn from those facts are correct. Yet, I have truthfully been writing nonsense. Specifically, I have given only *some* of the facts. Those facts that I have omitted alter the conclusions considerably.

I have presented only what is deemed possible by scientists from an energetic or thermodynamic point of view. An analogy would be for me to announce that I have calculated that in principle all men should be able to leap ten feet into the air. Obviously, such an announcement would not be followed by a sudden, frenzied, worldwide demonstration of people showing their leaping capabilities. Some people have sore feet; others have inadequate muscles; most haven't the slightest desire to leap into the air. The calculation might be correct, but the enthusiasm for jumping and the ability to jump might be very low. The problem is the behavior of people rather than that of inanimate matter.

We are confronted by the brutal fact that humanity today doesn't really know how to cope with the problems presented by three-and-a-half billion persons, let alone 333 billion. More than two-thirds of the present human population is poor in the material sense and is malnourished. The affluent one-third is, with breathtaking rapidity, becoming even more affluent. Two separate and distinct societies have emerged in the world, and they are becoming increasingly distinct and separated. Numerically the largest is the culture of the poor, composed of some 2,500 million persons. Numerically the smallest is the culture of the rich, composed of some 1,000 million persons. On the surface, the rich countries would appear to have it made; in historical perspective, their average per capita incomes are enormous. Their technological competence is unprecedented. Yet, they have problems that might well prove insoluble.

The most serious problem confronting the rich countries today is nationalism. We fight among each other and arm ourselves in order to do so more effectively. The Cold War has become a way of life, as is reflected in military budgets. Today the governments of the United States and the Soviet Union spend more on their respective military establishments than they do on either education or health—indeed a scandalous situation but, even worse, an explosive one.

All of the rich countries are suffering from problems of growth. Although the rates of population proliferation in these areas are not large, per capita consumption is increasing rapidly. Today an average "population unit" in the United States is quite different from one in the primitive world. Originally, a unit of population was simply a human being whose needs could be met by "eating" 2,500 calories and 60 grams of protein a day. Add to this some simple shelter, some clothing, and a small fire, and his needs were taken care of. A population unit today consists of a human being wrapped in tons of steel, copper, aluminum, lead, tin, zinc, and plastics. This new creature requires far more than food to keep it alive and functioning. Each day it gobbles up sixty pounds of coal or its equivalent, three pounds of raw steel, plus many pounds of other materials. Far from getting all of this food from his own depleted resources, he ranges abroad, much as the hunters of old, and obtains raw supplies in other parts of the world, more often than not in the poorer countries.

Industrial societies the world over are changing with unprecedented speed as the result of accelerated technological change, and they are becoming increasingly complex. All of them are encountering severe problems with their cities, which were designed within the framework of one technology and are falling apart at the seams within the framework of another.

The technological and social complexities of industrial society—composed as it is of vast interlocking networks of mines, factories, transportation systems, power grids, and communication networks, all operated by people—make it extremely vulnerable to disruption. Indeed, during the past year we have seen that the United States is far more vulnerable to labor strikes than North Vietnam is to air strikes. This vulnerability may eventually prove to be our undoing.

A concomitant of our affluence has been pollution. That which goes into a system must eventually come out; as our society has consumed more, it has excreted more. Given adequate supplies of energy and the necessary technology, such problems can be handled from a technical point of view. But it is by no means clear that we are about to solve these problems from a social or political point of view.

Although we know that theoretically we can derive our sustenance from the leanest of earth substances, such as seawater and rock, the fact remains that with respect to the raw materials needed for a highly industrialized society the research essential to the development of the necessary technology has hardly begun. Besides, it is less expensive for the rich countries to extract their sustenance from the poor ones.

As to the poor countries with their rapidly increasing populations, I fail to see how, in the long run, they can lift themselves up by their own bootstraps. In the absence of outside help commensurate with their needs, I suspect they will fail, and the world will become permanently divided into the rich and the poor—at least until such time as the rich, in their stupidity, blow themselves up.

One of the most difficult problems in the poor countries is that of extremely rapid population growth. If an economy grows only as fast as its population, the average well-being of the people does not improve —and indeed this situation prevails in many parts of the world. Equally important, rapid growth produces tremendous dislocations—physical, social, and economic. It is important to understand that the major population problem confronting the poor countries today is not so much the actual number of people as it is rapid growth rates. Clearly, if development is to take place, birth rates must be reduced.

Unfortunately, it is not clear just how birth rates can be brought down in these areas. Even with perfect contraceptives, there must be motivation upon the part of individuals, and in many areas this appears to be lacking. Some people say that economic development is necessary to produce the motivation, and they might be right. In any event, the solution will not be a simple one.

Although I am pessimistic about the future, I do not consider the situation to be by any means hopeless. I am convinced that our problems both here and abroad are soluble. But if they are ever solved, it will be because all of us reorient our attitudes away from those of our parents and more toward those of our children. I am convinced that young people today more often than not have a clearer picture of the world and its problems than do their elders. They are questioning our vast military expenditures and ask whether the Cold War is really necessary. They question the hot war in which we have become so deeply involved. They are questioning our concepts of nationalism, materialism, and laissez faire. It is just such questioning on the part of the young that gives me hope.

If this questioning persists, I foresee the emergence of a new human attitude in which people the world over work together to transform anarchy into law, to decrease dramatically military expenditures, to lower rates of population growth to zero, and to build an equitable world economy, so that all people can lead free and abundant lives in harmony with nature and with each other.

Suggestions for Writing

1. Write an ironic essay, with Swift your model. It need not be profound. Take some notorious collegiate fact or trait, and write, for instance, "A Modest Proposal to Encourage Recreation on Weekends." Imagine yourself a myopic do-gooder, and write an earnest, and modest, appeal to pry the students away from the books. Or, if you can keep the surface ironically cool, you may wish to try one of the burning issues of the day—the draft, student power, black power, classified research, inflation, free trade.

Build your essay, as Swift does, on a regular argumentative structure with beginning, middle, and end. Your thesis will be ironic, of course; but develop it as you would any argumentative thesis, using one of the *pro-con* structures on pages 60–61. Since irony depends on a shared understanding between writer and reader, you must pick some topic of common knowledge—or your irony will not be understood, and you will be talking in riddles. Since to write ironically you must be personally concerned, the world-shaking issues may be a little too impersonal for effective irony. If so, pick something perfectly familiar, something even playful and trivial, something like blind dates, roommates, dormitory food, eight o'clock classes, co-ops and communes, long hair and blue eyelids, style of dress, cluttering the walks with parked bicycles, or cluttering the lanes with parked cars.

2. Write an ironic sketch of someone overly admired by himself and others, borrowing some malicious hints from Carlyle.

3. Construct an essay after Harrison Brown, with both "ironic" and "straight" portions. Point up, as Brown does, a serious argument with its ironic counterpoint. Use as a subject for the essay one of the major topics suggested in question 1.

8½: *Fellini's Obvious Masterpiece* DWIGHT MACDONALD · 282
The Underground Man EUDORA WELTY · 295
The Cubist Epoch HAROLD ROSENBERG · 301

The Critical
Review

A critical review is a discovery and an evaluation.
It may evaluate any artistic work, but it usually
deals with books or, more recently, films. Three
critics, in this section, describe and evaluate a
film, a novel, and an art exhibit. Each critic tries
to locate a central meaning, since the novel and
the film act things out, in a kind of vocal
charade, rather than proclaiming their ultimate
significance, and an art exhibit presents moments
of visual perception in which the critic hopes to

11

find some integrated meaning. The review, like the essay, has its thesis—a combination of what the artist has implied, what that implication is worth, and how well he has implied it.

Thus Dwight Macdonald finds that Fellini's movie is a masterpiece precisely because it has *not* striven for deep meaning while yet implying the ironic richness and frustration of the artist's life in unusual psychological artistry; Eudora Welty finds that a detective story has shrewdly depicted modern society's wayward escapes into fantasy and hallucination; and Harold Rosenberg evaluates an art exhibit against the whole perspective of modern art.

As you read, notice how describing what is in each work not only conveys a sense of the work but also reinforces the critic's judgment of it.

8½ : *Fellini's Obvious Masterpiece*
Dwight Macdonald

I can't say that Fellini has been one of my favorite directors. *The White Sheik* I thought crude compared to Antonioni's comparable tragicomedy about a similar milieu, *The Lady Without the Camellias*. For all its poetic realism, *La Strada* left a sentimental aftertaste, mostly because of the performance of Fellini's wife, Giulietta Masina, which was praised for just the quality that put me off: her miming, which recalled all too faithfully the original creators of the style—Langdon, Keaton, and Chaplin. My favorite up to now has been *Cabiria* (1957), a Dickensian mixture of realism, pathos, and comedy; Mrs. Fellini also played the lead, this time with more restraint. The much-admired *I Vitteloni* (1953), I've seen only on a tiny 16-millimeter screen; it looked good, but my eye isn't practiced enough to know how it would look full-size.* The also admired *La Dolce Vita*, I thought sensationalized, inflated, and cinematically conventional, despite some brilliant episodes which (like the unbrilliant ones) made their point before they were half over. And Fellini's episode in *Boccaccio '70* was even worse than De Sica's: a stertorous laboring of a theme—censors are secretly prurient—that was probably considered hackneyed by Menander. But now Fellini has

---

* I have seen it full-size since this was written, and it *didn't* look good. I think it one of those historically important films like Visconti's *La Terra Trema*, Godard's *Breathless*, and (possibly) Resnais' *Hiroshima, Mon Amour* which haven't worn well because their innovations have become commonplace—too successful, in a sense—while there isn't enough else in them to engage our interest today. The antidramatic naturalism which fifteen years ago was exciting in *I Vitelloni* has become so familiar that the film now looks pedestrian, faded. [The footnotes in this review are Macdonald's.]

made a movie that I can't see any way not to recognize as a masterpiece.

This portrait of the artist as a middle-aged man is the most brilliant, varied, and entertaining movie I've seen since *Citizen Kane*. I saw it twice in as many weeks, and the second time I discovered many points that had escaped me in the first viewing, so headlong is its tempo, so fertile its invention. What I had found exciting the first time still seemed so, nor was I conscious of any *longueurs*, with two exceptions: the night visit to the tower (Guido's talk with Rosella merely verbalized what had already been shown to our eyes) and the scene in the car between Guido and Claudia (her "How big will my part be" would have been enough to make the point). A great deal is packed into every scene, like *Kane:* of well-observed detail; of visual pleasure; of fine acting in minor roles (Guido Alberti's The Producer, Edra's La Saraghina, Madeleine Lebeau's Actress). And finally, like *Kane,* it deals with large topics like art, society, sex, money, aging, pretense, and hypocrisy—all that Trollope wrote about in *The Way We Live Now*—just the opposite of these cautious little (though not short) art films that lingeringly explore some tiny area of impingement between three undefined characters or, if the director feels in an epic mood, four.

The action, or Argument, is as simple as its development is complex. Guido (played by Marcello Mastroianni with style, humor, and delicacy) is a famous director who has retreated to an Italian seaside health resort to avoid a breakdown and to finish the script of a spectacular of stupefying banality about the flight to another planet of the survivors of a nuclear war. The script is long overdue: a huge Canaveral launching tower has been erected on the beach—it cost a real $140,000 in the real film, we are told by the Joseph E. Levine handout which is also real, relatively—cast, producer, technicians, everybody is waiting around while costs tick along like a taxi meter as Guido tries to break through his Creative Block, and meanwhile to placate and if possible evade their persistent demands. His mistress arrives (a full-bodied, empty-headed soubrette right out of a Franz Lehar operetta—really wonderful performance by Sandra Milo) and is presently followed by his wife (Anouk Aimée manages to look astringent and attractive simultaneously), necessitating another series of evasions and placations that are all the more difficult because his relation to each is unsatisfactory since he is still, in middle age, trying to square the sexual circle: to possess without being possessed, to take without giving. His personal and professional lives are thus speeding toward catastrophe on parallel tracks. It happens. Mistress and wife finally clash in a scene of irretrievable social horror. The movie comes to smash at a huge publicity party the producer gives to force Guido's hand. Badgered by questions he can't answer, since the script is still hardly begun, Guido crawls under a buffet table and shoots himself. He springs back to life at once and begins to solve all his problems, emotional as well as cinematic, in a happy ending that has been widely deplored.

There are three kinds of reality in 8½, and the film proceeds with a constant shifting of gears between them. (Like *Marienbad,* but a secular version of that hieratic mystery: quick, humorous, jazzy, direct— you always know what gear you're in.) There is Guido's real present, as outlined above. There are his memories of his boyhood and of his dead parents. And there are his Walter Mitty daydreams of a harmonious realm of *luxe, calme, et volupté* in which all his problems are magically solved: the artist's world of creative fantasy. Its symbol is a beautiful young girl in white who keeps materializing and fading away throughout the film, and seems to be a kind of Muse. After his wife and his mistress have disastrously collided, Guido leans back in his café chair, closes his eyes (behind dark glasses), and revises the scene so that the wife compliments the mistress on her dress, and the two are presently waltzing together; since this works so well, Guido's editing goes all the way, and we have the lovely, and witty, harem fantasy, which poeticizes Freudian ideas about the libido even as it parodies them.

Everything flows in this protean movie, constantly shifting between reality, memory, and fantasy. Free association is its structural principle. A description of just what happens in two sequences may give some idea; I make no claim for detailed accuracy for these notes taken in the dark; they are merely what one viewer saw, or thought he saw. The first comes early in the film; the second covers the last half hour or so.

(1) A bedroom in a shabby hotel. Guido asks Carla, his mistress, to make up like a whore and go out into the corridor and come into the room as if to an unknown client. Carla: "Oh, good—we've never tried *that* before!" But she keeps spoiling the mood by chattering about her husband. (She's always trying to get Guido to give him a job: "He's serious, not pushy at all, that's his tragedy," she says in an earlier scene. "He knows more about Roman history than anybody. You'd like him.") Also by remarking, as Guido makes her up: "just like one of your actresses"; and, as she goes out, wrapped in a sheet, "I don't think I'd like that kind of life, I'm a homebody, really." (Cf. Proust's Charlus trying to get the hard-working youth he's hired to whip him in the male brothel to admit he's really a brutal criminal—the young man is shocked, he's the only support of an invalid mother, he insists, to Charlus's disgust.) She spoils it completely when she comes in, flourish-

ing a bottle of mineral water—"The landlady gave it to me for my stomach." It's a hopeless anticlimax when she flings wide the sheet. . . . Guido sleeps while Carla reads a comic book; both sleep. . . . A black-robed woman, seen from behind, appears; Guido wakes; she gestures to him to follow. . . . He is in a great weedy cemetery bounded by two long lines of high crumbling walls in which are niches and tombs. He talks with his dead father and mother (the woman in black). His father complains, in a reasonable tone and with precise gestures, as one explains why a new flat won't do, that his tomb is uncomfortably cramped; Guido listens sympathetically. . . . The producer and his assistant appear and complain to his parents that Guido is lazy and irresponsible; the parents agree he has always been a problem. . . . Guido helps his father back into his grave, tenderly, a dutiful son. He kisses his mother goodbye, she suddenly embraces him passionately and kisses him on the mouth, turning into a younger woman (his wife, as we find later).

(2) Interior of a movie theatre, empty except for Guido, who is isolated with his contemptuous collaborator; lower down we see his wife with her sister and friends, and the producer with his entourage. Guido must at last choose the cast, from screen tests; no more stalling, the producer warns, I can make it tough for you if you force me to. Wife's party murmur approval, everybody glares at Guido. The critic-collaborator, sitting just behind him, begins again to tell him how stupid his ideas are. Guido listens courteously, as always, then (beginning of shortest fantasy-sequence) raises one finger. Two assistants take the critic by the arms, lead him into the aisle, put a black hood over his face, a rope around his neck, and hang him. Back to reality: shot of Guido with his collaborator, undamaged, still sitting behind him. Producer calls for projectionist to begin; screen is lit by a blazing rectangle of light that is switched off at once. Beginning of longest fantasy, which lasts to the end, with dreams inside dreams inside dreams; from now on, despite some misleading illusions of reality, we are inside Guido's head. The screen tests are not for parts in the science-fiction movie Guido is supposed to be making, but for roles in his own story, i.e., in the movie we have been watching: wife, mistress, La Saraghina, etc. The producer sees nothing strange, since he's now in Guido's head too, and keeps demanding that a choice be made. But Guido says they're all bad. Only the originals will do, after all, since no matter how talented the massive actress who imitates La Saraghina, she isn't the real thing.

A man whispers to Guido, as he sits dejectedly watching the tests, that Claudia, whom he knew years ago as a young actress, wants to see him about a part. Guido follows him eagerly, is excited to find that

Claudia (played by Claudia Cardinale) looks exactly like the Muse (also played by Cardinale) he has already encountered several times in mysterious and frustrating circumstances. He takes her for a night drive in his sports car to talk it over. The first thing she says is, "How big will my part be?" . . . Cut to a provincial town square, old houses facing each other, a baroque gateway closing one end, the whole giving the effect of an oblong room open to the sky: camera peers through the only window that is lit, and we see Claudia the Muse, all in white, against white walls, setting a white table with fruit and wine —a lovely, poetic glimpse. (Gianni di Venanzo's photography alone would make 8½ worth seeing.) Guido and the other Claudia drive into the square, but now all the windows are dark—his Muse has fled before her earthly (and earthy) twin. Stopping the car, Guido tries to explain his troubles to Claudia. "It's because you don't know how to make love," she replies, with a smile implying she could teach him. No, you're wrong, he insists, a woman cannot change a man. "Then you brought me here, you cheated me, and there's no part for me?" "Yes, there's no part for you," he replies wearily, "and there's no movie." Suddenly they are blinded by the headlights of three cars that roar into the square, bearing the producer and his aides. The producer tells Guido he has decided to get things started with a big press conference and party at the launching tower tomorrow morning. They all get into the cars and drive off. . . .

The journalists and cast and guests are gathered at the tower on the beach; it is cold and windy. (Someone says, "You kept us waiting so long—look, it's almost winter.") Waiters behind long tables with elaborate foods and drinks. Guido arrives, tries to escape, is seized by the arms and dragged to the speaker's table, past a lineup of reporters shouting questions in various languages. Everybody surges up to the table—more questions, pleas, insults—skirts and tablecloths billow in the wind, which is getting stronger—bedlam, babel, a Mad Hatter's press conference. Guido refuses to say anything since he has not even cast the movie yet. Producer, venomous aside: "I'll break you, I'll see that you never make another picture, you're ruining me." Guido dives under the table, crawls along on hands and knees, people reach down to grab him, he pulls out a pistol, puts it to his temple, a loud report. . . .

Guido alone on the beach except for some workmen on the towers. "Take it down," he shouts up at them, "all of it." Collaborator-critic appears. Guido explains he's decided not to make the picture. "You're absolutely right," says the critic, "I respect you." They get into Guido's car; the critic drones on congratulating Guido on having the courage not to make a mediocre film "that will leave a mark on the sands of time like the deformed footprint of a cripple." As Guido starts to drive

away, the magician from an earlier scene—an old friend who seems
to have occult powers—appears in front of the car in his top hat and
tails, his face made up dead white with red lips and darkened eyes
like a clown, smiling his professional smile (manic yet gentle) and
pointing with his wand. Guido looks out of the car and sees his father
and mother, who wave to him, then Claudia the Muse, smiling and
beckoning, then the others from his past and present, all dressed in
white. (The critic is still explaining why it's impossible to create in
this age—he cannot see these people.) Guido gets out of the car,
takes up his director's bullhorn, and begins to arrange everybody; he
has decided to make an entirely different movie, about himself—his
memories, his women, his creative problems—in short, the movie we
have just seen. Like Prospero in another drama with a most implausible
happy ending, he summons them all: parents, wife, mistress, producer,
technicians, actors, the Muse Claudia, even himself as a boy who leads
a gay little parade of musical clowns. And they all come, walking up
from the sea, pouring down from the steps of the launching tower,
linking hands with Guido and his wife in a long line that dances along
a seawall to the tinny blare of the circus band. The last shot is of the
ten-year-old Guido, dressed in his seminarian's uniform (now white
instead of black), strutting along proudly in front of his band.

Most of the critics have objected to this finale as bogus, escapist,
sentimental, a specious "solution" that is incongruous with what has
gone before, a happy ending arbitrarily tacked on, etc. In a generally
favorable review in *Sight and Sound*, for instance, Eric Rhode writes
in solemn disapproval: "Both Guido and Fellini show themselves incapable of making a distinction between the truths of the mind and
those of behavior. The self-reflective spirit can swiftly turn narcissistic,
and although Guido may confront his inner world, he fails to confront
his social obligations." Or, as a psychiatrist objected to me: "He has
failed to integrate reality and fantasy." This is all true—no confronting
of social obligations, no integration of the real and the unreal, and
plenty of escapism. I didn't for a minute believe that Guido had
changed: the reconciliation with his wife—he asks her if their marriage
can't be "saved" and she replies, "I can try if you will help me"—was
unintegrated fantasy, as was the affectionate kiss he gives his mistress.
On the plane of real behavior, his wife will continue to be censorious,
his mistress will continue to be vulgar, and he will continue to betray
both of them and will still greedily try to get love without giving love.
The most that has happened in the "real" world is that Guido has
achieved some insight—"I am what I am and not what I want to be"—
which may or may not influence his future behavior; probably not.

But he has triumphed in the "unreal" world of fantasy, which for him is the real one, since it is there he creates. In the sphere of the imagination, he *has* faced up to his problems and resolved them, for there he has made a work of art that hangs together and is consistent with itself. (I could never understand why "art for art's sake" is usually sneered at—for what better sake?) All through 8½, Guido (and Fellini) are escaping from one kind of reality, but only in order to rush boldly and recklessly into another kind, the artist's kind. In this sense, the finale is consistent with what has gone before—and, in fact, its logical conclusion.

John Francis Lane wrote in a recent issue of *Sight and Sound:* "I'm afraid that however fond we may be of the director of *I Vitelloni,* we are not really deeply concerned about his intellectual and sexual fetishes. Fellini has been too honest, too courageous, too sincere. He has made a film director's notebook, and I am not surprised that directors everywhere (even those who usually hate Fellini's films) love this picture." I think the implication of self-indulgent narcissism in the first sentence is wrong. Granted that, as Fellini was the first to insist ("more than a confession . . . my testament"), Guido is himself and 8½ is his own Life and Hard Times, I think the miracle is how tough-minded his autobiography is, how he has been able to see himself at a distance, neither self-sparing nor self-flagellating, a wonderful Latin moderation throughout, realistic and ironic. Guido's hat, for instance, clerical black but worn at a lady-killing slant and with a worldly twist, is a perfect symbol of Fellini's own ambivalent feelings about the Church. Or there is the clowning he often uses to preserve his humanity in the movie jungle, such as kneeling between the marble lions at the foot of the hotel's grand stairway, salaaming and ululating gibberish salutations to the producer making his stately descent. Nothing duller than someone else's fetishes and neuroses, agreed, but I think in 8½ Fellini has found the objective forms in which to communicate his subjective explorations.

A major theme of the film is aging, which obviously worries Fellini. He expresses it not in Bergmanesque symbols or narcissistic musings, but in episodes that arise naturally out of the drama: the elderly patients lining up for the curative waters; the senile cardinal; Guido's friend, the aging diplomat (who looks very much like him, with a decade or two added) who is divorcing his wife to marry one of his daughter's school friends and whom we see, doggedly jaunty, doing the twist with his nymphet fiancée, sweat pouring from a face set in an agonized grin; the aging actress who desperately cries out to Guido as

he tries to escape politely: "I am a very passionate woman—you'll see!";
the magician reading the dowager's thoughts: "You would like to live
another hundred years." One of the most sympathetic traits of Guido
is the patience, gentleness, humor—the good manners of an old and
tolerant culture—with which he responds to the reproaches of everybody around him, reproaches all the more irritating because they are
justified. He is less patient, however, when the nerve of old age is
touched. He encourages an old stagehand with acting ambitions to
do a soft-shoe dance and croak out a song, then dismisses him brutally.
Memento mori. So with the half dozen dignified old men his assistant
has rounded up for extra parts: "How old are you?" he asks each.
"Seventy-one," "sixty-three," "eighty-four," etc. "You're not old enough,"
he says, turning away contemptuously. The theme is stated most fully
in a scene in the corridor outside the production office (where everybody has been working in a Kafkaesque-bureaucratic frenzy at three in
the morning) when Guido is waylaid by his elderly assistant director,
Conocchia, who begins by weeping into his handkerchief ("You don't
trust me, you won't let me help you, you tell me nothing, I was once
your friend"), and works himself up into a rage: "I've been in movies
thirty years—we used to do things you'd never dare!" Guido, who has
been listening with his usual ironical patience, like a man waiting for
a thunderstorm to pass, suddenly explodes: "Get out, leave me alone,
you . . . old man!" (Two young men from the production office poke
their heads out: "*Vecchio? Vecchio?*") But Conocchia has the last word.
"You're not the man you used to be!" he shouts as Guido walks away.

I hazard that 8½ is Fellini's masterpiece precisely because it is about
the two subjects he knows the most about: himself and the making of
movies. He doesn't have to labor his points, he can move freely, quickly,
with the ease of a man walking about his own home. And so much can
be suggested in so little footage! That tall, aristocratic blonde, for
instance, Guido glimpses several times in the hotel. She fascinates him
because she looks like the heroine of an international spy thriller; he
never meets her (the closest he comes is to put her into his dream
harem), but he does overhear her end of a long-distance telephone conversation, which sounds like a bad movie script but which vastly in-
trigues him. Several kinds of parody are intertwined in this tiny
episode: of movie clichés, of Guido's romantic eroticism, and—a feed-
back—of a man whose job it is to fabricate these glamorous stereotypes,
himself falling for them. Successful parody is possible only when the
parodist feels "at home with" (significant phrase) his subject. This
familiarity also means that Fellini is able to keep 8½ right down to
earth, so that what might have been one more labored exercise in fan-

tasy—like De Sica's *Miracle in Milan,* for instance—is spontaneous, lifelike, and often very funny. I think Fellini has become the greatest master of social comedy since Lubitsch.

8½ takes us further inside the peculiar world of movie-making than any other film I know. I once asked the Argentine director, Torre Nilsson, why important movie directors seem to lose their creative powers so much more often—and completely—than major artists in other fields. (I was thinking of Welles and Hitchcock.) He replied: "In movies, once you make a success, you become public property; you are overwhelmed with fame, money, women, admirers, promoters, and you can never get away from it. A painter or writer or composer creates by himself, but directors have to have hundreds of other people around all the time. So they burn themselves out early." When I saw 8½, I saw what he meant. Guido is distracted in the literal sense: "to divide [the mind, attention, etc.] between objects." They're all here: the highbrow journalist who asks about his philosophy, and also the lowbrow one— "Couldn't you tell me something about your love life?"; the producer who bullies him about the production schedule and the accountants who nag him about costs; the property man who begs Guido to take on as extras his giggling teen-age "nieces"; the playboy who wants him to sit up all night drinking; the man who waylays him in the lobby, waving a script: "It shows the necessity of universal disarmament; only a man of your courage and integrity could do it"; the press agents and tourists and mistresses, including his own. All there, and each wants a slice of him.

The reviews of 8½ in the newspapers and in magazines like *Newsweek* and *The New Yorker* have been enthusiastic. The public likes it, too. But the "little-magazine" critics have been cool and wary, as though they felt they were being conned. Their objections, remarkably uniform, suggest to me that the trouble with serious film criticism today is that it is too serious.

> All these sequences are so magnificently filmed that the breath is hardly left to voice a query as to what they mean. Gianni di Venanzo's black-and-white photography and Piero Gherardi's sets and costumes provide such visual magic that it seems pointless to make philosophical reservations on the film's content. Yet the sheer beauty of Fellini's film . . . is deceiving us. (John Francis Lane in *Sight and Sound.*)

He goes on to complain of "pretentiousness of subject matter" and "artistic inflation." It's true, beauty and art are deceivers ever. The pea is never under the shell Fellini has given us every reason to believe contains it. In James and Conrad, this is called ambiguity.

The trouble seems to come from another quarter—moral and intellectual content. Fellini's last three films seem to me to rank in merit according to the amount of "meaning" in each. *La Dolce Vita* fairly reeked of "meaning," with its Christ symbols, parallels to Dante, moral indictment of a contemporary life style, and what not. [This is not ironical—D.M.] The *Boccaccio '70* episode had its little fabulated moral. But *8½* has little or no intellectual content. The difference shows in the very titles. *La Dolce Vita* evokes a moral tradition of some kind. *The Temptation of Dr. Antonio* (with its echo of "The Temptation of St. Anthony") prepares us for religious allegory. But *8½* drives us right back into Fellini's biography. . . . The artist's promise of a moral or intellectual "point" bribes us (me) to take part in his (my) illicit fantasies. Without an intellectual superstructure, his personal fantasy fails to engage other persons. (Norman N. Holland in *Hudson Review*.)

It would be needlessly cruel to comment on these stiff-jointed lucubrations, though I can't help wondering what the quotes around meaning mean. Does he "mean" it? In addition to his other burdens, Mr. Holland groans under a massive load of primitive Freudianism. Maybe this explains why he dares to express openly a puritan nervousness when confronted by useless beauty that his colleagues express more discreetly.

Since *La Dolce Vita*, Fellini's films have been following a trend that certainly culminates in *8½*. [Briefest trend in cultural history since the only Fellini film between *Vita* and *8½* was the half-hour episode in *Boccaccio '70*—D.M.] It is the triumph of style over content. At the end of *8½*, we are excited not because Fellini has told us something significant about the artistic process, but because he has found such a visually exciting metaphor for his idea that it does not matter if this idea is not quite first-rate. . . . Nothing very significant is said about illusion and reality, dream and art. (Gary Carey in *The Seventh Art*.)

True that when it comes to making significant statements about illusion and reality and other high topics, Fellini is "not quite first-rate" compared to, say, Dr. Erwin Panofsky, of the (Princeton) Institute of Advanced Studies, whose 1934 essay, "Style and Medium in the Moving Pictures," is a classic. But I doubt that Dr. Panofsky, a modest and sensible man, would claim he could have made *8½*, any more than Fellini, also sensible if not modest, would aspire to a professorship of, say, Cinematic Philosophy. Mr. Carey ends his review on the usual sub-puritan note: "*8½* is really a visual experience, its only profundity resting there." And what better resting place?

Fellini's latest "autobiographical" oddity. . . . The nicest possible thing one could say is that he has had the guts to try and shove this particular form of lachrymose sexuality into the environs of art. . . . Of course, the result is horrendously pretentious. . . . She [Anouk Aimée as the wife] is where Fellini's vulgarity positively beckons us into attention and in so doing ruins a fantasy. He just can't deal with the grown-up issues she incarnates. But as a cinematic outlet for the imagination—the sort of stuff a director like Fellini *can* cope with . . . the film is extraordinary. . . . 8½ looks marvelous and doesn't matter much of a damn. (John Coleman in the London *New Statesman*.)

No comment.

The tone is never sure, but falters between irony and self-pity, between shamefaced poeticism and tongue-tied self-mockery. . . . The second failure . . . [is] ignorance. . . . 8½ piles problem upon problem, which is permissible; but sheds no light, which is not. . . . Fellini, apparently afraid of becoming a self-repeater with diminishing returns as so many famous Italian directors have become, tries for something new: symbolism, metaphysics, solid intellectual content. . . . What made Fellini's early films great . . . was their almost total avoidance of intellectualizing. (John Simon in *The New Leader*.)

The first sentence seems to me about as obtuse or perverse or both as you could get in eighteen words: I detected no self-pity, but on the contrary was impressed by the objectivity with which Fellini presented himself and his most personal worries; the poeticism was real poetry, and it was far from shamefaced, in fact it was blatant, exuberant; and any critic who could apply the adjective "tongue-tied" to Fellini, always fluent to the point of garrulity, must have an ax to grind. Mr. Simon's was a polemical one: his review is unique in finding nothing to praise in 8½. The closest he comes is: "Despite two or three good scenes [not specified] it is a disheartening fiasco." (It pains me to write thus, or should anyway, since I respect Mr. Simon's critical acumen so much that I wrote an introduction to his recent collection of essays, *Acid Test*.) Why "ignorance" is a fault in an artist, I don't see, nor why he has to solve any problems except those of constructing a work of art, which are difficult enough. Shakespeare was a bit of an ignoramous— "little Latin and less Greek"—nor do we expect *King Lear* to "shed light" on geriatrics. I agree that Fellini is no thinker, and that he is at his worst when he intellectualizes. I also agree that "all the principal characters . . . are sublimely dichotomous," that "the dialogue bulges with antinomies," and that Fellini isn't in the same league as "the great masters of ambiguity—Pirandello, Brecht, Valéry, Eliot." Compared to that Yankee lineup, he's a busher. But all this is beside the point since, at least as I read 8½, Fellini is *not* trying for "symbolism, metaphysics, [or] solid intellectual content."

This brings me to the crux of my quarrel with the all-too-serious critics (an exception was Jack Hirschman's jazzy paean in *Film Quarterly*) and indeed to what I see as the crux of the film itself. Because it is technically sophisticated, and because it deals with major areas of experience, these critics look for philosophical depths in a movie which is superficial—I think deliberately—in every way except as a work of art. They call Fellini a phony for not delivering the goods, but I don't see his signature on their bill of lading. On the contrary, some of the best comedy in his film is provided by intellectuals: the affected young beauty who has written a treatise on "The Solitude of Modern Man in the Contemporary Theater"; the highbrow British reporter who pesters Guido with questions like, "Is it that you cannot communicate? Or is that merely a mask?" And above all the collaborator who has been assigned to help Guido complete his script—an eyeglassed, beak-nosed superintellectual whose lean face is fixed in lines of alert, sour suspicion. This personage—listed in the cast credits as The Writer, and played with waspish authority by Jean Rougeul—is endlessly articulate about the script; it's narcissistic ("just another film about your childhood"), romantic, pretentious, tasteless, and mindless: "Your main problem is the film lacks ideas, it has no philosophical base. It's merely a series of senseless episodes. . . . It has none of the merits of the avant-garde film and all the drawbacks." How can a director make more explicit his rationale? Life imitated art, as elsewhere in this strange film* and the actual highbrow critics reacted to 8½ much as The Writer did to Guido's script. Several people I've talked to—and I must admit there is as much conversational as printed opposition to 8½—have suggested that The Writer is merely a ploy by Fellini to disarm his critics by making all their points in advance; they might have added the American woman who at the end shouts, "He's lost. He hasn't anything to say." Maybe. But he was a good prophet. For the "serious" critics have by now become habituated to profound, difficult films that must be "interpreted" from the language of art (what's on the screen) into the language of philosophy (what what's

---

* "Fellini found himself embarked, with costly sets built and stars under contract, on a kind of explanatory sequel to *La Dolce Vita*," reports *The New Statesman*. When he found this didn't work, he did what Guido did—switched to a film about himself, that is, about a famous director who finds himself blocked on a film. Reality came as close to overwhelming Fellini as it did Guido. According to *Sight and Sound:* "Two weeks before 8½ opened in Rome, he still hadn't made up his mind how to end it."

on the screen "really means"). It began with Bergman (whom I've always thought strongest at his shallowest) and reached a comic climax in the recent efforts of Franco-American *auteur* critics to read [Alfred Hitchcock's] *The Birds* as a morality play about Modern Civilization, and a pathetic one in the efforts of almost everybody to make sense out of that triumph of non- and indeed anti-sense, *Last Year at Marienbad* —everybody except its creators, who said they themselves disagreed on what it "meant."

The off-putting quality of *8½* for all but the less intellectualized critics (and the public) is that it is nothing but a pleasurable work of art which might have been directed by Mozart—and there were no doubt pundits in his day who deplored the frivolous way he played around with Masonic symbolism in *The Magic Flute*. It is a worldly film, all on the surface: humorous, rhetorical, sensuous, lyrical, witty, satiric, full of sharply realistic detail and also of fantastic scenes like the great one in the steam bath. The essence of *8½* is here: the visual panache of the movie-makers making their way down the stairs, swathed in sheets like Roman senators and wreathed in smoky steam like the damned going down to hell, terrific but also just a touch burlesque on Biblical spectaculars—the loudspeaker, "Guido, Guido. His Eminence will see you now"—the burlesque becoming strident as Guido's colleagues push around him, warning, "Don't hold anything back from His Eminence," while they ask him to put in a word for them, and then turning to satire, as Guido stands before the aged Cardinal (also wrapped in a sheet, bony neck and chest bare, mist swirling about him like God's mantle) and complains, "I'm not happy, Your Eminence." "Why should you be, my son?" the Cardinal replies with unexpected vigor. "That's not your job in life. . . . *Nulla salvatio extra ecclesiasm.* . . . That which is not of God is of the Devil." The scene closes with an exterior shot of a small cellar window that swings slowly shut as if excluding the sinner (*extra ecclesiam*) from the heaven within. There is plenty of symbolism here, indeed every shot is a metaphor, but they are all as obvious as the closing window. This is perhaps the difficulty; nothing for the interpretative tooth to mumble, no Antonionian *angst*, no Bergmanesque Godhead, no Truffaut-style existential Absurd to perplex us. Like Baroque art, of which it is a belated golden ray, *8½* is complicated but not obscure. It is more Handel than Beethoven—objective and classical in spirit as against the romantic subjectivism we are accustomed to. It's all there, right on the surface, like a Veronese or a Tiepolo.

One could drop still another name, the greatest of all. Is there not something Shakespearean in this range of human experience expressed in every mode from high lyric to low comic, from the most formal rhetoric to the most personal impressionism? And don't the critics remind one of those all-too-serious students who try to discover "Shakespeare's philosophy" and always fail because Shakespeare hadn't any; his "ideas" were all *ad hoc;* their function was to solve dramatic rather than philosophical problems. As Jack Hirschman writes: "Fellini has . . . come free of that awful psycho-philosophical air which pervades *La Dolce Vita.* . . . In 8½, people are on earth not because they are destined to be trapped by cultural despair, but because they are destined to play out the roles of their individual realities."

Finally, in 8½ Fellini steals from everybody, just like Shakespeare. "Theft" on this scale becomes synthesis: 8½ is an epitome of the history of cinema. His thefts are creative because they are really borrowings, which are returned with the fingerprints of the thief all over them. The childhood episodes are Bergmanesque chiaroscuro, as the great scene on the beach when La Saraghina dances for the schoolboys, which echoes, right down to the brutal beat of the music, an even greater beach scene, that between the soldiers and the clown's wife at the beginning of *Naked Night:* but this is a Latin Bergman, sensuous and dramatic and in no way profound. When Guido and his wife quarrel in the hotel bedroom, the bleak failure to make contact (and the austere photography) recall Antonioni, but *this* alienated couple don't suffer in silence, they yell at each other. The early scene in the rest-cure garden is full of heroic close-ups à la Eisenstein, but they are used (like "The Ride of the Valkyries" thundered out by the hotel band) for satiric counterpoint to the aging, prosaic faces of the invalids. The general structure—a montage of tenses, a mosaic of time blocks—recalls *Intolerance, Kane,* and *Marienbad,* but in Fellini's hands it becomes light, fluid, evanescent. And delightfully obvious.

The above text, revised slightly and expanded considerably from the original review in the January, 1964, *Esquire,* is that of my Afterword to Deena Boyer's *The Two Hundred Days of 8½* (Macmillan, 1964).

The Underground Man
Eudora Welty

Curled up, with an insulted look on his upturned face, and wearing a peppermint-striped shirt, the fresh corpse of a man is disclosed in a hole in the ground. From the scene of the crime, the victim's little boy is carried off, nobody knows why, by a pair of troubled teen-agers.

And at the same time, a deadly forest fire gets its start in these hills above Santa Teresa; whoever murdered Stanley Broadhurst must have caused him to drop his cigarillo into the dry grass. So opens the new novel by Ross Macdonald, *The Underground Man*. It comes to stunning achievement.

A Forest Service man looks into the killing to find out who was responsible for the fire; but Lew Archer goes faster and farther into his own investigation, for a personal reason. That morning, he had met that little boy; they fed blue jays together. He promises the young widow, the child's mother, to find her son and bring him back.

The double mystery of Santa Teresa cries urgency but is never going to explain itself in an ordinary way. For instance, it looks as if the victim himself might have dug the hole in which he lies. ("Why would a man dig his own grave"?—"He may not have known it was going to be his.") With the fire coming, Archer has to work fast. The corpse must be quickly buried again, or be consumed with his murder unsolved. This, the underground man of the title, waits the book out, the buried connection between present threat and something out of the past.

"I don't believe in coincidences," Archer says, as the investigation leads him into a backward direction, and he sees the case take on a premonitory symmetry. And it is not coincidence indeed, or anything so simple, but a sort of spiral of time that he goes hurtling into, with an answer lying fifteen years deep.

He is to meet many strange and lonely souls drawing their inspiration from private sources. On the periphery are those all but anonymous characters, part of the floating population of the city, evocative of all the sadness that fills a lonely world, like some California versions of those Saltimbanques of Picasso's ("even a little more fleeting than ourselves") drifting across the smoke-obscured outskirts. They are the sentinels of a case in which everybody has something to lose, and most of the characters in this time-haunted, fire-threatened novel lose it in the course of what happens—a son, or a husband, or a mountain retreat; a sailing boat, a memory; the secret of fifteen years or the dream of a lifetime; or a life.

Brooding over the case is the dark fact that for some certain souls the past does not let go. They nourish the conviction that its ties may be outlived but, for hidden reasons, can be impossible to outgrow or leave behind.

Stanley Broadhurst died searching for his long-lost father. The Oedipus story, which figured in Mr. Macdonald's *The Galton Case* and *The Chill*, has echoes here too. But another sort of legend takes a central place in *The Underground Man*. This is the medieval tale of romance and the faerie.

It is exactly what Archer plunges into when he enters this case. Finding his way, through their lies and fears, into other people's obsessions and dreams, he might as well be in a fairy tale with them. The mystery has handed him what amounts to a set of impossible tasks: Find the door that opens the past. Unravel the ever-tangling threads of time. Rescue the stolen child from fleeing creatures who appear to be under a spell and who forbid him to speak to them. Meet danger from the aroused elements of fire and water. And beware the tower.

But Archer's own role in their fairy tale is clear to him: from the time he fed the blue jays with the little boy, he never had a choice. There is the maze of the past to be entered and come out of alive, bringing the innocent to safety. And in the maze, there lives a monster; his name is Murder.

All along the way, the people he questions shift their stands, lie as fast as they can, slip only too swiftly out of human reach. Their ages are deceiving, they put on trappings of disguise or even what might be called transformations. As Archer, by stages, all the while moving at speed, connects one character with the next, he discovers what makes the sinister affinity between them.

"Robert Driscoll Falconer, Jr., was a god come down to earth in human guise," the older Mrs. Broadhurst, mother of the murder victim, has written in a memoir of her father, and here her Spencerian handwriting went to pieces: "It straggled across the lined yellow page like a defeated army." Mrs. Crandall, the mother of the runaway girl, is "one of those waiting mothers who would sit forever beside the phone but didn't know what to say when it finally rang." Another character being questioned plays "a game that guilty people play, questioning the questioner, trying to convert the truth into a shuttlecock that could be batted back and forth and eventually lost." And the violence and malice of another character "appeared to her as emanations from the external world."

These people live in prisons of the spirit, and suffer there. The winding, prisonlike stairs that appear and reappear under Archer's hurrying feet in the course of the chase are like the repeated questionings that lead most often into some private hell.

And of course unreality—the big underlying trouble of all these people—was back of the crime itself: the victim was obsessed with the lifelong search for his father; oblivious of everything and everybody else, he invited his own oblivion. In a different way, unreality was back of the child-stealing. "As you can see, we gave her everything," says the mother standing in her runaway daughter's lovely white room. "But it wasn't what she wanted." The home environment of the girl and others like her, Archer is brought to observe, was "an unreality so bland and smothering that the children tore loose and impaled themselves on the spikes of any reality that offered. Or made their own unreality with drugs."

The plot is intricate, involuted, and complicated to the hilt; and this, as I see it, is the novel's point. The danger derives from the fairy tales into which people make their lives. In lonely, fearful, or confused minds, real-life facts can become rarefied into private fantasies. And when intensity is accepted—welcomed—as the measure of truth, how can the real and the fabricated be told apart?

We come to a scene where the parallel with the fairy tale is explicit —and something more. It is the best in the book—I can give but a part.

"I made my way up the washed-out gravel drive. The twin conical towers standing up against the night sky made the house look like something out of a medieval romance. The illusion faded as I got nearer. There was a multi-colored fanlight over the front door, with segments of glass fallen out, like missing teeth in an old smile. . . . The door creaked open when I knocked."

Here lives a lady "far gone in solitude," whose secret lies hidden at the heart of the mystery. She stands there in "a long full skirt on which there were paint stains in all three primary colors." She is a painter— of spiritual conditions, she says; to Archer her pictures resemble "serious contusions and open wounds" or "imperfectly remembered hallucinations."

"'I was born in this house,' she said, as if she'd been waiting fifteen years for a listener." (And these are the fifteen years that have done their worst to everybody in the novel.) "It's interesting to come back to your childhood home, . . . like becoming very young and very old both at the same time.' That was how she looked, I thought, in her archaic long skirt—very young and very old, the granddaughter and the grandmother in one person, slightly schizo."

"There were romantic tears in her eyes" when her story is out. "My own eyes remained quite dry."

Fairy tale and living reality alternate on one current to pulse together in this remarkable scene. The woman is a pivotal character, and Archer has caught up with her; they are face to face, and there comes a moment's embrace. Of the many brilliant ways Mr. Macdonald has put his motif to use, I believe this is the touch that delighted me most. For of course Archer, this middle-aging Californian who has seen everything in a career of going into impossible trouble with his eyes open, who has always been the protector of the weak and the rescuer of the helpless, is a born romantic. Here he meets his introverted and ailing counterpart—this lady is the chatelaine of the romantic-gone-wrong. He is not by nature immune, especially to what is lovely or was lovely once. At a given moment, they may brush close—as Archer, the only one with insight into himself, is aware.

Time pressing, time lapsing, time repeating itself in dark acts, splitting into two in some agonized or imperfect mind—time is the wicked fairy to troubled people, granting them inevitably the thing they dread. While Archer's investigation is drawing him into the past, we are never allowed to forget that present time has been steadily increasing its menace. Mr. Macdonald has brought the fire toward us at closer and closer stages. By the time it gets as close as the top of the hill (this was the murder area), it appears "like a brilliant omniform growth which continued to grow until it bloomed very large against the sky. A sentinel quail on the hillside below it was ticking an alarm." Then, reaching the Broadhurst house, "the fire bent around it like the fingers of a hand, squeezing smoke out of the windows and then flame."

Indeed the fire is a multiple and accumulating identity, with a career of its own, a super-character that has earned itself a character's name —Rattlesnake. Significantly, Archer says, "There was only one good thing about the fire. It made people talk about the things that really concerned them."

What really concerns Archer, and the real kernel of the book, its heart and soul, is the little boy of six, good and brave and smart. He constitutes the book's emergency; he is also entirely believable, a full-rounded and endearing character. Ronny is the tender embodiment of everything Archer is by nature bound to protect, infinitely worthy of rescue.

When Archer plunges into a case, his reasons are always personal reasons (this is one of the things that make us so much for Archer). The little boy, for as long as he's missing, will be Archer's own loss. And without relinquishing for a moment his clear and lively identity, the child takes on another importance as well: "The world was changing," says Archer, "as if with one piece missing the whole thing had come loose and was running wild."

If it is the character of the little boy that makes the case matter to Archer, so it is the character of Archer, whose first-person narrative forms all Mr. Macdonald's novels, that makes it matter to us. Archer, from the start, has been a distinguished creation; he was always an attractive figure and in the course of the last several books has matured and deepened in substance to our still greater pleasure. Possessed even when young of an endless backlog of stored information, most of it sad, on human nature, he tended once, unless I'm mistaken, to be a bit cynical. Now he is something much more, he is vulnerable. As a detective and as a man, he takes the human situation with full seriousness. He cares. And good and evil both are real to him.

Archer knows himself to be a romantic, would call it a weakness— as he calls himself a "not unwilling catalyst" for trouble; he carries the knowledge around with him—that's how he got here. But he is in no way archaic. He is at heart a champion, but a self-questioning, often a self-deriding champion. He is of today, one of ours. *The Underground Man* is written so close to the nerve of today as to expose most of the apprehensions we live with.

In our day, it is for such a novel as *The Underground Man* that the detective form exists. I think it also matters that it is the detective form, with all its difficult demands and its corresponding charms, that makes such a novel possible. What gives me special satisfaction about this novel is that no one but a good writer—*this* good writer—could have possibly brought it off. *The Underground Man* is Mr. Macdonald's best book yet, I think. It is not only exhilaratingly well done; it is also very moving.

Ross Macdonald's style, to which in large part this is due, is one of delicacy and tension, very tightly made, with a spring in it. It doesn't allow a static sentence or one without pertinence. And the spare, controlled narrative, built for action and speed, conveys as well the world through which the action moves and gives it meaning, brings scene and character, however swiftly, before the eyes without a blur. It is an almost unbroken series of sparkling pictures.

The style that works so well to produce fluidity and grace also suggests a mind much given to contemplation and reflection on our world. Mr. Macdonald's writing is something like a stand of clean, cool, well-branched, well tended trees in which bright birds can flash and perch. And not for show, but to sing.

A great deal of what this writer has to tell us comes by way of beautiful and audacious similes. "His hairy head seemed enormous and grotesque on his boy's body, like a papier-mâché saint's head on a stick": the troubled teen-ager's self-absorption, his sense of destiny—theatrical but maybe in a good cause—along with the precise way he looks and carries himself, are given us all in one. At the scene of evacuation from the forest fire, at the bottom of a rich householder's swimming pool "lay a blue mink coat, like the headless pelt of a woman." A sloop lying on her side, dismantled offshore, "flopped in a surge like a bird made helpless by oil." The Snows, little old lady and grown son: "The door of Fritz's room was ajar. One of his moist eyes appeared at the crack like the eye of a fish in an underwater crevice. His mother, at the other door, was watching him like a shark."

Descriptions so interpretive are of course here as part and parcel of the character of Archer who says them to us. Mr. Macdonald's accuracy of observation becomes Archer's detection—running evidence. Mr. Macdonald brings characters into sudden sharp focus, too, by arresting them in an occasional archetypical pose. The obsessed Stanley is here in the words of his wife: "Sometimes he'd be just sitting there shuffling through his pictures and his letters. He looked like a man counting his money." And Fritz in the lath house, where Archer is leaving him, complaining among his plants: "The striped shadow fell from the roof, jailbirding him."

The Cubist Epoch
Harold Rosenberg

Modern art doesn't begin at any identifiable point, but the modern situation of art undoubtedly begins with Cubism. Among its other innovations, Cubism changed the relation of art to the public, and, in so doing, changed the nature of the art public itself. It excluded those who merely responded to pictures and replaced them with spectators who knew what made pictures important. The howls of indignation that greeted Cubist contributions to the Armory Show in New York in 1913 resound through the history of twentieth-century art as evidence that a genuine cultural revolution had taken place. The educated middle class had been challenged by a new power: the band of art professionals armed with advanced intellectual weapons. In Russia ten years later, a similar uprising was repulsed as a threat to the Party's control of taste and judgment.

Cubism ended the reign in art of what Gertrude Stein called "nature as everybody sees it"—that is to say, of common sense. Thenceforward, every art movement would propound its own conception of reality, and within the movement every artist would insist on his own uniqueness. A new public, open to doctrinal persuasion, would stand ready to welcome each effort toward expanded consciousness, while the majority could be counted on to reproduce what might be called the Khrushchev syndrome (or, recalling Theodore Roosevelt's reaction to Cubism at the Armory, the Roosevelt-Khrushchev syndrome) of denunciation. Instead of depicting things, or even fantasies or distortions, the Cubists made art esoteric by projecting into the mind of the spectator the secrets and problems of the studio.

Douglas Cooper, organizer of "The Cubist Epoch," a comprehensive survey exhibition of Cubism currently at the Metropolitan Museum, confirms that the problems of the artist constitute the content of Cubist paintings when he declares in his excellent catalogue for the exhibition that Braque and Picasso, co-founders of the new style, "thought more about forging the language of Cubism than about the aesthetic value of their subject-matter." A painting in a language-in-progress could not be understood simply by looking at it, and if it was not understood it could not be appreciated. Thus, Cubism launched the transformation of painting into an intellectual specialization, a compendium of old and new technical discoveries, methods, assumptions, errors to be corrected. The spectator was called upon to acquire this lore or to be guided by the knowledge of professionals. No more amateur gazing at pictures. Every manifestation of art since Cubism has depended for its reception on a phalanx of spectators governed by the opinions of their leaders. The quarrel between Gertrude Stein and her brother Leo as to whether to go on with Picasso after "Les Demoiselles d'Avignon" represents the archetypal drama of twentieth-century art appreciation.[1] Everyone must stop somewhere—the "Demoiselles" shocked even Braque—but there's always someone else to advance farther. With Cubism, the issue of the avant-garde in art was no longer a matter of responding to a new sensibility, as with Impressionism or Fauvism; Cubism built avant-gardism into the body of art as the principle of constant experimentation by which the aims and functions of art would be redefined.

The paintings in "The Cubist Epoch" actually consist in large part of challenges to Cubism (by Futurism, for example) and of deviations from it through insufficient comprehension (as by the Czech Cubists) or in the name of more advanced concepts (as by Mondrian). Cubism, says Cooper, was "a new pictorial language," but apparently only the "true" Cubists—Picasso, Braque, Gris, and, for a short while, Léger—could speak it; everyone else received it in mistranslation or proceeded to adulterate its meaning.

The esoteric nature of Cubism gave rise to the modern art audience, composed of experts, intermediaries (or explainers), and a mass recruited through publicity and art education to react to whatever is presented to it as art. Thus, Cubism inaugurated the enfolding of art creation within increasingly numerous layers of auxiliary professions, from showman-curators to art-movie makers—a process accelerated to the point of near suffocation by recent museum and foundation programs. The core of the new-epoch art audience, however, has consisted of individuals who have gained direct understanding of the innovating ideas through personal intimacy with the artists; Cooper himself is characterized in material issued in connection with the exhibition as "a close personal friend" of many of the Cubist painters, and this factor has no doubt contributed greatly to his success in tracing the changing attitudes responsible for different phases of Cubism. In its campaign against naturalistic art that tricks the eye, Cubism consolidated the po-

---

[1] The Steins were early collectors of Picasso's works. "Le Demoiselles d'Avignon" was the first important Cubist painting.—S.B.

sition of modern painting as creation based on ideology and directed toward concentric circles of insiders able to prefer art that, as Picasso said of Negro sculpture, "is not visually but conceptually true." The axiom that pictures cannot be checked against the visual world carried a corollary that art is for experts only. In the early days of Cubism, Cooper reports, Braque and Picasso kept largely apart even from other painters—in the last analysis, any spectator was an intruder.

The strength of Cubism lay in its by-passing of "false traditionalism" (as Braque put it) in order to express the modern world. Cooper is convinced, as Gertrude Stein was, that Cubism, despite appearances to the contrary, is a species of realism; its original ancestor, he contends, was Courbet. Cooper is a strict constructionist. Adherence to "solid tangible reality" is the criterion by which he distinguishes true Cubists from painters who merely "cubify" for decorative effect or who paint according to systems. Of Delaunay's "The City of Paris" Cooper says that it "is anti-Cubist by virtue of the unreality of its conception," and of Gleizes that "while using certain Cubist procedures," he "came more and more to disregard visual reality and evolved a predominantly decorative, formalized style of painting which was virtually abstract." The enigma of Cubism, which has baffled observers since its first appearance, is that while it seems to have originated abstract art and at times lacks an identifiable subject, so that to its foes it has been a "Navajo-rug" pattern of lines, shapes, and colors, it is essentially antipathetic to the nonrepresentational modes that evolved out of it.

In making the issue of reality central to his evaluation of Cubist creation, Cooper enters into direct conflict with the present-day school of formalist criticism, for which the meaning of Cubism consists in its handling of space, line, and color, and which applies Cubist-derived formulas as the measure of artists as different from one another as Ernst and Duchamp, Miró and Mondrian, Pollock and Frank Stella. This approach, diametrically opposed to Cooper's, is illustrated by a "Fact Sheet" on the exhibition distributed by the Metropolitan Museum. "Its lasting significance," this document declares of Cubism, "lies in its role as the origin and key to all subsequent styles of twentieth-century painting." Cubism is given a monopoly on formal innovations at the cost of being stripped of its contribution to the consciousness of our time. For Cooper, in contrast, the flattened pictorial space of Cubist paintings and the dissociation of pictorial elements, such as shapes and planes of color, were conceived not for their own sake but to attain a new grasp of reality, to provide "a viable alternative to naturalism." In Cooper's view, once this mission, begun in 1906, had been accomplished, the Cubist epoch was at an end; after 1920 its spirit survived only in the work of those artists who had been involved in its creation, and by about 1940 it had been "supplanted by artistic conceptions of a wholly opposite order."

The formalist view of Cubism as the mother of all twentieth-century styles is a simplification that has been accepted largely because of its usefulness in the audience-building processes of modern art—what could be more reassuring than a single "key," as the "Fact Sheet" calls it, to the art of the past fifty years? Yet Cooper's interpretation of Cubism as "concerned with the solid tangible reality of things" also presents difficulties. Isn't it odd that a realistic art engaged in investigating twentieth-century phenomena should have been compounded of Egyptian drawings, Iberian sculpture, and African figurines? Also, that Picasso, inventor of this advanced mode of apprehending reality, should in his late Cubist paintings have diluted it with naturalistic (commonly recognizable) ingredients and should finally have abandoned it entirely? A method for apprehending reality is rarely discarded until a more efficient method appears.

That Cubism provided a new pictorial language superbly suited to dealing with modern experience ought by this time to be apparent beyond question. In destroying the illusionism of painted apples and bodies, it exposed the illusory nature of actual apples and bodies. Through collage, it blended images with objects and made objects seem images. Collage is this century's outstanding contribution to mystification—it holds the seeds of events fabricated for the purpose of being described in the mass media, and of political personages reshaped by professionals to capture votes. The decentralized composition of Cubist painting and the derivation of its forms from geometry and from random objects—for example, Picasso's "Absinthe Glass, Bottle, Pipe, and Musical Instruments on a Piano"—resulted in the "democratization" of data and asserted that the identity of things lies not in the things themselves but in their placement and function. Cubist paintings and collages could contain anything—match folders, menus, wine bottles, contents of the artist's pocket—and this caused the everyday world to feel at home in art. Cubist disintegration of the object emphasizes that an apple in a painting may in actuality be the result of a hundred acts of looking and applying paint. In addition to the solution it offered to the problem of transposing objects from deep space to a flat surface, Cubism's replacement of linear perspective by two-dimensionality provided a metaphor of the psychic condition of modern man. Twentieth-century philosophers talk of the "flattening out" of the individual, and aspects of Cubism have reappeared in literature—Joyce, Pound, Eliot, Marianne Moore make use of collage, parody, and verbal "faceting"—and in music and the theatre. In sum, there *is* a Cubist epoch, and it is impossible to grasp the full dimensions of present-day experience without the Cubist reformulation of the sensibility, just as it is to hear sounds in extremely high and low ranges without electronic equipment.

But though Cubism has illuminated the modern world, and is not a mere episode in the history of aesthetics, I cannot detect what in Cubist paintings makes them represent "the solid tangible reality of things." In regard to objects, it seems to me that Cubist painting was involved in a contradiction: it wished to dissolve objects into directly appre-hended forms—the stem and the bowl of a pipe glimpsed separately—yet it wished to preserve the objects themselves as presences. Cooper describes how the "high" Cubist paintings of Picasso and Braque came to teeter on the edge of total abstraction, and he resorts to the rather silly suggestion that these paintings, elements of which were "primarily dictated by spatial considerations and pictorial necessity"—that is to say, by motives of abstract art, not by concern for tangible reality—can be recaptured for realism by finding the hint of a nose here, a watch chain there. Perhaps it was to mock the notion that in a Cubist paint-ing a rectangle is a cone is a nose that Gertrude Stein delivered her grand affirmation regarding the rose.[2] Guided by the belief that a paint-ing must represent objects, or perhaps out of instinct or habit, people still peruse a painting such as Picasso's "Clarinet Player" or Braque's "Still-Life with Dice and Pipe" in search of the clarinet or the dice, as if they were hunting for clues in a detective story or trying to find the cat in the tree in one of those puzzle pictures that used to appear in Sunday papers. The only merit, if any, in this type of scrutiny is that it repeats the activity of the Cubist painter in painting his picture. In Cubist painting, the object is grasped in tiny spurts of perception. It is a pile of clues submitted to an intuitive sense of order. Strictly speaking, the picture is never complete (another Cubist attitude passed on to later art modes) and it never reveals a "tangible reality."

Cooper's postulate of a recreated reality works very well for the de-tection of mixtures of naturalism and mannerism posing as Cubist paintings, as in Metzinger's "Cubist Landscape." Cooper fails to con-sider, however, that the "true" Cubist painting achieves not the reality of the object—why the reality of a pipe, in any case?—but an aesthetic generalization of it in terms of its appearance and its surroundings. In effect, the Cubist painting is a mask covering the model or still-life—though a mask composed of the model's own visual substance, as was the case with the mask-portrait of Gertrude Stein from which Picasso moved on to Cubism. Picasso himself, in a famous remark, noted that Cubist paintings were an anticipation of the camouflaged war machines he saw passing through the streets of Paris in 1914. Masked objects

---

[2] "A rose is a rose is a rose."—S.B.

represent the essential image of Cubist art. In the most literal sense, every Cubist painting and, even more obviously, sculpture is a masked entity. Cubism manipulates the physiognomies of things (and, for it, all sides are frontal) in order to dissipate the secrecy of Being into an organization of unprivileged facts; the "object art" and "thingish" novel of the sixties are resurrections of the Cubist spirit. With Picasso, the mask is an explicit theme, from the portrait of Gertrude Stein and the "high" Cubist "Portrait of D. H. Kahnweiler" to his late Cubist "Harlequin" and, of course, the celebrated "Three Masked Musicians," with which he closed his Cubist development, in 1921. Gris was also inclined to the harlequinade (the motif that connects Cubism with Picasso's Blue Period), while Braque suggests what might be called the masked still-life—in his 1912 oval "Guitar," a recognizable section of the instrument is repeated with vertical markings that transport it behind a series of columns and dissolve it under the lettering "ETUDE." In Cubism, the object is hidden behind shutters of forms that open and close at the will of the artist.

Despite any ambitions to capture reality, the ultimate aim of Cubism, as of all effective art movements, was not reality but art. (Later, Dada and Surrealism, despite their radical anti-art manifestos, also defected to art.) One might say that Cubism asserted the independent reality of painting in its relation to things, people, and landscapes. If, as Cooper says, the founders of Cubism clung to intuited reality, it was not for the sake of reality but for the sake of their painting. Indeed, a fundamental intimation of Cubism is that the art object is the only real object—nothing is anything until it has been reconstituted by the artist. It followed that, liberated by Cubism from the restraints of things "as everybody sees them," artists less dialectically subtle than Picasso and Braque were bound to believe that objects of the studio or the street— in fact, the entire objective world—could be dispensed with if the objects stood in the way of art. Logically, Cubism implies abstract, nonrepresentational art, and art history since 1920 has again and again taken the path of this logic. In reducing painting to its elements, Cubism made it possible to separate each element from the others and deal with it as sufficient for painting.

Not the least of the innovations of the Cubist epoch was its instigation of the crisis of the object in art, both as external reference (the finding of noses) and in regard to the work itself (as a product of craft); Duchamp's "ready-mades," which dispensed with the making of art objects, were already implied in collage. Cubism proper remained dedicated to making art objects; through paintings composed of colored papers it strengthened the idea of the "tableau-objet." Yet the ideal of Cubism was not the individual picture but a method of painting that could interpenetrate with the art of any time, place, or culture. In the years of the First World War, artists saw Cubism as the culmination of the era of picture-making, and postwar art movements from Dada to the Bauhaus were anti-Cubist in spirit, however much they took for granted the formal innovations of Cubism. The Cubist epoch consciously brought to an end the old European aesthetic culture. It brought itself to an end as the last period in which artists would engage themselves in reconstituting pictorially the reality of fruit bowls, pipes, and guitars. Since the close of Cubism, the crisis of the art object has been mounting from art movement to art movement.

Suggestions for Writing

1. With these reviews in mind, write a review of some book or movie you have strongly liked or disliked, preferably one by a director or writer whose work you have seen before. Try to locate in your recollected reaction just what displeased or delighted you, and why, transforming your reactions into reasons that would convince others.

2. Write a critical review of a concert, an evening of modern dance, a rock group or popular entertainer, a piece of sculpture, a painting, or an exhibit.

Murder Trial in Moscow JEREMY R. AZRAEL · *309*
What Is Wrong with the City? NORMAN MAILER · *321*
Democracy and Anti-Intellectualism in America RICHARD HOFSTADTER · *330*
Blueprint for a Silver Age: Notes on a Visit to America CYRIL CONNOLLY · *350*
The Challenge of Fear ALAN PATON · *361*

Evidence and the Author's Voice

Here a variety of voices respond to the modern scene, to the persistent problems of freedom and justice and how to obtain a fair society. A political scientist writes anecdotally about justice in Russia. A famous novelist tries his hand at politics, as a newspaper editor parallels his speech in conventional political prose. A historian deals with the broad crisis of the American intellectual. A literary critic records, in a brilliant notebook, his impressions of America twenty years ago. Finally,

12

a great South African novelist looks at the modern anguish of black and white. Each writes with equal conviction. Yet each speaks with a different voice, invoking different rhetorical powers, calling in different shades of evidence, to persuade his readers that his view is, in fact, true. These essays may stand in outline of the many styles and of the many possible ways of presenting evidence in support of a truth.

Here are some contrasts to notice. Azrael, relying on a swift narrative prose of straightforward sentences, uses little more than keen vignette and quotation. His essay is virtually all evidence, selected and pointed and reported at firsthand, which speaks for itself and carries you toward the thesis he does not state until the end, and then only obliquely. Stark figures of speech bloom like angry geraniums from Mailer's ferment, much more personal than Azrael's because this is his home town, this American city. And the roundly smoggy political prose, devised in parallel by an alert parodist, represents succinctly how our language can straddle the unbearable issue. Hofstadter offers a historical explanation for the stridencies of activist protest. Connolly, in the sparkling air just settled from the dust of World War II, sees a new America where, even though "there is a drunk in each so respectable family," nobody is poor and something idealistically important is about to happen. Then Paton's profound honesty tells us how far we have yet to go.

Murder Trial in Moscow
Jeremy R. Azrael

We first learned of the case of Aleksandr Ivanovich Bazhenov from an announcement on the bulletin board of Moscow University's law faculty which signaled forthcoming trials of special interest to aspiring Soviet jurists. However, despite this publicity, we were the only representatives of the university present in the small courtroom of the Moscow Oblast Court when, at 10 A.M. on November 10, the Bazhenov case was called. The rest of the audience consisted of sundry courtroom hangers-on, a sizable group of Bazhenov's neighbors, Bazhenov's wife, and the mother and several relatives of Bazhenov's victim. For Bazhenov was charged under Article 136a of the Criminal Code of the Russian republic, the article dealing with premeditated murder from base motives.

People's Judge Ivan Sergeyevich Shepilov summarized the bare details of the charge from the record of the pre-trial investigation which lay on his desk. First, however, he confirmed the identity and vital statistics of the accused, made sure that the latter did not object to the defense attorney who had been assigned him, and, after reading the law covering perjury, registered the witnesses who were slated to be heard.

Bazhenov, it was established, had been born in 1926, was a resident of a small village in Penza province, was of peasant origin and Russian nationality, was married but childless, had had six years of education, had served in the army from 1943 to 1950, was not a member of the Communist Party, had never before been accused or convicted of any crime, and, prior to his arrest, had been employed as a carpenter in a small factory. He was accused of having shot one Vladimir Silkin, aged fourteen, when the latter, along with three youthful companions, invaded his private apple orchard at midnight on August 9, 1958.

This was the sum and substance of the formal charge, although, informed as it was by such technical details as the number (78) and location (the chest) of the gunshot wounds found on Silkin's body, it took Judge Shepilov a full fifteen minutes to read it through. When he had finished, he asked Bazhenov whether he acknowledged the charge and asked the defense and prosecuting attorneys and the two people's assessors, lay jurymen assigned to decide the case along with him, whether they had any questions about it. Receiving an affirmative answer from Bazhenov and a negative answer from the attorneys and assessors, Shepilov requested the accused to rise and give his own version of the case.

Bazhenov, it quickly became clear, was precisely what his appearance suggested: a simple, inarticulate peasant. He was obviously bewildered and terrified by his current predicament and could scarcely speak. Moreover, he was given no opportunity to compose himself, for, at almost every word he uttered, Judge Shepilov interjected an acid comment or supercilious question, thus frightening and bewildering the accused yet further. As a result, Bazhenov's testimony added little to our knowledge of the events of the case. All it really did was give us our first insight into the character of Judge Shepilov, or, at least, into his attitude toward the case at hand:

BAZHENOV: I shot into the air.
SHEPILOV: But a man fell. Do you think we're fools? You shot at people.
BAZHENOV: I didn't want to kill anyone.
SHEPILOV: Really? Did you think that if you shot a man he would become healthier?
BAZHENOV: I didn't want to kill.
SHEPILOV: I didn't ask what you wanted.
BAZHENOV: I didn't want to.
SHEPILOV: Why did you do it, if you didn't want to?
(Silence)

SHEPILOV: Did you think nothing was more important than apples? Why did you kill?
BAZHENOV: On account of apples. . . .

BAZHENOV: I wanted to shoot up.
SHEPILOV: Where did you shoot?
BAZHENOV: In the air.
SHEPILOV: Impossible! That, you yourself fully understand. You are speaking nonsense. Where did you in fact shoot?
BAZHENOV: In the chest.
SHEPILOV: If you had wanted to shoot up, at most the head would have been hit. What was the direction of the shot?
BAZHENOV: Upwards.
SHEPILOV: You spent seven years in the army and didn't learn how to shoot? Really! Where did you shoot?

And so on. Bazhenov continued to insist that he had not wanted to kill and had fired into the air. Shepilov continued to insist that both propositions were nonsensical, and the merry-go-round went on for about twenty minutes.

The prosecutor, a sallow, self-satisfied-looking young man, also questioned Bazhenov. "You killed on account of apples? But what could your loss have been? Five or ten apples? Does that justify your shot?"

The examination of Bazhenov then passed into the hands of the defense attorney. Naum Viktorovich Bykovsky, with his carefully trimmed goatee, wavy gray hair, and comfortably well-groomed look, was the sort of elderly Russian who almost automatically inspires the confidence and trust of Westerners and frequently arouses the suspicion and hostility of Soviet activists. His questioning of Bazhenov was quiet and solicitous, and gave us our first substantial information about the circumstances of the Bazhenov case.

Bykovsky drew from Bazhenov the following history. The accused was dependent for half his income on the two cubic meters of apples which his small thirteen-tree orchard annually yielded him. However, ever since the orchard had begun to yield fruit, it had been beset by thieves. Often up to half the crop was stolen. During the past summer, Bazhenov testified, losses had been particularly heavy, reaching such proportions in the weeks immediately preceding the crime that he had finally taken to sleeping in the orchard in order to fend off the thieves.

Finally, only two weeks before Silkin's death, he had managed to catch two thieves in the orchard. However, when he attempted to detain them, he was set upon and badly beaten. He had reported this to the militia, but, so far as he knew, no investigation had been conducted. In any event, his assailants had not been apprehended. With this experience behind him, he had decided to buy a shotgun, and it was with this weapon that he had shot Silkin when, upon being awakened at midnight, he had seen four figures in the orchard. He had not, in the darkness, been able to perceive that the intruders were adolescents, but hc had given a warning whistle before firing, and he had fired—or, at least, had intended to fire—into the air.

With his client's version of the case fully recorded, Bykovsky closed his examination. Judge Shepilov thereupon started to call the first witness, but the prosecutor interrupted with a request to ask the accused just one more question. His purpose was not clarification but reiteration of what was clearly the foundation stone of the prosecution's case: "You intended merely to save apples, and that's all?" Again Bazhenov responded affirmatively, and the parade of witnesses was permitted to begin.

The first three witnesses were Silkin's companions on the fateful midnight raid. All three were sixteen-year-old factory apprentices; all three told substantially the same story. They were returning home from a public dance and, on passing Bazhenov's orchard, suddenly decided to filch a few apples. All testified that Silkin had been reluctant to take part in the foray but had finally followed them over the orchard's fence. All vigorously denied having stolen apples from Bazhenov or anyone else earlier. The only point on which they disagreed was whether or not the fatal shot had been preceded by a warning whistle.

The first of the boys to testify, the only one of the three who told his story clearly and coherently, claimed to remember such a whistle. The second, who insisted that the tragedy had occurred in July, not August, denied that there had been a whistle, and he was supported by the third. The point was clearly important to the attorneys as an index of Bazhenov's intent, and both pursued the issue vigorously. Apart from this question, however, the prosecutor examined the boys only cursorily, and Bykovsky sought to establish that the boys, each of whom earned three hundred rubles a month, could have afforded to buy apples.

The last witness was Bazhenov's wife, whose testimony confirmed that of her husband as to the care they had lavished on their orchard, its economic importance to them, the high losses they had sustained at the hands of thieves, the disruption of their normal lives brought about by the need for Bazhenov to sleep in the orchard, and the severity of Bazhenov's injuries from the incident two weeks prior to Silkin's death. She reported that when Bazhenov ran into the house on the fateful night and announced that he had just killed a man, her first words were, "You had better go to the militia," and this rang true to her general character as it was revealed in the tone of her testimony. She spoke without the least trace of emotion, throughout referred to Bazhenov as "he," and cast nary a glance toward the prisoner's dock. And yet one somehow felt that there was more of peasant fatalism than of conjugal distance or betrayal in all this.

When the witnesses finished their testimony, Judge Shepilov asked the attorneys whether they had any further evidence to introduce before beginning their summaries and pleas. The defense attorney introduced the accused's war record and work record. Bazhenov had won two citations for wounds received in battle and a First of May citation for good work. The mention of war wounds had obviously won the respect of the audience, but the mention of the work citation called forth a low roll of laughter that clearly said, "Who hasn't received such a certificate? You're really scraping the bottom of the barrel." It was, therefore, on a slightly less than overwhelming note that Bykovsky resumed his seat, and a ten-minute recess was declared before the court would reconvene for final arguments.

Like the majority of the courtroom spectators, we took advantage of the recess to stretch our legs in the corridor. However, despite the obvious desire of several of the spectators to talk to us, we moved off a bit and simply listened and watched.

The mother of the victim, Silkin, sat sobbing quietly on a bench just outside the courtroom door. She had already caused some commotion in the courtroom, first by fainting as Judge Shepilov read the indictment with its gruesome description of the state of the corpse, and then by going into hysterics during the testimony of her son's companions. On both occasions there had been a murmur of sympathy from the audience, which subsided only after Judge Shepilov rapped sharply for silence and warned that "This is a trial, not a spectacle."

Now, however, the sobbing mother seemed to arouse the ire of the waiting crowd. Several elderly men from among the courtroom hangers-on in the audience turned on her and began to upbraid her for having raised a thief. "What but a bad end," they demanded, "could be anticipated for such a son?"

The mother broke into yet louder and more bitter sobs. Over and over she shrieked, "No, no, he was a good boy." But her protests seemed simply to increase the vehemence of her tormentors, who let loose a flood of cruel, mocking laughter interspersed with asides about the fate of thieves, the just deserts of delinquents, the way children reflect their parents' character.

No one intervened, no one said, "Leave the poor, bereaved woman alone!" Even the woman herself did not plead to be left in peace.

Immediately upon reconvening the court, Judge Shepilov called upon the prosecutor to sum up his case. The latter spoke rapidly and without passion—indeed, almost without expression. His summation, which was chaotically organized, reinforced our impression that he was so certain of the outcome of the case that he attached little importance to its presentation. The main themes of his summation could, of course, have been predicted from his prior arguments, but what was surprising was the cavalier fashion in which he handled the two legal problems on which the outcome of the case would presumably hinge: was the murder premeditated and was it, as the relevant article of the code insisted it had to be, committed from base motives?

As for premeditation, the prosecutor's argument was simple: Bazhenov's intent to murder was proved by the fact that he had loaded his shotgun with live ammunition and had incontrovertibly, his professions to the contrary notwithstanding, fired not into the air but directly at a person. The fact that Bazhenov had perhaps not intended the specific murder which occurred was, he asserted, irrelevant.

The issue of motivation seemed to him equally clear-cut. Soviet law, he said, was always especially severe where the protection of life was concerned, but it had to be doubly so when life was taken in defense of a few apples. Bazhenov himself had admitted repeatedly that he had murdered for the sake of apples. "What," the prosecutor asked, "could be more miserly or base than to take the life of a fourteen-year-old boy for the sake of ten apples?" Bazhenov had a full range of defensive measures available for the protection of his orchard, but willfully chose to kill, and that without even a warning. The motive, the prosecutor reiterated, was to save a few apples; the victim was a young boy who had not even begun to live. "In the light of these facts," he concluded, "I ask for a finding of guilty under Article 136a of the Criminal Code and request that the court return the normal maximum sentence of ten years' deprivation of liberty."

The entire tone and style of the prosecutor's speech, which it had taken him only twelve minutes to deliver, contrasted sharply with that of defense attorney Bykovsky, who now rose to deliver his summation. The argument was both tightly organized and forceful, and skillfully blended four distinct elements. First, there was a careful reference to rulings and instructions from higher courts which bore on the case at hand. Second, there was a moving appeal, in the best tradition of Russian courtroom pleading, that the court put the case in the proper human perspective and judge only the individual who faced it. Third, there was a reinterpretation of the evidence in terms of the preceding elements—in terms of the rulings of higher courts and the individual circumstances of the accused. And finally, there was a striking reference to the possibilities of true justice, which had been introduced into

Soviet judicial practice after Stalin's death and were being put to the test in the present case.

Bykovsky stressed the fact that Bazhenov had been subjected to extreme provocation and that every Soviet citizen had the right to defend his property against thieves. However, he went much further. He opened his remarks by expressing his sympathy to Silkin's relatives. He spoke with great emotion of how blessed was the gift of life, of how easy it was to snuff out and how impossible to restore. And then, wheeling toward the bench, he reminded the court that, though Silkin's life was gone, Bazhenov was still alive, and that his fate, the fate of a living human being, rested now with the court.

Bazhenov, Bykovsky expostulated, was a poor and simple soul. He had given seven years of his life to the service of his country and upon returning to civilian life had sought, above all, peace and quiet. He had worked diligently and had devoted every spare moment to his small orchard. The orchard, Bykovsky argued, was much more than a source of profit to Bazhenov; it was a source of stability and personal satisfaction. However, as soon as the orchard had begun to flourish, it had been beset by thieves. Bazhenov had been forced to abandon his hearth and sleep amidst his precious trees in order to protect them and all they stood for. His whole life had been disrupted. And when he at last managed to catch some thieves, he had been badly beaten. Yet, even then the militia had done nothing except file a report on the assault.

It was only at this point, Bykovsky went on, only after he had been harassed, insulted, and injured, only after he had looked in vain to the public authorities for support, that Bazhenov, in desperation, had purchased a gun. There could be no doubt, Bykovsky asserted, that a Soviet citizen possessed the right to defend his property against hooligans and thieves. How, he demanded, could one attribute the exercise of this right to base motives, and hence bring it under Article 136a? Must one simply yield to a thief who demands one's clothing or watch? Could resistance to the thief in such a case be attributed to base motives?

Previously, Bykovsky remonstrated in a low voice, it had been an accepted part of Soviet court practice to attribute the worst imaginable motives to the accused and to avoid inquiry into the specific circumstances which surrounded an alleged crime. Then, Bykovsky continued, it had been customary to consider the trial nothing more than a ceremonial ritual, after which the accused was automatically given the severest possible sentence. But now, Bykovsky emphatically reminded the court, all that had changed. Apropos of the present case, one could see the change in the Judicial Instruction handed down in 1956 by the

U.S.S.R. Supreme Court, directing all lower courts to recognize that all citizens had the right of *active* defense of their property as well as their bodies and lives against hooligans.

How, Bykovsky thundered, could any prosecutor in 1958 claim that Bazhenov's act was one of premeditated murder from base motives? Try as he might, Bykovsky asserted, he could find nothing in any authoritative judicial text or contemporary directive which suggested that Bazhenov's act was anything more than active defense of property.

It was true, Bykovsky conceded, that active defense was justified only in response to a "socially dangerous attack," but that was precisely the nature of the robbery attempted by the unfortunate Silkin and his comrades. The boys could have bought apples, yet they stole; and Silkin was shot in the act of theft itself. "Socially dangerous? Of course! If one asks, 'Where can one go from apples?', the answer is, 'A long way. One can go to a watch, a jacket, a suit, and so forth.' The populace demands that the fruits of its labors be protected."

The only relevant question, Bykovsky maintained, was that of the degree of proportionality between attack and defense. The prosecutor, he insisted, was wrong to suggest that any question of proportionality between apples and lives was involved. No jurist would frame the question in this way. As for the really relevant question, Bykovsky went on, the defense itself was persuaded that Bazhenov had adopted a disproportionate defensive response. Bykovsky asserted that for this reason he himself did not consider it possible to recommend the simple acquittal of his client. However, the maximum sentence which could be tolerated was three years, and even that would be grossly excessive.

Bazhenov's crime clearly falls under Article 139 of the Criminal Code —the article which deals specifically with overly extreme measures of defense. Under this article, Bazhenov is guilty. He should have shot into the air or perhaps toward the boy's feet. But some sort of *active* defense was appropriate and necessary. Even if Silkin and his comrades had simply been innocently strolling through the orchard, the court would have to make a distinction between the objective situation and the motives of the accused. In even this hypothetical case, the relevant article would still be 139. In the actual case at hand, where not innocent strolling but criminal theft characterized the objective situation, there is clearly no way to go beyond Article 139. Neither sympathy for the relatives of the deceased nor outdated judicial habit should or can lead us to apply the wrong article.

The prosecutor, who was visibly stunned by the vigor of the defense, demanded rebuttal time. There was real wonder in his voice as he admitted, "My, my . . . so to speak . . . opponent is right about the instruction of the U.S.S.R. Supreme Court." However, the prosecutor went on to say that his "opponent" had failed to mention that the Criminal Code of the Russian republic, while not denying citizens the right to active defense of their private property, specifically directed that great caution be exercised where only gardens or orchards were involved. This, he argued, constituted a warning to the courts that such things as the theft of apples by children did not justify active measures of defense.

To this, Bykovsky, in his very brief rebuttal of the prosecutor's rebuttal, pointed out that at midnight on a dark night one could neither distinguish adolescents from adults nor be expected to ascertain the age of one's assailants before acting in self-defense. He did not contest the prosecutor's characterization of the Russian code, but simply reiterated the instruction of the U.S.S.R. Supreme Court and suggested that it was precisely because an orchard was involved that he had conceded Bazhenov's action was excessive. Certainly, Bykovsky concluded, there was nothing in the code to support the prosecutor's suggestion that action in defense of one's orchard was automatically tantamount to action inspired by base motives.

With the summations and rebuttals completed, Judge Shepilov declared a one-hour luncheon recess, to be followed by the final statement of the accused. As his four guards with their bayoneted rifles led Bazhenov from the room, we approached Bykovsky and congratulated him on his conduct of the case. We explained that we were American students of Soviet affairs and told him that it would be a pleasure to report that the quality of defense in Soviet trials was so high. We told him that, to our minds, he had made the prosecutor's case appear exceedingly flimsy.

Bykovsky thanked us with real warmth, but quickly changed the subject and began to inquire further about our special interests, our status in the Soviet Union, the nature of American legal training. Every time we tried to turn the discussion back to the Bazhenov case, he became distinctly ill at ease.

It was impossible, under the circumstances, to press him hard, but finally, after he had begun to glance at his watch, we asked what sort of decision he expected the court to return. We ourselves were quite optimistic, for we had by now adopted Bykovsky's case as well as been persuaded by it, and therefore were rather surprised when Bykovsky, after hesitating just a second, said in a voice that seemed to us strangely sober and resigned, "You will see." And with that he disappeared into his chamber.

After lunch, Bazhenov made his last statement in a whispered mutter. His head was cast down and his brow furrowed, and the words came out jerkily and expressionless: "I did not want to kill. I received two wounds in the war. I was beaten only ten days before the accident, and the militia did nothing. I loved my orchard and only wanted to protect it. I paid over six hundred rubles for my trees." And with this last exalted sentiment, Bazhenov resumed his seat. His mercenary conclusion surely had not been advised by Bykovsky and showed perhaps more clearly than anything else Bazhenov's own true character and total lack of sensitivity to the process in which he was caught up. It would, we feared, hardly turn the court's final deliberations in his favor. However, Judge Shepilov evidently did not contemplate that lengthy deliberations would be necessary in any case. Immediately after Bazhenov's statement, he announced that the court would reconvene for sentencing in fifty minutes.

When the court reconvened, Judge Shepilov immediately began to read an almost interminable but carefully organized decision which rehearsed all the facts of the case and all of the interpretations adduced. Two pages were devoted to a new description of the condition of Silkin's body after the shotgun blast. Shepilov's view of the case was clear-cut: the murder was ghastly, it was committed for the sake of a few apples, base motives were unmistakably at its root, it clearly fell under Article 136a, defining premeditated murder. The argument of the prosecution had carried the day, and the prosecutor leaned back in his chair with a sigh of satisfaction. Bykovsky did not raise his head from his papers. The audience waited for the sentence to be pronounced in a silence that was electric with anticipation.

"The crime," Judge Shepilov said slowly, "is not merely horrible; it is full of implications which justify our considering it a socially dangerous crime. In light of this fact, the crime falls outside the limits visualized in the scale of normal penalties attached to Article 136a. Because his crime was particularly socially dangerous, the court sentences the accused to the extreme measure of social defense, death by shooting." And then, fairly screaming at the defendant, "Clear enough?"

There was a gasp throughout the courtroom, and then, for the minute it took the shock to set in, there was silence. The first sound to be heard was a long, low sob from Bazhenov's wife, followed immediately, as if in response, by shouts of "Correct, correct, thank God, thank God" from Silkin's mother and several of her friends. These worn *babas* struggled to their feet and began frantically to cross themselves as they shouted. As the members of the bench filed out, these women pushed toward the aisle and reached out to touch Judge Shepilov as he passed, stern-faced, eyes straight ahead. "Thank God." "Correct, correct." "Thank you, thank you, thank you," they cried.

They turned with curses and imprecations on Bazhenov, who sat slumped in his seat. His wife, who had broken into uncontrollable sobs, they simultaneously belabored with derisive howls of glee and consoled with comments on her still young years and new-won freedom. Finally, they noticed us staring at them, and evidently they sensed a challenge in our look. "The verdict was right; the verdict was right, wasn't it?" several voices demanded.

We shrugged, but the demand was put again and again, more and more imperatively, and, at the same time, more and more imploringly, as if all their conclusions and the rectitude of all their actions hinged on our assent. At last, braving we knew not what, we said that we could not agree with either the verdict or the sentence. They must know as well as we, we said, that the fatal words "socially dangerous" were ordinarily applied only to crimes of high political import or to serious crimes committed by recidivists. The Soviet Union boasted to the entire world that to all intents and purposes it had no death penalty, and the entire world believed that this was so to all intents and purposes, even when it knew about the existence of the extraordinary provision dealing with "socially dangerous crimes."

There was a sudden silence, and then one wrinkled old woman leaned forward and, as the others drew around, whispered, "You don't know Bazhenov. He's a monster, a fiend. Why, just before he killed Silkin, he gnawed the hand from a five-year-old baby whom he caught in his orchard. He's a cannibal. He's had six children of his own, but he's boiled them all in oil. You don't know Bazhenov." The eyes of our aged confidante grew narrower as she spoke; her tone grew ever more mysterious. At first the crowd around us listened with as much wonder as we, but soon they began to nod vigorously. "He ate off a boy's hand," one repeated, "Boiled his own children," rasped another. A village legend, the legend of the monster Bazhenov, was being created. It was as if, having seen Bazhenov's fate, his neighbors had concluded that the accused had to be a satanic fiend. As if this were the only way they could make the outcome of the trial comprehensible. We were the catalysts that called their response forth, but once the moral was established, our belief or disbelief became irrelevant, and no one tried to detain us as we edged out of the circle.

It was only after we had found a café in which to collect our breaths and our thoughts that we realized that perhaps there was a sense in which the response of Bazhenov's fellow villagers was more than merely psychologically noteworthy. Perhaps the trial we had just witnessed had been intended not merely to uphold the law but to point a broader moral.

There was the fact that the Bazhenov case had been singled out for its special interest to law students. There was the whole tenor of Judge Shepilov's initial examination of the accused. There was the prosecutor's concentration on the nonjuridical aspects of the case and his obvious complacency about the outcome. There was the surprise shown at the vigor of Bykovsky's defense of the accused. There was Bykovsky's stress on the illegitimacy of ceremonial trials, coupled, however, with his unwillingness to ask that his client be acquitted. Finally, there was Bykovsky's message to us. Retrospectively, his "You will see" seemed to suggest: "No matter that you are persuaded and impressed by my defense; the key to this case lies outside my influence."

However, though they had, in a sense, been less naïve than we, Bazhenov's neighbors had surely drawn the wrong lesson from the trial. Their legend completely blunted the political and ideological moral the regime intended, which was not that Bazhenov was evil incarnate but rather that he had *become* evil incarnate under the corrupting influence of acquisitiveness and selfishness rooted in the possession of private property. It was not Bazhenov's having succumbed to evil instincts that was to be stressed, but his having succumbed to evil and "backward" instincts—the retrograde instincts of capitalism. The trial, we concluded, was very probably intended to serve as an especially significant object lesson in the regime's perpetual, and recently intensified, campaign against manifestations of the psychology of private ownership.

Yet there remained a puzzle. The regime's campaign against manifestations of the "bourgeois property instinct," while it had been energetic, had not been outrightly terroristic in recent years, especially where the rural population, with its deep-rooted attachment to its garden plots, was concerned. Judge Shepilov's sentence, however, had smacked of outright terrorism. It was, therefore, with some interest that we learned that on appeal by the *prosecutor* the Supreme Court of the Russian republic had reduced Bazhenov's sentence to ten years. Unfortunately, the Supreme Court did not explain the rationale behind its decision. What seemed likely, if our interpretative hypothesis was correct, was that at the original trial Judge Shepilov, aware that the case before him had special political and ideological significance, had overreacted. The purpose of the appeal, then, apart from salving the prosecutor's pride, was to rebuke the judge for his excessive zeal and the distortion of the "true" moral of the trial which was its consequence.

Another possibility was that the Supreme Court was striking against the continued presence of much wider tendencies on the part of some Soviet judges to invoke the "socially dangerous" escape clause in the law code as readily as they had prior to Stalin's death. The reduction of sentence might, that is, have been a partial vindication of legality in the Western sense—an attack on judicial terror in general and not merely on its clumsy use in a politically sensitive situation. But if this had been the intended implication, it would have been conveyed much

more effectively had the Supreme Court reviewed the case on an appeal
not from the prosecutor but from defense lawyer Bykovsky, or, at the
very least, had the Supreme Court followed Bykovsky's recommenda-
tions as to the proper article to apply to the case and the appropriate
sentence to impose. In short, we still felt that the Bazhenov case was
a miscarriage of justice and that the probable explanation lay outside
the legal system proper. Certainly Bykovsky was not formally vindicated by the Supreme Court. And yet we were aware that in a long-
term perspective, the most significant thing about the Bazhenov trial
might well be that Bykovsky's voice was heard.

What Is Wrong With the City?
Norman Mailer

How is one to speak of the illness of a city?
A clear day can come, a morning in early
May like the pride of June. The streets are
cool, the buildings have come out of
shadow, and silences are broken by the
voices of children. It is as if the neighborhood has slept in the winding street of the
past. Forty years go by—one can recollect
the milkman and the clop of a horse. It is a
great city. Everyone speaks of the delight
of the day on the way to work. It is hard
on such mornings to believe that New York
is the victim "etherized on a table."

Yet by afternoon the city is incarcerated
once more. Haze covers the sky, a grim,
formless glare blazes back from the horizon.
The city has become unbalanced again. By
the time work is done, New Yorkers push
through the acrid lung-rotting air and work
their way home, avoiding each other's eyes
in the subways. Later, near midnight, thinking of a walk to buy the *Times*, they hesi-

AS A REAL
POLITICIAN
PHRASES IT[1]

My fellow Americans, I
speak to you at a time of
crisis, a time not only of
crisis for our city but for
all America. It is a time
when great vision is called
for. Our cities have many
problems.

They are crowded.

Pollution is an ever-growing problem.

Our transportation net-
works are clogged and in-
adequate.

Honest citizens fear crime
in the streets as never before.

Out of this, a great cry
has been heard: "Some-
thing must be done." I have
heard your cry.

---

[1] The "real-politician" phrasing was added by the Detroit *Free Press*, which
printed Mailer's statements simultaneously with the New York *Times* on May 18,
1969. (Norman Mailer and James Breslin were candidates in the 1969 New York
City Democratic primary election for mayor and deputy mayor, respectively.
This primary, however, was won by Mario Procaccino, who lost the Fall mayoral
election to John Lindsay.)—S.B.

tate—in the darkness a familiar sense of dread returns, the streets are not quite safe, the sense of waiting for some apocalyptic fire, some night of long knives hangs over the city. We recognize one more time that the city is ill, that our own New York, the empire city, is not too far from death.

Recollect: When we were children, we were told air was invisible, and it was. Now we see it shift and thicken, move in gray depression over a stricken sky. Now we grow used to living with colds all year, and viruses suggestive of plague. Tempers shorten in our hideous air. The sick get sicker, the violent more violent. The frayed tissue of New York manners seem ready to splatter on every city street. It is the first problem of the city, our atrocious air. People do not die dramatically like the one-day victims of Donora[2], rather they dwindle imperceptibly, die five years before their time, ten years before, cough or sneeze helplessly into the middle of someone else's good mood, stroll about with the hot iron of future asthma manacled to their lungs.

That is our pervasive ill. It is fed by a host of tributary ills which flow into the air, fed first by our traffic, renowned through the world for its incapacity to move. Midtown Manhattan is next to impenetrable by vehicle from midday to evening—the average rate of advance is, in fact, six miles an hour, about the speed of a horse at a walk. Once free of the center, there is the threat of hourlong tie-ups at every bridge, tunnel, and expressway if even a single car breaks down in a lane. In the course of a year, people lose weeks of working time through the sum of minutes and quarter-hours of waiting to crawl forward in traffic. Tempers blow with lost schedules, work suffers everywhere. All the

Contaminants of our air have by now far exceeded acceptable levels.

Frankly, the great traffic networks which we viewed with such pride only a few short years ago are now totally inadequate.

---

[2] On October 30–31, 1948, a poisonous smog covering Donora, Pennsylvania, killed 20 persons and made 5,000 ill.—S.B.

while stalled cars gun their motors while waiting in place, pumping carbon monoxide into air already laden with caustic sulphur-oxide from fuel oil we burn to make electricity.

Given this daily burden, this air pollution, noise pollution, stagnant transport, all but crippled subways, routes of new transportation twenty years unbuilt—every New Yorker sallies forth into an environment which strips him before noon of his good cheer, his charity, his calm nerve, and his ability to discipline his anger.

Yet, beneath that mood of pestilential clangor, something worse is ticking away— our deeper sense of a concealed and continuing human horror. If there are eight million people in New York, one million live on welfare, no, the figure is higher now, it will be one million two hundred thousand by the end of the year. Not a tenth of these welfare cases will ever be available for work; they are women and children first, then too old, too sick, too addicted, too illiterate, too unskilled, too ignorant of English. Fatherless families and motherless families live at the end of an umbilical financial cord which perpetuates them in an embryonic economic state. Welfare is the single largest item in the city budget—two years ago it surpassed the figure we reserve for education, yet it comes down to payments of no more than $3,800 a year for a family of four. Each member of that family is able to spend a dollar a day for food, at most $1.25 a day.

Let me make myself perfectly clear. The entire system of welfare has broken down. It needs to be restructured along more realistic lines. More than that, we need to make welfare meaningful. We must learn not to give more, but how to give more efficiently.

Our finances are intolerable. If New York state delivers $17 billion in income tax and $5 billion in corporate taxes to the federal government, it is conservative to assume that $14 billion of the total of $22 billion has come from the people of New York City. But our city budget is about $7½ billion: of that sum only $3 billion derives from the

This city is now operating under an antiquated tax base . . .

state and from Washington. New York must find another $4½ billion in real estate and other local taxes.

Consider then: we pay $14 billion in income tax to the federal government and to Albany. Back comes $3 billion. We put out five dollars for every dollar which returns. So we live in vistas of ironbound civic poverty. Four of those lost five dollars are going to places like Vietnam and Malmstrom in North Dakota where the ABM will find a site, or dollars are going to interstate highways which pass through regions we probably will never visit. In relation to the federal government, the city is like a sharecropper who lives forever in debt at the company store.

We don't get our money's worth from Uncle Sam . . .

Yes, everything is wrong. The vocations of the past disintegrate. Jewish teachers who went into the education system twenty years ago to have security for themselves and to disseminate enlightenment among the children of the poor, now feel no security in their work, and are rejected in their liberal sociological style of teaching. The collective ego of their life-style is shattered. They are forced to comprehend that there are black people who would rather be taught by other black people than by experts.

America is still the great melting pot. Our differences are our strengths as well as our weaknesses. We must be able to give to people, whatever their ethnic persuasions, a sense of identity.

The need for authenticity has become the real desire in education. "Who am I? What is the meaning of my skin, my passion, my dread, my fury, my dream of glories undreamed, my very need for bread?"— these questions are now becoming so powerful they bring the pumps of blood up to pressure and leave murder in the womb of a dying city and a fury to discover for oneself whether one is victim or potential hero, stupid or too bright for old pedagogical ways. Rage at the frustration of the effort to find a style became the rage at the root of the uproar in the schools last year, and the rage will be there until the schools are free to discover a new way to learn. Let us not be arrogant toward the ignorant—their sensitivity is often too deep to dare the knowledge of numbers or the curlicue within a letter. Picasso, age of eleven, could still not do arithmetic because the figure 7 looked like a nose upside down to him.

Our parks deteriorate, and after duty our police go home to suburbs beyond the city —they come back to govern us from without. And municipal employes drift in the endless administrative bogs of Wagnerian systems of apathy and attrition. Work gets done at the rate of work accomplished by a draft army in peacetime at a sullen out-of-the-way post. The poverty program staggers from the brilliance of its embezzlements. But, of course, if you were a bright young black man, might you not want to steal a million from the feds?

Part of the tragedy, part of the unbelievable oncoming demise of New York is that none of us can simply believe it.

It's hard to believe it's happening to us.

Now all our problems have the magnitude of junkie problems—they are so coexistent with our life that New Yorkers do not try to solve them but escape them. Our fix is to put the blame on the blacks and Puerto Ricans. But everybody knows that nobody can really know where the blame resides. It is the only way he can have the optimism to run. So the prospective candidate writing these words has the heart to consider entering the Democratic primary on June 17 because he thinks he sees a way out of the swamp; better, he believes he glimpses a royal road.

A lot of us want to blame others, and run from the problem. But, my friends, I think together we can— and will—make things better.

The face of the solution may reside in the notion that the left has been absolutely right on some critical problems of our times, and the conservatives have been altogether correct about one enormous matter—which is that the federal government has no business whatever in local affairs. The style of New York life has shifted since the second world war (along with the rest of the American cities) from a scene of local neighborhoods and personalities to a large dull impersonal style of life which deadens us with its architecture, its highways, its abstract welfare, and its bureaucratic reflex to look for government solutions which come into the city from without (and do not work). So the old confidence that the problems of our life were roughly equal to our abilities has been lost. Our authority has been handed over to the federal power.

How can we begin? By the most brutal view, New York City is today a legislative pail of dismembered organs strewn from Washington to Albany. We are without a comprehensive function or a skin. We cannot begin until we find a function which will become our skin.

It is simple: our city must become a state.

We must look to become a state of the United States separate from New York state: the fifty-first, in fact, of the United States. New York city state, or the state of New York city. It is strange on the tongue, but not so strange.

Think on the problem of this separation. People across the state are oriented toward Buffalo or Albany or Rochester or Montreal or Toronto or Boston or Cleveland. They do not think in great numbers of coming to New York City to make their life. In fact the good farmers and small-town workers of New York State rather detest us. They hear of the evils of our city with quiet thin-lipped glee; in the state legislature they rush to compound those evils. Every time the city needs a program which the state must approve, the city returns with a part of its package—the rest has been lost in

It is simple: Our city must become a state.

What do the farmers care about urban problems? They don't like us anymore than we like them.

deals, compromises, and imposts. The connection of New York City to New York state is a marriage of misery, incompatibility, and abominable old quarrels.

Look, we have received no money so far for improving our city transit lines, yet the highway program for America in 1968 was $5 billion. Of this, New York state received at least $350,000,000 for its roads. New York City received not a dollar from Washington or Albany for reconstruction of its 6,000 miles of streets and avenues.

As a city-state we could speak to the federal government in the unmistakable tones of a state. We could claim that a comparable amount is required for our transportation problems which can better be solved by the construction of new rapid transit.

One suggestion is that we could spend our own money, rather than have it spent by all those farmers upstate.

We give to Washington and Albany almost five tax dollars for every dollar which returns; Mississippi, while declaiming the virtues and inviolability of states' rights, still gets four federal dollars for every income-tax dollar she pays up.

Power to the neighborhoods! In the new city-state, every opportunity would be offered to neighborhoods to vote to become townships, villages, hamlets, subboroughs, tracts, or small cities, at which legal point they would be funded directly by the fifty-first state. Many of these neighborhoods would manage their own municipal services, their police, sanitation, fire protection, education, parks, or, like very small towns, they could, if they wished, combine services with other neighborhoods. Each neighborhood would thus begin to outline the style of its local government by the choice of its services.

The grass roots must again be permitted to speak out. Where there is no grass, we must plant it. [laughter] I know what you young people are thinking.

Poorer neighborhoods would obviously look to establish themselves upon their immediate problems. So Harlem, Bedford-Stuyvesant, and the Barrio in East Harlem might be the first to vote for power to their

And so, I say we must return to self-determination. To control by the people of their own destiny.

own neighborhoods so that they might be in position to administer their own poverty program, own welfare, their own education systems, and their own—if they so voted—police and sanitation and fire protection for which they would proceed to pay out of their funds. They would then be able to hire their own people for their own neighborhood jobs and services.

Power to the neighborhoods would metan that any neighborhood could constitute itself on any principle, whether spiritual, emotional, economical, ideological, or idealistic.

To the degree that we have lost faith in the power of the government to conduct our lives, so would the principle of power to the neighborhoods begin to thrive, so too would the first spiritual problem of the twentieth century—alienation from the self —be given a tool by which to rediscover oneself.

In New York, which is to say, in the twentieth-century, one can never know whether the world is vastly more or less violent than it seems. Nor can we discover which actions in our lives are authentic or which belong to the art of the put-on. Conceive that society has come to the point where tolerance of others' ideas has no meaning unless there is benumbed acceptance of the fact that we must accept their lives. If there are young people who believe that human liberty is blockaded until they have the right to take off their clothes in the street—and more! and more!—make love on the hood of an automobile—there are others who think it is a sin against the eyes of the Lord even to contemplate the act in one's mind.

Both could now begin to build communities on their separate faith—a spectrum which might run from compulsory free love to mandatory attendance in church on Sun-

Whatever you believe, well, ladies and gentlemen, you could do your thing.

day! Grant us to recognize that wherever there is a common desire among people vital enough to keep a community alive, then there must be also the presence of a clue that some kind of real life resides in the desire. Others may eventually discern how.

Which is where we go now—into the campaign: To talk in the days ahead of what power to the neighborhoods will mean. We will go down the steps of the position papers and talk of jobs and housing and welfare, of education, municipal unions, and law and order, finance, the names of laws, the statistics of the budget, the problems of traffic and transportation. There will be a paucity of metaphor and a taste of stale saliva to the debates, for voters are hard-working people who trust the plain more than the poetic. How then can Mailer and Breslin, two writers with reputations notorious enough for four, ever hope to convince the voting hand of the electorate? What would they do if, miracle of political explosions, they were to win?

Well, they might cry like Mario Procaccino, for they would never have a good time again; but they would serve, they would learn on the job, they would conduct their education in public. They would be obliged to. And indeed the supposition could remain that they might even do well, better than the men before them. How else could they have the confidence to run?

As for the fact that they were literary men—that might be the first asset of all. They would know how to talk to the people—they would be forced to govern by the fine art of the voice. And best of all, what a tentative confidence would reign in the eye of New York that her literary men, used to dealing with the proportions of worlds hitherto created only in the mind, might now have a sensitive nose for the

You say we can't govern because of our background. Well, I say give us a try.

balances and the battles, the tugs, the pushing, the heaves of that city whose declara-
tion of new birth was implicit in the extraordinary fact that him, Mailer! and him,
Breslin! had been voted in.

Sweet Sunday, dear friends, and take a
chance. We are out of the lottery of the
years.

So let us try. Get out and
vote for us!

Democracy and Anti-Intellectualism
in America
Richard Hofstadter

Intellectualism and Democracy

American education today is in the midst of a great crisis, the general outlines of which I believe we can all recognize. About the first
part of this crisis, its financial aspect, I shall have nothing to say. A
second part of it comes from outside education, in the shape of tremendous pressures to conform, for we live in a society in which the most
dynamic force is provided by a small group of politicians who seek to
base careers upon the policing of opinion. About the problems of
freedom and conformity, I will speak briefly. The third part of this
crisis, which concerns me most, is internal; it is less dramatic and per-
ceptible than the others and it has been going on for a longer time. It
stems from an inner failure of nerve, for it is nothing less than the
growing loss of confidence among educators in the importance and
value of the life of the mind, a capitulation within the educational
world—indeed, in many quarters an eager capitulation—to the non-
intellectual or anti-intellectual criteria that many forces in our society
wish to impose upon education and which we might well consider it
the bounden duty of educators to resist. It is about this that I wish
primarily to speak; and I hope to suggest some relations between this
species of educational failure and our popular democracy.

Since I am speaking about education and intellectualism, I want to
make it entirely clear that I do not make the mistake of identifying
higher education in general with intellectualism. Quite the contrary; I
propose to emphasize the extent to which anti-intellectualism is ram-
pant within the educational community. But it is also probably true
that in America the greater part of the leadership of those who can be

called intellectuals lives and works in academic communities. And if higher education can be said to be under fire today, it can be said with greater certainty that the distinctively intellectual part of the educational community is the part that stands to lose most.

The crisis in higher education is also a crisis in the history of the intelligentsia. Today, everywhere in America, intellectuals are on the defensive. They have been identified with the now-defeated inheritance of the New Deal and the Fair Deal. That this identification should have been made is ironical, because the New Deal itself, for all its Brain Trusters, had its own streak of anti-intellectualism. But it has also been unfair: the intellectuals are never given credit for the successes of the New Deal, but they have had to take the blame for everything that has been charged up to the Democratic administrations of the past twenty years—with so-called creeping socialism, with the war, with the alleged failure at Yalta, even with treason. In the late presidential campaign a political leader who embodied the kind of traits that the intellectual would most like to see in our national leadership found the support of the intellectuals of slight value in overcoming the disadvantages of his party and his hour. During that campaign the nation also found the epithet for the intellectuals that it has so long wanted—"egg-heads."

Do not imagine, however, that the intellectual is going into permanent eclipse. He always has his day posthumously, for the very men who are most forward in proclaiming their dislike of living intellectuals are the most abject followers of the dead ones. They may not like contemporary intellectuals but they are often quite hypnotized by the intellectual leavings of Adam Smith or Herbert Spencer, or Edmund Burke, or Thomas Aquinas, or similar gods of the past. They have restored an old slogan of the frontiersman with a new meaning and a new object: "The only good intellectual is a dead intellectual."

But what is an intellectual, really? This is a problem of definition that I found, when I came to it, far more elusive than I had anticipated. A great deal of what might be called the journeyman's work of our culture—the work of engineers, physicians, newspapermen, and indeed of most professors—does not strike me as distinctively intellectual, although it is certainly work based in an important sense on ideas. The distinction that we must recognize, then, is one originally made by Max Weber between living *for* ideas and living *off* ideas. The intellectual lives for ideas; the journeyman lives off them. The engineer or the physician—I don't mean here to be invidious—needs to have a pretty considerable capital stock in frozen ideas to do his work; but they serve for him a purely instrumental purpose: he lives off them, not for them. Of course he may also be, in his private role and his personal ways of thought, an intellectual, but it is not necessary for him to be one in order to work at his profession. There is in fact no profession which demands that one be an intellectual. There do seem to be vocations, however, which almost demand that one be an anti-intellectual, in which those who live off ideas seem to have an implacable hatred for those who live for them. The marginal intellectual workers and the unfrocked intellectuals who work in journalism, advertising, and mass communication are the bitterest and most powerful among those who work at such vocations.

It will help, too, to make the further distinction between living for ideas and living for *an idea*. History is full of cases of great men with good minds, a capacity to deal with abstractions, and a desire to make systems of them—all qualities we associate with the intellectual. But when, as it has in many of them, this concern with ideas, no matter how dedicated and sincere, reduces in the end to the ingenious use of them for a central preconception, however grand, then I think we have very little intellectualism and a great deal of something else. A good historical illustration is that of Lenin, who, as his more theoretical works show, had in him a powerful element of intellectuality; but this intellectuality was rendered thin by his all-absorbing concern with certain very limiting political values. His book on philosophy, *Materialism and Empirio-Criticism,* a shrill work and an extremely depressing one to read, makes it altogether clear that the politician in him swallowed up the intellectual. I choose the illustration of Lenin because it helps me to make another point that seems unfortunately necessary because of the present tendency to identify intellectuals with subversives. That point is that the idea of a party line and political messianism is inherently inconsistent with intellectualism, and those few intellectuals who have in some way survived that tension are few, pitiable, and on the whole sterile.

The journeyman of ideas, and the janizary who makes a somewhat complicated but highly instrumental use of ideas, provide us with two illustrations of people who work with ideas but are not precisely intellectuals, as I understand the term. What, then, are the differences between the men who work with ideas but are *not* intellectuals and the men who work with ideas and *are* intellectuals?

Two things, that seem in fact to be mutually at odds, mark off the intellectual from the journeyman of ideas; one is playfulness, the other is piety.

Certainly the intellectual, if he is nothing else, is one who relishes *the play of the mind* for its own sake, for whom it is one of the major ends of life. The intellectual has a full quotient of what Veblen called "idle curiosity." His mind, instead of falling to rest when it has provided him with his girl and his automobile and his dinner, becomes even more active. Indeed if we had to define him in physiological terms, we might define him as the creature whose mind is *most* likely to be active after dinner.

I speak of playfulness too because of the peculiar nature of the relationship, in the intellectual's mind, between ideas and practicality. To the journeyman of ideas the be-all and end-all of ideas lies in their practical efficacy. Now the intellectual, by contrast, is not necessarily impractical; I can think of some intellectuals like Thomas Jefferson and Robert Owen and John Maynard Keynes who have been eminently practical, and I consider the notion that the intellectual is inherently impractical to be one of the most contemptible of the delusions with which the anti-intellectual quiets his envy—the intellectual is not impractical but primarily concerned with a quality of ideas that does not depend upon their practicality. He neither reveres nor disdains practical consequences; for him they are either marginal or irrelevant. And when he does talk about the practicality or the "relevance" of ideas, the kind of practicality that he is concerned with is itself somewhat different from the practicality of building a bridge, curing a disease, or making a profit—it is practical relevance to spiritual values themselves.

The best illustration of the intellectual's view of the purely practical that has recently come to my attention is the reaction of Clerk Maxwell, the great nineteenth-century mathematician and theoretical physicist, to the invention of the telephone. Maxwell was asked to give a lecture on the workings of this wonderful new instrument, which he began by saying how difficult it was to believe, when the word first came from America, that such a thing had actually been devised. But then, he said, "when at last this little instrument appeared, consisting, as it does, of parts, every one of which is familiar to us, and capable of being put together by an amateur, the disappointment arising from its humble appearance was only partially relieved on finding that it was really able to talk." Perhaps, then, this regrettable appearance of simplicity might be redeemed by the presence somewhere of "recondite physical principles, the study of which might worthily occupy an hour's time of an academic audience." But no; Maxwell had not met a single person who could not understand the physical processes involved, and even the science reporters for the daily press had almost got it right! The thing was a disappointing bore; it was not recondite, it was not profound, it was not complex, it was not *intellectually* new.

To be sure, what this illustration suggests is not merely that the telephone disappointed Maxwell as a pure scientist and an intellectual, but that the strain of intellectuality in him was not as broadly developed as it might have been. The telephone might well excite not merely the commercial imagination but the historical imagination. But my point is, after all, not that Maxwell was a universal intellectual, but that he was displaying the attitude of the intellectual in his particular sphere of interest.

The second element in intellectualism is its religious strain, the note of piety. What I mean by this is simply that for the intellectual the whole world of moral values becomes attached to ideas and to the life dedicated to ideas. The life given over to the search for truth takes on for him a primary moral significance. Intellectualism, although hardly confined to doubters, is often the sole piety of the skeptic. A few years ago a distinguished sociologist asked me to read a brief manuscript which he had written primarily for students planning to go on to advanced work in his field, the purpose of which was to illustrate various ways in which the life of the mind might be cultivated. The essay had about it a little too much of the how-to-do books, and my friend abandoned it. But the nub of the matter from the standpoint of our present problem was that I found myself to be reading a piece of devotional literature, comparable perhaps to Cotton Mather's *Essays to do Good* or Richard Steele's *The Tradesman's Calling*. My friend was trying to communicate his sense of dedication to the life of ideas, which he conceived much in the fashion of the old Protestant writers as a *calling*. To work is to pray. Yes, and for this kind of man, to think—really to think—is to pray. What he knows best, when he is at his best, is the pursuit of truth; but *easy* truths bore him. What he is certain of becomes unsatisfactory always; the meaning of his intellectual life lies in the quest for new uncertainties.

In a bygone day when men lived even more by dogma than they do now, there were two kinds of men whose special office it was to seek for and utter the truth; and they symbolize these two sides of the intellectual's nature. One was the angelic doctor, the learned schoolman, the conserver of old orthodoxies but also the maker of the new, and the prodder at the outer limits of received truths. The other was the jester, the professional fool, who had license to say on occasion for the purposes of amusement and release those things that bordered on lèse majesté and could not be uttered by others who were accounted serious men.

The fool and the schoolman are very far apart. No doubt you will ask whether there is not a contradiction between these two qualities of the intellectual, piety and playfulness. Certainly there is great tension between them; human beings are tissues of contradictions, and the life even of the intellectual is not logic, to borrow from Holmes, but experience. If you will think of the intellectuals you know, some will occur to you in whom the note of playfulness seems stronger, others who are predominantly pious. But I believe that in all intellectuals who have any stability as intellectuals—and that includes the angelic doctors of the middle ages—each of these characteristics is at some point qualified by the other. Perhaps the tensile strength of the intellectual can be gauged by his ability to maintain a fair equipoise between these aspects of himself. At one end of the scale, an excess of playfulness leads to triviality, to dilettantism, to cynicism, to the failure of all sustained creative effort. At the other, an excess of piety leads to fanaticism, to messianism, to ways of life that may be morally magnificent or morally mean, but in either case are not quite the ways of intellectualism. It is of the essence of the intellectual that he strikes a balance.

The widespread distrust of intellectuals in America reflects a tendency to depreciate their playfulness and distrust their piety. Ours is a society in which every form of play seems to be accepted by the majority except the play of the mind. It does not need to be explained to most people in America why sports, sex, liquor, gambling, motoring, and gourmandizing are all more or less legitimate forms of amusement for those who happen to find them amusing. The only forms of *mental* play that are similarly accepted and understood are those that do not involve the particular kinds of critical intelligence that are called into play by intellectualism; I refer, of course, to such highly cerebral amusements as bridge, chess, and the various forms of the crossword puzzle. I suppose that those who are inclined to find economic explanations will point out that the play of the mind, being the only kind that has not been susceptible to commercialization, has not been able to rally the support of a vested interest. I believe, however, that a large part of our common neglect of the humanities is attributable to the absence of a traditional and accepted leisure class which looks upon this kind of personal cultivation as a natural goal of life. The idea of leisured intellectual exercise, not put to the service of some external end, has been offensive to mass democracy. One of the best signs of this is the rhetoric adopted by college presidents and others who appeal to the public for support for education. Always these appeals tell how much education does for citizenship, science, technology, morals, or religion. Rarely do they point to the glories or pleasures of the human mind as an end in itself.

Just as the truly religious man is always a misfit in a secular society, so it is the piety of the intellectual that makes the greatest difficulties for him. Playfulness may be disdained or misunderstood, but it is not usually thought to be dangerous. Piety is another matter, for it is almost certain in the end to challenge something. It is the piety of the intellectual that puts iron into his nonconformism, if he happens to be a nonconformist. It is his piety that will make him, if anything does, a serious moral force in society. In our day the pressures operating against boldness in thought, as well as the sheer bureaucratization of intellectual life, bear hardest against the elements of piety in the intellectual. The temptation is very strong for some intellectuals to suppress the note of piety in themselves, to turn increasingly to the playful and generally more esoteric aspects of their work, to give up the office of spiritual leadership. Such self-suppression is psychologically and morally dangerous, and cannot be indulged in without paying a serious price. It does not become the intellectual, it is much too false to an important part of him, to give in altogether to playfulness and play the fool to the powerful. The jester had his prerogatives, to be sure, but we should also remember that he was usually a slave.

I have attempted thus far to define and elucidate intellectualism. Let me now explain what I mean by democracy when I say that in an important sense higher education and democracy have often been at odds. I do not mean by democracy simply the indispensable formal essentials of our society—constitutionalism, government by discussion, guarantees for the civil liberties of political minorities. These I neither challenge nor criticize; and I am sure that free higher education cannot in our time stand without them. But I do mean to criticize something that relates to the spirit of our politics, something that for lack of a better term I will call populistic democracy. Populistic democracy is neither progressive nor conservative, although it is in a perverse way equalitarian. Populistic democracy is the meeting ground, in fact, of the extreme left and the extreme right. It is government by or through the mass man, disguised behind the mask of an easy sentimentalization of the folk. It is the idea that anything done in the name of the people is *ipso facto* legitimate, even if the same act done in the name of a vested interest would be considered outrageous. It is the idea that a dozen postcards to a congressman from the wildest cranks should be given the same weight as a dozen reasoned letters from sober citizens. Transferred to the field of education, which is our concern, it is the idea that a university ought to cater to the needs of anybody who comes out of or pretends to represent the folk, whether or not he has any real need for or interest in the use of ideas. Put in terms of the state university, it is the idea that any graduate of the public high school should be accepted as a freshman no matter how dismal his prospects are as a student. Put in broader terms, it is the idea that any of the wants, real or fancied, of a mass society, should be absolute imperatives to its system of higher education.

We Americans are noted for our faith in both democracy and education. It has been our assumption that democracy and education, both being good, must be closely related and mutually reinforcing. We should have, it is argued, as much education and as much democracy as possible. It is also assumed that education serves democracy, and one of the most common shibboleths in our educational literature is the slogan "education for democracy." It is characteristically American that very few of us trouble to inquire whether democracy serves education. Whether it does indeed do so as fully and unambiguously as we might consider desirable is the question I insist we must face.

That there is any necessary relation between a vital system of higher education and a democratic society, one may readily deny on the basis of historical evidence. Two of the greatest periods in university history, that of the thirteenth and fourteenth centuries and that of the German universities in the nineteenth century, occurred in societies that were not notably democratic. In our own experience, I do not believe it incorrect to say that the great age of American university development from 1870 to 1910 was for the most part an age of political and economic oligarchy; and also that our finest universities and small colleges, by and large, have been those started and endowed by rich men and patronized chiefly by the upper classes.

All this does not mean, of course, that there is any necessary antagonism between democracy and higher education. Presumably there is no inherent or universally necessary opposition between a political democracy and a vital, respected, intellectually rich and alert university system. But I do wish to point out that there has been a historically persistent tension between our popular democracy and intellectualism that has been very sadly felt in the sphere of university and college life. The problem of how democracy and education can best serve and complement each other—as we would all, no doubt, like them to do—has not been nearly as constructively attacked as it might be for the simple reason that it has not often enough been candidly faced.

Long ago Tocqueville saw that the democratic culture that had emerged in the United States had brought with it pressures that were seriously hostile to the free use of the mind. He found that the democratic and equalitarian impulse had weakened the ability of the individual to resist the pressure of the opinion of the mass:

> The fact that the political laws of the Americans are such that the majority rules the community with sovereign sway, materially increases the power which that majority naturally exercises over the mind. For nothing is more customary in man than to recognise superior wisdom in the person of his oppressor. . . . The intellectual dominion of the greater number would probably be less absolute among a democratic people governed by a king than in the sphere of a pure democracy, but it will always be extremely absolute; and

by whatever political laws men are governed in the ages of equality, it may be foreseen that faith in public opinion may become a species of religion there, and the majority its ministering prophet.

Thus intellectual authority will be different, but it will not be diminished; and far from thinking that it will disappear, I augur that it may readily acquire too much preponderance and confine the action of private judgment within narrower limits than are suited either to the greatness or the happiness of the human race. In the principle of equality I very clearly discern two tendencies; the one leading the mind of every man to untried thoughts, the other inclined to prohibit him from thinking at all. And I perceive how, under the dominion of certain laws, democracy would extinguish that liberty of mind to which a democratic social condition is favourable; so that, after having broken all the bondage once imposed on it by ranks or by men, the human mind would be closely fettered to the general will of the greatest number.

Tocqueville found that in his time the most absolute monarchs in Europe were unable to prevent certain heretical notions from circulating through their dominions and even in their courts:

Such is not the case in America; as long as the majority is still undecided, discussion is carried on; but as soon as its decision is irrevocably pronounced, a submissive silence is observed, and the friends, as well as the opponents, of the measure unite in assenting to its propriety. The reason of this is perfectly clear: no monarch is so absolute as to combine all the powers of society in his own hands, and to conquer all opposition with the energy of a majority which is invested with the right of making and of executing the laws. . . .

I know no country in which there is so little true independence of mind and freedom of discussion as in America. In any constitutional state in Europe every sort of religious and political theory may be advocated and propagated abroad; for there is no country in Europe so subdued by any single authority as not to contain citizens who are ready to protect the man who raises his voice in the cause of truth from the consequences of his hardihood. If he is unfortunate enough to live under an absolute government, the people is upon his side; if he inhabits a free country, he may find a shelter behind the authority of the throne, if he require one. The aristocratic part of society supports him in some countries and the democracy in others. But in a nation where democratic institutions exist, organized like those of the United States, there is but one sole authority, one single element of strength and of success, with nothing beyond it.

While I do believe that Tocqueville was exaggerating the case of the United States in 1835, he pointed to the heart of the problem of majority tyranny over the soul. It is a problem that has grown still more acute in our own age, an age of mass communications and the mass man; for now the tyranny of the majority can be spread uniformly over the surface of a great nation otherwise well suited by size and diversity to a multiplicity of opinions, and it can be to some degree forged and manipulated from a few centers. If there were any horrors in that spontaneous, grass-roots variety of popular tyranny, as Tocqueville saw it, they must be greatly compounded by the artificial and centralized means of manipulation that the communications technology of our time has made possible.

But has there been substantial historical evidence in the development of American higher education for the validity of Tocqueville's fear of mass tyranny? I believe there is certainly enough evidence to warrant a reconsideration of our views of the relation between democracy and university culture. I propose to argue that while populistic democracy has been on the side of many educational improvements and reforms, it has often been aligned as sharply with forces tending to constrain freedom in higher education and to lower its devotion to intellectual goals.

Democracy and Higher Education

There may have been some popular upsurges in our history that have been auspicious for intellectualism in general, and for higher education in particular; but the popular movements that have been notable for their failure to understand the place of learning in our culture, or even on occasion for their hostility to it, are quite numerous. One of the first, the Great Awakening of the mid-eighteenth century, was notable for its hostility to a free and liberal-minded theological education such as was emerging in the older colleges; and while the Awakening must be in the end credited for enlarging the number of colleges, the goal sought at first in these enterprises was not an enhancement of the sphere of free learning but simply the creation of schools that would teach the right brand of theology. Jeffersonian democracy was not, on the whole, what I call populistic—at least not in its leadership. Its most constructive work in education, the founding of a liberal university in Virginia, was the work of aristocratic leadership. Jacksonian democracy, whatever its benefits in other areas, was identified with a widespread deterioration in the standards of professional education, masquerading under the ideology that easier access to these privileged areas of life must be made available to the people.

The founding of early state universities was badly hampered by popular hostility to advanced education that was held to be of use chiefly to the aristocrats, who, in fact, usually provided the basic impetus to the cultivation of the higher learning, whether in state-founded or private institutions. The movement that destroyed the old classical curriculum and made American universities, especially our state universities, the nurseries of all kinds of subintellectual practical skills of less than university grade was in its impetus very largely a popular movement; and while many of the consequences of that movement must be set to its credit as compensations, the undercurrent of vocationalism and anti-intellectualism was undeniable. Our history books tell us—to come toward our own time—that during the Populist-Bryan period the university professors who failed to accept the gold-standard economics of the well-to-do classes were often victims of outrageous interference; they do not usually trouble to tell us that when the Populists captured Kansas they raised hob with the University of Kansas in much the same way that they complained of so bitterly when the shoe was on the other foot. One of the most genuinely popular, and I believe democratic, political leaders in our history was William Jennings Bryan; and the sort of respect he showed for science and academic freedom is familiar to you all. His concept of the rights of the dissenting teacher reduces to his famous comment: "A man cannot demand a salary for saying what his employers do not want said."

My aim in stressing these facts is not to cast discredit upon popular democracy, whose merit in our whole scheme of things must be weighed by taking into account all its achievements as well as its deficiencies; I am simply trying to suggest that many of us have in the past made a mystique of the masses and have tended too much to attribute all the villainy in our world to the machinations of vested interests. I find it rather suggestive that the sole ruling group in our history that could be called a vested intellectual interest of any considerable power—I refer, of course, to the early Puritan clergy—has suffered the fate of being scandalously libelled by our "liberal" historians who have written in the tradition of V. L. Parrington.

Why this persistent tension between popular democracy and free higher learning? Obviously it is to some degree an aspect of social striving: a college education is a privilege that has not been open to all. While it can open up otherwise unavailable opportunities to the children of the less favored classes, it can also confirm the privileges of the upper classes by adding to those social, political, and economic advantages which are theirs by birth and family, the advantages of a superior education. Much of the early opposition to state universities was based precisely upon this argument. Why tax the poor, it was repeatedly asked, to educate the sons of the rich? No doubt there is such an element of resentment on the part of the lower classes for the privileges and attainments of the upper classes. But this, to my mind, will not get us very far in explaining why the United States in particular has been a happy hunting ground for anti-intellectualism. Class divisions exist in all western societies. Moreover, of all western nations, the United States has given by far the greatest proportion of its total population an opportunity to have a college education. In our more than 1700 colleges, for instance, we offer higher education, or a reasonable facsimile thereof, to about ten times as large a portion of our population as is done in the British Isles. Moreover, while we have always had our class stratification, class lines have been less sharp in the United States, and mobility between classes somewhat easier, than in European countries. By the showing of these facts, the United States should, in accordance with the class envy theory, have much less resentment of higher education as a source of privilege than any other country on the globe.

The evidence is all to the contrary, and this is enough to give us pause. It remains to be explained why, in a culture that seems to value education very highly, that has provided an enormous apparatus for the collegiate education of its youth, the genuine intellectual content of higher education is so little esteemed, why the teacher in general and the college professor in particular has so much less social status than he does almost anywhere else. I believe that the problem of status is, indeed, quite crucial, but that the situation cannot be explained in terms of broad assertions about the envy of manual for intellectual labor, the poor for the well-to-do, or the middle classes for the leisure classes. We must look to some of the unique factors of American historical development for our answers.

From the beginning the American people were confronted with rich resources, an immense task of continental settlement, and a shortage of labor. Their culture thus came to set a premium on practical achievement, the manipulation of material reality, and quick decision. It did not encourage reflection or a respect for the ultimate and irreducible disagreements of life. On the contrary, it suggested that it was to everyone's interest to arrive at a quick consensus, general enough to get the work done, that any disagreement on details was, in the light of the rich potentialities of organized work, unimportant. The American still sets a very high premium on such a consensus; he implicitly approaches broad intellectual and philosophical problems with that model of prompt decision in mind. "What can we agree on?" he wants to know. The wonderful persistence of irreducible differences of opinion, of the plurality of human dreams and perspectives, the exchange or contemplation of differences as an exercise in mutual understanding—all these are likely to be dark mysteries to him. He makes an ideology of normality; he asks not "What am I?" but "What is it customary and proper to be around here?" He *thinks* he is an individualist because he does truly and genuinely resent any rude coercive efforts to make him conform, but he cannot realize that he spends half his time trying to figure out how he can conform "spontaneously." One of the most appalling things in American life is the failure of those who prate most about individualism to develop any understanding of individuality. The loudest hosannas to individualism are sung by grim, regimented choruses.

The effects of our chronic shortage of labor have also struck quite directly at the teaching profession from grammar schools to graduate schools. Our historic abundance of land and other resources has continually beckoned to the inadequate resources of our labor power. The consequences of this for other areas of life than education have often been noted. Our agriculture, for instance, was dedicated from the outset to extensive and wasteful cultivation and rapid mechanization rather than to intensive and careful cultivation and farming as a settled way of life. Too little has been said about a similar trend in our educational history. I think we have cultivated man wastefully and mechanically too. The teaching of our young, for instance, has been all too regularly left over to those whose imaginations and energies were not absorbed—or not yet absorbed—in the more exciting and lucrative life of physical and economic conquest, or to those who for one reason or another were altogether incapable of entering upon it. Ichabod Crane was, I suppose, the archetype of the American schoolmaster— the timid misfit, the amiable failure, the man who was scared out of town; and when Brom Bones chased him that terrible night through Sleepy Hollow and frightened him almost to death with a pumpkin, he was passing upon him the characteristic comment of the American philistine upon the American teacher. If the teacher was not Ichabod Crane, then it was the lonely spinster, driven by desperation to take up teaching when all else failed. If not the spinster, it was the young man who was merely marking time, supporting himself before launching upon a more permanent career in business or some really serious profession. "The men teachers," wrote an observer of early Massachusetts schools—mind you, even Massachusetts schools—

> may be divided into three classes: (1) Those who think teaching is easier and possibly a little more remunerative than common labor. (2) Those who are acquiring, or have acquired, a good education, and who take up teaching as a temporary employment, either to earn money for pressing necessities or to give themselves time to choose deliberately a regular profession. (3) Those who, conscious of weakness, despair of distinction or even the means of subsistence by other

means. . . . They are often very young, they are constantly changing their employment, and consequently can have but little experience; and what is worse than all, they have never had any direct preparation for their profession. . . . No standard of attainments is fixed . . . so that any one *keeps school,* which is a very different thing from *teaching school,* who wishes to do it, and can persuade by herself or her friends, a small district to employ her. And this is not a very difficult matter, especially when the remuneration for the employment is so very trifling. . . . If a young man be moral enough to keep out of State prison, he will find no difficulty in getting approbation for a schoolmaster.

An exaggeration? Possibly. But in 1930–31, even after much had been done to improve standards of teacher training in the United States, the National Survey of the Education of Teachers showed that American teacher education, although only slightly inferior to that of England, was drastically inferior to that of France, Germany, and the Scandinavian countries. The teacher of a high school in the continental countries was found to be a much superior person, attracted by the relatively high social position, higher salaries, and advanced professional morale. And while I have been speaking here of the teaching profession below the university grade, most of what I have said will apply almost as well to American colleges down at least to the last three decades of the nineteenth century.

Let us look for a moment at those old colleges and the situation of their faculties. One of the first things that any observer of American higher education is struck by is the fact that the American professoriat is the only profession in the United States that is governed by laymen. Outside the continent of North America university faculties are nowhere governed, as they are here, by lay boards of trustees. Of course it is not easy to say whether the American professor lacks status because he is not self-governing or whether he has failed to get self-government in part because he lacks status. Genetically, however, it is not too difficult to explain how the curse of absentee government came to afflict American education. American colleges were called into existence before the community had the full means to support them amply, and indeed before there was a body of learned men professionally given to teaching. The great independent, self-governing universities of the middle ages, which established the pattern for early modern university government, came into existence only where there were well-established bodies of students and masters; they took their political form from the guild model of corporate self-control and the church's model of independence from the power of the state. The American colleges were founded in a Protestant milieu, which, no longer accepting the principles of hierarchy and corporate independence, had introduced lay government of churches. From this to lay government of colleges was a natural step, made the more natural by the fact that the greater part of the teaching personnel in early American colleges, for over a century and a half, consisted of young tutors, recent graduates, who were merely waiting and studying preparatory to entering the ministry. These men usually had no permanent interest in teaching as a profession, no permanent stake in its welfare. And they were considered by the philanthropic non-teachers who founded the colleges to be too young and too transient to be entrusted with the task of governing the colleges and managing their resources. Hence governmental powers were kept in the hands of trustees. The only working member of the college who held the full stature of a master of university learning was the president who, in the absence of the trustees, took over a larger and larger share of the task of determining college policy. Hence to this day the only person in the American community who enjoys a measure of prestige and respect comparable to that enjoyed by the university professor in most countries of Europe is our college or university president. Needless to say, with the development of the modern university, a great deal of the power to govern academic affairs has informally passed into the hands of faculties. But in almost all cases, such powers are delegated and may be legally retaken on any issue at any time by trustees. While few American university professors would argue for full self-government at this date, the legal inability of the American academic community to govern itself in matters bearing on academic freedom and tenure is a major disability in its struggle against the external forces of anti-intellectualism.

It may also be said in passing that the historic lack of prestige within the American academic community has tended to feed on itself. I am sure that no man anywhere whose primary desire is for a large share of the material goods of life enters the teaching profession with the idea that it will supply them with any abundance. He enters it because of other inducements: because he wants to pursue knowledge, because he values leisure (he will be lucky if he gets it), because he likes the idea of living in an academic community, or because of the prestige of the office. But American academic life, having so little prestige to offer, has failed to recruit a very large percentage of its professorial personnel from the upper classes, as does the professoriat in England or on the continent. The American college professor is characteristically drawn from the lower middle classes. I hope you will not imagine that I am being snobbish when I argue that this has been a signal disadvantage both to the freedom and the intellectualism of the academic community. Logan Wilson, in his study of *The Academic Man* in the United States, has pointed out that the recruit from the lower middle classes often comes from a background of cultural poverty in which, of necessity, the view taken of most things has to be profoundly affected by their material efficacy. I should also add that a man who comes from a well-established family with secure connections, and has perhaps in addition some personal resources to draw on, can confront the problems of free expression with far greater boldness than the man who feels that he must cling to his academic job at all costs. I have been impressed, in studying the development of a certain measure of liberalism in the American colleges of the eighteenth century, by the important role played by men who came to academic life from secure positions of social prestige, either in great commercial families or the ministry. One of the boldest men in early academic life was Professor John Winthrop, the great Harvard astronomer, and no little part of his boldness rested upon the security derived from the fact that he was, after all, a Winthrop in Massachusetts.

The low prestige of the professor in America was matched by the low prestige of the college itself. At the end of the eighteenth century and the beginning of the nineteenth, as the American population broke through the Allegheny mountains and began to spread across the continent, a process of educational fragmentation began which still profoundly afflicts our educational system. Every sect of Protestants wanted to have a little college to service every part of a great country. Localities thought that a community college would be good for local development. Parents welcomed the opportunity to educate their sons near at home in small schools whose annual tuition was often not much larger than the cost of transportation to a distant and perhaps more formidable seat of learning. They were advised, too, that the country college was socially democratic and that it protected their offspring from the corrupting atmosphere of great cities. This passion for breaking up the educational system into small units destroyed much of the potential strength and prestige of the old college. Where English colleges had clustered at a few university centers, American colleges were strewn across three thousand miles of continent. Innumerable colleges failed because they were so flimsily launched. Many that survived were much too tiny to maintain decent teaching staffs and adequate educational standards. It became a commonplace among serious educators before the Civil War that the American college was not, in the terms of international educational standards, a college at all, but a closer equivalent to the German gymnasium, the French lycée, the English public school.

After a time the old college became the butt of a great deal of criticism. It was, of course, devoted chiefly to the inherited classical curriculum, featuring Latin, Greek, and mathematics. This kind of schooling was increasingly held to be unadapted to the needs of American business, technology, and agriculture. It was held, and quite correctly, to be too limited and rigid to be adequate to the growing fund of human knowledge. Between the educational reformers, who were dissatisfied with the low level of work that the existing colleges were unable to transcend, and the practical reformers, who wanted to make American higher education work for the community in a clearer and more easily definable way, a curiously mixed transformation was finally effected in the last half of the nineteenth century. Universities, both state and private, were at last reared on adequate foundations; graduate and professional schools were created; schools of agriculture and engineering were founded; the curriculum was broadened; and the elective system was introduced.

Within only a few decades a curriculum system that had been too tight and too rigid was made too loose and too sprawling. All kinds of practical skills that had neither professional nor intellectual stature—no matter how necessary they might be to the community—were taught, or presumed to be taught, at universities. The president of a great state university was proud to say: "The state universities hold that there is no intellectual service too undignified for them to perform." Vast numbers of students without notable intellectual interests or skills flocked to the colleges and universities, availed themselves freely of the multitude of elective courses with little or no intellectual content, and passed out into the world with padded degrees. Much of the information thus inculcated may be thought to have no place in any system of formal education. A still larger part belongs to purely technical and mechanical education of the sort that can be properly taught in formal education but is not elsewhere considered proper to a university—the sort of thing that on the continent of Europe is to be found among the offerings of the German *technische Hochschule* and its many counterparts in other countries.

Now all this has taken place at serious cost to intellectualism. It is possible, of course, to argue that the professor of some field of pure learning is not interfered with in the pursuit of his work simply because his colleague in the school of agriculture is busy teaching farmers how to raise healthy pigs. Theoretically, no; but those who are familiar with the problems of university administration and finance know that these things have a way of pulling against or tripping over each other; and that when all kinds of skills of various levels are jumbled together and taught in one institution, the hierarchy of values that places intellectual accomplishment at the top, as one would expect to do in a university, is somehow broken and destroyed. Thus the universities, that we might have expected to stand as solid barriers against the undercurrents of

American anti-intellectualism, have actually intensified the push of the stream. How they could have resisted it, I do not honestly know. For one thing, our system of higher education is, unlike all the other systems in the world, a system of mass education, that today enrolls about 3,000,000 people. In a way, that is a preposterous figure, and I suppose it is altogether unreasonable to expect that students in such numbers will all get anything that could be called a common liberal education. All kinds of things pass for a college education in this country and will no doubt continue to do so for a long time to come. The difficulty is that we now have an educational system which rarely produces educators who will themselves dare to defend an education wholeheartedly directed to the goal of increasing intellectual power. The famous report of the President's Commission on Higher Education published in 1948—a report prepared by a representative group of American educators and laymen interested in education—had this to say on the subject:

> We shall be denying educational opportunity to many young people as long as we maintain the present orientation of higher education toward verbal skills and intellectual interest. Many young people have abilities of a different kind, and they cannot receive "education commensurate with their native capacities" in colleges and universities that recognize only one kind of educable intelligence.
> Traditionally the colleges have sifted out as their special clientele persons possessing verbal aptitudes and a capacity for grasping abstractions. But many other aptitudes—such as social sensitivity and versatility, artistic ability, motor skill and dexterity, and mechanical aptitude and ingenuity—also should be cultivated in a society depending, as ours does, on the minute division of labor and at the same time upon the orchestration of an enormous variety of talents.

I can think of no more shameful capitulation than this to the canons of anti-intellectualism: a group of educators urging that our de-intellectualized colleges become still more de-intellectualized by giving up their alleged preoccupation with "verbal aptitudes" and "a capacity for grasping abstractions"—that is, the power to think and to express thought—for a motley batch of skills which, however valuable, one does not have to go to college to learn; for "social sensitivity" that no doubt includes ballroom dancing and parlor games; for "motor skill and dexterity" that must clearly mean athletics if it does not mean the ability to wash dishes without dropping them; and for "mechanical aptitude and ingenuity" that may very well mean the ability to drive and repair an automobile. Worthy skills every single one of them, and no doubt a necessary part of our life; but why they have to be acquired in something that calls itself a college or university the Commission, whose business was supposed to be with *higher* education, did not take the trouble to explain. No doubt its members did not feel themselves to be on the defensive, for they were expressing the dominant point of view in American society.

At the top of our educational system this attitude threatens to weaken whatever intellectualism we have. At lower levels, in our grammar and high schools, it threatens to wipe out literacy altogether in the name of "progressive education" or education for "life adjustment." If you think I exaggerate, listen to the principal of a junior high school in Urbana, Illinois, speaking to a meeting of the National Association of Secondary-School Principals:

> Through the years we've built a sort of halo around reading, writing, and arithmetic. We've said they were for everybody . . . rich and poor, brilliant and not-so-mentally endowed, ones who liked them and those who failed to go for them. Teacher has said that these were something "everyone should learn." The principal has remarked, "All educated people know how to write, spell, and read." When some child declared a dislike for a sacred subject, he was warned that, if he failed to master it, he would grow up to be a so-and-so.
>
> The Three R's for All Children and All Children for the Three R's! That was it.
>
> We've made some progress in getting rid of the slogan. But every now and then some mother with a Phi Beta Kappa award or some employer who has hired a girl who can't spell stirs up a fuss about the schools . . . and ground is lost. . . .
>
> When we come to the realization that not every child has to read, figure, write, and spell . . . that many of them either cannot or will not master these chores . . . then we shall be on the road to improving the junior high curriculum.
>
> Between this day and that a lot of selling must take place. But it's coming. We shall some day accept the thought that it is just as illogical to assume that every boy must be able to read as it is that each one must be able to perform on a violin, that it is no more reasonable to require that each girl shall spell well than it is that each one shall bake a good cherry pie. . . .
>
> When adults finally realize that fact, everyone will be happier . . . and schools will be nicer places in which to live. . . .

Of course this speaker, unlike the President's Commission, does not seem to be entirely in harmony with the prevailing sentiments of the country—at least, not yet; for it is clear that he thinks himself to be a visionary whose notions are considerably in advance of the times but whose high ideals for the future of illiteracy will some fine day be realized. I must ask you, however, to try to envisage the minds of a generation of young Americans who receive their lower education under men of this stamp and their higher education under a regime fully conforming to the President's Commission's disdain for verbal aptitudes and abstractions.

What is it, I think we may properly ask, that brings our nation's educators to such depressing disavowals of the fundamentally intellectual purposes of education? Much the same thing, I believe, that has them cringing before the onslaughts of politicians who are beyond the pale of moral decency—and that is the lack of a self-confident dedication to the life of the mind. What the root of that failure of self-confidence is, no one really knows; but I venture to suggest that it has a great deal to do with our false piety for populistic democracy, our sense of guilt at daring to suggest that there is anything wrong with the mob, even when a large part of it has obviously been whipped up by demagogues to a state of frantic suspicion of everything it does not care to understand. I think it would help us all morally, even if it would do nothing else, to face the fact that the very idea of intellectualism implies an elite of some kind—not, to be sure, a ruthless elite with special privileges or powers, but simply a group of people who have interests not shared by everyone in the community and whose very special interest is in freedom. Not everyone really wants to belong to that elite. But the primary fact is that this elite must maintain a certain spiritual autonomy in defining its own standards. I am not optimistic enough to believe that in any calculable future the rest of society can be brought to recognize that intellectuals have their own rights and interests, not special rights or privileged interests, but of the same sort that any other group has. What the intellectual community can do is what any group of sensible people will do whose values are under attack—and that is not to try to find some plausible reason for abandoning those values because they are not shared by the majority; and not to try to convince themselves that they really agree with the majority after all—but to show cohesion and firmness under fire, until the point has been reached when it is no longer profitable to encroach upon them.

This world will never be governed by intellectuals—it may rest assured. But *we* must be assured, too, that intellectuals will not be altogether governed by this world, that they maintain their piety, their long-standing allegiance to the world of spiritual values to which they should belong. Otherwise there will be no intellectuals, at least not above ground. And societies in which the intellectuals have been driven underground, as we have had occasion to see in our own time, are societies in which even the anti-intellectuals are unhappy.

Blueprint for a Silver Age:
Notes On a Visit To America
Cyril Connolly

THURSDAY, 28 NOVEMBER. Nantucket light. In cold, sunny afternoon the bright red lightship bobbing to starboard is the first sign that our ten-day prep-school voyage is coming to an end; we are as happy as the discoverers of Virginia in 1584. "We found shoal water, where we smelt so sweet and so strong a smell, as if we had been in the midst of some delicate garden abounding with all kind of odoriferous flowers, by which we were assured that the land could not be far distant." No more dull dormitory life, eight to a cabin, no hurried monotonous meals (without drink, for our ship, the *Highland Governess,* is dry), no more scrambling for chairs, or searching for conversation, no more the pitching and tossing of the battered old bureaucrappy troopship over the endless empty heaving dishwater of the autumn Atlantic. Tomorrow our personalities will be handed back to us. . . .

To bed excited, with lights and lighthouses visible, and in the distance the Long Island beaches. All the voyage an immense euphoria about U. S. A., Baedeker alternating with Baudelaire: prospect of seeing California and far Southwest! Europe seems infinitely remote; England like a week-end cottage which one has abandoned with all the washing-up undone. I understand the New World motif. Actuality, the ideal of inhabiting a continuous present.

FRIDAY: Up at six to see New York in the darkness—sunrise, the Narrows, the first houses, the ferries, *"l'aurore rose et verte,"* the Statue of Liberty, skyscrapers in fog, general impression much more European than I had expected. Interminable wait before going ashore during which the passengers all look exactly as they did on the first day—"their sweating selves, but worse." Off about 12:30, then through customs and in taxi to hotel; my driver asks—and gets—six dollars. Tony and Wystan are there and we go off to lunch to a restaurant of my choice, exotic and rather bad; but Third Avenue, red and raffish, has a fascinating Continental charm. Auden warns us of the perils of the big city, he seems obsessed with hold-ups, the proper use of the subway system, and jumping to it at the traffic lights; his welcome is like that of the town mouse to the country mouse in the Disney film. I discover only later that his battle with the traffic lights is a kind of personal obsession with the machine age, a challenge to his desire to pass efficiently in the crowd. Hugging our wallets tightly and plunging over the crossings we proceed in short rushes to the Holliday bookshop, an oasis where carefully chosen books are sold like hand-made cushions; here Wystan introduces the two new mice and leaves us, with instructions on how to take the subway back.

That evening an elaborate dinner with Peter at Voisin's, much-anticipated on the *Highland Governess* (disappointing except for avocado pears). The new mice compare notes. Peter says the U. S. A. is a place where only the very rich can be the least different from anyone else, but where the poor are not crushed and stunted (as in England, where the upper class is twice as tall as the lower). Here, he said, the poor are picturesque and often beautiful—the true creators of the American dream—and that there was also great poetry about the country when one traveled over it. On the other hand it was awful seeing nothing but copies—of buildings, houses, furniture, pictures—and where the originals were in private hands they gave no intimacy. I found the skyscrapers depressing, a huge black ferro-concrete architecture of necessity shutting out the light from the treeless streets.

> Whose constant care is not to please
> But to remind of our, and Adam's curse
> And that, to be restored, our sickness must grow worse.

SATURDAY. To the Lafayette after a stroll round delicious Washington Square, which in the morning sun considerably revives me from the gloomy thoughts of the night before, sleepless beside the sizzling radiator. Greenwich Village, which reminds me more and more of Soho, is still cheap, and apparently not quite spoilt, "the one place in New York where different income groups are still mixed up, and where the queers and misfits from the Middle West can all find sanctuary."

"There is an immense cleavage here," says Tony at lunch, "between the intellectuals and everyone else, who are really quite uninterested in books, though they like to keep up with the best sellers. Intellectuals thus have to join political movements or attach themselves to causes or become dons, for they cannot otherwise survive. They become overserious, 'culture' requires one hundred per cent efficiency, it is a whole-time business, everyone becomes extremely bellicose and erudite; publishers work so hard that even they have no time for pleasure, and without pleasures the intellectual becomes uncivilized, a pedantic variation of the business man."

After lunch to the top of Rockefeller Center. Asked the bald elevator boy on the last lap why we were told to face outward. He made no reply at first, then broke down into helpless laughter; the only words to come from him were, "It's all so silly"—mountain sickness, perhaps. The view was the first beautiful thing I had seen in New York, where one can go for weeks without the knowledge of being surrounded by water. If one need never descend below the fortieth floor New York would seem the most beautiful city in the world, its skies and cloud-scapes are tremendous, its Southern latitude is revealed only in its light (for vegetation and architecture are strictly Northern); here one can take in the Hudson, the East River, the midtown and downtown colonies of skyscrapers, Central Park and the magnificent new bridges and curving arterial highways, and watch here the evening miracle, the lights going on over all these frowning termitaries against a sky of royal-blue velvet only to be paralleled in Lisbon or Palermo. A Southern city, with a Southern pullulation of life, yet with a Northern winter imposing a control; the whole Nordic energy and sanity of living crisply enforcing its authority for three of the four seasons on the violet-airy babel of tongues and races; this tension gives New York its unique concentration and makes it the supreme metropolis of the present.

Dinner with Auden's friend C. At last the luxury of poverty; stairs, no lift, leaking arm-chairs, a bed-sitting-room with bath-kitchenette curtained off, guests with European teeth (who was it said that Americans have no faces?), a gramophone library, untidy books not pre-served in cardboard coffins, an incompetent gas stove—an exquisite dinner cooked and served by C. Clam juice mixed with chicken broth, chops with a sauce and lima beans, liederkranz cheese and pumper-nickel, dry Californian wine. Argument afterward about poetry inter-spersed with selections from Wystan's favorite operas. They are many. Much conversation about the U. S., and W. continues to propound his point of view. Though very pro-British (his bedside bible remains a work on the mineralogy of the Lake District compiled by a friend of his father's), he reverts always to the same argument: that a writer needs complete anonymity, he must break away from the European literary "happy family" with its family love and jokes and jealousies and he must reconsider all the family values. Possibly he could do this in any large impersonal society, but only in America is it so easy for the anonymous immigrant to make money. He is, of course, extremely lonely, but then so is every American; "you have no idea," he says, "how lonely even the married are." I make the inevitable point that surely it is important to live in attractive surroundings, and in New York (where all want to live) only the rich can afford them. Why live an exile in a black slum, looking out on a fire-escape, in a city which is intolerable in winter and summer, when for the same money one might flourish in Regent's Park or on the Ile Saint Louis? But then, I imagine Auden replying, you would at once have the family all about you, and he concentrates on my return journey to Washington Square. Walking back from the subway station at two in the morning I find a second-hand bookstore open all night in West Eighth Street, I go in and buy more Cummings; to purchase early works of Cummings in the small hours, in the heart of

the little barbarous Greenwich perfumed fake

and march home with them in the frosty night, while the tugs hoot and central heating plants under the long black street puff away through its many manholes like geysers on the moon, that is to enjoy that anonymous urban civilization that Auden has chosen, and of which Baudelaire dreamed and despaired.

Long past diary-keeping now, I am slave of telephone and engagement book. Europe is a dream, and Auden's anonymity equally remote. We are plunged in New York literary life and try to analyze the swirl and eddy of that vigorous, intricate, cordial group of groupings. America is not Europe, in neither its places nor its people nor its values, and it is only by making the most desperate adjustment that a true European writer can remain himself here. Thus in the United States literature is fighting a losing battle against the Book Business which we can hardly comprehend. The crucial factor is the high cost of book production, which renders the printing of small editions (under 10,000) uneconomic; the tendency is therefore to go all out for the best seller and, with a constant eye on Hollywood, to spend immense sums on publicity to bring about one of these jackpots. But even without Hollywood there are large sums to be made from book-of-the-month clubs, cheap pulp editions, serial rights, and so the result of this pressure is a transformation of the literary scene into mass production. The American public are cajoled into reading the book of the month, and only the book of the month, and for that month only. Last year's book is as unfashionable as last year's car.

The standard of living among publishers is also ridiculously high; huge offices among skyscrapers employ armies of bright and competitive young men. I know of one whose lawyers forbade him to start a business of his own as his capital was but a hundred thousand dollars. The hunt for young authors who, while maintaining a prestige value (with a rôle for Ingrid Bergman), may yet somehow win the coveted jackpot, is feverish and incessant. Last year's authors (most of the names that have just reached England) are pushed aside and this year's—the novelist Jean Stafford, her poet husband Robert Lowell, or the dark horse, Truman Capote—are invariably mentioned. They may be quite unread, but their names, like a new issue on the market,

are constantly on the lips of those in the know. "Get Capote"—at this
minute the words are resounding on many a sixtieth floor, and "get him"
of course means make him and break him, smother him with laurels
and then vent on him the obscure hatred inherent in the notion of another's superiority.

"In Ngoio, a province of the ancient kingdom of the Congo," Frazer
relates, "the rule obtains that the chief who assumes the cap of sov-
ereignty is always killed on the night after his coronation." But in civilized Ngoio the throne is generally vacant. America is the one country
(greatly to its credit) where an author can still make a fortune for life
from one book; it is also the country where everyone is obsessed with
that idea, where publishers live like stockbrokers, and where authors,
like film stars, are condemned to meditate from minute to minute on
last year's income tax, next week's publicity. It is all part of the American tragedy—that, in the one remaining country where necessities are
cheap, where a room and food and wine and clothes and cigarettes
and travel are within everyone's reach, to be poor is still disgraceful.

The American way of life is one of the most effective the world has
known, but about the end of life Americans are more in the dark than
any people since the Gauls of Tacitus. What is the American way?

It may be summed up as a creed which is partly the effect of climate, partly of vitamins and calories, partly of pioneer experiences,
partly of the inherited memory of what was bad in Europe. The
American way assumes a world without God, yet a world in which
happiness is obtainable, but obtainable only through a constant
exertion of the will toward a practical goal and of the mind toward
solution of present problems. Riches and success are the outward
signs that this goal is being attained, that the human organism is
making full use of its energy and faculties; a whispering of wives,
expert at farewell (three is the lucky number), indicates that the
proper stages on the journey are being reached, and handsome,
healthy, indifferent children are present to carry on when the wage-
earner passes over; any moments of disquieting leisure are rendered
innocuous by extroverted social activities with colleagues of similar
status and their families, or sent flying by alcohol. The esteem of
society is enormously important and can only be held by a decent,
kindly, and acquisitive way of living. Courage, humor, hard work,
and the affectionate co-operation of uncles and cousins make endurable
the darker side: sickness, insolvency, hangovers, death, and mother.

Seldom has a more harmless or profitable philosophy of life been
evolved, a more resolute opponent of art, remorse, and introspection,
or one further removed from the futile European speculation about
the Soul or the Past, the moping about sin and death, the clinging to

moribund methods, ideals, relationships, the pangs of ennui. If one were but permitted to take human beings at their own valuation, the American way would seem the most desirable solution to our predicament, for it offers a full life built round the notions of freedom, independence, hard work, and the family; the personality without a thought stoically working itself out through action.

But the end? What is old age in America? After sixty, where do old people vanish? Why are the bustling battalions of unwanted Moms so elegantly pathetic? And the rich who have pocketed their winnings, why are they so glum? The rich in America are very aware of civilization, at the head of one of the most conscientious societies which the world has seen, and still largely owners of the means of production; yet in some way they appear grimly on the defensive. Public opinion is not behind this solemn patriciate as it is behind the boisterous and rising class. Cities like Boston and Philadelphia, which contain large bodies of rich rentiers living on inherited wealth but losing access to political power, are going off the boil, becoming august backwaters. Of all the Eastern cities only New York and perhaps Washington are on the upgrade, while the evolutionary dynamism of the "way" continues to expand in California and the far Northwest. The age of the Morgans, the Vanderbilts, the Mellons is over; the rich can do nothing with their money but give it away, and try to finance that artistic renaissance which their grandfathers by their exclusive cult of gold bricks and museum pieces did so much to destroy.

And what is this American "way," in reality, but forty years' drudgery in an office while the divorced wives play bridge together and the children drift apart? What is the getting of money but a constant source of ulcers and anxiety, till apoplexy or heart failure clamp down? And why does alcohol, which should oil the wheels of intercourse, so flood and clog them that there is a drunk in each so respectable family? And why the immense rush to psychiatry, the high rate of madness and suicide? Why, after midnight, do so many Americans fight or weep? Grown up while still a child, middle-aged at thirty, a boy only among his cronies of the golf course or the lunch club, coffined or cremated at about sixty-three, the American business male with his forceful, friendly, unlined face carries within him a dustbowl of despair which renders him far more endearing and closer to Europe than his dutiful efforts to conceal it. Action, often violent and destructive, not contemplation, is his remedy, but his awareness of the tragic human predicament goes very deep.

This leads us on to one of the finest traits in American character. At a time when the American way, backed by American resources, has made the country into the greatest power the world has known, there has never been more doubting and questioning of the purpose of the American process; the higher up one goes the more searching becomes this self-criticism, the deeper the thirst for a valid mystique of humanity. Those who rule America, who formulate its foreign policy and form its opinion, are enormously conscious of their responsibility and of the total inadequacy of the crude material philosophy of life in which they grew up. The bloody-minded, the smug, the imperialist, the fascist, are in a minority. Seldom, in fact, has an unwilling world been forced to tolerate, through its own folly, a more unwilling master.

The New York scene reveals many traces of this unrest. Insecurity reigns. Almost everyone hates his job. Psychiatrists of all schools are as common as monks in the Thebaid. "Who is your analyst?" will disarm any interviewer; books on how to be happy, how to attain peace of mind, how to win friends and influence people, how to breathe, how to achieve a cheap sentimental humanism at other people's expense, how to become a Chinaman like Lin Yu-tang and make a lot of money, how to be a B'hai or breed chickens (*The Ego and I*) all sell in millions. Religious houses of retreat merge imperceptibly into disintoxication clinics and private mental homes for the victims of traffic lights and nervous breakdowns. "Alcoholics Anonymous" slink like house detectives around the literary cocktail parties.

A most interesting phenomenon is the state of mind apparent in *Time, Life,* the *New Yorker,* and similar magazines. Thus *Life,* with its enormous circulation, comes out with excellently written leading articles on the dearth of tragedy in American literature or the meaning of suffering, and a closer acquaintance reveals them to be staffed by some of the most interesting and sensitive minds in that insensitive city.

It is easy to make fun of these three papers, but in fact they are not funny. Although they have very large circulations indeed, they only just miss being completely honorable and serious journals, in fact "highbrow." Hence the particular nemesis, ordeal by shiny paper, of those who manage them; they work very hard, and deliver almost the best work of which they are capable. But the gap is never quite closed between the public and the highbrow writer, because the American organism is not quite healthy. I mention this at some length because it indicates how very nearly New York has achieved the ideal of a humanist society, where the best of which an artist is capable is desired by the greatest number. Thurber's drawings, Hersey's *Hiroshima,* the essays of Edmund Wilson or Mary McCarthy, *Time's* anonymous reviews, show that occasionally the gap is closed; when it is closed permanently the dream will be near fulfillment.

But these anxiety-forming predicaments (*Time*-stomach is a common trouble) are for those who live in New York and have to earn their living. To the visiting noncompetitive European all is unending delight. The shops, the bars, the women, the faces in the street, the excellent and innumerable restaurants, the glitter of Twenty-One, the old-world lethargy of the Lafayette, the hazy views of the East River or Central Park over tea in some apartment at the magic hour when the concrete icebergs suddenly flare up; the impressionist pictures in one house, the exotic trees or bamboo furniture in another, the chink of "old-fash-ioneds" with their little glass pestles, the divine glories—Egyptian, Etruscan, French—of the Metropolitan Museum, the felicitous con-temporary assertion of the Museum of Modern Art, the snow, the sea-breezes, the late suppers with the Partisans, the reelings-home down the black steam-spitting canyons, the Christmas trees lit up beside the licorice ribbons of cars on Park Avenue, the Gotham Book Mart, the shabby cosiness of the Village, all go to form an unforgettable picture of what a city ought to be: that is, continuously insolent and alive, a place where one can buy a book or meet a friend at any hour of the day or night, where every language is spoken and xenophobia is un-known, where every purse and appetite is catered for, where every street and every quarter with the people who inhabit them are fulfilling their function, not slipping back into apathy, indifference, decay. If Paris is the setting for a romance, New York is the perfect city in which to get over one, to get over anything. Here the lost *douceur de vivre* is forgotten and the intoxication of living takes its place.

What is this intoxication? First, health. The American diet is energy-producing. Health is not just the absence of disease but a positive phys-ical sensation. The European, his voice dropping a tone every day, finds himself growing stouter, balder, more extroverted and aggressive, con-scious of a place in what is still, despite lip-service, a noisily masculine society. Then there is the sensation of belonging to a great nation in its present prosperous period of triumph. But in addition to "feeling good" the Americans are actively generous and kind, and it is this pro-fusion of civilities which ravishes the visitor. American hosts are not only thoughtful; it is almost dangerous to express a wish before them, to such unobtrusive lengths will they go to fulfill it. American hostesses bring their ingrained perfectionism into daily living. It is a society more formal, more painstaking, more glamorous, and more charitable than our poor old bitter, battered, pennywise European equivalent— one may pine inevitably for a whiff of honest English malice, out-spokenness, and bad manners; but one should not be proud of such nos-talgias—for we have largely forgotten the degree to which leisure, money, good will, and taste can still make life agreeable.

One thing alone seems to me impossible in New York—to write well. (My literary output over nine weeks amounted to a two-page letter.)

Not because the whirl and pleasurable bustle of the gregarious life built around writing is so irresistible, not because it is almost impossible to find a quiet room near a tree, or to stay in of an evening, not because intelligent conversation with a kindred spirit is hard to come by (it is not), but because this glowing, blooming, stimulating material perfection overexcites the mind, causing it to precipitate into wit and conversation those ideas which might set into literature. Wit and wisecrack, not art, are the thorny flowers on this rocky island, this concrete Capri; they call the tune for which our proud new bass is lent us. "Yah," one may say instead of "yes," but when "fabulous," "for Chris' sakes," "it stinks," "way off the beam," and "Bourbon over ice" roar off our lips, when one notices with distaste the Europeanism of others—it's time for flight, for dripping plane-trees, misty mornings, the grizzling circle of hypercritical friends, the fecund London inertia where nothing stirs but the soul.

What are the alternatives? One may stay on and coarsen—many English writers do—into shapely executives or Park Avenue brandy philosophers; one can fight like Auden for privacy and isolation, or grow bitter and Fitzrovian[1] in the "Village atmosphere," or one can try elsewhere. Cape Cod and Connecticut have their devotees, but these havens are the rewards of success, not its incubators. Boston, last stronghold of a leisured class, offers a select enlightenment of which a contemporary Englishman is just downright unworthy. Washington has immense charm, the streets of Georgetown with their ilexes and magnolias and little white boxes are like corners of Chelsea or Exeter, but a political nexus offers few resources to the artist who is outside the administration, and the lovely surroundings (the shores of the Chesapeake Bay and its tributaries form the most insidiously appealing of all American landscapes to the homesick European) are not places in which he can hope to earn a living.

Let us try California. The night plane circles round La Guardia, leaves behind the icy water of the Sound and that sinister Stonehenge of economic man, the Rockefeller Center, to disappear over the Middle West. Vast rectangles of light occasionally indicate Chicago or some other well-planned city till at six in the morning we ground in the snow of Omaha. As it grows light the snowfields over the whole agricultural region of the Middle West grow more intricate, the Great Plains give way to the Bad Lands, poison ivy to poison oak, the sinuosities of the Platte Rivers to the High Plains, the mountains of Wyoming, the Continental Divide. All semblance of European structure vanishes; Salt Lake appears as a radiant lunar landscape in the wan sunshine, the

---

[1] Fitzrovian—decayed Artists' Quarter between Soho and Bloomsbury.—S.B.

Great Salt Lake desert glistening beyond it, fading into other deserts, last, into the formidable Carson Sink. It is hard to picture the immense desolation of the West in winter, the wilderness of snow over fifteen hundred miles of plateau and mountain, till suddenly, unfrozen, among the pine woods of the Rockies a blue alpine lake appears, Lake Tahoe, and beyond a great glowing explosion of orange sky, woods without snow, green hills with no trace of winter, the darker patches of citrus orchard, the line of irrigation canals, the Sacramento Valley—California and the enormous pale Pacific.

San Francisco is a city of charming people, hideous buildings, mostly erected after the earthquake in the style of 1910, with a large China-town in which everything is fake—except the Chinese—with a tricky humid climate (though sunny in winter), and a maddening indecision in the vegetation—which can never decide if it belongs to the North or to the South and achieves a Bournemouth compromise. The site is fantastically beautiful, the orange bridge, the seven hills, the white houses, the waterside suburbs across the Golden Gate give it a lovely strangeness, the sunset view from the "Top of the Mark" is unique—but the buildings lack all dignity and flavor. Yet San Francisco and its surroundings, Marin County, Berkeley, Sausalito with its three climates, San Mateo where lemon and birch tree grow together, probably represent the most attractive all-the-year-round alternative to Europe which the world can provide. If I were an escapist—that is, rather more determined to escape—I would fly from the delirium and coma of the countries I love and settle in central California. There Europe is twice as far as from New York which itself is so remote that it becomes a kind of Europe, a delicious object of the annual holiday, yet the temperate European climate and way of life still prevail.

A hundred miles to the south is some of the loveliest country I have ever seen, the Monterey peninsula and the redwood hills of Big Sur. At Monterey the Pacific for once imitates the Mediterranean, the vast cold treacherous sail-less ocean flows in sunny, sandy coves round the pine and cypress woods of the peninsula, the enormous sea-lions bark all night off the shore. South of Carmel the wild Santa Lucia mountains with their forests of evergreen oak and holly roll southward for two hundred miles of green Dorset downs, five thousand feet high. Here the Pacific roars at the foot of inky cliffs, pouring in immense black strands of weed, whose roots bob like human heads, while out to sea the whales, drifting south in pairs, spout lazily by. On one of these cliffs surrounded by editions of Rimbaud lives Henry Miller with his wife and child. His house is a romantic shack, built by the convicts while making the road, for which he pays six dollars rent a month. A mile or so further is a hot open-air sulphur bath. Once a week the groceries come out from Carmel. There is some fog in winter, but generally it is sunny. The sea is there, the mountains, and a bathing pool in the redwood forest. Here is one writer who has solved the problem of how to live happily in America without hacking, writing unstintingly of himself and the Cosmos, decently impervious to this remote grandiose wilderness of mountain and sea.

Hollywood, Los Angeles are too well known to need description. On the whole those who have loved the Mediterranean will not be reconciled here in spite of the pot-pourri of talents and profusion of amenities, and those who really care for books can never settle down to the impermanent world of the cinema. Those who do not love the cinema have no business to come. There are exceptional cases of intellectual adaptation of which Huxley's is the most remarkable. The California climate and food creates giants but not genius, but Huxley has filled out into a kind of Apollonian majesty; he radiates both intelligence and serene goodness, and is the best possible testimony to the simple life he leads and the faith he believes in—the one English writer, I think, entirely to have benefited by his transplantation and whom one feels exquisitely refreshed by meeting. Huxley and Isherwood incidentally join hands with Auden in that all three believe (somewhat masochistically) that the peculiar horrors of America—its brashness, music at meals, and racial hysteria—by being emphasized there to a degree not found in other countries, force the onlooker into a rejection of the world which might otherwise come too late.

As Auden puts it, "the anonymous countryside littered with heterogeneous *dreck* and the synonymous cities besotted with electric signs . . . without which, perhaps, the analyst and the immigrant alike would never understand by contrast the nature of the Good Place nor desire it with sufficient desperation to stand a chance of arriving."

Miller, in his *Air-Conditioned Nightmare*, writes with more desperation: "In the ten thousand miles I have traveled I have come across two cities which have each of them a little section worth a second look—I mean Charleston and New Orleans. As for the other cities, towns, and villages through which I passed I hope never to see them again. Everything that was of beauty, significance, or promise has been destroyed or buried in the avalanche of false progress. We have degenerated; we have degraded the life which we sought to establish on this continent. . . . Nowhere have I encountered such a dull, monotonous fabric of life as here in America. Here boredom reaches its peak."

Well, maybe it does, perhaps Americans have destroyed their romantic wilderness on a grander scale than our own rodent attrition at the beauties of our countryside—but I feel a change is coming. Europe invented the Industrial Revolution, fathered the pattern of American ugliness; cities like Reading or Casablanca are worse than anything in America, more shabbily complacent, less conscious of the need for reform. For ninety per cent of Europeans America represents what they would like to be. Jazz is the folk music we have now lost, Hollywood is the dream we can't have, Wall Street the fortune we will never earn, Main Street the animation and plenty which elude us. Only a small minority may criticize without envy. But in America the percentage of the dissatisfied is higher. The enthusiasm which nearly made Prohibition possible still seeks an outlet. As Europe grows more helpless the Americans are compelled to become farseeing and responsible, as Rome was forced by the long decline of Greece to produce an Augustus, a Vergil. Our impotence liberates their potentialities. Something important is about to happen, as if the wonderful *jeunesse* of America were suddenly to retain their idealism and vitality and courage and imagination into adult life, and become the wise and good who make use of them; the old dollar values are silently crumbling, and self-criticism, experimental curiosity, sensibility, and warmth are on their way in.

For Americans change very fast. "Do they?" "Very fast and all at once," as Fitzgerald wrote, "and nothing ever changes them back."

The Challenge of Fear
Alan Paton

One of the big lessons that life has taught me is that my earlier understanding of man and his society was wretchedly inadequate. An extraordinary thing, is it not, that one should begin to acquire an understanding of them both when one is drawing near to the end of his acquaintance with them? The richer one grows in wisdom, the shorter becomes the time in which to use it.

Just how it happened that my understanding was so inadequate, I don't quite know. My parents certainly never taught me that man was growing better and better and that the future was therefore in some way assured. They certainly taught me to seek after righteousness, but they never taught me that righteousness would in a temporal and political sense be successful. Nor did I ever learn this at school. Yet that is what I grew up believing. Why should this be so?

I can only think that it was taught to me after all, not by father or mother or teacher or priest, but because it was a basic assumption of the pre-1914 society into which I was born. I am surprised to find that this view of man and life was shared by many all over the world who were born at that time. I am surprised because my own particular world was a very particular one indeed. It was the town of Pietermaritzburg, Natal, founded by the Afrikaner trekkers, but intensely British at the time of my birth in 1903, most of the trekkers having gone to the Transvaal after the British annexation of Natal. My world was intensely pro-Empire, devoted to the Royal Family, moved to excitement and pride when the red-coated soldiers of the British garrison marched down the street past our home, with arms swinging and drums beating and fifes blowing, to the old Polo Ground to parade for the King's birthday.

There were 30,000 people in Pietermaritzburg in my boyhood, more than half of them Africans and Indians, of whose existence we knew and of whose lives we did not. They were not persons. The Africans were servants, or they dug up the roads. The Indians sold fruit and vegetables, in baskets fastened one to the front end and the other to the back end of a flexible strip of bamboo carried on the shoulder, the baskets swaying up and down with a springy motion.

This faulty understanding of man and life has been called by some the romantic illusion, and can be entertained in different places and at different times in history, but in our illusion the might of the British Empire, the indomitable British Navy, and the *Pax Brittanica* were particular elements. The world was good, and it was going to stay good, perhaps even become better.

I had no conception at that age of the way in which man could create tremendous, noble-sounding slogans, and could shout them aloud while doing ignoble actions; and what is more, the louder the shout, the greater the ignobleness could be. I had no conception of the need of so much of mankind, while it was actually employed in self-seeking and self-securing, to cling simultaneously to unself-centered religion and altruistic ethics. Nor did I realize that man could so easily deceive himself that his highest religious and ethical values were identical with his own self-interest. And there must have been a great many people like me; otherwise why did George Orwell's *1984* create such a sensation among us?

The extraordinary thing about all this is that I ought to have known it. My parents gave me a religious upbringing, and the reading of the gospel story should have prepared me better for the world with its scribes and pharisees and the crucifixion of Jesus through the instruments of church and state. I take that story seriously, for I believe that in some societies one cannot be true to one's highest beliefs without paying for it in suffering. This is more true in the totalitarian and the semitotalitarian societies (of which Nazi Germany is an example of the first and South Africa an example of the second) than in countries such as America and Britain. In South Africa, one may say with safety that apartheid is misguided, but it is dangerous to say that it is cruel or to oppose it too vigorously.

Not only the Gospel, but history also should have taught me to know better. There is, for one thing, the tale of man's innumerable wars, and of his inhumanity to other men. The early Christians were persecuted by the state, but when Christianity became a state religion, it was not long before the church began persecuting and burning heretics. For centuries, the Jews suffered unspeakably at the hands of Christians, who had no difficulty in believing that they were doing a good thing, and doing it in the name of Christ, who taught that one must love one's neighbor as oneself and had made it very clear who one's neighbor was.

Not even the World War of 1914 shattered my pre-1914 world, though today to read of the terrible and useless slaughter of the bright youth of Britain, France, and Germany leaves one appalled. It was Adolf Hitler who finally destroyed for me—and for many others —the romantic illusion. Dachau, Belsen, Auschwitz—these places gave me an education which was not available in Pietermaritzburg. So one suddenly learns in age the truth of a saying heard in youth; namely, that life is the greatest teacher of them all.

What Hitler taught me about man and nature was sobering enough, but life taught me two further lessons. The first was that, whatever Hitler had taught me about man, I must on no account forget that all over the world men and women, both young and old, would offer their lives in the fight against totalitarian rule and the doctrine of race superiority because they believed them to be evil. The second lesson was quite different, and that was that some of these same men and women twenty years later would begin to support the very things that they had fought against, and to approve of the punishment without trial of those who opposed the doctrine of apartheid, but had committed no known offense.

And why do they behave like this? Have they suddenly, or even gradually, become corrupted? And if so, why? Surely the answer is that the nature of their security—and that means the nature of their self-interest—has changed. In 1939, their security was the British Empire and the Navy. In 1967, amid the turbulence and uncertainties of modern Africa, their security appears to them to lie in white supremacy and apartheid. With the change of one's self-interest, there comes also a change in one's ideology, one's values, one's principles.

This discovery of the complexity of human nature was accompanied by another—the discovery of the complexity and irrationality of human motive, the discovery that one could love and hate simultaneously, be honest and cheat, be arrogant and humble, be any pair of opposites that one had supposed to be mutually exclusive. This, I believe, is not common knowledge and would be incomprehensible to many. It has always been known, of course, by the dramatists and the novelists. It is, in fact, a knowledge far more disturbing to other people than to writers, for to writers it is the grist to their mills.

Nor was I aware when I was young (both as boy and as man) how powerful a motive is fear, even though I myself had many fears. As I write this, I am searching for an explanation of the fact that under some circumstances men readily admit fear, and under other circumstances do not. I assume that readiness to admit fear is part of a general readiness to look at the world as it is, and therefore at oneself as one is, while unwillingness to admit fear may be a strong element in self-esteem. One does not readily admit to a fear of which one is ashamed.

Now, while fear has its important uses, such as causing an outflow of adrenalin which helps one run away faster, it is a wretched determinant of conduct. There is nothing more pitiable than a human being whose conduct is largely determined by fear. Furthermore, it is a destroyer of reason and the rational life. What can be done to control it, check it, or even eliminate it?

Here I must use language which will be out of fashion for some, and I must use reasoning which will seem quite unreal to others. Life has taught me that John uttered the plain and simple truth when he wrote that there is no fear in love, but that perfect love casts out fear. In one sense, the opposite of fear is courage, but in the dynamic sense the opposite of fear is love, whether this be love of man or love of justice.

It is clearly not enough to tell a fearful man that if he would only love more, he would fear less. In an age when leprosy was feared much more than it is today, that rich and spoiled young man, Francis of Assisi, impelled by some sudden and irresistible emotion, got down from his gaily caparisoned horse and embraced a leper in the road. From that day, he feared nothing, and taught thousands of others to fear nothing. Yet few of us are visited by such irresistible emotion.

How does one help ordinary men and women, if not to eliminate fear, at least to keep it within bounds, so that reason may play a stronger role in the affairs of men and nations and so that men may cease to pursue policies which must lead to the very disasters they fear? To me, this is the most important question that confronts the human race.

I note that it is more and more widely held that poverty and inequality of opportunity are among the greatest causes of tension between man and man, between race and race, and between nation and nation. I believe that race tension in my own country would be amazingly abated if the disparity between average white income and average

black income were not so overwhelming. I believe that tension between
America and Russia has declined since Russia became one of the productive nations. Yet when men are ruled by fear, they strive to prevent
the very changes that will abate it.

Fear of change is, no doubt, in all of us, but it most afflicts the man
who fears that any change must lead to loss of his wealth and status.
When this fear becomes inordinate, he will, if he has political power,
abrogate such things as civil rights and the rule of law, using the argument that he abrogates them only to preserve them. In my own country, the government, in order to preserve Christian civilization, uses
methods incompatible with Christianity and abrogates values which
are essential to any civilization which calls itself Christian. If only a
man would say, "I do this because I'm afraid," one could bear it; but
when he says, "I do this because I'm good," that is a bit too much.

I see no hope for the peace of society or the peace of the world so
long as this fear of change is so powerful. And this fear will remain
powerful so long as the one side has so much to gain and the other
so much to lose.

I should like to make one point clear, and that is that I do not believe that a more equitable distribution of wealth will automatically
bring the Great Society. The point I am trying to make is that if it is
not done, there will never be any Great Society. Nor will there be any
peace for the world.

Can a school prepare our children for the complexity and waywardness of man? Is it not more likely that these lessons can be taught only
by living? There would be the danger that some children might learn
to believe a contrary illusion, namely, that man is cruel, cunning, and
deceitful. If I remember my childhood and boyhood correctly, and
perhaps even my experience as a young teacher, one actually protected
children against knowing too much of the worse sides of man's nature.
My readers know, no doubt, the story of the businessman who put his
young son on the roof of the house, and, standing below, said, "Jump,
son, and Daddy will catch you." So the boy jumped, and Daddy didn't
catch him, but instead said to him, "Son, that will teach you to trust
nobody." One could hardly do that. But one could, while holding up
the goals of honesty, kindness, loyalty, tolerance, integrity, tell children
a bit of what the world is like. I would also assume that the children
of 1967 know far more about man and his nature and society than did
the children of the pre-1914 days; it must be almost impossible for
children of today to cherish the old romantic illusion.

One must not suppose, however, that because children have lost the
romantic illusion and look upon life and the world and their parents
with a more calculating eye that they are now free of illusions. In South
Africa, many white children cherish the illusion that they are, in many

important ways, superior to other children, and I regret to add that many non-white children entertain the illusion that they are in many important ways, inferior to white children. Another powerful illusion handed down to many white children is that their country is perfect and their government wholly just and benign, so that they lose all faculty for self-criticism.

I have known people who, when their romantic illusion is finally destroyed, cease to believe anything except that man is bad and life intolerable; who feel that they have come, to use Thomas Wolfe's magnificent words, from the prison of their mothers' flesh "into the unspeakable and incommunicable prison of this earth." I presume they would say that this is what life has taught them. It is my fortune to be able to say that though life destroyed my romantic illusion, she did not teach me the contrary illusion. It would appear either that she does not teach the same lessons to everybody, or that other factors operate besides experience, such as temperament, character, religious faith, and sheer luck and good fortune.

I certainly had good fortune, in marriage and children and friends —especially those friends who, with me, have challenged the beliefs and practices of a color-bar society—and it is these personal relationships that have saved me from the melancholy that besets the wholly disillusioned. I call this my luck because it is very difficult, and perhaps impossible, to achieve such a state by act of will. You may say to a friend, "Don't worry; worry changes nothing," but that in itself will not stop him from worrying. Life has taught me—and this is my luck—that active loving saves one from a morbid preoccupation with the shortcomings of society and the waywardness of men.

I should again make it clear at this point that I am not saying that human society is unimprovable. What I am saying is that the problems of creating the Great Society are immensely greater than many of us were taught to believe and that we would have been better equipped to deal with them if we had understood their nature and difficulty better. To give up the task of reforming society is to give up one's responsibility as a free man. The task itself is endless, and large parts of it, sometimes the whole of it, must be performed anew by each succeeding generation.

Now, while life was teaching me these lessons, she was leading me in what would appear to be a quite contrary or at least contradictory direction. Here I must refer directly to my own local and particular situation as a white South African. While, on the one hand, I was discarding the romantic illusion about men and society, on the other I was beginning to rebel against the man-made barriers of race and color that divided man from man and to cherish a new ideal of society, which would be judged by some to be an illusion no less romantic than the one it was replacing.

When I first set out in this direction, the road was certainly unusual, whereas later it was to become dangerous, owing to the coming to power of a government which took to itself supra-legal powers enabling it to banish, silence, confine to small areas, debar from certain occupations and from attending any social or political gathering, any person who in the opinion of the Minister was "furthering the aims of Communism." Many non-Communists were dealt with in this way, without charge, trial, or sentence; some of these were my own fellow liberals, whose only offenses had been that they had ignored conventional race barriers or had been active in providing legal defense for political prisoners and aid for their dependents.

Whereas South Africa teaches many of its people to fear and to hate racial mixing (and I use the word "mixing" in its wildest, not its narrowest sense), here it was teaching me the opposite, and teaching me to see our future as being that of one nonracial society and not a collection of strictly separated and individual race groups. The whole philosophy of apartheid is based on the fundamental assumption that there can be no such thing as a nonracial society, and that each individual realizes himself only through his membership in his own racial group, and that, therefore, it is the duty of the government to preserve these racial differences, in language, education, sex, marriage, sport, entertainment, and so on and so on. The apostle of apartheid would further declare that it is only another romantic illusion to imagine that an Afrikaner Calvinist, an English-speaking Anglican (Episcopalian), a colored (that is, of mixed blood) Roman Catholic, an African Methodist, an African ancestor-worshipper, an Indian Hindu, and an Indian Muslim—not to mention those who profess no particular faith—could operate a common nonracial society. The apostle of apartheid says he is a realist and that a person like myself is a sentimental idealist. But when this apostle is angry with me he would call me dangerous, and could, if he wished, restrict my freedom in the ways I have mentioned above.

He will, almost certainly in 1968, make it an offense to operate a nonracial (and multiracial) political party. One learns the lesson at first hand that the practice of the art of political persuasion can be made impossible by the state. One learns how the whole character of a people can be changed by a powerful state. Having Germany in mind, I do not say fundamentally changed; but even if the change is not fundamental, it is terrible enough.

Yet, in spite of all this one goes on believing in a nonracial unity that can transcend racial difference. This is something that one has come to believe through experience of personal relationships, and it may be that what is possible in personal relationships is not possible in society. There have been many examples in history where two individuals from mutually hostile groups have greatly loved one another.

Now, is it possible or is it not possible to realize in society what one has realized in personal relationships? I believe one cannot answer the question. All that one can say is that there is within one an impulse to try to realize it, that this impulse is an integral part of one's self, and that it must be obeyed, for to disobey it is to do damage to the integrity of one's self. And what is more, one has fortunately already learned the lesson that a failure, or a measure of failure, to realize some social or political aim can be compensated for to a tremendous degree by the depth and warmth of one's personal relationships.

What has life then taught me after all? She has taught me not to expect too much, though not in the sense of the cynical beatitude, "Blessed is he who expecteth nothing, for he shall not be disappointed." Life has not taught me to expect nothing, but she has taught me not to expect success to be the inevitable result of my endeavors. She has taught me to seek sustenance from the endeavor itself, but to leave the result to God. And the strange thing is that my parents taught me all this more than half a century ago. It is a lesson that—for me—had to be learned at least twice. When I learned it in my youth, it meant Sir Galahad and the Holy Grail. When I learned it in my age, it meant Christ and the road to Golgotha. And looking back upon it all, I would not wish it otherwise. Indeed, I cannot see how it could have been otherwise.

To try to be free of self-deception, to try to see with clear eyes oneself and others and the world, does not necessarily bring an undiluted kind of happiness. Yet it is something I would not exchange for any happiness built on any other foundation. There is only one way in which one can endure man's inhumanity to man and that is to try, in one's own life, to exemplify man's humanity to man. "Teach me, oh Lord, to seek not so much to be consoled as to console."

Suggestions for Writing

1. With evidence from these five pieces, write an essay on the thesis "In the modern world, the individual is far from free."

2. With evidence from your own experience, write an essay on the pressures of conformity, such as "The Individual Versus the Sit-In," "The Bowling Club Versus Solitude," or "The Code of the Group."

3. Write an essay from your own observation about the fads in slang that make last year's circle look somewhat square.

4. Write a critique of Mailer's essay in which you analyze the source and means of its power, considering both thought and expression, for which the "political" phrasing alongside will give you some clues.

5. Write an essay patterned after Hofstadter, using his ideas where pertinent, on the subject "Education and the Curriculum at ——— (the college or university you know best)." After an introduction that establishes your thesis, present a definition of education that will then apply to the rest of your remarks about the particular curriculum.

6. Write an essay about the realities of student government (or of any kind of leadership), considering Hofstadter's reality as against the ideal Jefferson expressed in a letter of October 28, 1813, to John Adams:

> . . . I agree with you that there is a natural aristocracy among men. The grounds of this are virtue and talents. . . . May we not even say, that that form of government is the best, which provides the most effectually for a pure selection of these natural aristoi into the offices of government?
>
> . . . And had another [law] which I prepared been adopted by the legislature, our work would have been complete. It was a bill for the more general diffusion of learning. This proposed to divide every county into wards of five or six miles square, like your townships; to establish in each ward a free school for reading, writing, and common arithmetic; to provide for the annual selection of the best [students] from those schools, who might receive, at the public expense, a higher degree of education at a district school; and from these district schools to select a certain number of the most promising [students], to be [educated] at an University, where all the most useful sciences should be taught. Worth and genius would thus have been sought out from every condition of life, and completely prepared by education for defeating the competition of wealth and birth for public trusts.

7. Write a thorough critique of Connolly's essay, explaining everything important needing explanation (Why *blueprint?* Why *Silver Age?* Why *the ideal of inhabiting a continuous present?*). Where do Connolly's judgments of America seem true, where untrue? What license may you allow exaggeration? What of his attitude and his prose? Your aim will be to give an accurate description of his essay and his views, plus a judgment of them. But start from a thesis that expresses your judgment.

8. Write an essay on Paton's idea of "one's responsibility as a free man."

9. Write a research paper based on some issue raised by any of the esays in this book. Your problem will be essentially the same as that in an essay built of your own ideas alone: you will find a thesis and then lay it out in an essay with beginning, middle, and end. But you will go beyond your own speculations as you document and challenge your thesis with what

others have said. Pick some controversial topic, with much said on both sides, and make up your mind about where you stand. Contrary to common misconception, it is better to go into your researching with your own thesis (or hypothesis) clearly in mind, your own side chosen. Write out a thesis before you begin. Doing so will clarify your thought. But your mind need not be closed. As you read the *pro*'s and *con*'s of the matter, you may modify your thesis—or even switch to the other side. With no thesis beforehand, though, your mind may be too wide open for anything to stick.

Your thesis drafted, your reading done, and your notes taken, write an introductory paragraph, with thesis funneled at the end of it, and then proceed to set up your *con*'s and to knock them down with your *pro*'s. You will be writing your own argument, simply quoting and citing the arguments of others as you present your case.

Here are some suggested topics for research, stated as theses to attack or support:

a. Federal aid to our colleges means creeping dictatorship.

b. The cure for juvenile crime begins at home.

c. The American press is unfair to Russian justice (for example, the recent trials of dissenting writers).

d. The Peace Corps cannot teach democracy.

e. Schweitzer's Lambaréné did little permanent good.

f. The riot at (Columbia, Kent,————) was caused by injustice.

g. Euthanasia conflicts with Schweitzer's "reverence for life."

h. Racial desegregation by force denies democratic rights.

i. The Puritans were right in suppressing Christmas.

j. The Marshall Plan saved Europe for socialism.

k. Black Power means freedom for all.